HOLMAN
Old Testament Commentary

HOLMAN
Old Testament Commentary

I & II Samuel

GENERAL EDITOR

Max Anders

AUTHORS

Stephen J. Andrews
and Robert D. Bergen

HOLMAN
REFERENCE

NASHVILLE, TENNESSEE

Holman Old Testament Commentary
© 2009 Broadman & Holman Publishers
Nashville, Tennessee
All rights reserved

ISBN: 978-08054-9466-2
Dewey Decimal Classification: 222.4
Subject Heading: BIBLE. O.T. Samuel

Andrews, Stephen and Robert D. Bergen
    1, 2 Samuel / Stephen J. Andrews
    p. cm. — (Holman Old Testament commentary)
    Includes bibliographical references. (p.).
    ISBN 978-08054-9466-2
    1. Bible. 1, 2 Samuel—Commentaries. I. Title. II. Series.
                          —dc21

Printed in the Unites States of America
1 2 3 4 5 6 7 8 9 • 15 14 13 12 11 10 09
SB

*I*n memory of my father,
Rev. William Lee Andrews
(1927-2008),
who taught me
to love God's Word.
—Stephen J. Andrews

*T*o Martha and Wesley,
God's gifts of love,
inspiration,
and joy in my life.
—Robert Bergen

Contents

Contents

Editorial Preface

Today's church hungers for Bible teaching, and Bible teachers hunger for resources to guide them in teaching God's Word. The Holman Old Testament Commentary provides the church with the food to feed the spiritually hungry in an easily digestible format. The result: new spiritual vitality that the church can readily use.

Bible teaching should result in new interest in the Scriptures, expanded Bible knowledge, discovery of specific scriptural principles, relevant applications, and exciting living. The unique format of the Holman Old Testament Commentary includes sections to achieve these results for every Old Testament book.

Opening quotations stimulate thinking and lead to an introductory illustration and discussion that draw individuals and study groups into the Word of God. "In a Nutshell" summarizes the content and teaching of the chapter. Verse-by-verse commentary answers the church's questions rather than raising issues scholars usually admit they cannot adequately solve. Bible principles and specific contemporary applications encourage students to move from Bible to contemporary times. A specific modern illustration then ties application vividly to present life. A brief prayer aids the student to commit his or her daily life to the principles and applications found in the Bible chapter being studied. For those still hungry for more, "Deeper Discoveries" takes the student into a more personal, deeper study of the words, phrases, and themes of God's Word. Finally, a teaching outline provides transitional statements and conclusions along with an outline to assist the teacher in group Bible studies.

It is the editors' prayer that this new resource for local church Bible teaching will enrich the ministry of group as well as individual Bible study, and that it will lead God's people truly to be people of the Book, living out what God calls us to be.

Holman Old Testament
Commentary Contributors

Vol. 1 Genesis
ISBN 978-0-8054-9461-7
Kenneth O. Gangel and Stephen Bramer

Vol. 2 Exodus, Leviticus, Numbers
ISBN 978-0-8054-9462-4
Glen Martin

Vol. 3 Deuteronomy
ISBN 978-0-8054-9463-1
Paul Douglas McIntosh

Vol. 4 Joshua
ISBN 978-0-8054-9464-8
Kenneth O. Gangel

Vol. 5 Judges, Ruth
ISBN 978-0-8054-9465-5
Gary W. Phillips

Vol. 6 1 & 2 Samuel
ISBN 978-0-8054-9466-2
Stephen Andrews and Robert D. Bergen

Vol. 7 1 & 2 Kings
ISBN 978-0-8054-9467-9
Gary Inrig

Vol. 8 1 & 2 Chronicles
ISBN 978-0-8054-9468-6
Winfried Corduan

Vol. 9 Ezra, Nehemiah, Esther
ISBN 978-0-8054-9469-3
Knute Larson and Kathy Dahlen

Vol. 10 Job
ISBN 978-0-8054-9470-9
Steven J. Lawson

Vol. 11 Psalms 1-72
ISBN 978-0-8054-9471-6
Steven J. Lawson

Vol. 12 Psalms 73-150
ISBN 978-0-8054-9481-5
Steven J. Lawson

Vol. 13 Proverbs
ISBN 978-0-8054-9472-3
Max Anders

Vol. 14 Ecclesiastes, Song of Songs
ISBN 978-0-8054-9482-2
David George Moore and Daniel L. Akin

Vol. 15 Isaiah
ISBN 978-0-8054-9473-0
Trent C. Butler

Vol. 16 Jeremiah, Lamentations
ISBN 978-0-8054-9474-7
Fred C. Wood and Ross McLaren

Vol. 17 Ezekiel
ISBN 978-0-8054-9475-4
Mark F. Rooker

Vol. 18 Daniel
ISBN 978-0-8054-9476-1
Kenneth O. Gangel

Vol. 19 Hosea, Joel, Amos, Obadiah, Jonah, Micah
ISBN 978-0-8054-9477-8
Trent C. Butler

Vol. 20 Nahum, Habakkuk, Zephaniah, Haggai, Zechariah, Malachi
ISBN 978-0-8054-9478-5
Stephen R. Miller

Holman New Testament Commentary Contributors

Holman Old Testament Commentary

Twenty volumes designed for Bible study and teaching to enrich the local church and God's people.

Series Editor	Max Anders
Managing Editor	Steve Bond
Project Editor	Dean Richardson
Product Development Manager	Ricky D. King
Marketing Manager	Robin Patterson
Executive Editor	Tim Jordan
Page Composition	TF Designs, Greenbrier, TN

Introduction to

1 and 2 Samuel

BACKGROUND

During the period of the judges, the Hebrew tribal groups had settled in their territories. Life revolved around the groups. Everyone shared in the land's resources. No central government imposed restrictions on the tribes or made demands on them. But, likewise, no king and his army stood ready to defend them. This shortcoming was particularly evident when the Philistines developed into a powerful force that threatened to drive the Israelites out of their homeland.

Finally, the elders of the tribes approached Samuel and asked him to appoint a king to become their new leader (1 Sam. 8:5). The difficult process of moving from an old, established form of government to a new organization headed by a king brought disappointment to Samuel (1 Sam. 8:6). He described for the people what the new form of government would cost them (1 Sam. 8:10–18). But they were determined to have a king to provide military protection, so God instructed Samuel to "give them a king" (1 Sam. 8:22). The books of 1 and 2 Samuel describe this transition to a kingship under Saul and the eventual emergence of David as the ruler over a united Israel and the establishment of David's dynasty.

COMPOSITION OF 1 AND 2 SAMUEL

Substantially the work of the prophet Samuel, 1 and 2 Samuel were written in the eleventh century B.C. However, their obvious connectedness with 1 and 2 Kings, as well as literary clues in the text (e.g., mention of the length of David's reign [2 Sam. 5:4], use of the phrase "the kings of Judah" [1 Sam. 27:6], indication that a term used as late as the eighth century B.C. was out-of-date at the time of writing [1 Sam. 9:9]), indicate that these books reached their final form during the Babylonian exile or shortly thereafter and were written using at least one other written source (the Book of Jashar; see 2 Sam. 1:18).

The first readers of the finished form of 1 and 2 Samuel were Jews living in either the sixth or fifth century B.C. They were concerned about putting their nation back together again following the destruction of Jerusalem by Babylon. They were also interested in tracing out the historical roots of theological and political issues that affected their lives.

PURPOSES OF 1 AND 2 SAMUEL

The books of 1 and 2 Samuel were written to serve many different functions. First and most importantly, they were intended to be used in the Jewish religious community as Holy Scripture, that is, as the completely authoritative and trustworthy Word of God, providing guidance and encouragement to their hearers. As Scripture they reinforce the teachings of the Torah by providing historical examples of both obedience and disobedience to God's law. At the same time they lay a solid foundation for understanding the life and ministry of Jesus Christ, the ultimate son of David.

They also function as history. In this regard they describe Israel's transition to a monarchical form of government and provide information about Israel's last two judges and first two kings. These events took place over an indeterminate period of time stretching across parts of three centuries from the late twelfth century B.C. to the early tenth century B.C. These books also supply details about the religious history of Israel, including information about significant worship centers, priestly leaders, and the sacred ark of the covenant.

Another purpose for the writing of 1 and 2 Samuel was to defend certain leading figures in the Israelite monarchy against charges made against them. Three controversial situations arose during David's lifetime, and each of them needed an accounting. The issues were (1) displacement of Saul's family line by David's on the throne of Israel, (2) Solomon's rise to kingship even though he wasn't next in line to become king, and (3) the Abiatharites' loss of their role as leaders in Israelite worship. The books provide a justification for each of these outcomes in Israelite history.

STRUCTURE AND STYLE OF 1 AND 2 SAMUEL

The narratives in 1 and 2 Samuel center on three persons: Samuel (1 Sam. 1–7), Saul (1 Sam. 8–14), and David (1 Sam. 15–2 Sam. 20). Materials in these narrative sections are normally presented in chronological order.

An appendix at the end of these books (2 Sam. 21–24) provides materials that illustrate David's roles in his relationship with God. Materials in this appendix are in the form of narrative, lists, and poetry related to David's life. They are taken from various points in David's life and are, therefore, not part of the chronological scheme of the earlier portions of the books.

Originally composed in the Hebrew language using a classic narrative style, 1 and 2 Samuel richly draw portraits of the three leading characters. These books are among the most detailed in the Old Testament. In fact, David is the subject of more narrative verbs than any other character in the Old Testament—even more than Moses.

MESSAGES OF 1 AND 2 SAMUEL

Like other portions of the Former Prophets, Latter Prophets, and Writings (three of the four divisions of the Hebrew Bible), 1 and 2 Samuel were not written to inject new theological truths into Israelite society. Instead, they were carefully written to reiterate, reinforce, and clarify the theological truths of the Torah (the first five books of the Old Testament). Especially important in these books are the concepts of (1) the need for wholehearted obedience to God, (2) God's establishment of a covenant for the benefit of his people (in this case, covenantal provision of leadership for Israel through the family line of David), (3) the presence of God among his people (especially as it is connected with the ark of the covenant, and as God was with David), and (4) the relationship that exists between possession of the land of Israel and the people's obedience to God (when Israel sinned, enemies took control of portions of Israel; also David himself was forced to leave Israel for a time as a consequence of his sin with Bathsheba).

The books of 1 and 2 Samuel encourage and instruct us to live lives of wholehearted obedience to God (see 1 Sam. 15:22). Through the examples of Hannah and David, they teach us that God can use both women and men, who may be unappreciated or rejected by others, to do great things for him—if they have great faith in him.

These books also show us that sin brings its ultimate consequences. Take, for example, the lurid example of Amnon's rape of Tamar and its effects (2 Sam. 13). As David's oldest son, Amnon would normally have been in line to succeed his father. Instead, his sinful act led to his assassination and the exile of his brother, Absalom.

The books of 1 and 2 Samuel also magnify the grace of God that is greater than all our sin. There is no clearer demonstration in the Old Testament that we are valued by God "while we were still sinners" (Rom. 5:8) than the account of David's sin. It is a testimony to God's grace that David overcame his sin to become the model for all future kings (1 Kgs. 15:5; 2 Kgs. 18:3). This affirmation of God's continuing love even for those who sin (2 Sam. 7:15) became the foundation block of the messianic hope that God would not leave his people without a Savior.

OUTLINE OF 1 AND 2 SAMUEL

I. Samuel, Last of the Judges, First of the Prophets (1 Sam. 1:1–8:22)
   A. Family Background: Birth and Dedication (1 Sam. 1:1–2:11)
   B. Failure of Eli, the High Priest (1 Sam. 2:12–3:21)
   C. War with the Philistines (1 Sam. 4:1–7:14)
   D. Judgeship of Samuel and Demand for a King (1 Sam. 7:15–8:22)

II. Saul, Israel's First King (1 Sam. 9:1–15:35)
   A. Saul's Early Success as King (1 Sam. 9:1–12:25)
   B. Consolidation of Saul's Kingship (1 Sam. 13:1–14:52)
   C. Campaign Against the Amalekites (1 Sam. 15:1–35)

III. Rise of David (1 Sam. 16:1–31:13)
   A. Selection of David (1 Sam. 16:1–23)
   B. David and Goliath (1 Sam. 17:1–54)
   C. David's Relationship with Saul (1 Sam. 17:55–20:42)
   D. David's Exile (1 Sam. 21:1–25:44)
   E. Gradual Eclipse of Saul (1 Sam. 26:1–30:31)

IV. David's Activities After Saul's Death (2 Sam. 1:1–4:12)
   A. An Amalekite Messenger's Account of Saul's Death (2 Sam. 1:1–10)
   B. David's Lament for Saul and Jonathan (2 Sam. 1:11–27)
   C. David in Hebron as King of Judah (2 Sam. 2:1–11)
   D. Fateful Meeting of Abner and Joab (2 Sam. 2:12–3:1)
   E. A Note on David's Family (2 Sam. 3:2–5)
   F. Abner's Quarrel with Ish-bosheth; His Overtures to David (2 Sam. 3:6–21)

1 Samuel 1:1–2:36

The Faithfulness of Hannah

I. **INTRODUCTION**
For This Child I Prayed

II. **COMMENTARY**
A verse-by-verse explanation of these chapters

III. **CONCLUSION**
Hannah's Blessing
An overview of the principles and applications from these chapters

IV. **LIFE APPLICATION**
A Faithful Role Model
Melding these chapters to life

V. **PRAYER**
Tying these chapters to life with God

VI. **DEEPER DISCOVERIES**
Historical, geographical, and grammatical enrichment of the commentary

VII. **TEACHING OUTLINE**
Suggested step-by-step group study of these chapters

VIII. **ISSUES FOR DISCUSSION**
Zeroing these chapters in on daily life

| Quote |

"*W*hen you know what God has said, know what he is about to do, and have adjusted your life to him, there is yet one remaining necessary response to God. To experience him at work in and through you, you must obey him. When you obey him, he will accomplish his work through you; and you will come to know him by experience."

Henry T. Blackaby

GEOGRAPHICAL PROFILE: RAMATHAIM

- Name means "two heights"
- Located in the hill country of Ephraim
- Modern location of site is unknown
- May be the same place as Ramah, hometown of Samuel (1 Sam. 1:19; 7:17)

BIOGRAPHICAL PROFILE: ELKANAH

- A descendent of Zuph, an Ephraimite
- Worshiped the Lord Almighty at Shiloh
- Husband of two wives, Hannah and Peninnah
- Father of Samuel, the prophet

GEOGRAPHICAL PROFILE: SHILOH

- Modern Seilun, located nine miles north of Bethel
- Since days of Joshua, Israel worshiped the Lord here
- The tent of meeting or tabernacle was set up here (Josh. 18:1)
- The tabernacle was still used here in Eli's time (1 Sam. 2:22)

1 Samuel 1:1–2:36

I N   A   N U T S H E L L

The first two chapters of 1 Samuel describe the unique birth and upbringing of Samuel. Hannah, one of the two wives of Elkanah, was barren. Taunted and provoked by Peninnah, the other wife of Elkanah who had children, Hannah cried out to God for a son. With an unselfish heart and pure motives, Hannah offered to give her son back to the Lord. Hannah fulfilled her commitment, and God established her son Samuel as a mighty prophet in Israel. Because of her faithful actions, Hannah remains a role model for all believers.

The Faithfulness of Hannah

I. INTRODUCTION

For This Child I Prayed

The year was 1932, and a brand-new mother was listening to a special church service on a little battery-operated radio on a farm in Indiana. The speaker was Harry Ironside, pastor of the famous Moody Memorial Church in Chicago. Moody Church was conducting a special dedication service. During the service, Dr. Ironside invited parents to come forward to present their children to the Lord.

This was a new experience for the Indiana mother. She was so moved by the service that she went to the crib of her newborn child, picked him up, and carried him into her little kitchen. There she knelt, and along with the parents participating in the church service one hundred miles away in Chicago, she dedicated her son to the Lord.

Years later, the mother revealed to her son, Dr. Gene Getz, what she had done that day on the farm in Indiana. Getz, a pastor, radio commentator, and prolific Christian author, firmly believes that God answered his mother's prayer—a prayer that has impacted his life to this very day (Getz, *Samuel*, 30–31).

The first two chapters of 1 Samuel introduce us to the powerful prayer of Hannah, the mother of Samuel. Hannah prayed to God for a son. God answered her prayer and she gave birth to Samuel. She wanted so much to have a son that she promised she would give him back to the Lord. Hannah fulfilled her vow to the Lord, and Samuel became one of the greatest prophets of God the world has ever known.

II. COMMENTARY

The Faithfulness of Hannah

MAIN IDEA: *Samuel is born to a faithful, previously barren woman who dedicates him to the Lord. After a prayer of thanksgiving, she leaves him with Eli, the high priest, to be reared in the temple. Eli's sons are wicked, and a prophet prophesies judgment against them.*

🄰 Hannah's Sorrow (1:1–8)

SUPPORTING IDEA: *Hannah, the wife of Elkanah, is harassed by Elkanah's second wife for being barren.*

1:1–2. The first two verses of 1 Samuel introduce us to a certain man by the name of **Elkanah** ("God has created"). In quick succession, we learn about his place of origin, his lineage, and his marital status. **Ramathaim** ("twin heights") in **the hill country of Ephraim** is regarded by some scholars to be a variation of Ramah ("height"), a town listed in the territorial allotment given to the tribe of Benjamin (Josh. 18:25). Other scholars suggest that Ramathaim is the same as Arimathea in the New Testament (Bergen, 63). The actual location of Ramathaim is not known.

Elkanah's genealogy reveals something very important about his heritage. Verse 1 lists four generations of his ancestors. But according to 1 Chronicles 6:22–28,33–38, Elkanah was from the family line of Kohath, the son of Levi. This means that Elkanah was a Levite.

It might seem a bit odd to tell us about Elkanah's marital status so soon after introducing him. The truth is, however, that these apparently insignificant matrimonial details are extremely important for the rest of the book, as well as God's future dealings with his people, Israel. Sometimes, God operates quietly in the small details. When we ignore the small things, we run the risk of missing the opportunity of recognizing God at work.

There are several significant statements in verse 2. First, Elkanah had two wives. Second, their names were **Hannah** ("Gracious") and **Peninnah** ("Pearl"). Since Hannah is named first, she was probably the first wife. Finally, Peninnah had children, but Hannah was barren.

Since polygamy is certainly not the biblical norm (Gen. 2:24), why did Elkanah take a second wife? This may be a case where an individual took a wife who apparently turned out to be infertile. Desiring an heir, and perhaps lacking faith, this individual might then take a second wife. Elkanah may have taken a second wife because Hannah, his first wife, was barren.

The inability of a wife to produce an heir was a serious issue in ancient Near Eastern societies. An heir not only maintained the family line but also provided for the preservation of the father's estate within the clan and the tribe. In addition, the heir would provide for his mother after the death of the father as a kind of Social Security of that culture.

The ancient Code of Hammurabi contains four laws permitting the taking of a second wife in the event the first was unable to produce an heir (Bergen, 65). In the Bible, Sarah gave Hagar to Abraham in hopes of having a child through her (Gen. 16:1–2). Rachel did the same with Bilhah (Gen. 30:3).

Hannah is not the only barren wife mentioned in the Scriptures. Sarah (Gen. 11:30), Rachel (Gen. 29:31), Samson's mother (Judg. 13:2), and Elizabeth (Luke 1:7) were all initially barren. As we read further, we find out that God did not forget Hannah. Elkanah may have tried to solve the problem by taking a second wife, but God tended to work otherwise. Dale Ralph Davis notes it is one of God's basic principles to begin to bless at the point of our hopelessness and helplessness: "When God's people are without strength, without resources, without hope, without human gimmicks—then He loves to stretch forth His hand from heaven" (Davis, *Heart*, 17).

1:3–7. Year after year Elkanah, Hannah, and Peninnah and her sons and daughters would make a pilgrimage to **Shiloh** to worship and offer sacrifice to the Lord. As a Levite, Elkanah would possibly be called upon to serve before the tabernacle at Shiloh. The Old Testament law required every Israelite to appear before the Lord three times a year (Exod. 23:14–19; 34:23; Deut. 16:16–17).

But as the years passed, these times of festive celebration became more and more burdensome for Hannah. The plight of her childlessness became increasingly heavy. Perhaps she saw Eli's two sons, **Hophni** and **Phinehas**, who served as priests before the Lord, and they reminded her that she had no son to serve as a Levite.

Hannah's family didn't help matters. When it came time to serve his family during the sacrificial meal, Elkanah gave sufficient portions to Peninnah and her children. But to Hannah, he gave what most translations call a "double portion" (v. 5). The Hebrew text is difficult to read at this point, and scholars are not sure exactly how to translate it (Bergen, 66). Regardless of whether it was a "special portion" or a "double portion," Elkanah gave it to Hannah because he loved her, even though the Lord had closed her womb.

Surely Peninnah saw how Elkanah loved Hannah, and this angered her. As Elkanah "doubled" Hannah's portions, Peninnah "doubled" her efforts to irritate and provoke her rival. This went on year after year until Hannah could stand the pain no longer. Peninnah's abuse during these times was so intense and painful that Hannah would often burst into tears and became so emotionally distraught that she couldn't eat—"a sign of intense anxiety and depression" (Getz, *Samuel*, 22–23). Hannah was in great sorrow.

1:8. Gene Getz has called Elkanah's response to Hannah's emotional turmoil both humorous and embarrassing. She needed empathy and sincere understanding, not a typical male self-centered approach. Getz notes that Elka-nah's four questions in verse 8 indicate his inability to relate to her feelings:

1. "Hannah, why are you weeping?" (as if he didn't know).
2. "Why don't you eat?" (as if he didn't understand the reason).
3. "Why are you downhearted?" (again, as if he wasn't aware of what was happening).
4. "Don't I mean more to you than ten sons?" (Getz, *Samuel*, 23).

In one way, Elkanah's last question probably reflects his fear that his efforts at loving Hannah were being rejected. The reference to the "ten sons" may be an allusion to the sons born to Jacob during the period of Rachel's barrenness (Gen. 29:31–30:22). In saying this, Elkanah may have been try-ing to tell Hannah that he loved her like Jacob loved Rachel. If this is true, then we can also perceive how the statement at the same time foreshadows a happy ending because Rachel eventually had children. Bergen expresses it this way: "The circumstance of having a beloved wife who was incapable of bearing children links Elkanah with the Torah patriarchs Abraham, Isaac, and Jacob. To the reader familiar with the Torah the connection is a favorable one, for it suggests the possibility—later realized—that a child of great sig-nificance to God's kingdom may ultimately result" (Bergen, 65).

B Hannah's Supplication (1:9–20)

> **SUPPORTING IDEA:** *On a trip to the temple, Hannah prays silently for a son. Eli thinks she is drunk, but when she explains, he affirms her. Upon returning home, Hannah conceives and bears a son, Samuel.*

1:9–11. Peninnah's abuse may have been designed to goad Hannah into complaining to God. Instead, it drove her to her knees. Here we see Han-nah's greatest act as a faithful role model for all believers. She could have cursed God, challenged his motives, or rejected him for a miserable life of bitterness. She reminds us to let our sorrows and travails drive us to our knees before the great throne of grace.

Deeply distressed, Hannah **wept** and cried out to the Lord. While Eli the old priest sat nearby on a chair at the doorpost of the tabernacle, Hannah uttered a serious and solemn vow. With a broken heart, Hannah offered an amazing prayer.

In verse 11 Hannah addressed her prayer to the LORD **Almighty**. The first time the phrase "the Lord Almighty" is used in the Old Testament is in verse 3 of this same chapter. But Hannah is the first individual in Scripture to use this phrase to address God. She recognized that the Lord alone is the giver of life. Thus she came to him with a proper respect, believing that he would help her in her distress. Hannah called on the name of the Lord seven times in her prayers in chapter 1 (1:11,15,17,26–28). Contrast this with Eli, who used the more distant phrase "God of Israel" (1:17).

Hannah also came to the Lord with a proper attitude. Although a few translations do not show it, Hannah referred to herself three times in the prayer with a term that is normally used to describe a female household slave. Hannah humbled herself before the Lord: "She understood that the proper position of a believer in relation to the Lord is that of absolute subjection" (Bergen, 68).

Furthermore, Hannah came to the Lord with a proper request. Many of our prayers are one-sided. We tend to come to the Lord to ask for something. However, in his little booklet on prayer, E. W. Price Jr. reminds us that along with supplication—seeking for others and ourselves—surrender is also necessary. Effective prayer requires "a fresh commitment of everything in our lives to God" (Price, 31). Specifically, what Hannah asked from the Lord as her heart's desire, she was willing to give back to him.

Hannah set her prayer in the form of a **vow**, a very special and unique vow. Women were permitted to make vows (Num. 30:3–16), as long as their father or husband agreed (as Elkanah apparently did later; see 1:23). No other example of a woman making a vow is found elsewhere in the Old Testament.

In her vow, Hannah promised two things to God. If God would give her a son, she would **give him to the Lord for all the days of his life, and no razor will ever be used on his head**. The second phrase is very important because it indicates that Hannah was giving her son to the Lord as a Nazirite (Num. 6:1–21; see "Deeper Discoveries"). This statement reminds us of Samson, who lost his strength when the Philistines shaved his head (Judg. 16:1–22). His parents had made the same vow (Judg. 13:2–5), and he did mighty things for God until he violated his Nazirite vow.

Normally, a Nazirite vow was temporary. However, Hannah was so committed to the Lord that she made it permanent. She vowed that she would give her child to God "all the days of his life." Just to have the experience of giving birth, she would give the child back to the Lord. God heard Hannah's prayer and honored her request.

1:12–18. Elkanah was not the only person to misunderstand Hannah's heart. Old Eli sitting on a chair by the doorpost of the tabernacle started watching her. He saw her lips move, but he didn't hear a word. He thought she was drunk (1:13). He accused her of freely pouring out the wine. But Hannah was praying in her heart. She defended herself. The only thing she was "pouring out" was her soul to the Lord. She was deeply troubled and was praying out of her great anguish and grief.

The one person who should have been sensitive to Hannah's sorrow was Eli, the priest of God at Shiloh, supposedly a man of great spiritual maturity. Instead, we see him as spiritually blind and emotionally insensitive. Concerning Eli's character at the beginning of 1 Samuel, Bergen really hits the nail on the head: "He was a man who watched lips instead of perceiving hearts, who judged profound spirituality to be profligate indulgence in spirits, who heard nothing when the Lord spoke (1 Sam 3:4,6), and who criticized his sons for abusing the sacrificial system yet grew fat from their take (2:22–24; 4:18). Fittingly, in the end his powerful career was surpassed by those who were 'nothing'—a socially powerless rural woman and a child" (Bergen, 69).

Still, Eli was able to recognize his blunder, and he did validate Hannah's prayer with a blessing and a benediction that the God of Israel would grant her request (1:17). Hannah seemed to know then that God had heard her prayer. She went back to the family and sat down and ate something (1:18). In her trusting attitude, the depression disappeared, and her sorrow melted away. Hannah's spiritual victory was gained through the anguish of tearful prayers. In the end, Hannah trusted completely in God's will for her life.

1:19–20. On the last day of the feast, Elkanah and his family worshiped the Lord one more time and then left for home. When Elkanah and Hannah enjoyed the marriage bed, the Scripture tells us that **the LORD remembered her** (1:19). The womb that was closed by the Lord (1:5) was now opened. In the course of time, Hannah conceived and bore a son (1:20). When used with the Lord as the subject, the verb "to remember" (*zakar*) points to the beginning of a major new work initiated by God on behalf of his people (Gen. 8:1; Exod. 2:24).

Hannah had asked for this son, so she gave him a name that would help her and everyone else remember her bold prayer and the Lord's gracious response. The meaning of the name **Samuel** has been something of a puzzle to several generations of scholars (see "Deeper Discoveries"). The point of Hannah's request was that God would hear her and act to open her womb and give her a child. As it stands, "Samuel" can mean "the name of God." Since the word *name* in biblical Hebrew can mean "reputation" or "fame" or "memorial," it doesn't seem so farfetched to assume that Hannah wanted a name that focused praise on God for what he had done and not on anything she may have done.

![C] Hannah's Surrender (1:21–28)

SUPPORTING IDEA: *Hannah takes Samuel to the temple and dedicates him to the Lord.*

1:21–23. After the birth of Samuel, Elkanah again prepared his family to make the pilgrimage to offer the annual sacrifice at Shiloh. Hannah stayed home with the baby Samuel to nurse him and care for him until he was **weaned**. Weaning a child in those days could take up to three years or longer.

Elkanah appeared to be a little cautious at this point. Hannah promised that she would pay her vow after Samuel was weaned. She was straightforward in saying, **I will take him and present him before the LORD, and he will live there always** (1:22). She was determined to give back to the Lord what he had given to her. Elkanah encouraged Hannah to do what seemed best to her. But he was serious about paying the vow.

Her husband had a right to be concerned. The God-given love of a mother for a child is powerful and relentless. Hannah had prayed so hard for this child. It's a wonder she could give him up at all. Perhaps Elkanah's statement, **Only may the Lord make good his word**, was intended to remind Hannah of her vow and to ask the Lord to strengthen her in her resolve.

1:24–28. Even if there is a question in the reader's mind about Hannah's sincerity, that notion is dismissed in quick fashion as we learn that she took the young child and a generous sacrifice to **Eli** at **Shiloh** for the next annual feast (1:24). In fact, Hannah's determination is seen in the generosity of the offering brought along for this special occasion. The NIV follows the Septuagint and the Dead Sea Scrolls in listing the sacrificial offering as a **three-year-old bull, an ephah of flour and a skin of wine** (Bergen, 73). But the Hebrew text actually says "three bulls." The large amount—a full ephah and a whole skin—of flour and wine is more appropriate for a sacrifice of three bulls than for one. Hannah wanted to do this sacrifice right.

True to her word, Hannah brought the boy to Eli. She reminded him of her vow and declared that this was now the payment: **So now I give him to the LORD.** For his whole life he would be given over to the Lord. Hannah prayed for this child, and God granted her request. Now she was giving Samuel back to God.

Hannah serves as a faithful role model for all Christian parents. Children are gifts from the Lord (Ps. 127:3). We should seriously desire that each of our children be "given over to the Lord." God's gifts should be given back to him. It is not coincidence that many churches hold special dedication services to help parents present their children to the Lord.

D Hannah's Song (2:1–10)

SUPPORTING IDEA: *Hannah prays a prayer of thanksgiving to the Lord for his blessing and exalts him for his great works.*

2:1. The first part of chapter 2 contains the second prayer of Hannah. The contrast between her first prayer (1:11) and this one is profound. The first was a vow, the result of bitter anguish; the second, a song of praise and thanksgiving for God's gracious gift of a son. The song can be divided into four sources of joy (Kaiser, 69).

First, Hannah rejoiced in her own experience. She exalted **in the LORD**. Samuel was a gift from God. He was not the product of her strength or her own achievement. The term **horn** symbolizes strength (2:10; see also Pss. 89:24; 112:9; 132:17). "In the LORD" her strength was **lifted high**. She could boast over her enemies, but her boasting was in the deliverance of the Lord.

2:2–3. Hannah also rejoiced in her God. At Shiloh, she felt a profound sense of God's holiness. **There is no holy one like the LORD**, she stated. **There is no one besides you.** Ancient Canaan was full of Astarte idols. These small clay figurines were prayed to and worshiped with a hope that they would increase the fertility of their owners. But Hannah did not pray to a figurine; she prayed to the Lord. He was her rock, and he had established her lineage.

Standing before a holy God requires humility. She had to humble herself before the Lord in her anguish and bitterness. Here Hannah turned her attention beyond her own immediate experience. Since her prayer was spoken in a public worship at Shiloh, she warned her fellow Israelites (and us for that matter) not to be proud and arrogant. Hannah called for us to humble ourselves. God is aware of our thoughts and he judges our deeds.

2:4–8. Hannah also rejoiced in God's way of justice. God weighs the deeds of man and, if necessary, humbles and exalts (2:7). The proud and the haughty will not stand. In a series of contrastive actions, Hannah describes five areas of life where God may prove himself to be the great "reverser of fortunes." These areas include military might, famine, fertility, life and death, and economic status.

The very **foundations of the earth** belong to a sovereign Lord. He has set the world upon them. Hannah saw God's justice prevailing because God had created and established the world. God is on the throne of life, and his heart is with the poor and lowly. God chooses to work this way, and he did so in Hannah's life.

2:9–10. The final section of Hannah's song rejoiced in her future hope. That hope is expressed in both the temporal and mundane world as well as the eternal world to come. Travel in the ancient world was accomplished mostly by foot over difficult and rocky trails. Hannah proclaimed that the Lord will **guard the feet** of those who are faithful to him. The wicked, however, will perish. No one will be able to succeed by their own strength, and anyone who tries to oppose God in the eternal court of judgment will lose their case. Ultimately, **the LORD will judge the ends of the earth**.

In her closeness to the Lord, Hannah caught a prophetic glimpse of the coming Messiah, the exalted King who will be the judge of all the earth. Through the Lord's anointed, true justice will reign on the earth and throughout eternity. By the power of the Holy Spirit, Hannah could see in her own experience the way the Lord would provide for the consummation of his kingdom. It is perhaps no coincidence that there are some remarkable similarities between Hannah's song and that of the virgin Mary's Magnificat (Luke 1:46–55).

E Hannah's Son (2:11–36)

> **SUPPORTING IDEA:** *Eli's sons are wicked, and while Eli makes a feeble attempt to correct them, they are undaunted. As a result, a prophet comes to the temple and prophesies judgment against Eli and his family.*

2:11. Elkanah and his family returned home. But this time they were missing one important person. Samuel remained at Shiloh to live **before the LORD**. Hannah gave Samuel to minister "before the LORD," and this is what he did for the rest of his life (see 1 Sam. 2:18,21; 7:6; 10:19; 11:15; 12:3,7; 15:33).

2:12–17. For the last part of chapter 2, most commentaries focus on the wickedness of **Eli's sons** and the prophecy of judgment raised against Eli's house. But this is only part of the story. There are a number of pivot points in the narrative where Samuel's growth in ministry is contrasted with the religious and moral depravity of the sons of Eli. This fact suggests that the textual unit is primarily about Hannah's son and God's purpose in calling him to replace the corrupted house of Eli.

Davis calls these brief notes about Samuel "silent witnesses of Yahweh's provision" (Davis, *Heart*, 31). They point out that the Lord will indeed judge the wickedness of Hophni and Phinehas and lift up the humble Samuel. Davis notes that this quiet work of God can be seen in the following structure:

Samuel serving, 2:11
Liturgical sins, 2:12–17
Samuel serving, 2:18–21
Moral sins, 2:22–25
Samuel growing, 2:26
Prophecy of judgment, 2:27–36
Samuel serving, 3:1a (Davis, *Heart*, 31)

Two things are said about Hophni and Phinehas in verse 12. First, they were **wicked** (lit. "sons of Belial"), and second, they had **no regard for** (lit. "did not know") the Lord. But these two sons of Eli were supposed to be "priests of the LORD" (1:3).

This disregard for the Lord can be seen in the way Hophni and Phinehas took advantage of their liturgical office for personal gain. According to Leviticus 7:28–36, priests were allowed to have the "breast" and the "right thigh" of a sacrifice. Instead, Hophni and Phinehas devised the use of a **three-pronged fork** to take whatever they wanted from the Israelites who came to offer sacrifices at Shiloh (1:13–14).

Hophni and Phinehas went even farther in their total disregard for the Lord's sacrificial regulations. Priests were allowed to take their share only after the fat portions of the sacrifice had been burned on the altar. These two priests would send their servants and demand their meat **before the fat was burned** (2:15). If anyone resisted, the servant was instructed to take it **by force** (2:16).

The sin of Hophni and Phinehas was a travesty in the sight of the Lord. They abused their priestly office, and they had contempt for the Lord's offering. Leviticus 10:1–11 records the seriousness with which the Lord takes priestly misconduct. A holy God would not allow this to go on without punishment.

2:18–21. In contrast to the wickedness of Eli's sons, the narrative breaks sharply away to remind us of Samuel's progress in ministering before the Lord. In his daily ministrations, Samuel wore a **linen ephod**, a type of garment worn by the Levites. In addition, every year Hannah would make him a type of **robe** also worn by the Levites in priestly service (Lev. 8:7). Eli recognized that Hannah still cared very much for Samuel, and he pronounced another blessing over Elkanah and Hannah (2:21). God responded by blessing Hannah with **three sons and two daughters**. In the meantime, Samuel grew up with the Lord.

2:22–25. The same narrative technique used previously in 2:18 to turn our attention to Samuel is used in verse 22 to return our thoughts to **Eli** and his sons. As if their liturgical sins were not enough, the brothers added moral sins to their catalog of priestly misconduct. Eli heard that they were sleeping with the women who served at the entrance to the Tent of Meeting, and he sought to confront them.

Eli tried to reason with them, and as a judge he used the imagery of a legal dispute to warn his errant sons. He examined two cases. In the first case, Eli reminded them that if a man sinned against another man, God himself would mediate the case. But, if, as in the second case, a man sinned against God, there would be no one capable of interceding on behalf of the sinner, and condemnation would follow. Since Hophni and Phinehas had committed capital offenses (Lev. 7:25; 22:9), they could expect the death penalty to be brought against them.

2:26. Again, the narrative switches abruptly and briefly back to **Samuel**. But it would be wrong to think that this short notice is insignificant. In fact, a strong contrast is drawn. As the sins of Hophni and Phinehas were growing in magnitude, and God and society were condemning them, the good standing of Samuel was increasing. Samuel's growth in **stature** and in **favor** with God and men foreshadowed the boyhood development of Jesus (Luke 2:52).

2:27–36. Finally, God sent an unnamed person to reveal his judgment against Eli's house. It is clear that this individual was a prophet. The phrase **man of God** is the second most common designation for a prophet in the Old Testament. The messenger also began his statement with the classic prophetic introduction "Thus says the LORD."

The prophetic judgment speech contains three parts. In verses 27–28 God summarized the grace he had extended to the line of Aaron. God chose Aaron to be his priest, to attend to the altar in the tabernacle courtyard, to burn incense in the holy place, and to perform all other official priestly functions while wearing an ephod. All this was done in God's presence. In addition, God ordained that the sacrificial meat portions given to him by the Israelites were to be eaten by the priests. This great office was to be taken seriously because in the handling of sacrifices, the priests were to mediate between God and man.

Verse 29 identifies the sin of Eli and his sons. God condemned Hophni and Phinehas for their presumption in taking the fatty portions of every offering that was to be burned in the fire. Eli was also condemned for honoring his sons more than God. He verbally reproved them (2:23–24), but he took no decisive action to restrain them (3:13) or remove them from their office. Eli was willing to tolerate sin. He seemed to profit by growing fatter himself (4:18). God could not allow this to go on.

The last section of the prophetic speech (vv. 30–36) begins with an ominous **therefore**. The Lord, the God of Israel announced the judgment against Eli and his house. God proclaimed that he would **cut short** Eli's strength and the lineage of his **father's house** (v. 31). This would happen in two ways. First, the current generation of Eli's family would suffer. Hophni and Phinehas would **die on the same day** (v. 34). Second, future generations of Eli's family would suffer. His descendants would die untimely deaths (v. 33) and lose their livelihood (v. 36).

The message is clear. God will punish those who use their religious positions to further their own selfish and sinful purposes (Getz, *Samuel*, 66). The fall of the house of Eli stands as a stark warning to those who minister in the church.

In the place of Eli and his house, God declared that he would raise up a faithful priest (v. 35). This new priest would walk completely in God's will, acting in accordance with God's wishes and purposes. In turn, God would do two things for him. First, God would build for him a "faithful house." That is, his descendents would remain true to their priestly calling. Finally, as a measure of honor, this **faithful priest** would minister before the Lord's Messiah forever.

The identity of this faithful priest is uncertain. Some have suggested Samuel. Others have looked to the priestly line of Zadok to fulfill the prophecy (1 Kgs. 2:26–27,35). If Zadok is the faithful priest, then David and his successors must be understood as the Lord's anointed.

The contrast continues into the next chapter. God will continue to prepare Samuel, Hannah's son, to replace Eli and his wicked sons. The moment has not yet arrived, but it will soon come.

> **MAIN IDEA REVIEW:** *Samuel is born to a faithful, previously barren woman who dedicates him to the Lord. After a prayer of thanksgiving, she leaves him with Eli, the high priest, to be reared in the temple. Eli's sons are wicked, and a prophet prophesies judgment against them.*

III. CONCLUSION

Hannah's Blessing

In the first two chapters of 1 Samuel, we have watched Hannah struggle with the sorrow of childlessness. Instead of letting bitterness consume her,

Hannah prayed in her pain and anguish to the Lord. All she wanted was a child and nothing more. What she wanted most in life, she was willing to give back to the Lord. After giving birth to Samuel, Hannah was faithful in her vow and returned him to serve before the Lord. Because of Hannah's faithfulness, God blessed her beyond her initial request. God blessed her with more sons and daughters. In addition, God raised up Samuel, Hannah's first son, to serve as a mighty judge and priest in Israel.

PRINCIPLES

- All children are a gift from the Lord and should be the most precious and central part of a parent's life.
- Walking with Christ does not take away life's problems; he desires to give us victory over our problems.
- God can produce miracles even from a dysfunctional family.
- Prayer is measured by intensity and not by time.
- Great things come from God when we are obedient and follow our commitments to him.
- When we are faithful, God will bless us with more than we ask.

APPLICATIONS

- Dedicate your children to the Lord.
- If you have no children, ask God to show you what is at the center of your life and then dedicate this to the Lord.
- Yield every problem to the care of the Lord. He knows exactly how to handle them.
- Ask God to help you learn to pray with a broken heart for his will to be done, for others to know him, and for your own personal Christian walk and witness.
- Thank God and praise him for his salvation and blessings in life.
- Seek the discernment of the Holy Spirit to reveal any actions in your ministry and service that arise from self-serving or personal motivations.
- Reject any impure reasons for Christian service and replace them with a simple desire to seek to glorify God in all your actions.

IV. LIFE APPLICATION

A Faithful Role Model

By the age of 25, Tiger Woods was already a golf legend. He made his debut at age two by putting on the *Mike Douglas Show*. When he was three years old, he shot 48, and by the time he was five, he was featured in *Golf Digest*. Woods later won a record three-straight junior amateur titles, three-straight U.S. Amateur titles, and the NCAA individual crown for Stanford University. Woods became the first player of color to win the Masters tournament in 1997. Three years later he won the Masters again, as well as the PGA championship, the U.S. Open, and the British Open, becoming the first player ever to hold all four crowns at the same time.

But despite his great achievements, Tiger's father said that he is a better person off the course and loves setting a good example for children. Tiger and his father, Earl Woods, have offered clinics for minority youngsters and have started a nationwide program to teach kids how to become role models to others. At one of the clinics, Tiger said, "Today, I'm going to speak to you from the heart. You have chosen me as a role model. I didn't ask for it, but I accept the responsibility. If I can do it, so can you."

Whether we ask for it or not, God has called us to be role models of faith and to encourage others to be the same. Our witness for Jesus is at stake. The world must see our faithfulness. Hannah provides us with a faithful role model.

In the midst of trouble in her life, she suffered faithfully. Instead of complaining or blaming others, she took her heart to the Lord in prayer and put her cares on him. Hannah promised her most cherished desire to the Lord. And when the time came to make good on the promise, she dedicated her son to God's service.

Through all of this, Hannah was faithful to praise and exalt God. In her song, she thanked God for his salvation and blessings in life. She remained faithful by providing her son with physical needs as he grew in the presence of the Lord. Hannah's faithfulness provides us with a role model of trust and commitment that we should emulate. Our goal in life should be to hear from our Lord, "Well done, thou good and faithful servant."

V. PRAYER

Heavenly Father, teach us to throw our cares upon you. Take away worry and fear from our lives. Search our hearts and reveal to us that which we deeply cherish. Help us to dedicate all things totally to you, whether it is our spouse, children, job, or any possession or thing. Like Hannah, help us to be faithful role models for others, but by your power, not ours. Help us to show others the trust we place in you daily. Amen.

VI. DEEPER DISCOVERIES

A. The Time of the Judges (1:1)

The book of 1 Samuel describes the period between the judges and the monarchy, a transitional time in Israelite history. After the death of Joshua, Israel sinned against God and worshiped idols (Judg. 2:10–11), and he handed them over to surrounding nations that oppressed them. But in his compassion, God raised up various judges to deliver Israel from her enemies (Judg. 2:16). As long as the judge lived, God was with the judge and saved Israel from the hands of their enemies (Judg. 2:18).

But when the judge died, the people of Israel turned their backs on God and became even more corrupt than their fathers (Judg. 2:19). Israel fell into a downward spiral of sin. Eventually, even the judges became corrupt. Nevertheless, God still remained faithful. Concerning this period of transition, Eugene Merrill concludes: "Just when it seemed the nation would cave in on its own rottenness, God intervened and in response to godly Hannah's prayer gave young Samuel to her and the nation. Samuel's strong leadership as judge, prophet and priest provided respite to the people for both their internal and external threat" (Getz, *Samuel*, 12).

B. Levites (1:1)

The genealogy of Elkanah in 1 Chronicles 6:22–28,33–38 identifies him as a Levite. The Levites were the descendents of Levi and were set apart for the service of the sanctuary (Num. 3:11–13). They were selected for this purpose because of their zeal for the glory of God (Exod. 32:26).

The Levites were the special guardians of the tabernacle (Num. 1:51; 18:22–24). It was their duty to move the tent and carry the parts of the sacred structure from place to place. Since they were wholly consecrated to the service of the Lord, they had no territorial possessions. The Lord was their inheritance (Num. 18:20; 26:62; Deut. 10:9; 18:1,2). The Levites were grouped according to their ancestors, the three sons of Levi: Gershon, Kohath, and Merari. Elkanah was of the Kohathite clan.

C. The Lord Almighty (1:3)

This verse contains the first Old Testament use of the phrase "LORD Almighty." In addition, Hannah is the first person to utter this special name for God in prayer (1:11). The Hebrew *yhwh tsbaoth* is sometimes translated "Yahweh of Armies/Hosts." The KJV and other versions translate the term as "LORD of hosts." The phrase proclaims the Lord's dominion over all spiritual entities and points to his unmatched sovereign authority (Bergen, 65). It is used more than 240 times in the Old Testament, primarily in the writings of the prophets, including especially Isaiah (62 times), Jeremiah (79 times), Zechariah (53 times), and Malachi (24 times).

D. "No Razor Will Ever Be Used on His Head" (1:11)

Hannah's use of this phrase has led many scholars to believe that she was dedicating her son to be a lifelong Nazirite. According to Numbers 6:1–21, three conditions were attached to the Nazirite vow. First, the individual must abstain from wine and all other fermented drinks. Second, no razor was to be used on the head of a Nazirite. Finally, the individual must not go near a dead body. Throughout the days of this vow, the Nazirite was considered to be holy unto the Lord. Samson was a Nazirite (Judg. 13:3–5). Paul apparently took a Nazirite vow (Acts 18:18; 21:23–24). It is possible also that John the Baptist was a Nazirite.

The Septuagint, an early Greek translation of the Old Testament, and one of the Dead Seas scrolls (4QSam[a]) contain additional textual material at verses 11 and 22. Both versions have Hannah also stating her son would not taste wine or strong drink. In verse 22, 4QSam[a] has Hannah clearly saying that she was giving Samuel to be a Nazirite before the Lord (Bergen, 69, n. 21).

E. The Meaning of Samuel's Name (1:20)

The meaning of the name Samuel has perplexed scholars to this day. Suggested meanings include: "His name is El," "Name of El/God," "Heard of God," "Asked of God," "He Who Is from God," "Offspring of God," and "El Is Exalted" (Bergen, 71, n. 24). The problem arises when scholars try to connect the name (*shemuel*) and the verb "asked" (*shaal*) which Hannah used in giving the reason why she named the boy Samuel: "Because I asked the LORD for him."

Perhaps it is better to remember that Samuel can mean "The Name of God." Since the word *name* in biblical Hebrew can mean "reputation," "fame," or "memorial," it doesn't seem so farfetched to assume that Hannah may have chosen a name that exalted God for his gracious gift.

VII. TEACHING OUTLINE

A. INTRODUCTION

1. Lead Story: For This Child I Prayed
2. Context: The first two chapters of 1 Samuel introduce us to two families living in Israel during the time of the judges. One family enjoys a grand religious heritage and prestige. The other is the family of a lowly but faithful Levite. While Israelite society all around them plunges downward in a continuing spiral of sin and rebellion against the Lord, only the family of the Levite remains faithful. But because of the faithfulness of Hannah, the wife of the ordinary Levite, God is going to do an extraordinary miracle in their lives.
3. Transition: Hannah functions in these two chapters as an excellent role model of faith. As she struggles with her sorrow and her anguish, it is important to examine her actions. What she wanted most in life, she was willing to give back to God. When God gave her a son, Hannah was faithful to her word and returned him to serve before the Lord. Hannah only wanted a son, but God blessed her with six children. God used that first son, Samuel, to bring all Israel back to himself.

B. COMMENTARY

1. Hannah's Sorrow (1:1–8)
   a. Elkanah and his family (1:1–2)
   b. Family squabbles at Shiloh (1:3–7)
   c. Elkanah's Response (1:8)
2. Hannah's Supplication (1:9–20)
   a. Hannah's vow (1:9–11)
   b. Eli's mistake (1:12–18)
   c. A miracle child (1:19–20)
3. Hannah's Surrender (1:21–28)
   a. Hannah waits at home (1:21–23)
   b. Hannah fulfills her vow (1:24–28)

4. Hannah's Song (2:1–10)
    a. Hannah rejoices in her own experience (2:1)
    b. Hannah rejoices in her God (2:2–3)
    c. Hannah rejoices in God's way (2:4–8)
    d. Hannah rejoices in a future hope (2:9–10)
5. Hannah's Son (2:11–36)
    a. Hannah's son ministers before the Lord (2:11)
    b. The religious sins of Eli's sons (2:12–17)
    c. Hannah's sons and daughters (2:18–21)
    d. The moral sins of Eli's sons (2:22–25)
    e. Hannah's son grows before the Lord (2:26)
    f. The judgment against Eli's sons (2:27–36)

C. CONCLUSION: A FAITHFUL ROLE MODEL

VIII. ISSUES FOR DISCUSSION

1. Do you pray from a broken and sincere heart? Have you recognized that God must be approached humbly on your knees?
2. Is there something in your life that God has refused to give you and you are bitter about? Will you confess that to God right now?
3. Have you dedicated all your children to the Lord, realizing that even if they are grown, it is still not too late? Will you pray that they will be committed to doing God's will in every respect?
4. Have you made a vow to the Lord that you have not fulfilled? In what ways can you fulfill it now?
5. Have you watched God humble someone who has exalted themselves? Has this happened to you? What steps can a Christian take to avoid spiritual pride?
6. Have you tried to fight a spiritual battle on your own? How can a Christian avoid doing this?
7. Do you know of situations in which Christians have suffered because they have chosen to allow sin to control their lives? What can we learn from these examples?

1 Samuel 3:1–21

The Call of Samuel

I. **INTRODUCTION**
"Speak, Lord, for Your Servant Is Listening"

II. **COMMENTARY**
A verse-by-verse explanation of this chapter

III. **CONCLUSION**
Samuel's Lesson

An overview of the principles and applications from this chapter

IV. **LIFE APPLICATION**
When God Speaks

Melding this chapter to life

V. **PRAYER**
Tying this chapter to life with God

VI. **DEEPER DISCOVERIES**
Historical, geographical, and grammatical enrichment of the commentary

VII. **TEACHING OUTLINE**
Suggested step-by-step group study of this chapter

VIII. **ISSUES FOR DISCUSSION**
Zeroing these chapters in on daily life

| Quote |

"*W*hen Christ calls a man, he bids him come and die."

D i e t r i c h   B o n h o e f f e r

GEOGRAPHICAL PROFILE: DAN TO BEERSHEBA

- Common phrase used to refer to the whole land of Israel
- Dan is located in the far north of the country
- Beersheba is in the south
- The expression is often found in Samuel, Kings, and Chronicles

1 Samuel 3:1–21

 I N   A   N U T S H E L L

*C*hapter 3 describes how God called Samuel to be a faithful prophet. As a young lad Samuel ministered before the Lord under Eli's tutelage. Prophetic revelation was rare in the days of the judges, but late one night God called Samuel. The word that God gave to Samuel was difficult to bear, but Samuel was faithful and shared the prophecy with Eli. The Lord was with Samuel as he grew. God established him as a faithful prophet at a time when Israel desperately needed to hear the word of God. The church needs faithful servants who will listen for God's call and be obedient to it.

The Call of Samuel

I. INTRODUCTION

"Speak, Lord, for Your Servant Is Listening"

In his book *Listening*, Norman Wakefield tells about a "Dennis the Menace" cartoon that emphasizes the difference between *hearing* and *listening*. Dennis runs into Mr. Wilson's house and sees him sitting down and reading a newspaper. Immediately, Dennis greets him with a warm, "Hello, Mr. Wilson." But Mr. Wilson does not respond. Again, Dennis speaks, but this time a little louder, "Hello, Mr. Wilson." No response comes from his neighbor behind the newspaper. Finally, Dennis blasts forth with a long "HEL-LOOO, MR. WILSON!" Still Mr. Wilson does not answer. So Dennis turns to leave and in a normal voice says, "Well, then, goodbye, Mr. Wilson." Mr. Wilson replies, "Goodbye, Dennis." As he walks out the door Dennis remarks, "There's nothing wrong with his hearing, but his listening's not so good" (Wakefield, 23–24).

The young child that Hannah and Elkanah had dedicated to the service of the Lord was growing in stature and favor with God and man. Samuel continued to minister at the tabernacle of the Lord Almighty, the God of Israel. But Samuel had not yet met the Lord of that tabernacle. Samuel could hear, but he had not listened for God's call.

One night God spoke to him, but he thought it was old Eli calling. Finally, Eli realized that the Lord was calling Samuel. So Eli taught Samuel to reply, "Speak, Lord, for your servant is listening." In chapter 3 we discover how well Samuel listened.

II. COMMENTARY

The Call of Samuel

MAIN IDEA: *The Lord calls Samuel to be a prophet, and blesses him so that all Israel recognizes him as a "prophet of the Lord."*

A The Call of God Is Rare (3:1)

SUPPORTING IDEA: *During a time when visitations from the Lord were rare, Samuel ministered to the Lord under Eli.*

3:1. The text tells us that Samuel had grown since his parents had left him at Shiloh. Now he was a young lad ministering **before the LORD**. Eli continued to teach him.

The end of verse 1 states that the word of the Lord was **rare** (lit., "precious"). Prophetic visions were not "breaking through." Between Joshua and Samuel there were only three prophets mentioned (Judg. 4:4; 6:8; 1 Sam. 2:27–36) and five revelations given (Judg. 2:1–3; 6:11–23; 7:2–11; 10:11–14; 13:3–21). Why did God stop speaking?

Because Israel rebelled against him, God handed them over to their enemies (Judg. 2:14). The absence of the word of God may have been a sign of God's judgment. God was displeased with the corrupted priesthood of Eli's sons. The downward spiral of sin kept God and man separated. When there is no prophetic word, society degenerates quickly (Prov. 29:18). The cycle is difficult to break: sin keeps us from listening to God, and sin will keep God from listening to us (Ps. 66:18).

B The Call of God Is Personal (3:2–4)

SUPPORTING IDEA: *One night as Samuel is sleeping, the Lord speaks to him.*

3:2–3. These verses describe what must have been a typical night for Eli and Samuel at Shiloh. Eli's **eyes** were growing **weak**, and he was lying down in his usual place (v. 2). The reference to Eli's eyes is intended to cause us to pause and wonder about his spiritual sight.

The mention of the **lamp of God** and the **ark** of the covenant points out two things. First, the fact that the lamp had not yet gone out indicates that God spoke to Samuel in the predawn hours (Exod. 27:21). Perhaps this is also symbolic of God's presence still remaining in the Shiloh complex, even though it was run by Hophni and Phinehas, the corrupted sons of Eli.

The reference to Samuel **lying down in the temple** near the ark of God is important. As Bergen has pointed out, Samuel was of all the Israelites the closest to the Lord's throne (Bergen, 86). This was at least true physically, if not spiritually.

3:4. Being so physically close to the Lord's throne, Samuel was bound to meet him. All of chapters 1 and 2 has led up to this point. God was going to do something wonderful with this young man who was dedicated by his parents to minister before the Lord.

Here was the moment of contact. Here was God's call. It was personal and face-to-face. It was private when no one else was around. It came in God's house in the early morning. Samuel answered, **Here I am**. He responded to the divine call in a similar manner as Abraham, Jacob, and Moses had done (Gen. 22:1,11; 31:11; Exod. 3:4). But he didn't know who called him. He heard, but he wasn't listening.

C The Call of God Is Persistent (3:5–10)

> **SUPPORTING IDEA:** *Samuel thinks it was Eli calling him. Eli instructs him to ask the Lord to speak to him further.*

3:5–6. Can you imagine Samuel waking up old Eli? Samuel thought Eli had summoned him, so he ran to Eli and repeated again, **Here I am**. For good measure he added, **You called me**. Perhaps Eli sleepily grumbled his reply, "I didn't call you! Go back to bed!"

God is certainly persistent. The verb *call* occurs eleven times in verses 4–10. Anyone who has ever experienced a call from God can tell you that sometimes it is relentless. God does not give up. This time God spoke his name, **Samuel**. Again, Samuel awakened Eli: "Here I am; you called me." Again, Eli denied the summons and sent him back to bed.

3:7–8. Samuel had an excuse for making a mistake about the call. It had never happened to him before. Samuel had never heard God speak. He had never before received a prophetic revelation of the word of God. Getz points out, "Since this was a new experience for Samuel, he had no way of understanding and interpreting what was happening" (Getz, *Samuel*, 73). He did not know how to respond, so when God's call came the third time, Samuel went again to wake up Eli.

Eli, on the other hand, had no excuse. It took him three tries to figure out what God was doing. This was certainly not a good reflection on Eli's spiritual insight. But finally, Eli realized that God was calling Samuel.

3:9–10. Eli's directions were sound. If God should call again, Samuel was to respond, **Speak, LORD, for your servant is listening**. The next time Samuel would be ready.

He needed to be ready because the fourth time was extraordinary. To begin with, God called the boy's name twice, **Samuel! Samuel!** In addition, verse 10 indicates that the Lord came and stood in Samuel's presence. What an awesome experience!

In the early hours of the morning, the Lord called Samuel and gave him a message of judgment. Perhaps it is understandable that Samuel neglected to repeat one word in the phrase that Eli taught him. Samuel said, "Speak, for your servant is listening." Maybe Samuel forgot to say "Lord" because he didn't have to. The Lord was standing right in front of him!

𝔻 The Call of God Is Painful (3:11–17)

SUPPORTING IDEA: *The Lord gives Samuel a prophecy against Eli and his sons.*

3:11–14. The message God gave to Samuel confirmed the prophetic judgment delivered previously by an unknown man of God (2:27–36). God reiterated that he would punish Eli's house because of sin. It would make the **ears** of everyone who heard about it **tingle**.

God's judgment would be complete. Just as he had promised, God would destroy Eli's lineage. This was not just the fault of Hophni and Phinehas. Eli knew about their sin. They had made themselves **contemptible** to God, but Eli had failed to restrain them (v. 13). There was no amount of **sacrifice or offering** that would make atonement for the sins of the house of Eli.

3:15–17. The message was troubling to Samuel. He returned to bed and went about his regular chores in the morning. He was **afraid to tell Eli** what God had said (v. 15).

The prophetic call of God is both a joyous occasion and a painful one. On the one hand, the prophet is called to speak a message of hope to Israel. But on the other, the message could also be one of doom and destruction.

Jeremiah experienced this in his call (Jer. 1:4–19). Six verbs were used to describe Jeremiah's ministry. The last two were positive: "to build and to plant." The first four, however, were negative: "to uproot and tear down, to destroy and overthrow" (1:10).

No one likes to be the bearer of bad news. Nevertheless, the gospel, the "good" news, does contain a negative aspect. The good news is that Jesus died on the cross to save us from our sins. Receiving salvation means enjoying eternity with the Lord. The bad news is that rejecting Christ ends in eternal damnation and punishment in hell.

Eli did not let Samuel off the hook. He called Samuel and demanded to know what God had said to him (v. 17). Even though the prophecy was against Eli and his house, Eli knew that Samuel must share it, that the prophet is compelled to proclaim the word of God. Eli's admonishment taught Samuel to be faithful in speaking God's word. Samuel "must never withhold or soften God's message to sinful humanity—even if it hurt those closest to him" (Getz, *Samuel*, 74).

🄴 The Call of God Is Perfect (3:18)

SUPPORTING IDEA: *Eli accepts the prophecy issued by the Lord through Samuel.*

3:18. One might expect Eli to respond in a negative way to the prophecy revealed to Samuel. But Eli knew enough to teach Samuel one more lesson. He wanted Samuel to know that he was dealing with a holy and sovereign God. The Lord had said there would be no atonement for Eli's sins. Eli took full responsibility for his actions.

At this point, Eli probably realized that God had chosen Samuel to be his successor. Eli had been able to teach Samuel. Perhaps he did not want Samuel to repeat the mistake that his own sons had made. Eli knew that the judgment of God was righteous. Eli submitted to the perfect will of God.

Samuel needed to hear Eli's words because they taught him to accept the call of God on his life as perfect and right. God will **do what is good in his own eyes**. God's will for his servant is perfect and good in every way.

🄵 The Call of God Is Powerful (3:19–21)

SUPPORTING IDEA: *God blesses Samuel and gives him great stature in Israel.*

3:19. The power of God's call on Samuel's life is shown in the faithfulness of God's presence with his ministry. God did not leave Samuel alone to fulfill his calling by himself. Samuel did not need to get by on his wits or good looks.

Verse 19 says two important things. First, as Samuel grew up, God was with him. It also states that God **let none of his words fall to the ground**. What exactly does this mean?

Obviously, the phrase refers to Samuel's prophetic ministry. Whatever Samuel proclaimed as a word from the Lord came to pass. But don't get the idea that this suggests Samuel could predict anything he wanted to and God was obligated to make it happen. The sentence really means that Samuel learned the first lesson of his call very well. That is, Samuel learned to say, "Speak, LORD, for your servant is listening" (v. 9).

Samuel did not use his call for fame or personal gain (cp. 1 Sam. 12:3–4). He did not try to twist God's commands to suit himself or his friends. He listened and spoke as God spoke to him. He had the courage to be faithful to the message of God, no matter what. And because he did, God blessed his ministry and confirmed his prophecies. Samuel's words were trustworthy because they were the Lord's words (Bergen, 88).

3:20–21. Since Samuel was faithful to listen to the Lord and obey him, his reputation as a prophet spread throughout the land. Like Moses before him (Num. 12:7), Samuel was now considered a **prophet of the LORD** in all Israel. The famine of hearing the word of Lord (Amos 8:11) was over. No longer was the word rare or uncommon. The Lord continued to reveal himself to Samuel at Shiloh. Samuel had truly learned to say, "Speak, LORD, for your servant is listening."

> **MAIN IDEA REVIEW:** *The Lord calls Samuel to be a prophet, and blesses him so that all Israel recognizes him as a "prophet of the Lord."*

III. CONCLUSION

Samuel's Lesson

The child whom Hannah and Elkanah had given back to the Lord was growing up at Shiloh. God was ready to call Samuel to serve him, but Samuel needed to learn an important lesson. Samuel did not know that God was calling him until Eli taught him to say, "Speak, LORD, for your servant is listening." When Samuel learned this lesson and continued to apply it through his many years of service, God was able once again to speak through a faithful prophet to his people, Israel.

PRINCIPLES

- God speaks to us clearly and regularly through the Scriptures.
- Sin keeps us from listening to God's voice.
- In order to listen to God, Christians must develop spiritual listening skills.
- God desires to have a personal relationship with us.
- No matter what, God's will is always perfect for us.
- God wants faithful servants to proclaim his word throughout the world.

APPLICATIONS

- Make Bible study and prayer priorities in your life.

- Ask the Holy Spirit to teach you how to listen to God and how to be sensitive to the needs of others.
- Develop your spiritual listening skills so you can be ready when God calls.
- When God does call, surrender your heart and life to him.
- Confess your sins to God, especially those that keep you from listening to him.
- Seek every day to nurture your personal relationship with God.
- Learn to trust completely in God. Trust that his will is always good and perfect for you.
- Ask God to provide opportunities for you to share the gospel daily with people in your world.

IV. LIFE APPLICATION

When God Speaks

Years ago, the brokerage firm of E. F. Hutton developed a series of successful television ads. The circumstances were always different, but the message was the same. In a crowded room, restaurant, or other location, a small group of people are busy talking about some financial investment.

Generally, one individual was not saying much, but in the course of the conversation that person was finally asked what he thought. The person always responded in every ad by saying the same thing, "Well, my broker is E. F. Hutton, and E. F. Hutton says . . ." Immediately, the person stopped speaking and realized that all activity around them had stopped, everything had become silent, and all ears were stretched to catch the next words out of his mouth.

In fact, everyone surrounding the speaker was straining to hear the latest financial tip or advice. At this point, an announcer broke in and said, "When E. F. Hutton speaks, people listen." Of course, the implication was clear. E. F. Hutton was so successful in the investment business that people would stop everything they were doing just to listen to what the broker had to say.

When you think about it, it seems sad that this doesn't happen to God. It ought to be that when God speaks, people listen. Unfortunately, this is not the case. The world is too busy to stop and listen.

Nevertheless, God is the creator and sustainer of life. He gave his only Son to die on the cross in order that we might have life. He gave us the Bible, God's instruction book on life. He desires to guide us through this life and eternity. The least we can do is to learn to say like Samuel, "Speak, LORD, for your servant is listening."

V. PRAYER

O Lord, your word will stand forever! Teach us to listen to you—to listen through Scripture, through the Holy Spirit, and through your Son, Jesus. Show our sins to us so that we may humble ourselves and confess them, especially the ones that keep us from hearing your voice. Teach us how to listen to others, to discern their needs. Give us the courage to share the gospel with them that they may listen to you, too. Help us to trust you completely. Lead us to serve you faithfully whenever and wherever you call. Amen.

VI. DEEPER DISCOVERIES

A. The Lamp of God (3:3)

The lamp mentioned in this verse is the golden lamp stand found among the tabernacle's furnishings. This lamp stand stood opposite the bread of the presence in the holy place (Exod. 25:31–40). It was a violation of the priestly regulations to allow this flame to go out before morning (Exod. 27:21).

B. The Tabernacle of the Lord (3:3)

Although the Hebrew text uses the term for "temple" *(hecal)*, the portable tabernacle is meant (Exod. 26). In 1 Samuel it is also called "the house of the Lord" (3:15), "the Tent of Meeting" (2:22), and "my dwelling" (2:32). Since the tabernacle may have been located at Shiloh for 40 years (the length of Eli's judgeship; see 4:18), a larger, more permanent building complex may have grown up around it. This would justify the use of the term *temple*.

C. The Ark of God (3:3)

The ark of God, a chest of acacia wood overlaid with gold inside and out, symbolized the presence of God with Israel (Exod. 25:10–22). Two cherubim sat on top of the mercy seat on the ark, and the Lord Almighty was said to be enthroned between them (1 Sam. 4:4). The ark led the people of Israel through their wilderness journeys and into the promised land. It was kept in the most holy place of the tabernacle behind a curtain (Exod. 26:33).

D. "He Let None of His Words Fall to the Ground" (3:19)

God saw to it that all of Samuel's words were reliable. Consequently, Samuel was recognized as a prophet who spoke the word of the Lord. At Shiloh, the Lord continued to reveal himself to Samuel through his word (3:21); then Samuel's word was accepted by all Israel (4:1).

VII. TEACHING OUTLINE

A. INTRODUCTION

1. Lead Story: "Speak, Lord, for Your Servant Is Listening"
2. Context: Chapter 3 details the growth of Samuel as he ministers before the Lord at Shiloh. He is still under the tutelage of Eli, and he learns a very important lesson. Much of the action takes place one night when God seeks to call Samuel.
3. Transition: The lesson Samuel learned is important for every believer. We can send more students to seminary, call out more missionaries, and start more programs in church. But all this will be for nothing if we do not listen to the Lord and faithfully obey him. Eli taught Samuel to respond to God's call by saying, "Speak, LORD, for your servant is listening." Samuel never forgot that lesson. God used him to call a nation back to faith and to establish the Messiah's line. What do you think God could do with us if we were willing to say, "Speak, LORD, for your servant is listening"?

B. COMMENTARY

1. The Call of God Is Rare (3:1)
2. The Call of God Is Personal (3:2–4)
3. The Call of God Is Persistent (3:5–10)
4. The Call of God Is Painful (3:11–17)
5. The Call of God Is Perfect (3:18)
6. The Call of God Is Powerful (3:19–21)

C. CONCLUSION: WHEN GOD SPEAKS

VIII. ISSUES FOR DISCUSSION

1. Are you a good listener? What kinds of skills are necessary for "spiritual listening"?
2. Has God ever spoken to you? What were you doing, and what did God say?
3. Do you read the Bible daily, asking the Holy Spirit to speak to you through the Word of God?
4. Is it difficult to trust God with your life completely? Do you remember a time when you did this? What did God do?
5. Do you think God may be calling you to Christian service? What does it mean to be "called" by God?

1 Samuel 4:1–7:17

Arkeology

I. **INTRODUCTION**
The Cross along the Nile

II. **COMMENTARY**
A verse-by-verse explanation of these chapters

III. **CONCLUSION**
Just a Piece of Jewelry
An overview of the principles and applications from these chapters

IV. **LIFE APPLICATION**
Bernard Coffindaffer
Melding these chapters to life

V. **PRAYER**
Tying these chapters to life with God

VI. **DEEPER DISCOVERIES**
Historical, geographical, and grammatical enrichment of the commentary

VII. **TEACHING OUTLINE**
Suggested step-by-step group study of these chapters

VIII. **ISSUES FOR DISCUSSION**
Zeroing these chapters in on daily life

Q u o t e

"If God is God, He's big, and generous and magnificent, and I can't see that anybody can say they've made a 'corner' in God, or shut Him up in their particular box."

J . B . P h i l l i p s

FAITH PROFILE: THE ARK OF THE COVENANT

- A chest of acacia wood overlaid with gold (Exod. 25:10–22; 37:1–9)
- Two cherubim hovered over the top of the mercy seat on the ark (1 Sam. 4:4)
- Symbolized the presence of God with Israel (1 Sam. 4:4)
- Kept in the most holy place of the tabernacle behind a curtain (Exod. 26:33)
- Led the people of Israel through their wilderness journeys and into the promised land (Num. 10:35; Josh. 3:6)

PEOPLE PROFILE: THE PHILISTINES

- People with this name had lived in Palestine since the time of Abraham (Gen. 21:32; 26:1; Exod. 23:31)
- Became militarily active during the time of the judges (Judg. 3:31; 10:6–8; 13:1–16:30)
- The Philistines of Samuel's day may have migrated from the Aegean region along with other Sea Peoples about 1200 B.C.
- The battles of the Sea Peoples with the Egyptian Pharaoh Ramesses III are depicted on the famous wall paintings of Medinet Habu

RELIGION PROFILE: THE GOD DAGON

- An important god in the Semitic pantheon of deities
- Attested as early as the third millennium at Mari

- He was worshiped by the Assyrians in Mesopotamia and by the people of Ugarit on the Mediterranean coast.
- One of the gods of the Philistines (Judg. 16:23; 1 Chron. 10:10)
- Dagon is often identified as a god of grain, but this is uncertain.

GEOGRAPHICAL PROFILE: THE FIVE CITIES OF THE PHILISTINES

- All five cities were situated in a coastal plain west of the Shephelah, the foothills of the Judean plateau
- These five cities were often called the Philistine Pentapolis
- Ashkelon was located on the Mediterranean coast
- Ashdod and Gaza were about three miles inland on the coastal highway called the *Via Maris*
- Ekron and Gath were further inland in the foothills of the Judean mountains

1 Samuel 4:1–7:17

IN A NUTSHELL

Chapters 4–7 of 1 Samuel relate the painful lessons the nation of Israel had to learn in what Dale Ralph Davis calls the subject of "Arkeology" (Davis, Heart, 49). Through the misuse of a sacred religious symbol, the ark of the covenant, the people of Israel tried to win a battle against the Philistines by manipulating God for their own purposes. As a result, the sinful regime of Eli's sons, Hophni and Phinehas, came to a tragic and inglorious end. The ark, the powerful symbol of God's presence with his people, was captured by the Philistines. And although the ark was eventually recovered, it was effectively lost to Israel for many years until its return to its proper place of glory in David's reign. A little while later, without the ark, Samuel led the people to repentance, and God decisively delivered them from the Philistines.

Arkeology

I. INTRODUCTION

The Cross along the Nile

*I*n January 1999 Dr. Mark Coppenger, then president of Midwestern Baptist Theological Seminary, invited me to go on an unusual mission trip. The plan was to bicycle along the upper Nile River in Egypt from Luxor to Aswan. Escorted by Egyptian tourist police, we rode more than 152 miles along the Nile in four days. We distributed literature telling about our cycling team as well as evangelistic tracts and Scripture portions to the Egyptian people we met in the many small towns along the way. Coppenger also provided the team with a specially designed jersey featuring the logo of the seminary. The jersey also displayed the silhouette of a large cross woven into the colorful pattern on the front. For the bikers the cross functioned as a symbol of faith—the visible sign of God's invisible presence and redeeming grace.

In addition, Coppenger brought along an instant camera to take pictures of the team and the local folks. In each photograph he made sure that one of us with our special jersey was standing front and center. Then he would give away these photos to the local people. In this way he prayed that after we had cycled along to the next town, the proud owner of the photo would look at the picture and see the cross—see not only the friends who had visited, but also the Savior who died on that cross for them.

Religious symbols can be a powerful testimony to someone's faith. But such symbols can also be abused and misunderstood. The Israelites misunderstood the purpose of the ark of the covenant. The ark was the symbol of God's presence with his people. The ark was not God. Nor could the Israelites manipulate God or guarantee his presence by moving the ark wherever they pleased. Israel learned this the hard way. Chapters 4 through 7 document the lessons Israel had to learn on the subject of "Arkeology."

II. COMMENTARY

Arkeology

> **MAIN IDEA:** *The ark of the covenant is captured by the Philistines, then eventually returned, and the Israelites learn appropriate respect for this sacred object.*

🅰 The Error of God's People (4:1–11)

> **SUPPORTING IDEA:** *The Philistines capture the ark of the covenant when the Israelites carry it into battle.*

4:1–4. Scholars disagree on the place of the beginning of verse 1 of 1 Samuel 4. Some suggest that the first part of the verse, **and Samuel's word came to all Israel**, should be connected to the end of chapter 3 as a summary statement of Samuel's new role as a mediator of God's revelation to his people. In this case, we should begin our reading of the next section of Scripture with, **Now the Israelites went out to fight against the Philistines** (4:1b). If this is so, Samuel's leadership was ignored, and the Israelites decided by themselves to fight against the Philistines. The Israelites alone then were to blame for seeking to do battle without first seeking the will of the Lord in the matter.

A few older Bible commentaries, however, regard the two clauses in verse 1 to be logically associated with each other. This would mean that Israel went out to do battle against the Philistines because Samuel gave them the wrong advice. Gene Getz believes this is what happened (Getz, *Samuel*, 84). Getz thinks that Samuel did not listen for the Lord's direct revelation, but gave Israel his own word. If this is true, then Samuel stepped out in front of God and made a bad judgment. Samuel would then face part of the blame for the defeat of the Israelites and the capture of the ark.

In either case, the text does not tell us that Israel sought the Lord's will on whether to go up against the Philistines. We are simply told that they went out to fight against them at **Aphek**. Samuel, himself, was absent from the battle, and he remains out of the picture until chapter 7. This was their first error in judgment.

This initial battle went badly for the Israelites as the Philistines killed **four thousand of them** (v. 2). When the soldiers reported on the outcome of the battle to the elders of Israel, the elders asked the right question! Why did the Lord defeat them before the Philistines? Unfortunately, Israel's elders didn't bother to seek the answer. If they had taken the time to do so, they would have learned their first valuable lesson in "Arkeology."

Why did God bring defeat upon the Israelites? In God's covenant relationship with his people, all battles were to be fought under God's rules of war. First, God himself, as sovereign king, was to lead Israel out into battle. He could be trusted in this because he was a warrior who would fight for Israel (Exod. 15:3). Also, in a crisis and before a battle God was to be sought to determine if it was his will for Israel to fight or not (1 Kgs. 22:5–12; 2 Kgs. 3:11). The text never tells us that Samuel or the people asked for God's direction or leadership. It does say that Israel instigated the matter (4:1b). This wasn't God's battle; it wasn't his time or his place. Therefore, Israel suffered a crushing defeat.

But the rules of holy war also required solemn and consecrated preparation on the part of the people of God (Josh. 3:5) before the ark of the covenant led them out into battle. Nowhere in 4:1–4 do we find Israel confessing sins or consecrating themselves for battle. Without asking God and without preparing themselves, their effort was doomed to failure.

Instead of stopping to answer their own sobering question, the **elders** jumped to a conclusion and proceeded to offer their own solution. They made a foolish decision to fetch **the ark of the LORD's covenant** from Shiloh (4:3b). The people forgot that the ark represented God's *shekinah*-glory, the presence of God as it dwelt among his people. In the 22 verses of chapter 4, the ark is mentioned 12 times. As important as the ark was, the glory of God was not a commodity or item that resided in it. The ark was seen as the footstool of the throne of the Almighty God.

The confusion of the people in this matter is shown in the NIV translation of the pronoun in the phrase, **so that it may go with us and save us from the hand of our enemies**. The Hebrew text allows the translation of "he" instead of "it" in this verse (as an NIV footnote shows). The Israelites may have thought that God was coming into the camp.

Who or what were they bringing into the camp? A box of acacia wood? Or God? How could the ark save them? Did they think that the ark was God? The great Presbyterian preacher Andrew W. Blackwood pointed out the very easy progression of sinful thought: "First, men said that God was in the Ark. Then they insisted that God *was* the Ark. Later they assumed that the Ark was God. Hence they relied on the Ark as a substitute for the God of their fathers" (Blackwood, 48).

The people of God put their trust in a religious symbol! Apparently, they thought they could manipulate the very presence and power of God by controlling the ark. If the ark came into the camp, they were certain to win the battle. It seems that they thought they had God in a box, that he could be directed and brought to wherever they deemed necessary.

The people of Israel had not prepared themselves for God's presence to come into their midst. The text makes no mention that they had consecrated themselves as they did before crossing the Jordan River in the days of Joshua (Josh. 3:5–6). In fact, we are told that the wicked sons of Eli **were there with the ark of the covenant** (1 Sam. 4:4).

The lack of spiritual insight of the leadership of Israel and the foolish decision to bring the ark into the camp would have devastating consequences. Believers must never think that God's presence and power can be controlled or presumed upon. We may tend to rely on rituals or symbols in our worship and daily walk to guarantee that God will bless us. Like Israel preparing for holy war, we too must consecrate ourselves before God's *shekinah*-glory can be released in our midst. His redeeming power will be shown when we humble ourselves, seek his face, and follow his will (2 Chron. 7:14).

4:5–11. At first the Philistines were terrified at the **great shout** raised by Israel when the ark came into the camp. They thought that **a god** had **come into the camp**. The Philistines mistakenly thought that Israel had more than one god. To them, these were the gods that brought the plagues against the Egyptians (4:8). Instead of running, the Philistines resolved to **fight** (4:9), and fight they did. The Israelites were **defeated** and left the field of battle (4:10).

Three disastrous results followed from Israel's folly in believing that God's presence and power could be controlled on that day. First, the families of the people of God suffered a great loss. It was bad enough to lose four thousand men initially to the swords of the Philistine (4:2). But this second blunder caused them the loss of more than seven times that many (4:10). Thirty thousand families mourned the deaths of their loved ones. Sinfully presuming upon God's presence can destroy the fellowship and witness of God's people.

Second, the ark of the covenant, the great symbol of God's *shekinah*-glory, was lost to Israel (4:11). It would be more than 20 years before David would rescue the ark out of obscurity in Abinadab's house in Kiriath-Jearim and restore it to its central role in the worship of the sovereign God of Israel. When we presume upon the presence of God—when we seek to control his power—we run the risk of losing the focus of our worship. God is not in a box, an order of worship, a type of music, or a building.

Finally, the leadership of Israel died. Both **Hophni and Phinehas** were lost in the fateful battle (4:11). Their deaths were the fulfillment of the prophecy brought against Eli's house for their sins (2:31). Their loss reminds us that when as leaders we think we can manipulate and control God—in our worship style, service, or just plain arrogance—we run the risk of a disaster. Above all, leaders in the church must humble themselves, wait on God, seek his presence, and desire to be his servants. God will not be mocked (Gal. 6:7); he will not allow his *shekinah*-glory to be manipulated. Any leader who seeks to do this will face the consequences.

B The Heartbreak of God's Departure (4:12–22)

SUPPORTING IDEA: *Eli dies when he learns that the ark has been captured and his sons have been killed by the Philistines.*

4:12–18. A **Benjamite** messenger returned to **Shiloh**. His clothes were torn and he had dust on his head. Both were signs of mourning. He found Eli sitting by the side of the road waiting and watching (4:13). Eli must have known that this business of leading the ark into battle would end in disaster. Verse 13 tells us that **his heart feared for the ark of God**.

Eli was very old and nearly blind. When he heard the outcry in the town, he demanded to know what had happened (4:16). We don't know if the messenger's voice quivered as he spoke or with what emotion he related the terrible news. But he did tell Eli the three things that had happened. Interestingly, the order of the bad news was changed for Eli.

The messenger first stated that Israel had **fled before the Philistines** and suffered heavy losses. Then the news came that Eli's sons, **Hophni and Phinehas** were dead. The third statement of the messenger had a deadly effect. When he mentioned that the ark had been captured, Eli, a heavy old man, **fell backward off his chair**, broke his neck, and died (4:18).

4:19–22. Eli's death was not the end of the tragedy. Eli's **daughter-in-law**, Phinehas's wife, also heard the tragic news. She was pregnant, and the news of the deaths of her husband and father-in-law and the capture of the ark caused her to go into labor and give birth (4:19). The labor was too much for her, and she died as a result of the childbirth (4:20).

She lived long enough to name her son (4:21–22). The son's name would be **Ichabod**. This was not a name of joy for the birth of a male child. It was one of sadness and pain, because the Hebrew name means "No Glory," or "Where (is) the Glory?" She repeated her reason for giving that name twice. She named her son Ichabod because "the glory has gone into exile from

Israel" (4:21). She believed that the *shekinah*-glory of God had **departed from Israel** because of the death of her husband and father-in-law and the capture of the ark.

H. L. Ellison maintains that she was wrong. The glory had departed from Israel, but not because Phinehas and Eli had died, nor even because the ark had been captured. Instead, "the ark had been captured because the glory had already departed" (Davis, *Heart*, 55). Think about it. Hophni and Phinehas were wicked, and Eli refused to discipline or censure them. The ark was sacred but still a box. God had removed his glory because Israel had sinned against him. Such a thing would happen again when the glory of God departed from the temple in the days of the prophet Ezekiel (Ezek. 10:18).

Andrew W. Blackwood tells a story about Joseph Parker, pastor of the City Temple in London, England. Parker once declared in a burst of eloquence that if anyone ever preached any other gospel at the City Temple, someone should write the word "Ichabod" across the front of the church. According to Blackwood, several years later someone actually did paint the word "Ichabod" across the front of the City Temple, and people passing by were startled to see it (Blackwood, 48–49).

One wonders whether "Ichabod" could be written with justification across the front of many of our church sanctuaries today. God's presence and power can't be found in a box. Through his Holy Spirit, he desires to reside within his humble and faithful people (1 Cor. 3:16). But we must never arrogantly presume upon this promise of faith.

▣ The Supremacy of God's Glory (5:1–6:12)

> **SUPPORTING IDEA:** *The Philistines return the ark of the covenant to Israel after they suffer several calamities that they believe are caused by the ark.*

5:1–5. The Philistines took their captured trophy from the now-abandoned Israelite camp at **Ebenezer** and placed it beside the image of their god **Dagon** in his temple at **Ashdod**. This was one of the five cities of the Philistines. Due to the fact that the ark was brought to the temple there, Ashdod may have been the preeminent site for worship of Dagon.

The purpose of this act was clear. Yahweh as the defeated God would stand in service before the victorious Dagon. The ark represented the Lord's presence. The Philistines may also have regarded the ark as Israel's God (4:7), but more likely they recognized it as the visible throne of an invisible deity. At any rate, the Philistines believed that since they had won the battle, their god Dagon must have defeated the God of the Israelites on the divine battlefield. Now just as Israel would serve the Philistines, Yahweh would serve Dagon. The Philistines soon found out that they were wrong.

Early the next morning, the people of Ashdod found Dagon lying **face down on the ground** in obeisance before the ark of the Lord. Dagon's new posture reflected an act of reverence and submission before the Lord, the true God enthroned above the ark (Num. 7:89). Dagon would serve Yahweh!

What kind of god was Dagon? The so-called victorious god now needed the help of man to regain his pedestal. Perhaps tongue in cheek, and certainly with understated humor, the narrator tells us matter-of-factly that the Philistines had to put Dagon **back in his place** (5:3). Dagon, like all the other pagan gods of that time, needed the help of man to sustain him.

The next morning Dagon's humiliation was repeated, but this time with a major difference. Dagon was again lying face down on the ground before the ark. Now, however, **his head and hands had been broken off** (Heb. "cut off") and were **lying on the threshold** (5:4). Bergen notes that this treatment suggests a military execution (1 Sam. 17:51; 31:9; 2 Sam. 4:12; Bergen, 97–98). In respect to their fallen deity, the priests and worshipers of Dagon avoided stepping on the threshold of his temple (5:5).

While this account is truly humorous, it is intended to teach another important lesson in "arkeology." Dale Ralph Davis argues that the contrast between Dagon and Yahweh is deliberate (Davis, *Heart*, 58). Unlike Dagon, Yahweh does not need anyone to set him up again. He can fight the Philistines by himself. The ark won't need to be rescued; he will bring it back by himself. In fact, Israel won't need to carry Yahweh. Yahweh will carry Israel (Isa. 46:1–4). The supremacy of Yahweh is independent of Israel (Davis, *Heart*, 59).

Certainly, God wants us to serve him; but it would be arrogant to assume that God is dependent on us to do his will. God works where he will, and it is our responsibility to find out where he is working and join him (Blackaby, 78).

5:6–12. The Philistines mistakenly thought Israel had more than one god, and that these gods had brought all kinds of plagues against the Egyptians (4:8). They were about to experience firsthand the power of Israel's God. We learn that God **afflicted** them with **devastation** and **tumors** (5:6). The disease producing the tumors or boils was apparently carried by rats (6:4–5). Scholars are divided over the exact nature of the malady (Bergen, 98, n. 67). But one thing is certain—the once humorous episode with the inanimate idol Dagon had now turned deadly. The people of Ashdod were not sure what kind of god the ark represented. They did come to realize, however, that neither they nor their god Dagon could stand up to Yahweh (5:7).

Their solution was to call a council of Philistine rulers to decide what to do with the ark (5:8). The rulers concluded that the ark should go on a road trip to **Gath**, another one of the five cities of the Philistines. But the same reign of terror immediately broke out there (5:9). When this became too much for the inhabitants of Gath, they sent the ark off to **Ekron**.

The Philistines at Ekron, however, were wary of the devastation this box of acacia wood had caused at Ashdod and Gath. As soon as the ark entered their city, they **cried out** (5:10). This trophy turned out to be a menace. No sooner did the ark enter Ekron than the plague fell upon them (5:11–12). In a true perception of reality, the people of Ekron recognized this war trophy meant death for them. They argued that it should be sent **back to its own place**, or it would surely kill them. The hand of the Lord was **very heavy** upon them.

Now the pagan Philistines began to have the respect for the ark that Israel should have had at the beginning. They were playing with fire, and they needed to know what to do. The Philistines were learning lessons in "arkeology" the hard way.

6:1–12. The Philistines took seven months to figure out that keeping the ark was a bad idea. They turned to their priests and diviners (religious fortune-tellers Israel was forbidden to consult, cp. Deut. 18:10,14) to tell them how to send the ark back (6:2). They had learned a painful lesson in "arkeology."

The Philistine priests recognized that they had sinned against God by taking the ark of the covenant. Sending it back was no easy matter. They dare not risk more offense to Israel's God. So the matter had to be handled with care. The religious leaders warned the Philistine leaders not to harden their hearts like the Egyptians, but to pay "honor" to Israel's God (6:5–6). The Hebrew word *chabod* translated "honor" in this passage in the NIV is the same word found in Ichabod's name (4:21–22). The Philistines were directed to give "glory" to Israel's God. The irony of this is that the glory that Israel refused to ascribe to God (Ps. 29:2) by trying to use the ark for their own purposes would be offered to him by the pagan Philistines. The glory of God will be declared among the nations.

The priests recommended that a **guilt offering** (cp. Lev. 5:15–6:7; 7:1–6) be sent along with the ark to atone for their sin and to compensate for the violation of the Lord's honor. According to the diviners, this act of reparation would heal the Philistines, and as a consequence determine why God was afflicting them (6:3). If the Philistines knew that the God of Israel desired a guilt offering, they certainly did not know what kind. The diviners recommended **five gold tumors and five gold rats** corresponding to the number of the Philistine rulers and cities (6:4,17–18).

Perhaps the rulers of the Philistines really did not want to believe that Israel's God was responsible for their affliction, or perhaps the priests and diviners just wanted to hedge their bet. At any rate, a test was devised to verify whether it was Yahweh who brought these plagues upon them rather than a coincidence of nature. In reality, the Philistines stacked the deck against Yahweh.

A **new cart** was prepared. Then two cows that were suckling calves and had **never been yoked** before were chosen to pull the cart (6:7). The calves were to be taken away and penned up. Both the ark and the chest containing the guilt offering were placed on the cart (6:8), and the cart was sent on its way. If the whole entourage headed out toward Beth Shemesh in Israelite territory, then it was certain that Yahweh had brought **this great disaster** upon them. But if not, then the Philistines would know that all of this happened **by chance** (6:9).

Under normal circumstances these "mothers" would never leave their young. But this was the hand of Yahweh. The noisy cows went straight up toward Beth Shemesh. **They did not turn to the right or to the left** (6:12). This was a clear miracle—what Dale Ralph Davis calls a "cow-revelation" (Davis, *Heart,* 62). The Philistines witnessed what occurred (6:12,16) and learned another lesson in "arkeology." Yahweh had spoken. He had destroyed their god, their land, and their bodies. He was sending the Philistines the message that he was the one true sovereign God.

Ⓓ The Reverence of God's Holiness (6:13–7:1)

SUPPORTING IDEA: *The Israelites of Beth Shemesh send the ark to Kiriath Jearim after they treat it with disrespect and are stricken by the Lord because of their irreverence.*

6:13–18. When the **people of Beth Shemesh** looked up from their harvesting and saw what must have been an amazing site—two noisy cows pulling a new cart with the ark of covenant—they rejoiced. The destination was no coincidence. Beth Shemesh was one of the Levitical cities and was set aside for the clan of Kohath, the Levitical family in charge of caring for the ark (Num. 4:4,15). Beth Shemesh was also one of the designated homes of the descendants of Aaron (Josh. 21:13–16). So it stands to reason that the people of Beth Shemesh would have real cause to rejoice. They would also know how to treat the ark of the covenant as the symbol of God's holy presence—or at least they should have known.

Joshua of Beth Shemesh probably never dreamed that a **large rock** in his wheat field would become famous (6:14,18). But there the cows stopped and the cart came to rest. The Levites took the ark and the chest containing the gold objects sent by the Philistines off the cart and set them on this rock (6:15). The people used the wood from the cart and the cows to sacrifice a **burnt offering** to the Lord (6:14).

Robert D. Bergen points out that only male animals were to be used in burnt offerings (cp. Lev. 1:3). Did these Levites not know better? Then why did they allow the people to sacrifice the Philistine heifers? This reckless act in not precisely following the sacrificial regulations of God "serves as an early indication of impending divine judgment" against the people of Beth Shemesh (Bergen, 102).

The Israelites offered other burnt offerings and sacrifices to the Lord (6:15), and the **five rulers of the Philistines** watched the festivities from a distance (6:16). We can only imagine what they said to their people when they returned to Ekron. Their attempt to hedge their bet had failed. It was the hand of the Lord that brought the plague of tumors against them (6:9).

6:19–20. The joy of the people of Beth Shemesh, however, soon turned to mourning. One can imagine the scene. There on the rock were the ark and the golden objects on display for all to see. The people were rejoicing and laughing, and no doubt, "eyewitnesses" were retelling how they looked up and saw the miraculous sight and sound of the noisy cows headed right for them. Many of the men were milling around, and some made their way up to the rock to catch a sight of the famous ark of the covenant. A few curious and courageous souls even tried to lift the lid to check out the ark's contents. Sounds fairly innocent, doesn't it?

The problem, however, is that no Israelite outside of the Aaronic priesthood was ever to be permitted to see even the outside of the ark, let alone the inside (Num. 4:5–6). The Levitical Kohathites who were charged with carrying the ark were even forbidden to touch or view the ark. They transported the covered ark with poles (Exod. 25:13–15; 37:5). The first obligation of the Levites and priests of Beth Shemesh was "to hide the ark from view while avoiding any physical or visual contact with it" (Bergen, 103).

The act of sacrilege committed by **some of the men of Beth Shemesh** (including priests and Levites) brought a swift and devastating judgment from the Lord. Because of their shameless disregard of the sanctity of the ark, the God of Israel struck them down. The same Hebrew verb (*nkh*) is used here as is in the case of the pagan Philistines (cp. 5:6,9). God afflicted the Philistines for not respecting his holiness as symbolized in the ark. Why should he not do the same to the Israelites who supposedly knew better?

According to the Masoretic text and the Greek Septuagint, 50,070 men from Beth Shemesh died (cp. KJV, NKJV, and NASB). The NIV and other modern versions follow a few Hebrew manuscripts that read only 70 men. Bergen argues that the larger number fits better theologically—if the military might of the Philistines could kill 30,000 Israelites (4:10), in his holiness the sovereign God of Israel could destroy 50,000 (Bergen, 103).

Just like the elders of Israel at Ebenezer (4:3), the people of Beth Shemesh first asked a profound and correct theological question and then followed the question with the wrong solution (6:20). The first question, **Who can stand in the presence of the LORD, this holy God?** was appropriate. The answer was "no one." The response of faith would be to bow in repentance and reverence before a holy God. But the people of Beth Shemesh had already shown their true colors by mourning **the heavy blow the LORD had dealt them** instead of their sin. So it is not surprising that their second question signified the wrong solution. Like the Philistines (5:8,10), all the Israelites were concerned about was sending the ark off to the next city. There was no self-searching, no confession of sin. This act confirmed the spiritual darkness of their hearts

6:21–7:1. So the devastated citizens of Beth Shemesh sent a short, cryptic message to the people of Kiriath Jearim (modern Abu Ghosh), an otherwise obscure village about 15 miles east of Beth Shemesh, to **come down and take** the ark **up to your place** (6:21). The men of Kiriath Jearim accepted the offer and moved the ark to Abinadab's house. Eleazar, Abinadab's son, was consecrated to guard or keep the ark of the Lord (7:1). The ark would remain there until David took it to Jerusalem (2 Sam. 6:2).

Dale Ralph Davis has pointed out that believers can fall into this same Beth Shemesh mode of thinking (Davis, *Heart*, 65–66). We want our God to be casual and easygoing. He is "the man upstairs" rather than the Lord of Hosts, chummy rather than holy. We want God to be the copilot, and we get worried when he wants to fly the plane.

But God wants us to bow before his holiness with respect and reverence. There is a danger in being in the presence of the Lord of Hosts, especially when we come into his presence with arrogance or apathy. We must come before his presence with quiet humility and brokenness. Perhaps the prophet

Habakkuk said it best: "The LORD is in his holy temple; let all the earth be silent before him" (Hab. 2:20).

𝔼 The Power of God's Mercy (7:2–17)

SUPPORTING IDEA: *Samuel leads the people to repent before the Lord, and Israel wins a decisive battle against the Philistines.*

7:2–6. Twenty years passed while the ark remained at **Kiriath Jearim**. But the people were not silent. Instead of mourning over "the heavy blow the LORD had dealt them" (6:19), they now lamented after the Lord (7:2). Samuel arrived back on the scene. He had been absent since the time that Israel had gone out to fight the Philistines at Ebenezer (4:1b). What takes place in this chapter is in direct contrast to the first debacle at Ebenezer. Samuel led Israel to follow the proper steps in seeking God's help. The difference is clear, and the result was dramatic.

In order for God to help them against the Philistines, Samuel called Israel to a holy repentance before God (7:3). The language used here is similar to that of Jacob (Gen. 35:2–4) and Joshua (Josh. 24:14–15). Several factors are involved in true repentance.

Israel's repentance must be genuine. They must return to God with all their hearts. It must also be tangible. The people of God must rid themselves of the foreign gods in their homes and in their hearts. Since these gods were often represented in idol form, this must be a concrete action, physically removing and destroying the idol. In this they were to follow the first commandment (Exod. 20:3).

Their repentance would also be difficult because it would fly in the face of the surrounding culture. Samuel clearly stated that the Ashtoreths must also be forsaken. Ashtoreth was the name of the goddess known in Canaan as Ashtar or Astarte, the consort of Baal. Canaanite religion was essentially a fertility cult. Sexual rites were part of its worship.

From the time of Joshua's death and onward, Israel was tempted to believe that the Baals and the Ashtoreths were responsible for the growth of their crops (Judg. 2:13). Only "establishing" their hearts (**commit yourselves**) to the Lord and serving him would help Israel stand against such temptation. The people of Israel responded positively to Samuel's call for repentance by putting away their idols and worshiping only the Lord (7:4).

Israel completed the first step (repentance) in seeking God's will. They were ready for the next step, so Samuel called a solemn assembly at **Mizpah** (7:5). This town was located about five miles north of Jerusalem on the main north-south road through the central highlands. The solemn assembly included prayer, fasting, and confession of sin.

Israel also performed a water libation before the Lord (7:6). This is the only time Israel did so in a religious convocation, and its significance must not be overlooked (cp. Jonah 3:7; 2 Sam. 23:16). Bergen suggests that this was Israel's "confession that the Lord's favor was more important to them than life-sustaining water" (Bergen, 107).

Now for the first time in the book, Samuel is identified as a "judge" or **leader** of Israel (7:6b). His ministry was accepted here at Mizpah. He would follow in the footsteps of the best of the judges before him, and he would lead Israel to the one from whose seed the Messiah would come.

7:7–11. While Samuel and Israel were busy seeking the Lord, the Philistines caught wind of the assembly at Mizpah and decided to attack. Instead of trying to manipulate God with the ark, this time Israel turned to intercession. They pleaded with Samuel to continue to cry out to the Lord for them (7:8).

Quickly Samuel offered a blood sacrifice, a suckling lamb as **a whole burnt offering to the LORD** (7:9). While he was doing so, the Lord heard his cry on behalf of repentant Israel and answered him. The Lord **thundered with loud thunder against the Philistines** (7:10). They were thrown into such a panic that the Israelites routed them and pursued them all the way **to a point below Beth Car** (7:11). The location of Beth Car is not known, but what is certain is that God gave the Israelites a mighty victory that day. Without the ark at hand, God turned the shame of the defeat of chapter 4 into the rejoicing of triumph.

Dale Ralph Davis has noted that a formal parallel exists between the actions in chapter 4 and chapter 7. The contrast between what Israel could not do and what God did may be seen in the following chart (Davis, *Heart*, 73):

Chapter 4	Chapter 7
Israel "struck down" (Heb. *nāgap*) by Philistines (vv. 2,3,10)	Philistines "struck down" (Heb. *nāgap*) by Israel (v. 10)
Manipulation: "Let it save" (v. 3)	Repentance: "Let him deliver/save" (vv. 3,8)
Philistines hear (v. 6)	Philistines hear (v. 7)
Result: "Ichabod" (v. 21)	Result: "Ebenezer" (v. 21)

7:12–14. In the wake of Israel's rout of the Philistines, Samuel set up a stone monument, a new religious symbol. Samuel named it **Ebenezer** and explained its significance: **Thus far has the LORD helped us** (7:12). The Ebenezer mentioned here is regarded by many as a different place than the site mentioned in 4:1.

By doing this Samuel sought to keep the memory of God's deliverance current in Israel's mind. He wanted Israel to remember the past and be thankful for God's help. Remembering God's help in the past also encourages hope for the future, and hope sustains faith. The popular hymn "Come Thou Fount of Every Blessing" alludes to this idea at the beginning of the second verse:

> Here I raise mine Ebenezer;
> Hither by Thy help I'm come;
> And I hope by Thy good pleasure
> Safely to arrive at home.

The Philistines were subdued, and throughout Samuel's lifetime the **hand of the LORD** was against them (7:13). The towns captured by the Philistines were restored to Israel. The Philistines ceased to be a dominant power in the area, and there was **peace** (7:14).

7:15–17. These verses summarize Samuel's career as a **judge**. The Hebrew verb "judge" (*shapat*) occurs in each verse. Samuel continued to judge Israel **all the days of his life**. He became a circuit rider, annually going from Bethel to Gilgal to Mizpah and back to Ramah (7:16). Since Samuel built an altar at Ramah, it is most likely that Shiloh had been destroyed by the Philistines. Robert D. Bergen summarizes the faithful ministry of Samuel by noting five major points about his career (Bergen, 109):

1. He was a prophet (3:20; 4:1).
2. He led in repentance and recommitment to the Lord (7:3,5).
3. He was recognized as a judge (7:15; 8:4).
4. He was chosen to select Israel's first king (10:17–25).
5. He was mourned when he died (25:1).

May God bless the church with more leaders like Samuel!

MAIN IDEA REVIEW: *The ark of the covenant is captured by the Philistines, then eventually returned, and the Israelites learn appropriate respect for this sacred object.*

III. CONCLUSION

Just a Piece of Jewelry

Many years ago while visiting the Sea of Galilee, I stopped a girl wearing a small silver cross as a necklace. Jerusalem crosses were sold as souvenirs in the Holy Land, and they were considered fashionable to wear among Christians. Because of the cross necklace I thought she might be a Christian. But she wasn't; to her the cross necklace was just another piece of jewelry. It didn't mean anything to her, and she didn't understand the meaning behind the symbol. I did have the chance to tell her about the Savior who hung on the cross, but she seemed to regard her necklace more as a good luck charm than a symbol of the redemptive grace of God.

Religious symbols can be a powerful testimony to a person's faith. But such symbols can also be abused and misunderstood. The Israelites misunderstood the purpose of the ark of the covenant. The ark was the symbol of God's presence with his people. The Israelites could not manipulate God's presence by carrying the ark into battle. They were to come before the ark with reverence and respect. It was not to be treated as a trophy or a curiosity. The Philistines learned this lesson too.

The ark pointed to the glory and power of God, but the ark was not God. Only when Israel repented and confessed their sins could they finally see the awesome, holy, and merciful God behind the symbol. God did not need the ark to save his people. He needed his people to put away their false idols and seek him. Israel learned these lessons in "arkeology" the hard way. God grant that we may learn from Israel's example.

PRINCIPLES

- The ark of the covenant was a powerful testimony of God's saving presence with Israel.
- We must be careful not to think we can manipulate God's presence and power. This is especially true of those in the church who are called on to lead the congregation.
- Since God is holy, we cannot presume to come into his presence with an arrogant and sinful attitude.
- We must remember that while God wants to work through us, he is not dependent upon us.

- We should never fail to honor God and give him the glory for all he does in our lives.
- God desires that we confess our sins and seek him with all our hearts.

APPLICATIONS

- Reject any false images in your life, especially the religious symbols, attitudes, and traditions by which you have knowingly, or unknowingly, tried to make God accomplish your will.
- Ask God to teach you true reverence.
- Thank God and praise him for his awesome and sovereign majesty.
- Praise God for the trials in life through which we learn, sometimes the hard way, to trust solely in him.
- Surrender completely to the will of the Father.
- Thank God for the redemptive work of our Savior on the cross.
- Be ready to share the true meaning of the cross.
- Ask God to help you identify any sinful behavior in your life, to confess it, and to turn from it.
- Thank God for his protection and bountiful mercy.
- Seek to serve the Lord with all your heart.

IV. LIFE APPLICATION

Bernard Coffindaffer

While most people have never heard of Bernard Coffindaffer, many have seen the results of his work. Born in 1935 in Craigsville, West Virginia, and orphaned at the age of ten, Coffindaffer managed to finish high school at age fourteen, serve six years in the U.S. Marines, and go on to graduate from the University of Charleston with a degree in business. He established a coal-washing business and made a small fortune in the mountains of West Virginia.

But the coal-washing business is not the work of Coffindaffer that has touched the hearts of so many people. This work began when he became a Christian at the age of 42. He soon became a minister and served seven small churches in Pocahontas County, West Virginia. His most profound ministry began when Coffindaffer had what he called "a genuine, marvelous, glorious vision."

Coffindaffer had sold his business and netted nearly three million dollars. The Holy Spirit gave him a vision to take that money and erect sets of three large crosses along the highways and roads of the United States and the world. And starting in 1984 that's what he did. In the last nine years of his life, Coffindaffer set about erecting clusters of three crosses in 29 states, the District of Columbia, Zambia, and the Philippines. Because of his vision a total of 1,864 clusters of crosses now stand by interstates and local highways and country lanes.

Maybe you have seen some of them, these silent witnesses for Jesus Christ. The crosses are made of California Douglas Fir with the center cross painted gold befitting the royalty of the Messiah. The crosses on the left and the right are painted pale blue. There are three nails in each cross, one at each of the cross arms and one halfway down the main shaft of the cross. Each nail represents where the hands and feet of the crucified were nailed. At the erection of each set of crosses, a service of consecration was held. Scripture would be read and a prayer of dedication would be offered.

In 1993 Bernard Coffindaffer died penniless of a heart attack at the age of 68. He left a tremendous legacy for all to see. He said the crosses were erected for only one reason: "To remind people that Jesus was crucified on a cross at Calvary for our sins." He was happy if the crosses "would make one person stop and think."

Most of Coffindaffer's crosses remain today as powerful religious symbols. They point to a decision that must be made by all people. Instead of erecting just one cross, Coffindaffer remembered that three men were crucified on that fateful day. On one hung the Savior, but on the other two were two ordinary men. The difference between these two was in a decision. One decided to pray to the Savior; the other rejected that Savior (Luke 23:39–43). May we never take the cross, the symbol of the sacrificial death of our Savior, for granted!

V. PRAYER

Heavenly Father, teach us never to presume upon your indwelling presence. Help us to see the real meaning behind symbols of our faith. Give us awe and wonder for your shekinah-glory. Enable us to cherish and reverence your presence in our lives, in our families, and in worship. Show us how to place our faith in you even when our enemies are pounding at the door. Help us to be truly thankful for your mercy and grace. Amen.

VI. DEEPER DISCOVERIES

A. Shiloh (4:3)

Shiloh has been identified as Khirbet Seilun, a site halfway between Bethel and Shechem. The site, a little over seven acres in area, benefited from fertile lands, a good water source, and access along the main north-south road through the central highlands. Iron Age I ruins and evidence of destruction by fire have been discovered in the remains of the site. Jeremiah 7:12–15 refers to the destruction of Shiloh. It is possible that the Philistines destroyed it (4:12). The facts that the ark was eventually taken to Kiriath Jearim instead of Shiloh (7:1) and that Samuel built an altar in his home-town of Ramah (7:17) also lend credence to this possibility.

B. God's Shekinah-Glory (4:4)

Although the word *shekinah* does not occur in the Bible, the term was used in rabbinic literature to signify God's presence. The Hebrew verb *shakan* is found many times, particularly in the noun *mishkan* ("dwelling" or "tabernacle") and the name Shecaniah ("Yahweh dwells"). At Sinai God offered his divine presence as a guarantee of the covenant (Exod. 29:45–46). When the tabernacle (*mishkan*) was completed, the cloud of God's glory descended upon it as evidence of the divine presence (Exod. 40:34–38). God's presence was particularly associated with the holy of holies in the tabernacle where Yahweh sat enthroned between the cherubim above the ark (2 Sam. 6:2; Ps. 80:1). Thus wherever the ark went, it signified the place of the divine *shekinah* (Num. 10:35–36).

C. Dagon and the Ark (5:3–4)

The fall of Dagon's statue was a clear indication that Yahweh was not defeated in the battle at Ebenezer. The Philistines put the ark in the temple of Dagon to humiliate the Israelites. However, the cutting off of the hands and head of Dagon symbolized the destruction of the Philistine idol. Displaying the head of a conquered foe was done typically to confirm his death (1 Sam. 17:51–54). Cutting the hand off of a dead enemy was a common practice in the ancient Near East for counting casualties (Judg. 8:6). Egyptian monuments show piles of hands gathered after a battle.

D. Ebenezer (7:12)

The Ebenezer mentioned here is regarded by many as a different place than the site mentioned in 4:1. Samuel apparently used the name for two reasons. First, as the meaning of the name implies, this "stone of help" functioned as a memorial stone. It possibly marked the new boundary between the Philistines and the Israelites. Examples of memorial stones marking territorial limits are common in the ancient Near East. But second, Samuel may have chosen the name Ebenezer to declare God's victory over the Philistines in contrast to the humiliating defeat suffered at the first Ebenezer (4:1). According to Bergen, "All that was lost through sin in the first Ebenezer event was restored through repentance in the second" (Bergen, 108).

VII. TEACHING OUTLINE

A. INTRODUCTION

1. Lead Story: The Cross Along the Nile
2. Context: Eli's wicked sons still lead Israel. Without seeking the will of the Lord, the elders call for the ark to be carried into battle against the dreaded Philistines. The ark is captured and Eli's house is destroyed as prophesied. God will not allow the Philistines to treat the ark as a trophy, and he afflicts them with a devastating plague. When the ark is returned, God does not allow the people of Beth Shemesh to treat it as a mere curiosity. The ark is hidden away in Kiriath Jearim, and God shows his people through the mediation of Samuel that they didn't need the ark to win the fight; they simply needed to seek God with all their heart and humbly bow before him.
3. Transition: The ark of the covenant functions in the first three chapters of 1 Samuel as a focal point representing God's powerful presence. Its absence from the main events of chapter 7 underscores the lesson God intended to teach Israel about wholeheartedly seeking him. Israel learned these lessons in "arkeology" with some difficulty. The church needs to consider these lessons for today. What do you think would happen if believers humbled themselves and sought the Lord with all their hearts?

B. COMMENTARY

1. The Error of God's People (4:1–11)
2. The Heartbreak of God's Departure (4:12–22)

3. The Supremacy of God's Glory (5:1–6:12)
4. The Reverence of God's Holiness (6:13–7:1)
5. The Power of God's Mercy (7:2–17)

C. CONCLUSION: BERNARD COFFINDAFFER

VIII. ISSUES FOR DISCUSSION

1. Do people today take religious symbols for granted? How many religious symbols can you name, and what are the basic meanings behind them?
2. Can you list any religious symbols, traditions or attitudes—sacred cows—that tend to take on a life of their own and become like God to some people?
3. How would you feel if someone wrote "Ichabod" across the front of your church? Would they be justified in doing so?
4. What does it mean to reverence and fear God?
5. How can we turn to the Lord with all our hearts? What specifically can we do?
6. Is it easy to trust God in all things? Name some ways and steps that we could take to show our trust.

1 Samuel 8:1–11:15

The Call for a King

Q u o t e

"What we need today are men and women of convic-

tion, men and women who are not wishy-washy, men and

women who say, 'I don't care if everybody's doing it. . . . I'll

do what's right and not let the world squeeze

me into its mold.' "

R i c k   W a r r e n

BIOGRAPHICAL PROFILE: SAUL

- Son of Kish, a Benjamite (1 Sam. 9:1)
- A handsome young man taller than others (1 Sam. 9:2)
- Reigned approximately 1020–1000 B.C.
- Died in battle against the Philistines (1 Sam. 31)
- He was beheaded and his body hung on the walls of Beth-Shan

GEOGRAPHICAL PROFILE: GIBEAH

- Hometown of Saul (1 Sam. 10:5, 26)
- Probably Tel el-Ful, three miles north of Jerusalem
- Saul made it the capital of his kingdom (1 Sam. 11:4)
- Saul's base of operations in fighting the Philistines and other ene-
  mies of Israel (1 Sam. 13–14)

GEOGRAPHICAL PROFILE: MIZPAH

- A town in the territory of Benjamin (Josh. 18:26)
- Location uncertain—perhaps Tel en-Nasbeh, seven and one-half
  miles north of Jerusalem

- Samuel gathered Israel to pray here in light of the Philistine threat (1 Sam. 7:5–11)
- One of the towns of Samuel's judging circuit (1 Sam. 7:15)
- Saul publicly chosen king here (1 Sam. 10:17–25)

PEOPLE PROFILE: THE AMMONITES

- Descended from Lot (Gen. 19:38)
- Lived east of the Jordan River near the upper regions of the Jabbok
- Rabbath-Ammon was the capital city
- Fought against Israel in the time of the judges (Judg. 3:13; 11:4–32)
- Saul defeated Nahash, king of the Ammonites (1 Sam. 11:1–11)
- David later defeated and subjugated them (2 Sam. 10:6–19)

IN A NUTSHELL

Samuel appoints his own sons as judges, but they turn out to be corrupt. Samuel of all people should have known that the task of choosing Israel's leaders belonged to the Lord. Desiring to be like the surrounding nations, Israel asks for a king. Samuel warns the people what the reign of a king will be like, but they ignore him and insist on a king. The Lord directs Samuel to anoint Saul as Israel's first king. God's choice is confirmed when Saul leads Israel to victory over the Ammonites.

The Call for a King

I. INTRODUCTION

Jumping on the Bandwagon

P. T. Barnum is credited with the first known use of the term *bandwagon* in print in 1855. The bandwagon was an ornate horse-drawn wagon carrying a band of musicians playing loud, catchy tunes. Bandwagons were used in the parade before the show to attract crowds to the circus grounds. Nobody knows for sure if Barnum was the first to come up with the idea for a bandwagon, but he certainly took advantage of its use in drawing a crowd to "the greatest show on earth."

Most likely the promoters of the circus would have the important citizens and politicians in a small town ride on the bandwagon in the circus parade. This would garner the favor of the city fathers and encourage the local folk to attend the circus. Later bandwagons were used to lead important parades and political rallies. Political candidates would ride through the town, and those who wished to show their public support were incited to jump or climb on the bandwagon. Eventually jumping on the bandwagon came to mean that a person was following the crowd or was just there for the entertainment or excitement, rather than from deep or firm conviction.

Chapters 8–11 of 1 Samuel contain another example of jumping on the bandwagon. Israel wanted to follow the crowd of the surrounding nations by having Samuel give them a king. Israel had rejected God as their king. God did give them a king, but it was a king of God's own choosing. God would later use their rejection to raise up the Messiah from David's line, but first Israel had a lot to learn about choosing faithful servant leaders—God-called leaders who would not jump on the bandwagon to follow the crowd, but would seek the will of the true King of Israel.

II. COMMENTARY

The Call for a King

MAIN IDEA: *Samuel anoints Saul as the first king of Israel. The Israelites under Saul's leadership defeat the Ammonites.*

Ⓐ Asking for a King (8:1–22)

SUPPORTING IDEA: *Samuel warns the people about the problems they can expect with an earthly king as their leader.*

8:1–5. What was Samuel thinking? Had he forgotten the moral failure of Hophni and Phinehas? (2:12–17). Did he not remember the sorrow of Eli and the judgment of God against Eli's house? (2:27–36). In appointing his own **sons as judges**, perhaps Samuel did not believe that they would turn aside for dishonest gain.

Judges were to be appointed for each tribe and town (Deut. 16:18–20). But judges were to be fair and impartial. They were to "pursue justice" (Deut. 16:20). Samuel's sons were appointed to serve in Beersheba in the Negev. But Joel and Abijah **did not walk** in Samuel's ways. They **perverted justice** by accepting **bribes** (8:3). But to Samuel's credit they **turned aside** only after they were appointed. Their immoral behavior was certainly a departure from God's will, and it was bound to create problems. It could not be ignored.

Complaints must have reached the ears of the **elders**, and perhaps the elders did not want to cause a scene with Samuel. But they needed to do something. The last time the elders of Israel are mentioned as a group occurs in Deuteronomy 31:28. But now they **gathered together** in some type of ruling council or official delegation to address the problem. The people would not tolerate another series of failed judgeships.

The elders, however, chose to correct a wrong with another wrong. There was no praying and seeking of the Lord's face. There were no solemn assemblies—no crying out to God. The elders simply demanded that Samuel **appoint a king** to lead the nation, **such as all the other nations have** (8:5).

First and foremost in the request was the desire for uncorrupt judges. The Hebrew infinitive translated "to lead" in the NIV is literally "to judge." They wanted a king to administrate the legal system. Perhaps the elders felt that a king would hold local judges more accountable. A second concern was certainly political (8:20). The elders wanted a political monarch who would defeat oppressive enemies. They wanted a king just like the surrounding nations.

Everybody else was doing it. Why shouldn't Israel jump on the political bandwagon and have a king? The trouble was that, as Bergen has noted (Bergen, 115), a fundamental teaching of the Torah was that Israel was to be distinct from all the other nations (Lev. 20:26; Num. 23:9). God, and God alone, was Israel's king (Exod. 15:18; Pss. 10:16; 24:10; 93:1; 95:3).

8:6–9. The request of the elders for a king **displeased Samuel** (8:6; lit. "was evil in the eyes of Samuel"). But Samuel wisely took the request to the Lord. The tendency today is to answer immediately, to "shoot from the hip." Samuel knew, however, that wisdom came from God (Prov. 2:6; see also James 1:5; 3:17).

God's response to Samuel's prayer was direct and to the point (8:7–9). He directed Samuel to respond in three ways. First, God told Samuel to **listen** to the voice of **the people** (v. 7). The Hebrew verb "to listen" contains the idea of "heeding" or "obeying." In an emphatic way, God wanted Samuel to know that Israel had not rejected him as judge, but they had **rejected** God as **king**.

God's response to Samuel in verse 8 shows that the motivation of the elders was wrong. The request was self-centered and carnal. They wanted a king like "all the other nations." What was in operation here was a long-standing pattern of sinful rejection. Israel had continuously rejected God. From the day he rescued them **out of Egypt** until then, they had turned their backs on him and served other gods. Samuel was now getting a taste of what Israel had done for generations.

Secondly, God wanted Samuel to warn them solemnly (v. 9a); the Hebrew text says literally, "warning you shall warn them." The rejection of God and his covenant involved serious consequences (Josh. 24:19–20). God wanted to remind them that covenantal promise of the land was conditional. Finally, God wanted them to know the actions and deeds of the king who would reign over them like the other nations (v. 9b).

8:10–18. Samuel did just what God asked and repeated **all the words of the LORD to the people** (8:10). Bergen points out that this section of 85 Hebrew words is the third-longest recorded speech by Samuel in the Bible (Bergen, 117). This sober description tells the people what they could expect from a king. Four times the Hebrew text uses the verb "he will take" (vv. 11, 13, 14, 16). In reality, "kings would be 'takers' who would diminish others to further their own interests" (Bergen, 117).

Samuel's description reveals that a king would establish a permanent bureaucratic institution based on two primary branches of government. First, the king would call up a permanent military. Israelites would be forced to serve in the royal honor guard (v. 11), in the cavalry (v. 11), in the officer corps (v. 12), in the production of weapons (v. 12), and in the production of the army's food supply.

Second, Samuel noted that a king would need administrative support. From the ranks of the general population would come **perfumers** (v. 13), **cooks and bakers** (v. 13), and general laborers and draft animals (v. 16). In order to support all this, the king would need to appropriate the best **fields and vineyards** (v. 14). The "subjects" would have to pay a **tenth** of their grain, vintage, and flocks (vv. 15,17). In effect, the people would become the king's **slaves** (v. 17). Through Samuel, God warned Israel that they would soon **cry out for relief** from the king they were demanding (v. 18). But on that day, the Lord would **not answer** them.

8:19–22. Despite the solemn warning of Samuel, the people still refused to listen (v. 19). They demanded a king! They wanted to follow the crowd, to be **like all the other nations** (v. 20). They wanted a human king to judge them and to lead them into battle.

Samuel repeated the words of the people **before the LORD** (v. 21). The Lord then agreed to **give them a king** (v. 22). In response, Samuel dismissed the elders and men to return to their towns. God would give them a king, but he would do it his way.

B Acquiring a King (9:1–27)

SUPPORTING IDEA: *The Lord reveals to Samuel that Saul is his choice as the person to become Israel's first king.*

9:1–2. The irony of the process of choosing Israel's king is that it didn't follow our logic. Remember, God's ways are not our ways (Isa. 55:8). There were no nationwide searches, beauty contests, or tests of skill. It actually began with lost donkeys! Donkeys may have been lost, but Israel found a king.

We are first introduced to Kish, **a Benjamite** with a good pedigree. He was a mighty man of valor (**a man of standing**; v. 1). His son Saul was **an impressive young man** who stood **a head taller than any of the others** (v. 2).

9:3–14. Here the donkeys come in. After the brief introduction of Kish and Saul, we are told that Kish's **donkeys** were lost (v. 3). We are not told how they were lost. We don't know whether someone left the barn door open or if they broke the enclosure down and escaped by themselves. How they were lost is not important. Donkeys as beasts of burden in those days were very valuable. So Kish sent out Saul and an unnamed servant to look for the lost animals. Saul did not know that looking for lost animals on that day would lead to an anointing!

Saul and the servant searched through five different territories with no luck. The donkeys were nowhere to be found (vv. 4–5). When they reached the land of **Zuph**, Saul was ready to give up. He recognized that they had been gone a long time and that his father would **start worrying** about them (v. 5). After all, they had been gone for three days (see v. 20).

At this point the servant made a suggestion that would change Saul's life. It seems that in a nearby town (probably Ramah; see 7:17) there lived **a man of God** (v. 6). It wouldn't hurt to stop in and see if he could be of help. After all, this man was **highly respected, and everything he says comes true.** Perhaps he could tell them where to search for the lost donkeys. Apparently, neither Saul nor his servant knew that this prophet was Samuel.

Three terms are used to describe the special office Samuel held in Israel. He is first referred to as **a man of God** (v. 6). A little later in the text we are told that he was **a seer**, and that the word *seer* was an older term for **prophet** (v. 9). Based on what happened next, the servant's statement attesting to Samuel's prophetic foresight—"everything he says comes true"—must have echoed over and over in Saul's mind.

After deciding what to give the man of God, Saul and his servant set out to find him (vv. 7–10). In searching for the seer, they met some young women heading for a well to draw water. From these young women, Saul learned that Samuel was in town for a special occasion. The people were to **have a sacrifice at the high place** (v. 12) and Samuel **must bless** it (v. 13). If they hurried they would find him. In God's timing, Saul met Samuel **coming toward them on his way up to the high place** (v. 14). This was no chance meeting. It had been planned by God.

9:15–17. At this point the action of the narrative stops, and we are told about a revelation Samuel had the day before this meeting (vv. 15–17). The emphasis in the Hebrew text of verse 15 is on the Lord: "Now the LORD uncovered the ear of Samuel." The Lord gave Samuel the spiritual skill to hear what he was about to reveal to him. **Tomorrow**, God said, Samuel would meet a Benjamite. God's commandments were clear: **Anoint him leader** (Hebrew *nagid;* see "Deeper Discoveries") **over . . . Israel** (v. 16). This individual would **deliver** (lit. "save") **my people from the hand of the Philistines**. God had heard the cry of his people.

On his way up to the high place, Samuel caught sight of Saul (v. 17). Immediately, the Lord spoke to Samuel: **This is the man I spoke to you about**. God told Samuel that this one would **govern** Israel. Bergen points out that God's words to Samuel are filled with irony (Bergen, 123). The Hebrew verb translated "govern" in the NIV can also mean "restrain" or even "imprison." In fact, in the majority of the 46 times this verb occurs in the Bible, the connotation is negative. The only time it is taken to mean "rule" is here in this passage. The use of this verb foreshadows Saul's career as a difficult king. He would "imprison" or "hold back" God's people from receiving the providential blessing designed for them.

9:18–27. The action of the narrative resumes at verse 18. Saul approached Samuel to ask directions to the seer's house. In verses 19–20 Samuel responded to Saul's request for directions in four ways. First, rather than send him off to wait at his house, Samuel identified himself as the seer. Second, Samuel offered Saul a personal invitation to a sacrificial meal. Third, Samuel offered free information on the lost donkeys. Finally, Samuel hinted about the significant destiny awaiting Saul. Samuel told Saul that he was **the desire of Israel** (v. 20).

Again, Samuel used a word that can have two meanings. Besides the positive idea of desire used here, the word can mean "sinful craving" (Bergen, 124, n. 19). Saul was to be Israel's answer for a king like all the other nations. Saul was a little perplexed by Samuel's unexpected statements. He was also a bit confused because he recognized that he was from **the smallest tribe of Israel**, and his clan was **the least of all the clans** of Benjamin (v. 21).

Nevertheless, Samuel brought Saul into the festival hall and seated him at the head of the guests of honor (v. 22). He instructed the cook to bring Saul the choice piece of meat (vv. 23–24). Imagine the looks on the faces of the other invited quests. Samuel brought in a nobody and seated him as the guest of honor. This must have made an impression on the guests as well as Saul.

Saul stayed with Samuel for the rest of the night (vv. 25–26), and the next morning Samuel prepared Saul to go on his way. Just as they reached the edge of town, Samuel sent the servant on ahead (v. 27) and told Saul that he had a **message from God** for him. This message—an anointing—came as a complete surprise to Saul.

C Anointing a King (10:1–27)

SUPPORTING IDEA: *In a public ceremony at Mizpah, Samuel anoints a reluctant Saul as Israel's first king.*

10:1–8. After the servant had walked away, Samuel took out a **flask of oil** and anointed Saul. The familiar Hebrew term *messiah* is derived from the same verb *mashach* ("anoint") used here. From this point on the king became known as "the Lord's anointed" or "the Lord's messiah" (1 Sam. 24:6,10; 26:9,11,16,23). David would also be known as the Lord's anointed (2 Sam. 19:21). Ultimately, Jesus, the Messiah, came from David's lineage.

Samuel anointed Saul to be **leader** (Hebrew *nagid*) over the Lord's **inheritance**. Note that Samuel conveyed this to Saul in a question. Samuel did not stop to explain all the ramifications of this significant action. Instead, he immediately told Saul that four signs along the way would confirm that God had indeed chosen him as king of Israel:

1. *The Message of Two Men* (v. 2). **Two men** were to meet Saul near Rachel's tomb. They would tell Saul that the lost donkeys had been found and that Saul's father was now worried about him.

2. *The Gift of Three Men* (vv. 3–4). **Three men** would meet Saul by **the great tree of Tabor**. These men would be making a pilgrimage to Bethel and carrying three goats, three loaves of bread, and a skin of wine. They would offer Saul two loaves of bread which he must accept.

3. *The Procession of Prophets* (v. 5). When Saul returned to Gibeah, he would meet a **procession of prophets** carrying various instruments. They would be prophesying.

4. *The Power of the Spirit* (v. 6). At that point, the **Spirit of the LORD** would come on Saul, and he would prophesy with the prophets. He would be changed into a different person.

In verse 7 Samuel told Saul that after **these signs** were **fulfilled** he could do whatever the occasion demanded. Samuel then assured Saul that God would be with him. Finally, Samuel directed Saul to precede him to Gilgal and to wait for him there for seven days. Bergen points out that this was Saul's first lesson about the relationship he was to have as Israel's first king with the Lord's prophet. "Samuel and the later prophets had the right to prescribe royal behavior (cf. 1 Kgs 20:13,22)." In fact, "the plans of Saul (and all Israelite kings who would come after him) were to be subordinate to the prophetic word" (Bergen, 128).

10:9–13. God did not wait for the signs to come to pass; we are told that he immediately **changed Saul's heart** (v. 9). Still, the signs **were fulfilled that day**. Just as Samuel had said, **a procession of prophets** met Saul at Gibeah. There **the Spirit of God came upon him in power** (see "Deeper Discoveries"), and he started to prophesy with them (v. 10).

Saul's uncharacteristic behavior shocked his friends. Three questions were raised as a result. Some wanted to know what had **happened to the son of Kish**. Others couldn't believe that Saul had joined the ranks of the prophets.

One local man responded with the final not-so-clear question (v. 12): **And who is their father?** This cryptic question is difficult to understand, and scholars do not agree about its meaning or intent. Some see it as a derisive and degrading attempt to question the circumstances of Saul's birth (Bergen, 129–30). Others have suggested that the father mentioned in the question is to be identified with the Lord. That is, if the Lord "is the one who inspires the prophets in their praises, then surely he is able so to grip Saul and cause him to do the same" (Davis, *Heart*, 96–97). This then suggests a positive sense of surprise at the wonder wrought by God. Whenever something unusual or unexpected happened in Gibeah the people would respond with something equivalent to "wonders never cease!" (Davis, *Heart*, 96).

10:14–16. Saul's **uncle** was the first to meet Saul and question him about his adventure looking for the **donkeys**. Saul sought to placate his uncle by giving him a few details about the trip. The mention of Samuel's name brought a response from his uncle (v. 15), but Saul only told him a part of the story (v. 16). Saul's divine selection remained a secret until God revealed it publicly later. A two-stage pattern of God's call is established here. David's confirmation to the kingship would also follow this same "two-stage beginning" (Bergen, 131). First, God privately called a leader and then publicly set him apart for his service.

10:17–24. In time Samuel **summoned the people of Israel** to come before the Lord **at Mizpah**. In his introductory speech, Samuel reminded them that they had **rejected** the God who brought them out of the land of Egypt and delivered them from their enemies during the time of the judges (vv. 18–19). Israel had demanded a king, so now was the time to do so by presenting themselves before the Lord by their tribes and clans.

The exact process used in selecting the king is not revealed; although the Urim and Thummim may have been used to do so (Exod. 28:30). Samuel knew that the leaders who coveted the kingship would not be satisfied with his testimony alone. God would have to do the choosing. As Bergen has pointed out, the important fact is that the king was chosen "by divine prerogative, not human manipulation" (Bergen, 132). The only other individual identified by the use of a similar method was Achan, who stole from the Lord (Josh. 7:16–18).

We are not told what may have gone through Saul's mind as the public convocation began. The climax was the dramatic selection of a king. Out of all the tribes of Israel, Saul's tribe of **Benjamin** was chosen. Then, when the clans of Benjamin were brought forward, Saul's **clan** was chosen. Certainly the drama was intensified. Who among this clan would be chosen?

Finally, the lot fell on Saul, the **son of Kish**. But when they looked for him he was nowhere to be found (v. 21). Perhaps they couldn't believe that God would choose a man who hadn't even shown up. Further inquiry was sought from the Lord, and unbelievably, it turned out that Saul was hiding **among the baggage** (v. 22). Saul's shyness may account for his actions. But it is also possible that his refusal to step forward may foreshadow his later lack of commitment to take up the responsibilities that fell upon a godly ruler. Samuel appears to deflect the shy behavior of Saul by pointing out his unusual height, and the people confirmed the choice (v. 24) by shouting, **Long live the king!**

10:25–27. Many scholars see the action listed in verse 25 as one of the crucial turning points in Israel's history (cp. Bergen, 132–33). The narrative passes over the significant event with a mere statement of seven Hebrew words. We are simply told that Samuel declared **the regulations of the kingship** to the people. He first declared these to the people, and then he wrote them down in a **scroll**. The exact contents of the document are unknown. It possibly contained the stipulations for a king laid down by Moses in Deuteronomy 17:14–20 (see "Deeper Discoveries"). Samuel may have given a copy to Saul, but the original was deposited at the Mizpah sanctuary. The purpose of this Mizpah covenant was to distinguish Israel's kingship from that of the surrounding nations. It would remind Saul to fear the true King of Israel.

Having finished the convocation, Samuel dismissed the people. An unknown number of **valiant men** went with him (v. 26). God had touched the hearts of these men, and they were willing to make a difference.

God's chosen leaders are not without their detractors. Several **troublemakers** publicly objected to Saul's coronation. They refused to give Saul the customary tokens of goodwill. Saul responded with grace. He kept silent (v. 27). Further confirmation of his leadership would come in the days ahead.

D Affirming a King (11:1–15)

SUPPORTING IDEA: *Saul leads the Israelites to victory over the Ammonites, and the people express their confidence in him as their new leader.*

11:1–11. Some time after Samuel dismissed the people, the first crisis of Saul's leadership arose. Perhaps **Nahash the Ammonite** wanted to test the resolve and stamina of the new Israelite king. Maybe he was after what he thought would be quick and easy plunder. We cannot be sure. At any rate, he attacked Jabesh Gilead, an Israelite town east of the Jordan River in the tribal allotment of Manasseh.

At first, **the men of Jabesh** offered to make **a treaty** with Nahash. The terms of the treaty were generous. They offered, in effect, to become the servants or vassals of Nahash. Nahash did not want to negotiate. His sole desire was **to bring disgrace on all Israel**. He refused the offer and posed a grisly stipulation in its place. Nahash would make the treaty on the condition that **the right eye of every one** of Jabesh was gouged out (v. 2).

In desperation the elders of Jabesh asked for seven days to **send messengers throughout Israel**. Their hope was that some tribe or leader would come **to rescue** (lit. "save") them (v. 3). If no one arrived within that time, the elders agreed to **surrender** to Nahash and submit to his demands. When word arrived at Gibeah of the plight of Jabesh Gilead, Saul was out working in the fields (v. 5). The people **wept aloud** at the news. Just then Saul returned and asked why the people were weeping. They repeated the frightful message of the men of Jabesh.

Two things happened when Saul heard the words of the messengers. First, the Spirit of God **came upon him in power** (v. 6; see "Deeper Discoveries"). Second, he **burned with anger**. This was righteous anger on behalf of God's chosen people, Israel. This anger led Saul to cut **a pair of oxen**—valuable agricultural animals—into pieces and to send the pieces throughout the borders of Israel to call the Lord's army together. Saul promised the same fate for the oxen of those who refused to come and **follow Saul and Samuel** (v. 7). A similar act was performed by a Levite in the book of Judges (Judg. 19:29).

The call had a chilling effect on the people, and **the terror** (lit. "fear") **of the LORD fell on** the Israelites. **When Saul mustered them at Bezek**, they numbered 330,000 (v. 8). Bezek was located west of the Jordan River north of Shechem. This site was chosen because it was within quick striking distance of Jabesh Gilead.

Verses 9–11 reveal some of Saul's skill as a military strategist. He took advantage of a ruse, divided his forces into **three divisions** for better effect (cp. Judg. 7:16; 9:43), and used a surprise attack. First, Saul sent encouragement to the inhabitants of Jabesh Gilead (v. 9). We are not told so, but Saul may have instructed the men of Jabesh to tell the Ammonites that they would surrender the next morning (v. 11). This ruse would give Saul time to divide his troops and attack the Ammonites by surprise during the last watch of the night (from 2:00 a.m. to 6:00 a.m.).

Saul's strategy worked. He **broke into the camp of the Ammonites** and defeated them. The survivors scattered. In the victory over the Ammonites, God had confirmed Saul as king.

11:12–15. Standing on the east side of the Jordan River in the midst of the battlefield, savoring the victory, several of the people remembered the troublemakers who despised Saul and doubted his call (v. 12; cp. 10:27).

Now they approached Samuel and demanded the death of those who had questioned the choice of Saul as king. Two things need to be said about this problem. The first involves Saul's response, and the second concerns the reality of leadership.

Saul's refusal to put anyone to death shows a gracious sense of mercy (v. 13). Saul's mercy was based on a profound theological understanding. Saul knew that he himself did not save Jabesh Gilead. Instead it was the Lord who had rescued them. No matter how good our leadership is, no matter how skillful we are, it is the Lord who builds and blesses the church.

The reality of leadership is that leaders must be consistent. Although the people were willing to put to death anyone who doubted Saul's kingship, this enthusiasm was based on one victory. Samuel knew this. There would be more crises to come. God would need to confirm Saul's leadership again and again. This may have worried Samuel. In order for God to confirm Saul's leadership, the king would have to prove himself faithful, and Saul would soon show himself to be unfaithful.

At this point (v. 14) Samuel called the people to **reaffirm the kingship** at Gilgal. In another public convocation, Israel **confirmed Saul as king**. Together they **sacrificed fellowship offerings** and **held a great celebration** before the Lord.

MAIN IDEA REVIEW: Samuel anoints Saul as the first king of Israel. The Israelites under Saul's leadership defeat the Ammonites.

III. CONCLUSION

Bandwagons on Madison Avenue

Years ago in a ninth grade civics class, I first learned about the Institute for Propaganda Analysis (IPA). This organization was created in 1937 to educate the American public about the widespread nature of political propaganda. The IPA was best known for identifying seven basic propaganda devices: Name-Calling, Glittering Generality, Transfer, Testimonial, Plain Folks, Card Stacking, and Bandwagon.

Our teacher was not so interested in finding these types of propaganda in political speeches or documents. Instead he wanted us to see how the advertising agencies of Madison Avenue used these same devices to sell products to the American public. We were assigned one of the types and required to go home and describe and document as many television commercials as we could find which utilized that particular propaganda device to sell a product.

I drew Bandwagon. While I can't remember the exact commercials I found, I do remember that the basic goal was to convey the idea that everyone—or at least everyone who mattered—was using their product. In fact, the message was given that once you found this out, you would certainly want to climb on the bandwagon and not be left behind. To be successful you had to follow the crowd without question.

Israel looked around and saw the surrounding nations. They had a monarchial form of government with the power vested in one man—a leader who led them into battle and whose word was law. This type of government appeared to be tangible, real, and concrete. Israel, on the other hand, was to be different—chosen by God—and operating under a theocracy, a rule by God. The Lord was Israel's king. He led them into battle and judged them. Israel rejected God's kingship and hastened to jump on the bandwagon pulled by the surrounding nations.

By his mercy, God gave Israel an anointed king. Israel was to learn that climbing on the bandwagon was not all it was cracked up to be. God grant that as believers we follow the Lord's Messiah and not the crowd.

PRINCIPLES

- God wants us to grow spiritually so that we do not follow the crowd by blindly jumping on the bandwagons of fame, fortune, power, and other worldly desires.
- God, and God alone, must remain King of kings.
- The covenant of kingship is brought to fulfillment in Jesus the Messiah.
- We must trust God to raise up chosen leaders even when we are tempted to do something about ungodly leaders with our own devices.
- God will privately call a servant before that servant makes God's call public.
- God will publicly confirm a call in a servant's life and ministry.

APPLICATIONS

- Ask God to show you clearly the difference between his leadership and jumping on the popular bandwagon.

- Ask the Holy Spirit to reveal to you any areas of your life where you have been following the crowd after worldly desires.
- List these worldly desires in a spiritual journal and confess and repent of the sin of rejecting the King of kings as you pray over these desires each day.
- Surrender completely to God as King and Jesus as Lord in your life.
- List ways you can praise God as King, and share these ways with others.
- If you think God may be calling you to serve him, seek this secretly first and trust God to reveal it publicly in his time.
- If you have been called, ask God for the grace to trust him to publicly confirm your call and not to seek the approval of men.
- Ask God to give you the courage to stand against the crowd whenever necessary.
- Thank God and praise him for his awesome and sovereign majesty.

IV. LIFE APPLICATION

The Eighteen Benedictions

My first experience with Orthodox Jews saying their morning prayers came in the wee hours of the morning on a transatlantic flight from New York to Tel Aviv. I was going on my first archaeological excavation in Israel, and I was too excited to sleep. The last of several in-flight movies was playing, when one observant Jew down toward the screen stood up. He was wrapped in a prayer shawl, a kippah, and tephilin. He began to sway back and forth in the direction of Jerusalem right in the middle of the movie screen.

Several passengers voiced their displeasure at the interruption of the movie. But since I had never seen this before, I asked another passenger what the man was doing. "Oh, he's just saying the Eighteen Benedictions," he replied. I guess my blank stare encouraged my neighbor to elaborate. "You know," he said, "the *Amidah*, the morning prayers." I think I said "Oh," and that ended our conversation. But I had no idea what he was talking about, and it would take me many years before I found out.

Observant Jews are faithful to pray three times a day. The daily prayers contain two foundational parts. The first is the recitation of Deuteronomy 6:4–8 and 11:13–22 and Numbers 15:37–42. This part is known as the

Shema. The name *Shema* comes from the Hebrew imperative used at the beginning of Deuteronomy 6:4: "Hear, O Israel."

The second part of the morning prayer is the rabbinical Eighteen Benedictions or blessings also know as the *Amidah* (The Prayer Said Standing). The benedictions cover a wide variety of life, and they are uttered as praise to God. They thank God for his power and holiness. They intercede for human needs, for wisdom and knowledge, and for man's return from his misguided path. They ask for God's forgiveness and help and the healing of the sick. Finally, they plead for justice and righteousness as well as judgment against arrogance, evil, and hypocrisy. These prayers are said by some scholars to date back to A.D. 100.

As Christians we are not obligated to say these prayers. But what strikes me as a believer is the profound two-part formula found at the beginning of almost all of the benedictions. The most common benedictions begin, "Blessed art thou, O Lord our God, king of the universe." Early rabbis said that each benediction must contain the name of God and must state the attribute of God's kingship. That says two things to me.

First, all of the petitions offered in the benedictions are prefaced with a recognition of God's kingship. While Israel rejected God as king in Saul's day, Israel in the Diaspora will not. All of our petitions and supplications must be based on God, and God alone, as King of kings. Second, the Eighteen Benedictions are repeated three times a day, every day, by faithful Jews. Of course, prayers can become meaningless repetitions. But they should remind us of the awesome and sovereign God whom we serve. Such repetition might serve the church well. Can you imagine what might happen if believers everywhere regularly, daily, and repetitively based all their requests on a recognition of the kingship of God? Maybe it would help us strive less to be king in our personal lives and in our ministries and let God be King.

Now when I see an observant Jew stand up to recite the morning prayers on transatlantic flights, I know what he is doing. I don't worry about the movie. In fact, I allow it to call me to prayer—to say my own benedictions, celebrating the King of the universe and his anointed Son.

V. PRAYER

Blessed art thou, O Lord, king of the universe! Reveal to us the depths of your majesty and sovereignty. Teach us to follow and trust in your kingship! You will lead us out to battle, and you will judge our hearts. Give us the strength and courage to stand against the crowd. Thank you for your Messiah, Jesus. Show us how to proclaim to others the righteousness of your kingdom. Amen.

VI. DEEPER DISCOVERIES

A. Anointing Saul as *Nagid* (9:16; 10:1)

God directed Samuel to anoint Saul *nagid* over Israel (1 Sam. 9:16; see 10:1). David (1 Sam. 13:14), Solomon (1 Kgs. 1:35), Jeroboam (1 Kgs. 14:7), Jehu (1 Kgs. 16:2), and Hezekiah (2 Kgs. 20:5) were also anointed (*mashach*) or appointed (*tsavah*) *nagid*. The word can mean "prince" or "ruler." When speaking about the kings of Israel, it is often translated "commander" (cp. NKJV). It is possible that *nagid* comes from a Hebrew verbal root (*nagad*) that means "declare" or "make clear." If this is so, *nagid* would point to the "one declared (by the Lord) to lead," and would emphasize the divine election of the king as leader of God's people.

B. The Breaking Out of the Spirit (10:6,10; 11:6)

During the period of the judges, God's Spirit fell upon chosen individuals and empowered them to deliver Israel and accomplish special tasks (Judg. 3:10; 6:34; 11:29; 13:25; 14:6,19, etc.). Samuel predicted that Saul would also experience the coming of the Spirit in power (1 Sam. 10:6,10; 11:6). Saul would then prophesy and be changed into a different person.

In most places the text mentions that the Spirit simply came upon a judge. But in the cases of Samson (Judg. 14:6,19; 15:14), Saul, and David (1 Sam. 16:13), the Hebrew text is more vivid. The verb used here (*tsalach*) carries the stronger meaning to "break out" or "break upon." Hence, the NIV translates that the Spirit "came" upon them "in power." Another option would be to say that the Spirit "powerfully came" upon them. Davis suggests the idea that the Spirit came "rushing" upon Saul. "The 'rushing' of the Spirit indicates his equipping for the tasks of leadership. In this sense Saul is another man, receiving what he had not had before" (Davis, *Heart*, 95, n. 11). Under God's Spirit, Saul would be prepared for leadership.

C. Regulations of the Kingship (10:25)

Samuel explained the regulations of kingship to Israel during the public convocation at Mizpah. He also wrote them down in a scroll. The exact contents of the document are unknown. It most likely contained the stipulations for a king laid down by Moses in Deuteronomy 17:14–20. This text implies that a request for a king was not wrong in itself. God gave Moses the prophetic foresight to stipulate the characteristics of the ideal king for Israel. He must be a man of the Lord's choosing and a brother Israelite (17:5). He was not to have the same privileges that were characteristic of other kings: a standing army, multiple wives, and massive wealth (17:16–17). Above all, Israel's king was to be subservient to God's law (17:18–20).

VII. TEACHING OUTLINE

A. INTRODUCTION

1. Lead Story: Jumping on the Bandwagon
2. Context: Israel is frustrated with the corruption of Samuel's sons who were appointed to be judges. Instead of trusting God to correct the situation, Israel looks to the surrounding nations and follows their example by demanding a king. In doing this, God reveals that Israel has not rejected Samuel. Instead, they have rejected the kingship of God. Samuel privately anoints Saul as king. Later, God publicly chooses Saul as king and confirms his choice by giving him a great military victory over Nahash the Ammonite. All Israel reaffirms Saul's kingship at Gilgal.
3. Transition: Israel tries to correct a wrong by committing another wrong. Instead of trusting God to provide godly leaders, Israel jumps on the kingship wagon like the surrounding nations. God acquiesces to the plan, but uses the rejection of Israel as occasion for mercy. Israel might reject God as king, but God will choose the new king and divinely confirm his choice. What do you think would happen today if pastors, deacons, and church members would all bow the knee to seek first the kingdom of God and his righteousness? (Matt. 6:33).

B. COMMENTARY

1. Asking for a King (8:1–22)
2. Acquiring a King (9:1–27)
3. Anointing a King (10:1–27)
4. Affirming a King (11:1–15)

C. CONCLUSION: THE EIGHTEEN BENEDICTIONS

VIII. ISSUES FOR DISCUSSION

1. Is it especially difficult for Americans living in a democratic society to understand the concept of kingship? Can we acknowledge God as King and still function within a democratic society?

2. Name some of the bandwagons that we are tempted to climb on in modern society. Does the Bible help to identify bandwagons? How can we avoid jumping on a bandwagon? How can we help those who have already climbed aboard?

3. Why is it often difficult to stand against the crowd? Name some ways believers can help other believers do so.

4. A process for God's private and public calling of a servant-leader appears to be found in chapters 8–11 of 1 Samuel. What are the steps in this process?

5. Can we trust God to provide the church with faithful servant-leaders? What should believers do when their leaders are not faithful?

1 Samuel 12:1–15:35

The Disobedience of Saul

I. INTRODUCTION
Contract with America

II. COMMENTARY
A verse-by-verse explanation of these chapters

III. CONCLUSION
The First One Hundred Days

An overview of the principles and applications from these chapters

IV. LIFE APPLICATION
The Lawn Chair Pilot

Melding these chapters to life

V. PRAYER
Tying these chapters to life with God

VI. DEEPER DISCOVERIES
Historical, geographical, and grammatical enrichment of the commentary

VII. TEACHING OUTLINE
Suggested step-by-step group study of these chapters

VIII. ISSUES FOR DISCUSSION
Zeroing these chapters in on daily life

┤ Q u o t e ├

"*G*od does not call us to be successful,

but to be obedient."

B i l l y   G r a h a m

BIOGRAPHICAL PROFILE: JONATHAN

- Eldest son of King Saul and Ahinoam (1 Sam. 14:49–50)
- Revealed exceptional courage in battle with Philistines at Micmash (1 Sam. 14:1–16)
- Had a close friendship with David (1 Sam. 18:1–4)
- Acknowledged David as the next anointed king (1 Sam. 23:16–18)
- Died in battle with Saul at Mount Gilboa (1 Sam. 31:1–13)

GEOGRAPHICAL PROFILE: GILGAL

- Perhaps modern Khirbet Mefjir located approximately one mile east of Jericho
- First camp established by Joshua after crossing the Jordan River (Josh. 4:19)
- Served as the border between Israel and Judah (Josh. 15:7)
- Became an administrative and religious center for Israel (Josh. 5:2–10; 14:6; 1 Sam. 7:16)
- Saul's kingship was reaffirmed here (1 Sam. 11:15)

GEOGRAPHICAL PROFILE: MICMASH

- Modern Mukhmas located seven miles northeast of Jerusalem
- Name means "Hidden Place"
- Site of an Israelite victory over the Philistines (1 Sam. 14:20)
- Exiles returning from Babylon later resettled the city (Neh. 7:31; 11:31)

ETHNIC PROFILE: AMALEKITES

- A nomadic tribe, descendents of Amalek, grandson of Esau (Gen. 36:12)
- Lived in the Negev and northeast Sinai Peninsula
- Attacked Israel after the exodus at Rephidim (Exod. 17:8–16)
- Saul was commanded by God to exterminate the tribe, but he disobeyed (1 Sam. 15:2–3).
- Finally defeated late in the eighth century (1 Chron. 4:43)

1 Samuel 12:1–15:35

IN A NUTSHELL

After Israel's victory over Nahash the Ammonite, Samuel calls the people to Gilgal to reaffirm the kingship. Samuel delivers a farewell speech emphasizing the sin of Israel in asking for a king. He calls upon the Lord to reconfirm the covenant with Israel by sending thunder and rain. Then Samuel warns the people to serve the Lord faithfully with all their heart. Saul begins his reign with a lack of courage and faithfulness. He disobeys the command of the Lord to wait for Samuel and offers up a burnt offering before the Lord without Samuel. Jonathan, Saul's son, demonstrates great courage in the face of the Philistine threat, but Saul continues to act foolishly, making unwise decisions. Again Saul disobeys God's command to destroy the Amalekites. As a result, Samuel tells Saul that God has rejected him as king over Israel. Samuel leaves for his home in Ramah never to see Saul again.

The Disobedience of Saul

I. INTRODUCTION

Contract with America

*O*n September 27, 1994, on the steps of the U.S. Capitol, Newt Gingrich and Dick Armey led the Republican members of the House of Representatives and over 360 Republican candidates for Congress to sign their names on a political pledge to the citizens of the United States. Known as the "Republican Contract with America," this document listed eight major reforms to be enacted on the first day of the 104th Congress and ten major bills to be presented within the first one hundred days of the session. The reforms and bills would, of course, only be possible if a majority of Republicans were elected to the House of Representatives. Prior to the election, these candidates publicly pledged: "If we break this contract, throw us out."

A number of Americans responded by giving the Republican Party its first majority in the House of Representatives in 40 years. Although it is debated how well they actually met their goals, the House Republican leadership in a remarkable legislative flurry did most of what they said they would do in the contract. In the years to come, historians will probably reflect back upon the Contract with America as one of the most significant developments in the political history of the United States at the end of the twentieth century.

In the Old Testament, a contract is called a covenant. God made a covenant with Israel at Sinai and prepared and provided leaders who would carry out its terms and stipulations. These leaders included Moses, Joshua, and Samuel. Now Israel had demanded a king, and God gave them one. This king, however, was not to rule outside or above the covenant. Chapters 12–15 reveal the type of covenant leadership needed by Israel. Unfortunately, Saul failed to live up to this need and God rejected his leadership.

II. COMMENTARY

The Disobedience of Saul

MAIN IDEA: *In spite of his good start as king, Saul soon falters by refusing to obey the Lord's clear commands. Samuel declares that the kingship will be torn from him and given to another person.*

Ⓐ Samuel's Farewell (12:1–25)

SUPPORTING IDEA: *In a long farewell speech, the elderly Samuel calls on the people to follow the Lord and to remain faithful to the covenant between him and his people.*

12:1–5. Speaking before all Israel gathered at Gilgal, Samuel started by confirming that he had done what the people had asked and **set a king over them** (12:1). This is no insignificant statement. According to Bergen, this chapter "represents one of the theological climaxes of the Former Prophets, and takes its rightful place alongside such similarly toned sections as Joshua 24, Judges 2, 1 Kings 8, and 2 Kings 17" (Bergen, 140). Here Israel again stood at a crossroad of faith and must ultimately choose in which direction to go. The choice would have far-reaching consequences.

Three interpretive issues underscore the power of this chapter. First, three of Samuel's six longest discourses are recorded here, including his longest (205 words in Hebrew). Second, the poignancy of Samuel's urgency is heard in his use of the Hebrew particle "now" in verses 2, 7, 13, and 16. Each use of "now" divides the chapter into its four major subsections. Finally, three literary devices are interwoven in the passage. What appears at first to be a farewell speech quickly moves into a prophetic oracle as Samuel issued stern warnings, called on heavenly portents, and challenged Israel to reject the sins of the past. At the same time, underneath the speech and prophetic oracle is a renewal ceremony emphasizing Israel's accountability to the covenant.

Samuel began by declaring that Israel now had a king. He recognized that he was **old and gray** (12:2). This starts out sounding like a farewell speech. The new leader is here; it is time for the old to retire, to depart from the political scene. But suddenly Samuel turned to the people and declared, **Here I stand** (12:3; Heb. "Behold me!"). The great judge of Israel now placed himself on trial. He challenged anyone to testify against him that he had stolen, cheated, oppressed, or taken a bribe. Far from assuming that he would be instantly vindicated, Samuel declared that if it turned out he had done any of these things he would **make it right**.

The people responded by affirming Samuel's faithfulness to the Torah's standards of conduct (Lev. 6:2–4; Deut. 16:19). Samuel's reference to the **donkey** (12:3) may have been intended to say that as a leader he followed the example of Moses (cp. Num. 16:15). Samuel, however, was not satisfied with mere words. Instead, he asked the people to swear a formal covenantal oath declaring that the Lord and his **anointed** as witnesses had found Samuel innocent of any charge (12:5).

In essence, Samuel's actions show that covenant leadership must be held accountable on three levels. First, Samuel appealed to the Lord as a **witness** (12:5). Ultimately, he knew that as a covenant leader he was first and foremost accountable to the God of Israel. Servant leaders must remember that their ultimate accountability is to God (Ezek. 34:10; Matt. 12:36–37; Rom. 3:19; Heb. 9:27).

Samuel also appealed to the Lord's anointed (12:5). In the immediate context, this meant Saul, the king, who was anointed to rule over Israel. Samuel the judge opened his ministry to Saul's scrutiny. In the same way, servant leaders are also to be accountable to one another (James 5:16).

Finally, Samuel began his farewell speech by inviting the people to examine his public ministry (12:3). Samuel was in fact declaring that he was subject to the same ethical standards as the people. By this we learn that covenant leadership is also accountable to the people of God. Servant leaders are not above the people; the same standards by which the people are judged also apply to them.

12:6–12. Having exonerated himself as a judge, Samuel next turned to address Israel as a prophet (Bergen, 141). The longest single quotation attributed to Samuel in the Hebrew Bible begins here and runs through verse 17. This quotation may be divided into three parts: a historical introduction (12:6–12), followed by a warning (12:13–15), and a portent of God's covenant-making power (12:16–25).

In verse 6, Samuel reminded Israel that the Lord established **Moses and Aaron** as leaders to bring their **forefathers up out of Egypt**. As Samuel stood on trial before the people to give an account of his covenant faithfulness (12:1–5), so too it was time for Israel to **stand** and be confronted with the evidence of **all the righteous acts performed by the LORD** on their behalf (12:7). The trial motif of verse 3 is maintained, but this time the people are the defendants.

A very interesting covenant pattern can be seen at work in Samuel's brief history lesson (12:8–12). During a period of crisis (whether because of enslavement in Egypt or because of the sin of idolatry), Israel would repent and cry for help. Then the Lord would hear their cry and send a covenant leader to deliver them (Davis, *Heart*, 121).

The threat of Nahash the Ammonite was no different than before (12:12). But this time, Israel lost faith in God's divine pattern of deliverance. Instead of trusting the Lord to provide their salvation, Israel demanded a king like the nations around them. In effect, Israel broke the covenant by rejecting the Lord God as their true king.

Samuel held Israel accountable to the covenant pattern of deliverance and found them wanting. Unfortunately, church history is full of cases where God's people rejected his divine plan by looking to other means of salvation. Believers must learn to trust in the Savior of the new covenant, the Lord Jesus Christ (John 14:1).

12:13–15. Continuing his speech, Samuel turned and pointed to Saul and identified him as **the king you have chosen, the one you asked for** (12:13). The NIV misses the strong disjunctive force of the next phrase. There should be a strong "but" added before the next line (cp. NKJV, "and take note"). This may be the king that Israel asked for, but he only served as king because the Lord had set him over them and confirmed him (10:20–21). Israel was not to think that the covenant was done away with because God had given them a new type of leader. The king, too, was subject to the stipulations and requirements of the covenant. All leaders must remember that they serve at the pleasure of Almighty God.

The blessings and curses of the Sinai covenant are summarized by Samuel in the conditional sentences of verses 14–15. If Israel, and the new king, fear, serve, and obey the Lord—if they do not rebel against God's commands—then Israel will continue to walk after the Lord (12:14). But if they **do not obey the Lord**, then God's hand will be **against** them just as it was **against** their fathers (12:15). God intended for the covenant relationship to continue. Not only were the people to be held accountable to its stipulations, but so also was the new king.

12:16–25. Samuel again exhorted the assembled Israelites to **stand still** and consider the meaning of his speech (12:16). The Lord was about to do a **great thing** before their eyes. Samuel called upon God to bring thunder and rain upon the earth as a divine portent of his covenant-making power. The portent was designed not only to cause awe before the people, but also as a means of punishment for the sin of asking for a king (12:17–18).

This was no mere thunder and rain. It rarely rains in Israel during the wheat harvest. Thunder and rain at this time would have been a very unusual event. It would also have damaged the heads of the ripe grain, causing the harvest to be reduced. God had also spoken in thunder and lightning on Mount Sinai (Exod. 19:16).

The heavenly display produced a contrite confession of sin (12:19). Israel had wanted a king in order to trust in a human deliverer. Samuel consoled them, reminding them that **for the sake of his great name, the LORD will not reject his people** (12:22). Samuel encouraged the people to learn **the way that is good and right** (12:23). Israel would survive if they continued **to fear the LORD and serve him faithfully** with all their heart (12:24). Samuel's last words in the chapter offered an ominous and serious warning. Israel would still be held accountable to the covenant; but if they persisted in evil, Israel and the new king would **be swept away** (12:25).

B Saul's Folly (13:1–23)

SUPPORTING IDEA: *Defeated in a battle with the Philistines, Saul sins by offering sacrifices himself instead of waiting for Samuel to perform this ritual.*

13:1. This chapter begins with a typical chronological notation about Saul's age at the time he ascended to the throne and the duration of his reign. This type of note is found in reference to other kings elsewhere in Samuel and Kings (Bergen, 147, n. 53). The Hebrew text literally reads, "Saul was one year old when he became king, and he ruled over Israel two years." The NIV guesses that Saul was about **thirty** when he took the throne and gives the length of his reign as **forty-two years**, based on Paul's statement in Acts 13:21.

13:2–7. Saul began his career by doing just what the elders of Israel had demanded—serving as king to lead and fight Israel's battles (8:20). Apparently, soon after the covenant renewal at Gilgal, Saul chose an army of **three thousand**. Two thousand warriors went with Saul to **Micmash** overlooking a pass leading up to the city of Geba. One thousand camped with **Jonathan**, Saul's son, at Gibeah, the capital of Israel at the time. The rest of the recruits he sent back home. This is the first time Jonathan is mentioned in Samuel.

Saul's military objective was **the Philistine outpost at Geba** (13:3). Geba was located just a few miles from Gibeah, Israel's new capital. It was also a city set aside for the priesthood (Josh. 21:27). Saul may have discussed this strategy previously with Samuel at Gilgal (13:11; cp. 10:8), but the text does not indicate that Saul sought the Lord before attacking the garrison. Perhaps this was the first mistake.

Saul's plan was to attack the outpost and then assemble all Israel at Gilgal to repel the Philistine counterattack. Jonathan actually led the assault on Geba, and Saul remained with the larger body of troops. Why did Saul not go out before Israel? Again, this small issue may foreshadow a future problem with Saul's leadership as king. At any rate, Jonathan was successful and Israel became **a stench to the Philistines** (13:4). How bad a stench this turned out to be can be seen in the unexpected Philistine response.

Israel was unprepared for the serious reaction of their enemies. The Philistines fielded **three thousand chariots** (the NIV follows a few Septuagint Greek texts; the Hebrew text has "thirty thousand"), **six thousand chariot-**

eers, and an overwhelming number of infantry (13:5). The sight of such a large army assembled against them created a panic among the Israelite forces. They must have left Micmash in a hurry. They hid in caves, thickets, rocks, pits, and cisterns (13:6). Some of the troops retreated over the Jordan River, and even Saul and **all the troops with him were quaking with fear** (13:7). Saul's action did not inspire confidence. Saul had lost his courage.

13:8–15. Saul remained at Gilgal **seven days** waiting for Samuel to arrive and offer the sacrifices to prepare Israel's army to go out to war (Andrews, 775). On the seventh day, Samuel had not come and Saul's men had begun to scatter. Saul then called for the **burnt offering** and the **fellowship offerings**. He himself began the offerings and had finished offering the burnt offering when Samuel arrived (13:10).

Samuel did not exchange pleasantries with Saul. He asked him directly, **What have you done?** Saul blamed his action on three things: the men scattering, Samuel's tardiness, and the Philistines at Micmash (13:11). Saul again showed a lack of courage.

Davis says that Saul's sin was "an act of insubordination, a failure to submit to Yahweh's word through his prophet" (Davis, *Heart*, 130). He had usurped Samuel's prerogative to seek guidance from the Lord and to give instructions about the conduct of the battle (cp. 10:8). By his action Saul implied that it was not necessary to wait on the Lord or seek his will. He could function by himself. He did not need the covenant.

Samuel condemned Saul's action as foolish (13:13). No excuse could justify disobedience to the Lord. Saul had not been faithful to the covenant, to **the command** the Lord had given him. The term *command* (Hb. *mitsvah*) specifically refers to the stipulations of the Torah (cp. Exod. 24:12), and it is used here to indicate that Samuel's words spoken in his role as a prophet are to be equated with those of Moses on Mount Sinai (Bergen, 150). Saul had failed to remain faithful to the covenant.

Saul's disobedience produced two consequences (13:14). First, God had intended to give Saul a dynasty, but now because of his sin his dynasty would **not endure**. Saul would be the last of his line to rule over Israel. Second, the Lord had already taken measures to seek out **a man after his own heart**. This individual would be appointed as **leader of his people**. The same word *leader* (Hb. *nagid*) used to describe Saul's position (9:16; 10:1) is used here. Clearly, Saul's leadership position was based on his faithful obedience.

It appears that Samuel then left Gilgal without offering any sacrifices (13:15). Saul was left with just a few men. The "three thousand" had dwindled down to about **six hundred**. The situation looked very bleak for Israel.

13:16–23. The remainder of the chapter presents an informational aside to describe the position the rag-tag Israelite army faced. First, we learn that they were just about surrounded. The Philistines sent out three **raiding parties** to control three of the roads that provided access to Micmash (13:17–18). Later, a Philistine detachment moved to **Micmash** (13:16). These actions not only secured their positions at Micmash, but also sealed off Saul's camp from receiving reinforcements (Bergen, 154).

If this wasn't bad enough, we learn that the weapons arsenal held by the Israelites was technologically inferior. The Philistines controlled the metal trade and charged high fees to sharpen and repair **plowshares, mattocks, axes and sickles** (13:20). They refused to make iron or bronze weapons for the Israelites (13:19). Only Saul and Jonathan had swords and spears. The rest of the army had weapons made of wood or stone—arrows, slings, clubs, or stone knives. The situation appeared hopeless.

Ⓒ Jonathan's Faithfulness (14:1–23)

> **SUPPORTING IDEA:** *Saul's son, Jonathan, leads a courageous attack against the Philistines and rallies the Israelite army to stand firm against the enemy.*

14:1–14. It is often said that the acorn doesn't fall far from the tree. But this was not the case with Saul's son, **Jonathan**. While Saul was not faithful to the covenant and disobeyed the Lord, Jonathan took courage and remained faithful. In the face of overwhelming opposition, Jonathan's fearless faith activated the Torah promise of Deuteronomy 28:7: "The LORD will grant that the enemies who rise up against you will be defeated before you. They will come at you from one direction but flee from you in seven."

The Lord used the courage of one individual as a starting point to rescue his people (14:23). In the face of overwhelming opposition, believers are called to stand faithfully and courageously for God's kingdom.

While Saul held court under a pomegranate tree on the outskirts of Gibeah with a small contingent of 600 men, Jonathan and his armor bearer quietly launched a small, covert military foray **to the Philistine outpost on the other side** (14:1–3). Bergen notes that Jonathan's plan defied all military logic. He gave up the element of surprise, refused to fight the Philistines if they abandoned their strategic position on the hilltop to come down to him, and then decided on a path of attack that would require him to scale a rock wall and then hit them head-on (Bergen, 156).

Jonathan did not, however, decide on this action on his own. Each step is punctuated by the acknowledgment of God's will. Jonathan began by reminding his young armor bearer of his hope that the Lord would act on their behalf. He believed that **nothing can hinder the LORD from saving** (14:6). Jonathan looked for a **sign that the LORD has given them into our hands** (14:10). When that sign came, he knew the Lord was with him, and he took courage to fight the foe (14:12). The plan succeeded only because Jonathan had the courage to determine the will of the Lord and to follow it. Jonathan and his armor bearer fought and killed **some twenty men in an area of about half an acre** (14:14). The Lord would use Jonathan's faithfulness as a catalyst for a great salvation.

14:15–23. Jonathan's surprising victory started a panic that **struck the whole army**. A perfectly timed earthquake confirmed that this was **a panic sent by God** (14:15). Saul's lookouts saw the dispersion of the Philistine army, and it was discovered that Jonathan and his armor bearer were missing. At first Saul called for the priest to bring the ark and address the army (cp. Deut. 20:2–4), but then he could not wait and stopped the priest and led the small number of Israelites that he had into battle (14:18–19).

A lack of concern for the direction of the Lord remained an ongoing problem with Saul's leadership. Covenant leadership requires courage, but it also requires waiting on the Lord. Saul's haste cost him a great victory over the Philistines, and it nearly lost him a son that day.

Saul's small army did not defeat the Philistines that day. To remind Israel not to trust in human ability, the Lord orchestrated the battle in such a way that the victory could only be assigned to him. Jonathan's bravery triggered the panic. Then Hebrew mercenaries who had joined the Philistine encampment went over to Saul and the Israelites during the confusion (14:21). In addition, the Israelites who had fled and hid themselves in the hill country (13:6–7) heard of the rout and **joined the battle in hot pursuit** (14:22). Israel, however, did not get credit for the victory, for **the LORD rescued Israel that day** (14:23). Believers must remember and take courage that the Lord will lead us out and fight for us (Deut. 20:4; Josh. 10:14,42; Judg. 4:14).

Ⓓ Saul's Fast (14:24–52)

> **SUPPORTING IDEA:** *Saul orders his warriors to observe a fast, although they are exhausted from battling the Philistines. His stubbornness almost causes the death of his son, Jonathan, who was not aware of Saul's orders. But Jonathan is rescued by members of the king's army.*

14:24–30. Some time before or during the battle, Saul **bound the people under an oath** (14:24). This was the first of four oaths uttered on that day (cp. 14:39,44–45). The first three would show Saul's lack of compassion and selfish pride as the new king of Israel. The last oath spoken by the leaders of the army would redeem Saul's son Jonathan from death.

The troops were not allowed to eat any food before evening. Saul's use of the term **cursed** (Hb. *arur*) signaled that any violation of the oath would be dealt with in a serious manner. It is possible that Saul wanted to gain the Lord's favor by requiring Israel's soldiers to fast during the battle. However, Saul's aim appears to be personal and selfish. Note the threefold use of the first person pronouns in Saul's statement, **Before I have avenged myself on my enemies**. The oath does not focus on God's honor or Israel's national security. Saul showed his self-centeredness by foolishly denying his soldiers the food they would need to be strong in battle. Saul's self-centered style of leadership lacked the compassion required of a covenant leader.

As the battle moved on into the woods, the soldiers noticed **honey** on the ground, probably in hives disturbed by the quickly retreating Philistines. The troops **feared the oath** and did not touch the honey (14:26). Since Jonathan had not heard his father's oath, he dipped the end of his staff **into the honeycomb** and sampled some of the sweet nectar. Immediately, Jonathan was reinvigorated as **his eyes brightened** (14:27).

Jonathan's response on being told about the oath is consistent with this section's contrast of Saul's foolish decisions with Jonathan's faithful wisdom. Jonathan recognized that this oath meant **trouble for the country** (14:29). In fact, this same term for trouble (Hb. *akar*) was used to describe the sinful action of Achan in contributing to Israel's devastating loss at Ai (Josh. 7:25). Jonathan realized that his father's lack of compassion prevented an even greater **slaughter of the Philistines** (14:30). Kingdom leaders are commanded to clothe themselves with compassion (Col. 3:12).

14:31–35. Saul's foolish oath had further devastating consequences. It would cause Israel to break the covenant kosher laws and sin by eating blood, and it would nearly cost him the life of his oldest son.

After chasing the Philistines nearly 15 miles from Micmash to Aijalon, the Israelites **were exhausted** (14:31). They were also hungry. Since the time of the oath had expired, the men **pounced on the plunder** and butchered whatever sheep, cattle, or calves they could find. In their haste and exhaustion, they slaughtered them on the ground, which allowed the blood to remain in the carcass (14:32). This act violated the covenant kosher laws (cp. Deut. 12:16; Lev. 3:17; 7:26–27).

When Saul discovered what the men were doing (14:33), he ordered a large stone to be rolled over at once. Butchering the animal on the elevated stone permitted the blood to drain properly. As an added precaution Saul built there **an altar to the LORD**. We are also told that **it was the first time he had done this** (14:35). The narrator is possibly condemning Saul here for taking the time to build an altar. Saul may have been afraid that the Lord would punish Israel for their sin in eating blood. So perhaps he built the altar as a precautionary measure to try to avoid the wrath of God.

14:36–46. Soon after the Israelites were refreshed and fed, Saul suggested a night raid against the Philistines (14:36). The people were willing, but the priest recommended that Saul **inquire of God** (lit. "draw near to God"). Saul agreed and wanted to know two things: should he attack the Philistines that night and would God deliver them into Israel's hand? Scholars generally believe that Ahijah the priest used the Urim and Thummim (Exod. 28:15–30) to seek an answer from the Lord at this point and later in choosing Jonathan (14:42; cp. 28:6). Note that Saul received no answer that day (14:37). His experience suggests that three outcomes are possible when we seek the will of the Lord: yes, no, and no answer.

Some scholars maintain that God did not answer because Saul's oath had been broken in the battle that day. But perhaps the Lord was silent because he was displeased with someone's actions (cp. Bergen, 160). At first glance we might think that God was angry with Jonathan for breaking the oath, but in reality it was Saul's selfish actions that displeased God.

Saul called all the leaders of the army together to determine **what sin has been committed** (14:38). Saul swore a second oath. This oath appealed to the Lord, and Saul implied that the offender would be executed. Even if Jonathan was the offender, **he must die** (14:39). The men of the army said nothing.

Verses 40–42 describe the process of determining guilt by casting lots. This process began with Saul separating himself and Jonathan from the leaders of the army. Saul then **prayed** to the Lord demanding a "perfect" response, or a **right answer**. Lots were cast and eventually **Jonathan was taken** (14:42).

Saul responded by commanding Jonathan to explain what he had done (14:43). In the Hebrew text, the sentence construction of Jonathan's confession emphasizes two extremes. In the first part of his response Jonathan stated that he had *merely* tasted a *little* honey (emphasis mine) with the end of his staff. That is, his act was minimal. He had done this without knowledge of the oath. In the second part, Jonathan asked, **And now must I die?** The Hebrew again emphasizes that Jonathan must pay the ultimate penalty.

At this point, the heart of any parent would break. But the reputation of Saul's kingship was at stake. He had spoken two oaths. What would he do? Unbelievably, Saul uttered a third oath (14:44): Jonathan must die. The foolishness of Saul's impassioned quest for revenge now threatened to destroy his own son.

Fortunately, the leaders of the army recognized the heroic action of Jonathan in battle that day. They uttered the fourth and last oath: Jonathan will not die! This oath appealed to God and recognized the true strength of Jonathan's deeds: **for he did this today with God's help** (14:45). The NIV states next that **the men rescued Jonathan, and he was not put to death.** But the term translated "rescue" (Hb. *pdh*) literally means "redeemed." The people redeemed Jonathan.

At stake here was the will of a human king versus the will of the divine King. Despite the desire of the people to have a king like the other nations, the power of that king was still subject to Israel's true King. As Bergen notes, human kings could utter curses and oaths but ultimately they lack the power to bring them to fulfillment. "Jonathan's faith-filled actions had inadvertently brought about the defeat of two enemies of Yahweh's purpose—one external, the Philistines, and one internal, a misguided Israelite king" (Bergen, 161). In the end Saul let the remaining Philistines escape (14:46). Perhaps the opportunity for a greater victory was lost. Later, Saul and Jonathan would lose their lives fighting the Philistines (cp. 31:1–6).

14:47–52. Chapter 14 ends with a summary of Saul's achievements and his family line. The fact that a career summary comes at this point is puzzling. Bergen points out that Saul loses his anointed status in the very next chapter. "From the narrator's perspective Saul was no longer Israel's true king, though he would function as head of state for years to come" (Bergen, 162). Saul may have been a successful military leader, but he was a failure as a covenant leader.

🄴 Saul's Failure (15:1–35)

SUPPORTING IDEA: *Saul fails to carry out the Lord's orders to destroy the Amalekites and all the spoils the Israelites took in battle. Samuel declares that this disobedience will cost Saul the kingship.*

15:1–9. Since chronological notes are not given at the beginning of chapter 15, it is impossible to determine when the events narrated here occurred. They may have been early in Saul's career. Unfortunately, Saul displayed the same willful disobedience as before. As a result God rejected Saul as king over Israel.

Samuel came to Saul with a **message from the LORD** (15:1–2). The time had come to fulfill the prophecy made in the days of Moses about the treachery of the Amalekites (cp. Exod. 17:14–16; Num. 24:20). The command of the Lord was simple: Go and attack the Amalekites and **totally destroy everything that belongs to them** (15:3).

In verses 8, 9, 15, 18, and 20 the NIV uses "totally destroy" or a variation of the phrase "completely destroy" to translate the Hebrew verb *charam*. The noun derived from this root (Hb. *cherem*) also occurs in verse 21 and is translated here as "what was devoted." This Hebrew root has a very important technical sense in holy war and was to be practiced only against peoples who had come under God's severest judgment (Andrews, 775; Bergen, 168; cp. "Deeper Discoveries"). In a holy war, the people and possessions of an entire city would be set apart or devoted to God and destroyed. God's command to Saul was straightforward and explicit. Everything was to be devoted to God and destroyed: **men and women, children and infants, cattle and sheep, camels and donkeys** (15:3).

Saul needed only to obey God's command. But in mustering the troops and attacking the Amalekites, he spared their king, Agag, **and the best of the sheep and cattle, the fat calves and lambs** (15:9). The Israelite army destroyed the weak and despised and kept the best. Saul was given a chance to show his covenant leadership by being obedient to this assigned task, but he disobeyed.

15:10–21. Immediately, the Lord told Samuel that he was **grieved** that he had made Saul king (15:11). The NIV uses the term *grieve* here and in verse 35 to translate the Hebrew verb *naham*, which generally means "to have compassion" or "pity." In verse 29 the NIV translates the same verb as "change his mind" (cp. NKJV "regret" and "relent"). Genesis 6:7 states that God was grieved when he observed the wickedness of mankind.

Saul's actions **troubled** Samuel (lit. "became angry"), and he prayed all night. Early in the morning he went to find Saul. But he was told that Saul had the gall to **set up a monument in his own honor** at Carmel in the Negev and had returned to Gilgal. This act of self-centeredness was typical of Saul's entire life.

When Samuel finally reached Saul, the king was ready to defend himself. He claimed that he had **carried out the LORD's instructions** (15:13). Samuel would not put up with a lie. Saul had not carried out the instructions of the Lord. Samuel asked Saul a question: what was the bleating and lowing of the animals he was hearing? Both Saul and Samuel knew where the animals had come from.

Saul tried to put the blame on the **soldiers,** as if he could do nothing to stop it. Besides, Saul reasoned, they had kept the **best** to **sacrifice** to Samuel's God (15:15). Note especially from here on Saul used the second person pronoun in referring to the Lord—he was Samuel's God (cp. 15:21,30). Samuel stopped Saul from giving excuses and revealed to him what the Lord had told him.

The matter was simple. The Lord had taken a nobody and made him **the head of the tribes of Israel** (15:17). He had anointed him **king over Israel.** He had sent Saul out on a mission to bring God's judgment against the Amalekites and wipe them out. Samuel asked Saul two questions. Why did he fail to **obey the Lord?** Why did he **pounce on the plunder** and thereby do evil in God's sight? Pouncing on the plunder is exactly what the famished Israelite army had done after their battle with the Philistines (14:32). Their hunger had led them to sin against the Lord by eating the blood with the slaughtered animal. Here the greed of Saul and the people led them to sin against the Lord by failing to carry out his instructions.

Again, Saul protested—he **did obey the LORD.** He just brought back **Agag** the Amalekite king. The soldiers took the best of the sheep and cattle in order to sacrifice to the Lord. Saul just didn't get it. God had given him explicit instructions, but he didn't carry them out to the letter. Perhaps, in Saul's mind he improved on God's words. To have an Amalekite king bow down to him would be great sport at a victory celebration. Selfish people don't often see where they have gone wrong.

15:22–23. Samuel wasn't buying the excuse. At issue was complete obedience to God. As covenant leader, Saul was to lead the nation to follow the Lord's direction and commands. In this eloquent poetic quotation, Samuel pronounced God's judgment against Saul's kingship.

To **obey** and heed the Lord God was far better than **burnt offerings** or the **fat of rams.** The term translated **rebellion** has to do with pressing one's case (cp. Deut. 31:27). Samuel referred at this point to Saul's attempts to justify and excuse his actions. Samuel compared this with the sin of divination. Divination attempted to gain control of a deity by foretelling what would please the god. Saul believed he knew what would please the Lord. Saul would later use divination (cp. 28:7–9).

The term translated **arrogance** is used when someone is trying to force a certain course of action. Samuel equated this with idolatry, using the specific word *teraphim* (cp. Gen. 31:19). Food and gifts were presented to teraphim (apparently small hand-made idols) in an attempt to manipulate a god into granting requests or bestowing blessings. Samuel implied that Saul was attempting to manipulate Yahweh with the best of the Amalekite flocks just like the pagan idol worshipers (Walton, Matthews, and Chavalas, 304).

There is no reason to suppose that Samuel was rejecting sacrificial worship (cp. Bergen, 172, n. 11). After all, Samuel was a Levite (cp. 1 Chron. 6:22–26) and often performed ritual sacrifice himself (1 Sam. 10:8; 11:15; 16:3–5). Samuel recognized that for a sacrifice to be effective, it must be offered with complete obedience. Worship that counts must result in obedience to the will of God (see "Deeper Discoveries"). Because Saul had rejected the Lord, the Lord had rejected him as king.

15:24–31. Saul finally admitted that he had sinned, that he had **violated** (lit. "transgressed") the Lord's command and Samuel's instructions. Instead of fearing the Lord, Saul was **afraid of the people**. Saul begged for forgiveness, but Samuel was adamant. Samuel must have felt that Saul had not really repented. Saul again was concerned with appearances. He wanted the people to think that everything was all right.

When Samuel turned to leave, Saul grabbed the hem of Samuel's robe and it tore. Samuel used this as an illustration: the Lord had **torn the kingdom of Israel** from him (15:27). The **Glory of Israel** would not change his mind (cp. Num. 23:19); Saul was rejected from being king. Even through this exchange, Saul still thought about appearances. He continued to plead his case that Samuel would **honor** him before the **elders** and return with him. Samuel reluctantly agreed. Note again Saul's use of the second personal pronoun in verse 30 to refer to Samuel's God (cp. 15:15,21).

15:32–35. What Saul had failed to do, Samuel carried out. When they returned, Samuel called for Agag, the Amalekite king. Agag thought that by this time, **the bitterness of death** had passed, that the Israelites would not put him to death. But Samuel declared an oracle of judgment against him and put him to death as the Lord had commanded. After this Samuel left for Ramah. The men did not see each other again before Samuel died. Samuel continued to mourn for Saul, and the Lord regretted that he had made Saul king over Israel.

> **MAIN IDEA REVIEW:** *In spite of his good start as king, Saul soon falters by refusing to obey the Lord's clear commands. Samuel declares that the kingship will be torn from him and given to another person.*

III. CONCLUSION

The First One Hundred Days

According to presidential historians, concern over the first 100 days of a president's tenure began in 1933 when Franklin Roosevelt took office. Roosevelt ushered in a great wave of reform and sent bill after bill to Congress. Sometimes Congress passed them without even reading them. At the beginning of the Depression this flurry of activity in Roosevelt's first 100 days provided a great psychological boost for the country.

Since then the first 100 days of every president's term have been scrutinized, examined in detail, and debated by political analysts and media pundits. As a result, presidential candidates, if elected, have often promised detailed plans and actions for their first 100 days in office. When they do, they are judged on how well they live up to their promises in that time.

Saul was Israel's new king. The first 100 days of his reign were not promising. He may have enjoyed some success as a military commander. But he was a failure as a covenant leader. A covenant leader must be accountable and faithful. Covenant leadership requires courage and compassion. Above all, a covenant leader must be obedient. From the very beginning of his reign, it was clear that Saul did not submit to the covenant God of Israel.

PRINCIPLES

- God, and God alone, must remain King of kings.
- Believers must be accountable to God, church leadership, and one another.
- God requires us to remain faithful regardless of the circumstance.
- Believers must seek to accomplish God's will with courage.
- Compassion is a necessary skill of covenant leadership.
- God is more concerned with obedience to his will than any type of worship or praise.
- Those who lead must first seek to be led by God.

APPLICATIONS

- Thank God and praise him for his sovereign kingship.
- Surrender your will in obedience to God.
- Seek to trust God's strategy in all things.
- Ask the Holy Spirit to clothe you in compassion (Col. 3:12).

- Develop accountability groups with close friends, church members, and pastors.
- Ask the Holy Spirit to teach you faithfulness and courage in hard circumstances.
- Reject the sin of pride and ask God to help you become an obedient kingdom leader.
- Identify and reject any worship rituals that are done out of habit and not obedience.

IV. LIFE APPLICATION

The Lawn Chair Pilot

People do some crazy things. Take, for example, Larry Walters, the 33-year-old lawn chair pilot. In July 1982, Larry tied 42 helium-filled weather balloons to a Sears lawn chair in San Pedro, California. He wanted to sail across the desert and hopefully make it to the Rocky Mountains. He took supplies with him, including a parachute, a citizens band radio, and a BB gun to shoot the balloons when he was ready to descend.

Larry's flight didn't go as planned when they released the tethers holding down the lawn chair. Larry and the lawn chair shot into the sky at over 1,000 feet per minute. Eventually he leveled out around 16,000 above sea level. The flying lawn chair was spotted by TWA and Delta Airline pilots. They both radioed the tower that they were passing a guy in a lawn chair at 16,000 feet.

When Larry's hands became numb he began to shoot out a few balloons to start his descent. But then he dropped the BB gun overboard. He used the radio to call in a mayday, before his flying lawn chair became tangled in a power line. Larry was able to get down safely, but he did succeed in blacking out a small area in Long Beach, California.

Larry set the altitude record for gas-filled clustered balloons. But for flying his lawn chair, Larry was arrested for violating Los Angeles airspace and fined $1,500 from the FAA. He also won the top prize that year from the Bonehead Club of Dallas and appeared on several TV talk shows. Perhaps the fame was too much for Larry. Eleven years later, he hiked into a remote spot of the Angeles National Forest and committed suicide.

It is easy to laugh at Larry Walters and his dream of flying a lawn chair lifted by weather balloons. Larry didn't realize that so many balloons would catapult him to such a height. None of us would dream of trying such a stunt.

We also know better than to disobey God and his perfect will for our lives. Still, we do crazy things. Like Saul, we allow our egos and self-centeredness to control our thoughts and actions. When that happens we shoot up to some dizzying heights, but we will lose control and crash. It's easier to say that we are covenant leaders than actually to be accountable, faithful, courageous, and compassionate. The next time we try to fly our lawn chairs of pride, we need to stop and consider that the kind of leadership that pleases God can only be built through obedience to his will.

V. PRAYER

O Lord, our King of kings, teach us that true leadership begins with submission to your perfect will. Help us be accountable to you and each other in Jesus. Help us to learn the skills of covenant leadership: faithfulness, courage, compassion, and obedience. Thank you for the example of our anointed Savior, Jesus, who became obedient unto death, even the death of the cross (Phil. 2:8). In Jesus' name we pray. Amen.

VI. DEEPER DISCOVERIES

A. Israel's Preparation for War (13:8–15)

Before the armies of Israel went out to war, several preparations were necessary. The priest would come forward and address the army (Deut. 20:2). A sacrifice would be offered to God (1 Sam. 7:9; 13:9), and his guidance would be sought (1 Sam. 14:36; 2 Sam. 5:23–24). The warriors who marched into battle had to be pure and consecrated to God (Josh. 3:5). Those who had built a new house or vineyard or who had become betrothed in marriage were allowed to return home. The fearful and faint-hearted were also excused (Deut. 20:5–8). The presence of God in the arena of battle was symbolized by the ark of the covenant (1 Sam. 4:5–7; 14:18). After the victory, praises were offered to God in a victory celebration (Exod. 15:1–3).

B. The Ban (15:3)

As the final act of battle, Israel was sometimes required to dedicate everything in a "ban" (Hb. *cherem*), which meant that the people and possessions of an entire city would be set apart for God and destroyed (Deut. 7:2; 20:17; Josh. 8:2; 1 Sam. 15:3). Only the metal objects were saved (Josh. 6:18–24). Those who transgressed the ban faced dire consequences (Josh. 7).

Why would a loving God order the wholesale extermination of the nations living in the promised land? There is no simple answer to this difficult question. Three points, however, need to be remembered.

First, the concept of the ban is also found among the nations surrounding Israel. In war, every living being and every piece of property was to be dedicated to the deity.

Second, the rules for placing the spoils of war under the ban appear to apply only to the cities of the nations within the promised land God had designated as inheritance for Israel (Deut. 20:16–18).

Finally, it must be remembered that Israel was only allowed to drive out the nations living in the promised land because of their sinful abominations (Deut. 9:4–5; 18:9–14; 20:16–18). In this sense, Israel served as the instrument of God's judgment against these sinful nations. In like manner, God would later allow another nation to march against Judah in judgment (Hab. 1:6–11).

C. Requiring Obedience Rather than Sacrifice (15:22–23)

Several passages of Scripture appear to reject Israel's sacrificial and ritualistic worship (Pss. 15:1–5; 40:6; 51:16–17; Isa. 1:10–15; 66:3; Jer. 6:20; 7:21–26; Hos. 6:6; 9:9; Amos 5:21–24; Mic. 6:6–8). But behind all these passages is the clear consideration that sacrifice is acceptable only when brought with an attitude of obedience and devotion to God and his covenant commandments. This is made clear in Samuel's response to Saul: "To obey is better than sacrifice" (15:22; cp. Jer. 7:23).

Often the rituals we use in worship are taken for granted. They become commonplace. We find ourselves going through the motions, and their deeper meaning is lost. The prophets did not reject sacrifice, solemn assemblies, and feast days. They did, however, reject vain and shallow worship— worship that did not result in obedience.

VII. TEACHING OUTLINE

A. INTRODUCTION

1. Lead Story: Contract with America
2. Context: At Gilgal, Samuel delivers a farewell speech emphasizing the sin of Israel in asking for a king like the other nations. He calls Israel to remain accountable to the covenant with the Lord, their great king. Saul begins his reign with indecision, a lack of courage, and unfaithfulness. He disobeys the Lord by offering up a burnt

offering without waiting on Samuel. Jonathan, Saul's son, displays great courage and faith in the face of the Philistine threat, but Saul continues to act foolishly. Finally, Saul again disobeys God's command and misses the opportunity to fulfill God's prophecy against the Amalekites. As a result God rejects Saul as king. Samuel leaves for his home, never to meet Saul again.

3. Transition: The new king was not to be above the covenant. He was to remain accountable to its ethical standards and to stand faithful to its stipulations and requirements. As a covenant leader, the new king was to display courage in the face of overwhelming odds. He had to believe and trust that the Lord God would fight for his people. Finally, as a covenant leader, the new king was to be obedient to every point of God's command. He could not second-guess God or adapt the divine command to his own liking or will. Saul failed as a covenant leader, and God grieved that he had made Saul king over Israel. These same principles hold true in the new covenant for the kingdom leader. Kingdom leadership can only be built through obedience to God's will. The kingdom needs good and faithful servant leaders.

B. COMMENTARY

1. Samuel's Farewell (12:1–25)
2. Saul's Folly (13:1–23)
3. Jonathan's Faithfulness (14:1–23)
4. Saul's Fast (14:24–52)
5. Saul's Failure (15:1–35)

C. CONCLUSION: THE LAWN CHAIR PILOT

VIII. ISSUES FOR DISCUSSION

1. Name some of the leadership skills needed in God's kingdom today. How can leaders learn these skills?
2. In what specific ways should a kingdom leader be held accountable? How can the church facilitate accountability for all of its leaders?
3. How can a kingdom leader remain faithful to the will of God? What specific activities must be done to assure faithfulness?

4. Can courage be learned? How do kingdom leaders look to the Lord for courage? List some situations or circumstances today that especially require courage.

5. Do leaders need compassion? List some of the ways Jesus as a leader showed compassion. How are we as his disciples and kingdom leaders to exercise compassion in leading?

6. Why is obedience to the Word of God more important than worship rituals? Worship that counts should result in obedience. How can our worship result in obedience?

1 Samuel 16:1–17:58

The Heart of David

"It is not the size of a man but the size of his heart that matters."

E v a n d e r   H o l y f i e l d

BIOGRAPHICAL PROFILE: DAVID

- Eighth son of Jesse (1 Sam. 16:10)
- Born and raised in Bethlehem
- Anointed by Samuel (1 Sam. 16:13)
- Had a close friendship with Jonathan (1 Sam. 18:1–4)
- Entered into Saul's service (1 Sam. 16:21)
- Reigned over Israel and Judah for 40 years (1 Kgs. 2:11)

GEOGRAPHICAL PROFILE: BETHLEHEM

- A small village five miles south of Jerusalem
- Known to Jacob as Ephrath (Gen. 48:7)
- A few Iron Age (1200–586 B.C.) remains were found here
- Called the "town of David" in the New Testament (Luke 2:4)
- Birthplace of Jesus (Mic. 5:2; Matt. 2:1; Luke 2:4–7)

GEOGRAPHICAL PROFILE: THE VALLEY OF ELAH

- Generally identified with modern Wadi es-Sant, about 15 miles west of Bethlehem
- Used by the Philistines to gain access to central Palestine
- Scene of David's victory over Goliath (1 Sam. 17:2; 21:9)
- Name Elah means "terebinth"

1 Samuel 16:1-17:58

IN A NUTSHELL

After God rejects Saul as king over Israel, the Lord directs Samuel to anoint one of the sons of Jesse as king. Jesse brings his sons one by one before Samuel, but all are rejected until David, the youngest son, arrives. God reminds Samuel of the biblical truth that God looks on the heart and not the outward appearance. Samuel anoints David in the presence of his brothers. Then, since David has a reputation as a harp player, he is chosen by Saul to help soothe his tormented spirit. Soon after, Israel's armies are paralyzed with fear before the Philistine champion Goliath. But David's heart is enraged by the blasphemous boasts of the giant, and he defeats Goliath with a sling. God gave David the victory, and the army of Israel is able to slaughter the Philistines and plunder their camp.

The Heart of David

I. INTRODUCTION

Two Bananas

The entire church listens with rapt attention when our pastor calls the kids forward for the children's message. One Sunday, he held up two bananas. The first was discolored with brown and black spots all over the skin. The second banana was smooth and yellow with no blemishes. The first appeared spoiled and over-ripe; the second looked just right to eat.

The pastor had previously prepared these two bananas for the object lesson. The first banana he placed in the refrigerator where the skin blackened and discolored. Then he prepared the second banana by poking a toothpick carefully many times along one of its sides to bruise and spoil its fruit.

Our pastor said, "I have two bananas, but I can't tell which is good and which is bad. Maybe you can help." First, he held up the brown and black one and asked how many would eat this banana. None of the children's hands went up. A few of them responded with sounds of distaste and rejection. Then he held up the first nice-looking banana and asked how many would eat this one. Every one of the children's hands went up.

Then our pastor said, "Sometimes fruit may look good on the outside when it's really rotten on the inside." Next, he peeled the yellow banana with no blemishes. Even though it looked good on the outside, inside the fruit was very bruised and spoiled. None of the kids said they would eat that fruit.

Then our pastor peeled the banana with the brown and black spots. This was the banana that at first no one wanted. Its fruit was firm and ripe and ready to eat. Everyone wanted a taste of this banana.

Our pastor spoke again: "When God told Samuel to anoint one of Jesse's sons to be king over Israel, Samuel began to look on their outward appearance, thinking God wanted someone who was tall and strong. But God wanted David, who was young and still growing, to be king. In 1 Samuel 16:7 God told Samuel, 'Man looks at the outward appearance, but the LORD looks at the heart.' God is not concerned with how we look on the outside. He wants us to have faithful hearts."

Because Saul was unfaithful, God had rejected him as king. Now he wanted to teach Samuel a lesson on how to look for a good king who would serve him with a faithful heart. Chapters 16–17 reveal that this king would be David, the son of Jesse.

II. COMMENTARY

The Heart of David

MAIN IDEA: *Because of Saul's failure as king, David is selected by the Lord through Samuel as the new king of Israel. David proves his leadership ability by defeating a Philistine giant and giving credit for the victory to the Lord.*

🄰 Searching for a New King (16:1–5)

SUPPORTING IDEA: *Samuel is commanded by the Lord to search for a new king by going to the home of Jesse in Bethlehem.*

16:1–3. God had **rejected** Saul's leadership because Saul had rejected the word of the Lord (1 Sam. 15:23). Samuel had returned home to Ramah. It grieved God that he had made Saul king, but Samuel mourned for him (1 Sam. 15:34–35). Now it was time to stop mourning because God had one very important task for Samuel to do. This task turned out to be the most important one of his entire career. Samuel was going to set apart the person through whom the Messiah would eventually come. Samuel's task reminds us that leaders are to be chosen by God.

Samuel was commanded to fill his **horn with oil** and go to Bethlehem. God had **chosen** one of Jesse's sons to be king over Israel. The word translated "chosen" by the NIV comes from the Hebrew root *ra'ah*, which literally means "to see." It is used here in the sense of "provide." The same idea is found in Genesis 22:8 where Abraham told Isaac that the Lord would "provide" a lamb for the sacrifice.

How far the rift between Samuel and Saul had grown can be seen in Samuel's response to God's request. Saul no longer sought God's will but his own. Even though God had rejected him, Saul was still the most powerful man in Israelite society. Samuel was afraid Saul would kill him (16:2). So God assigned Samuel an additional task that would help mask his journey to Bethlehem and not raise undue suspicions (Bergen, 178). Samuel was to **take a heifer** with him **to sacrifice to the LORD**. He was also to **invite Jesse to the sacrifice** (16:3).

16:4–5. Samuel did what the Lord had commanded him. When he arrived at Bethlehem the elders **trembled** to meet him. Samuel assured them that he had come **in peace**. Then he commanded them to get ready for the sacrifice by consecrating themselves before the Lord. Samuel also consecrated **Jesse and his sons and invited them to the sacrifice**. Consecration before a sacrifice required ritual cleanness. This normally involved bathing, changing into clean clothes, avoiding contact with anything dead or unclean, and refraining from all sexual activity (Exod. 19:10,14–15; Josh. 3:5).

B Selecting a New King (16:6–13)

SUPPORTING IDEA: *The young David is selected from among all Jesse's sons to be the new king of Israel because David had the right kind of heart.*

16:6–10. When Jesse and his sons arrived at the sacrifice, Samuel was ready to anoint the new king of Israel, the man after the Lord's own heart (1 Sam. 13:14). But Samuel did not know the intent of God's heart, and he made a fundamental mistake. Samuel looked only skin deep. Samuel's mistake leads us to consider that faithful leaders must have the right kind of heart.

The first of Jesse's sons to be considered was **Eliab**. He must have been tall and handsome. Samuel was impressed and was sure this was **the LORD's anointed**. But he was wrong. God was not concerned with height or appearance. What God said to Samuel is one of the most important statements in all of Scripture.

It is a fundamental truth of the Bible that God's ways are not our ways (Isa. 55:8–9). God does not value or judge the same things that man does. Man is shallow and often fickle. He judges by what he can see, **the outward appearance**. The Hebrew text literally says man looks at "the eyes" (16:7). Man cannot see the thoughts, emotions, and intents of another. Only God has the ability to observe and judge these things because **the LORD looks at the heart**. God desires his servants to have the right kind of heart.

One by one Jesse had seven of his sons pass before Samuel. But none of them had the right kind of heart. The Lord rejected each one. This was certainly perplexing since the Lord had clearly stated that he had chosen one of Jesse's sons to be king (16:1). But Samuel knew that God's word to him was true, so there had to be another son.

16:11–12. Samuel asked Jesse, **Are these all the sons you have?** No, there was one who was **tending the sheep**. The NIV labels him **the youngest**, but the Hebrew text literally says "the smallest" (16:11). The NIV's translation is certainly legitimate because the Hebrew language does express the idea of the youngest in this way. But many scholars have also noted the irony in the contrast between David's stature and that of his brothers and Saul as well (16:7; Bergen, 179). They were tall; he was not.

The Lord's anointed was sent for. When he arrived Samuel took note of his features. He was **ruddy** (either sun-tanned or having red-tinted hair) **with a fine appearance and handsome features** (16:12). David's physical characteristics were nice, but since God had already told Samuel how he judged (16:7), they were irrelevant. Instead, God looked at David's heart. David had a desire to search after God's own heart (Acts 13:22). Immediately, the Lord told Samuel to arise and **anoint** David. Jesse's youngest son was **the one**.

16:13. Samuel took **the horn of oil** and poured its contents on David's head in the presence of his brothers. It is not certain whether anyone else witnessed the anointing. Anointing was the symbolic act used to set apart priests, kings, altars, and even the tabernacle and the ark. It signified that the individual or thing was consecrated for God's use.

This consecration was further confirmed with the gift of God's Spirit upon David **in power** (16:13). This represents a sudden change because the Hebrew text states that the Spirit "rushed" upon him. When Saul was anointed the Spirit also "rushed" upon him (1 Sam. 10:10). But the difference here is that the Spirit stayed with David **from that day on**. This would make David's anointing superior to Saul's (Bergen, 180). From that day on the political landscape of Israel would be changed forever.

Ⓒ Soothing the Troubled Spirit of a Rejected King (16:14–23)

SUPPORTING IDEA: *David uses his musical skills to soothe the troubled spirit of King Saul.*

16:14–15. Much controversy has arisen over the meaning of 1 Samuel 16:14–15 (Arnold, 242–243; Bergen, 182–184). The idea that God would plague Saul with an **evil spirit** is perplexing to the Christian mind. But several things need to be kept in mind.

First, the contrast here concerns the Spirit of God coming upon David from the moment of his anointing onward. That Spirit remained with David and blessed him. The same Spirit had left Saul only to return for a brief moment later (1 Sam. 19:23). Now God had sent a different spirit upon Saul. The Hebrew term *rā'ah* translated as "evil" by the NIV has a wide range of meanings, from "misery" to "morally evil." Here it could mean "distressing" (NKJV) or "injurious" (see NIV marginal note).

Second, the great Sinai covenant was still in effect. Israel's king was expected to walk in that covenant and obey it (Deut. 17:18–20). By obeying, Saul would have chosen life and blessing; in disobeying, Saul chose death and curses (Deut. 30:15–20). In choosing to disobey, Saul was calling God's judgment upon himself. God chose this means to punish Saul.

Third, the Hebrew verb *bā'at* used here and translated as **tormented** can be understood to refer to an emotion of extreme fear (Bergen, 182, n. 36). As the sovereign Creator, God can choose to punish with physical illness or psychological affliction. Such a punishment would show itself in fear, paranoia, suspicion, and indecisiveness.

Finally, the grammatical construction of verse 14 is unusual. This suggests the narrator wanted to call our attention to the text or "highlight" it (Bergen, 183, n. 39). God used this circumstance to highlight David's character. The irony is that the newly anointed king came to serve the disobedient and rejected king. Saul's plight actually created the need for David's service. This is not a fact to be overlooked.

16:16–17. This important point is often overlooked in the controversy surrounding the text: David used his God-given skills to serve Saul. This will not be the first contrast drawn between the character of Saul and that of David. These contrasts are deliberate and should be well noted. Even though David had been anointed king, he still chose to use his skills to serve others. Saul's **attendants** recognized the dilemma Saul was in. They recommended the soothing effect of music to alleviate the torment of the spirit (16:16). Musicians are well attested at royal courts throughout the ancient Near East. One of the servants of Saul just happened to know about a young son of Jesse of Bethlehem who would serve nicely.

16:18–22. This servant described David as one **who knows how to play the harp** (16:18). This probably refers to the lyre, a stringed instrument with two arms rising up from a sound box. David was also **a brave man and a warrior**. He was handsome and spoke well. But most importantly, the servant noted that **the LORD was with him**. This key statement underscores the changing circumstance in Saul's kingdom. The Lord was with David, but not with Saul.

Saul sent for David, and his father, Jesse, complied. The food sent with David was either a gift for Saul or provisions for David along the way. David arrived and entered Saul's **service** (16:21; lit. "stood before him"). It was not long before Saul was so impressed that he made David **one of his armorbearers**. Saul came to love David. He asked Jesse to **allow David** to **remain** in his service.

16:23. Whenever the spirit came upon Saul, David would play for him. As a result of the soothing music, **relief would come to Saul.** David was a skilled musician. He is called "the sweet singer of Israel" (2 Sam. 23:1 NCV), and many of the biblical psalms are attributed to him. When David played, Saul **would feel better**, and the **evil spirit** would depart from him.

Note that David was "a loyal, trustworthy servant of Saul who used his abilities to benefit the king" (Bergen, 184). Throughout his entire service to Saul, David made no attempt to usurp Saul's throne or bring down his dynasty. Saul would soon seek David's life, but David would be a true servant of Saul. Faithful leaders are called to serve others. Faithful leaders must use their abilities, skills, and talents to serve the people of God.

🄳 Shrinking from the Challenge of the Enemy (17:1–11)

SUPPORTING IDEA: *Saul's army cowers in fear before the taunts and insults of a Philistine giant named Goliath.*

17:1–3. From this point on in 1 Samuel, the disobedient leadership of Saul is contrasted with the obedient faithfulness of David. Since the Lord was with him (16:18), David began to prosper as he demonstrated what it meant to be a leader after God's own heart (13:14). In the first part of chapter 17, the old enemies of Israel, the **Philistines**, returned to threaten the peace. But this time, a young David stood up to the challenge.

We do not know how much time elapsed between the end of chapter 16 and the beginning of 17. It may have been only a short time later because David is still a boy (17:42). Nevertheless, chapter 17 opens with the serious news that the Philistines had **gathered their forces for war** and encamped on one side of a valley **at Ephes Dammim, between Socoh and Azekah.** Saul and the Israelites encamped on the other side of the valley and **drew up their battle line** against the Philistines. This was exactly the circumstances for which Israel wanted a king. Saul and his army would be put to the test.

17:4–7. Out from the ranks of the Philistines stepped **a champion named Goliath.** His name is possibly of Hittite or Lydian origin (Bergen, 188). In November 2005 the name Goliath was found written on a pottery shard at Tell es-Shafi, Israel. Tell es-Shafi is generally regarded to be the location of the ancient city of Gath, Goliath's hometown.

Goliath's great height was not a figment of Israelite imagination. An Egyptian letter on Papyrus Anastasi I (thirteenth century B.C.) describes fierce Canaanite warriors of seven to nine feet in height. In addition, two female skeletons about seven feet tall and dating from the twelfth century B.C. were discovered at Tell es-Sa`ideyeh in Transjordan (Walton, 306–7).

The NIV follows the Masoretic Hebrew text by translating the literal "six cubits and a span" as **over nine feet tall** (a cubit was approximately eighteen inches). Several ancient Greek texts and one copy of the Dead Sea Scrolls (4QSam^a), however, state that Goliath was "four cubits and a span" or roughly six feet, nine inches (Hays, 703–4). Regardless of his height, Goliath was formidable and frightening, an awesome foe. Saul, who was also a head taller than the normal Israelite and closer to Goliath's size, was elected king of Israel to face just such a foe (1 Sam. 10:13). Unfortunately, he and the rest of Israel's warriors cowered in fear before Goliath.

As a soldier, Goliath was well equipped with a **bronze helmet**, bronze body armor weighing over 125 pounds, **bronze greaves**, and a bronze scimitar or **javelin**. He had the latest in weaponry and armor. Metal was scarce at that time, and it was regulated by the Philistines (1 Sam. 13:19–22). The average soldier was not equipped with armor. Apparently, only Saul and Jonathan had the armor to match that of Goliath (17:38–39). The giant also had a spear **like a weaver's rod**. The iron spear point weighed about 15 pounds. Hays and others point out that this spear may have had a loop of cord attached to the end, making it possible to throw it harder and farther (Hays, 708).

In the spiritual battles faced by believers every day, leaders are often called upon to face awesome and frightening foes. These foes look bigger and appear to be so much better equipped for battle. To be honest, our initial response may be like Saul's and the Israelite warriors'. But we must also remember that the battle is the Lord's (1 Sam. 17:47). He is mighty in battle (Ps. 24:8), and we can defeat any foe through him.

17:8–11. Several cases of individual combat are attested in the ancient Near East (Walton, 307). Two champions were chosen to do battle as representatives of their respective armies. The outcome of the battle would be regarded as the judgment of the gods. Goliath demanded that Israel field their champion: **Choose a man and have him come down to me** (17:8). Goliath's words were meant to defy Israel in three ways (cp. Bergen, 190).

First, Goliath questioned their resolve to do battle by taunting them about lining up for battle (17:8). Second, his words chided Israel about champion combat (17:9). Israel may have been aware of this type of individual combat before (2 Sam. 2:14–16), but here Goliath challenged them to send out someone to do battle with him. His boasting may have sounded like he didn't expect to lose and, perhaps, rang hollow as the Philistines later reneged on the idea (see 18:30). Finally, Goliath insulted the Israelite warriors: **This day I defy the ranks of Israel** (17:10). The Hebrew verb translated "defy" by the NIV literally means "to heap shame."

The sight of Goliath with his height, armor, and weapons was certainly frightening, but we are told that when Saul and the Israelites heard the words of this overwhelming enemy they **were dismayed and terrified** (17:11). Enemies choose their words carefully to invoke such a response. Believers, and especially leaders, must not regard the insolent and lying words of the enemies of God.

As we shall see, David, on the other hand, trusted God and rose to the challenge. He believed that the same God who had delivered him from the lion and the bear would also deliver him from this blasphemous Philistine (17:37). Many times God calls us to face awesome and seemingly overwhelming enemies. Leaders who are called by God will not shrink from the challenge but will stand up to the enemies of God.

E Standing up to the Enemies of God (17:12–32)

SUPPORTING IDEA: *David arrives in Saul's camp and expresses outrage that Goliath is defying the Lord and taunting the armies of Israel.*

17:12–15. In contrast to Saul's response to the Philistine threat, the narrative now turns to David. In these few verses we are reintroduced to David, the eighth son of Jesse, **an Ephrathite** (Ruth 1:2; 1 Chron. 2:19; 4:4) from Bethlehem. **Jesse's three oldest sons** had gone to war with Saul, but **David went back and forth** from Saul and the army to help tend his father's sheep.

17:16–24. The standoff between the Israelites and the Philistines lasted for **forty days**. At the beginning and end of each day, Goliath would come forth and taunt Saul and the Israelite army (17:16). The length of the hostilities meant that David's brothers would soon run out of whatever provisions they were able to carry with them. Each family was expected to supply the needed rations for their sons in service. So Jesse sent David to resupply his brothers with an **ephah of roasted grain** and **ten loaves of bread**.

Jesse also sent a gift of **ten cheeses to the commander of their unit** (17:18). David was also sent with instructions to find out about the safety and well-being of his brothers. Jesse also wanted **some assurance** or "token" that the cost of the provisions would be reimbursed or covered by the spoils taken from the Philistines in the event of an Israelite victory (Bergen, 191–92).

After leaving his father's flock with another shepherd, David reached the Israelite camp in the **morning**, just in time to see them draw up in battle lines opposite the Philistines (17:20). The Philistines responded in like manner to oppose the Israelites, but this had been a formality every morning and perhaps every evening for 40 days. Just as David reached his brothers and began talking with them, Goliath came out of the Philistine lines and shouted his **usual defiance** (17:23; cp. 17:8–10). David watched his fellow Israelites run from him **in great fear**.

17:25–32. Since Saul was afraid to fight Goliath, he did a predictable thing—he offered a big reward to anyone who did. Saul promised three things to the warrior who would defeat the giant: great wealth, marriage into his family, and exemption from taxes. Saul's desperate lack of leadership is revealed in the extreme nature of the reward. All of the Israelites were talking about the reward. It promised instant wealth, status, and economic stability. They were talking about it, but not doing anything about it.

David's response was one of incredulity. He appeared astonished to hear that the king of Israel, the Lord's covenant community, would even offer such a reward. To David this Philistine was daring to heap shame on or **defy the armies of the living God** (17:26). For David this was equal to defying the living God himself.

David appears to have made quite a stir with his questioning. **Eliab, David's oldest brother**, overheard him speaking with some of the soldiers (17:28). Eliab accused David of leaving their father's flock in the desert because he, David, had a **conceited** and **wicked** heart. He assumed that David only wanted to come and watch the battle. And now, he misunderstood David's concern for the honor of Israel's God.

David, however, was consumed with the matter, and he kept bringing up **the same matter** to anyone who would listen (17:30). Soon what David said was overheard and reported to Saul (17:31). His outrage at the blasphemies of Goliath did not go unnoticed (Bergen, 193). Saul sent for David, and what he said to Saul confirms that David's heart was in the right place. David reassured Saul that they need not **lose heart** because of this Philistine (17:32). Instead, David astonished everyone by declaring that he himself would **go and fight** Goliath.

David was outraged that anyone would be allowed to impugn the honor of the living God of Israel. Since David was a man after the Lord's own heart (1 Sam. 13:14), he was also zealous for God's honor. Unlike Saul, David was not willing to allow the pagan Philistine to defy God and speak against his covenant community. To do so would be to refuse to acknowledge God's kingship and reign. David knew that he must stand in the gap and fight for God. He also believed that God would deliver him from Goliath (17:37).

Christian believers must be zealous for the honor of God and his Son, our Savior Christ Jesus. This is especially true of Christian leaders, who must not shrink before the challenges of God's enemies. We cannot afford to ignore their threats and be silent before their lies and half-truths. Leaders cannot hide by offering rewards for fighting the battles that are rightly theirs. Leaders must stand in the gap and fight for the honor of God.

F Securing the Victory for God (17:33–58)

SUPPORTING IDEA: *By trusting in the Lord, David brings down Goliath with a stone from his trusty shepherd's sling.*

17:33–37. The contrast between Saul's way of thinking and David's is clear in the way Saul responded to David's offer to fight Goliath. Saul first rejected David's offer (17:33). It is clear that Saul was considering the outward appearance. He was unable to fight Goliath because David was still a boy and Goliath was a giant. Besides, Goliath had been a soldier **from his youth**. David, however, looked like a shepherd.

But David rejected this line of reasoning. He protested that he had had sufficient experience in battling the **bear** and the **lion** (17:34). David was aggressive in going after these ferocious animals. Since Goliath defied the Lord God, he was no more than an animal (17:36). David was certain that just as the Lord had delivered him from the paws of the lion and the bear, he would also deliver him **from the hand of this Philistine**. David wanted Saul to look at the heart, a heart filled with trust in a God who would deliver him in battle. Saul seemed to acquiesce and offered a blessing to David (17:17).

17:38–40. Still it would appear that Saul did not understand David's offer to fight. He tried to make David into something he was not by outfitting him with the equipment of a soldier. Saul dressed David **in his own tunic** and found a **coat of armor** and **bronze helmet** for him. David fastened on a sword and tried to walk around. The scene must have been humorous. Here was David, a small boy, dressed in the same type of armor worn by the giant Goliath. Saul actually believed that David needed these things in order to fight the Philistine. This was how it was done; this was how all the kings and soldiers fought!

But David knew that Saul's armor would be a detriment to him. He was **not used to them** (17:39). Instead, David picked up his familiar **staff** and chose **five smooth stones** from the wadi. He took his sling and approached

Goliath. David had a different way of looking at things. Since David trusted in God to deliver him, David trusted in God's strategy. God would have David do battle with the weapons he already had, a shepherd's staff and a sling. God would use David's own heart to win the battle! David trusted that the Spirit of God would be with him as he stood before the enemy and that God's Spirit would win the battle (Zech. 4:6). Christian leaders need to learn to trust God when facing difficult enemies. This means trusting God's strategy as well as trusting that God will give us the weapons we need to win.

17:41–47. Note that the initial confrontation between David and Goliath consisted of words. When David came within his eyesight, Goliath noted that David **was only a boy, ruddy and handsome**. This infuriated Goliath, and he let loose with an insult and a curse. Such insults and curses were typical features in ancient Near Eastern warfare (Walton, 308–9). They were designed to demoralize and intimidate the opponent (cp. 2 Kgs. 18:17–36).

Winning a battle against such a poorly armed opponent would not be such an impressive accomplishment, so Goliath **despised** David (17:42). Goliath insulted David's shepherd's staff by calling it a **stick**. He also cursed David by his gods (17:43). This latter curse was theologically significant. As Bergen points out (p. 195), the readers of this text would know "that by cursing this son of Abraham, Goliath was bringing down the Lord's curse on himself (cf. Gen. 12:3)." Goliath then boasted that he would kill David, humiliate his corpse, and deny him an honorable burial. Individuals who dishonor God are quick to bring threats against God's people. Since they do not possess the truth, they employ intimidation to win. But believers and Christian leaders must recognize that such threats are empty and powerless.

David responded to Goliath's threats by speaking the truth. David was not disturbed by Goliath's insults. He launched a verbal counterattack of his own. But there is one fundamental difference. David offered no idle or proud threats. He was not alone in the battle, because the Lord would fight with David against the Philistine giant. David completely trusted the battle to God.

There is much in David's reply that commends itself to the Christian leader. First, David had no delusions about the strength of his enemy. He acknowledged that Goliath came against him with **sword and spear and javelin** (17:45). But David's weapon was far superior. He came in the name of the **Lord Almighty, the God of the armies of Israel**. Against such no human weapons can stand! Goliath had insulted the God of Israel, and David wanted him to know that he would not get away with it. Bergen points out that the penalty for blaspheming was stoning (Lev. 24:16; cp. Bergen, 195). This may have influenced David's choice of the sling and stone.

Second, David realized that the skill of the human combatants is of little consequence in this confrontation. Goliath, the giant, could not stand against the Lord of all creation. David informed this mighty Philistine that the Lord would **hand him over** to him that day! Because the Lord would fight for him, David knew that he would be able to strike his enemy down and cut off his head (17:46).

Third, David knew that the Lord would not only be able to win this battle, he would also win the war. David may have been suspicious that the Philistines would not acquiesce to Goliath's call for a decision by champion battle (17:9). Still, it did not matter. Goliath boasted that he would dishonor David's corpse (17:44). David knew that the result of this battle would bring Goliath's insult on the entire Philistine **army**—their carcasses would become fodder for **the birds of the air and the beasts of the earth**.

Fourth, David was aware that the purpose of the battle was broader in scope than Goliath realized. Goliath's goal was to subjugate the Israelites in servitude. But David recognized that God's honor was at stake. Goliath had insulted God and his chosen covenant people. This battle and war was to set the record straight. At its conclusion, the **whole world** would **know that there is a God in Israel**. The Hebrew verb *yāda‘* ("to know") carries the idea of personal experiential knowledge. David argued that everyone would know in their hearts this Almighty God.

Finally, David recognized that God's strategy is perfect. Human prowess with sword and spear is irrelevant and often unnecessary. Think about it! A small boy armed with a staff and a slingshot should be no match for a gigantic, seasoned warrior equipped with the latest and best armament. But God's ways are not our ways. The Christian leader who seeks after the Lord's own heart must acknowledge this (Zech. 4:6). The battle is the Lord's, and he would give all of the Philistines—not just Goliath—into the hands of David and the Israelites.

17:48–54. The words stopped and the conflict moved quickly. Two champions faced each other, the giant and the young man. The giant walked toward David, but David went on the attack and **ran quickly** to meet Goliath. Choosing **a stone** from his bag, David **slung it** and hit Goliath **on the forehead**. The impact was strong enough to sink the stone into the Philistine's brow, and **he fell facedown on the ground**.

David ran to Goliath and **stood over him** (17:51). He took the Philistine's own sword from its scabbard and cut off Goliath's head. Young David, with no armor, no coat of mail, no shield, and no sword had defeated the Philistine hero. God gave David a stunning victory with **a sling and a stone** (17:50).

It must have taken only a moment for the impact of what had happened to sink in. When the Philistines saw what had happened to Goliath, **they turned and ran**. The Israelites followed in pursuit to **the entrance of Gath and to the gates of Ekron** (17:52). David's confident words had come true—their dead bodies were strewn along the road. The Israelites plundered the Philistine camp, and David received the giant's armor and sword.

17:55–58. Bergen considers the presentation of David to Saul at this point important for two reasons (198–99). First, if by chance David succeeded in defeating Goliath, Saul needed to know the name of David's father in order to declare his house exempt from taxes (17:25). The proof of David's success was the head of Goliath in his hand. David had trusted God, and God had given him a magnificent victory.

Second, this passage shows again the growing difference between Saul and David. Since the Lord's Spirit was no longer with Saul, the king was growing more and more incompetent. Saul did not remember David (cp. 1 Sam. 16:21–22). But David was patient and civil (17:58).

MAIN IDEA REVIEW: *Because of Saul's failure as king, David is selected by the Lord through Samuel as the new king of Israel. He proves his leadership ability by defeating a Philistine giant and giving credit for the victory to the Lord.*

III. CONCLUSION

Blue or Gray?

Appearances are important, but what matters most is the heart. There is a Civil War legend that tells of a confused soldier who put on the Confederate gray coat, and the Union blue trousers. From his appearance it was impossible to tell where his sympathies were. So when he went into battle he got shot at from both sides! The Federals shot him in the coat, and the Confederates shot him in the seat of the pants!

Believers and Christian leaders come in all shapes and sizes. What matters most is not the appearance, but the heart. God does not take aim at us based on our appearance. He looks at the heart! He chose David because of his faithful and trusting heart. Saul was rejected because his heart was not completely committed to serve Israel's God. Jesus warned us that where our treasure is, there our heart will be also (Matt. 6:21). God wants to use kingdom leaders who long after God to glorify and honor him.

PRINCIPLES

- God desires leaders to seek after his own heart.
- God alone chooses those he wants to lead his people.
- Leaders must be servants who minister to the needs of their people.
- At times, leaders must face frightening enemies.
- Leaders must be zealous for the Lord and trust his strategy.
- The battle belongs to the Lord.

APPLICATIONS

- Daily seek the Lord's heart on all matters.
- Ask the Holy Spirit to show you where pride and self-centeredness hinder your trust in God.
- Repent of pride and self-centeredness so that God can use you in his service.
- Ask God to show you how you can be a servant to someone today.
- Ask the Holy Spirit to help you be zealous for God's honor and to be strong to stand when his name is profaned.
- Seek to trust God's strategy and plan for your life.
- Ask God for courage to face the frightening enemies you face today.
- Learn to trust that the battle belongs to the Lord.

IV. LIFE APPLICATION

He's Making Coffee

Dr. James Dobson tells the story of a three-year-old girl who told her mother one day that she learned that Jesus will come to live in the hearts of those who invite him. This is obviously a difficult concept for a child so young to grasp, and the mother was somewhat amazed. Before she could respond her three-year-old came over to where she was sitting on the couch and put her ear to her mother's chest.

"What are you doing?" asked the mother.

"I'm listening for Jesus in your heart," replied the child.

The mother let the little girl listen for a few seconds and then asked, "Well, what do you hear?"

"He's there," replied the little girl, "and it sounds to me like he's making coffee."

As king over Israel, Saul turned his heart away from obedience to God's will. And as a result, God rejected him (1 Sam. 15:22–23). David, on the other hand, faithfully sought after the heart of God. This is why God chose him to be the next king of Israel (1 Sam. 13:14).

When we come to Christ, we say that we invite him to live in our hearts. But as believers, and even more so as leaders, our own hearts must be consumed with knowing the heart of the Savior and seeking to make his will our own. We laugh when we think of the little girl listening to hear if Jesus was in her mother's heart. But the truth of the matter is that many around us listen to our hearts with spiritual stethoscopes every day to ascertain its condition and direction. Not only must Jesus be there; he must be percolating!

V. PRAYER

O heavenly Father, our King of kings, teach us how to humbly seek your heart. Help us to be consumed with you, to treasure nothing else save knowing you and your will for us. Help us to be offended when you are blasphemed. Teach us how to trust your strategy. Guide us to see how with little you can accomplish mighty miracles. Through the Holy Spirit, enable us to make Jesus our first priority. In the name of our Savior, Jesus Christ, we pray. Amen.

VI. DEEPER DISCOVERIES

A. Inheritance of the Firstborn (16:11–12)

Ancient Near Eastern societies generally gave special inheritance rights and leadership roles to the firstborn son. In the Bible, God often chose those overlooked and ignored in the line of succession. Abraham, Jacob, Joseph, Moses, and Solomon were younger brothers whom God blessed in spite of their birth order.

B. David's Harp (16:18,23)

The musical instrument played by David is not like a modern harp as we would imagine but is really a lyre. David's lyre had two arms rising up from a sound box. Strings were attached between the arms. Examples of this type of lyre have been found at Megiddo.

Israel's musical heritage is inextricably linked with David. He was the "sweet singer of Israel" (2 Sam. 23:1 NCV) and the author of at least 73 psalms. He also was responsible for establishing music as a major part of the temple worship in Jerusalem (1 Chron. 25).

C. The Weaver's Rod (17:7)

Among the weaponry used by Goliath was a spear said to be like a weaver's rod. This spear had an iron point weighing over 15 pounds. Traditionally, it has been thought that this description referred to the size and weight of the shaft of the spear. Weaving looms of that period may have used a large shaft in the making of cloth. Knowing this, the ancient reader would easily and quickly understand the comparison.

Recent studies have suggested that the reference to the weaver's rod meant that Goliath's spear, like a rod used by the weaver, had a loop of cord or string attached to its end (Bergen, 189). Aegean javelins dating from the Mycenaean period down to the fifth century B.C. had this same kind of loop. The spinning motion caused by the loop effectively increased the distance and accuracy of the spear.

D. Champion Warfare (17:8–10)

Depiction of individual combat is found in Egypt and Canaan from the early second millennium onwards. But on occasion individual combatants from each army were chosen to meet in battle. The outcome of the fight would signify the judgment of the gods on the matter. The type of champion warfare advocated by Goliath is known from ancient Greek and Hittite sources. Israel also may have used this type of warfare in 2 Samuel 2:14–16.

E. Five Smooth Stones (17:40)

The sling was used alongside the bow and spear in warfare in the ancient Near East. Pictures from Egypt and Mesopotamia depict slingers and archers standing side by side in battle scenes. The militia of Benjamin were especially known for their proficient left-handed slingers (Judg. 20:16).

Excavations in Israel have revealed hundreds of sling stones at many fortified sites. They are typically the size of tennis balls and weigh about a pound each. An accomplished warrior could sling a stone this size at a rate of 100 to 150 miles an hour, making it a very lethal weapon. It is most likely that David chose stones from the dry stream bed of this size and weight. As a shepherd David knew how to use a sling, and he was probably very proficient in its use.

VII. TEACHING OUTLINE

A. INTRODUCTION

1. Lead Story: Two Bananas
2. Context: After God rejects Saul as king, God tells Samuel to go and anoint a new king, one after God's own heart. Samuel finds and anoints David, the son of Jesse. David enters Saul's service and helps soothe his troubled heart. Ever zealous for the Lord, David offers to fight the Philistine giant who is insulting Israel and blaspheming God. With a sling and a stone, David is given a spectacular victory by the Lord. Israel pursues the Philistines and then returns to plunder their camp. David is again presented to Saul, and he stands before Saul with Goliath's head in his hand.
3. Transition: Saul failed as king over Israel because he was self-centered and disobedient. God rejected him and took away his Spirit from him. When a leader rejects God, God rejects him for another. God wants kingdom leaders to seek after his own heart. That is, to seek his will, his wishes, and his honor. Kingdom leaders will face frightening enemies, but they must stand up to those adversaries and be zealous for God's name. Kingdom leaders must believe and trust that the battle belongs to the Lord.

B. COMMENTARY

1. Searching for a New King (16:1–5)
2. Selecting a New King (16:6–13)
3. Soothing the Troubled Spirit of a Rejected King (16:14–23)
4. Shrinking from the Challenge of the Enemy (17:1–11)
5. Standing Up to the Enemies of God (17:12–32)
6. Securing the Victory for God (17:33–58)

C. CONCLUSION: HE'S MAKING COFFEE

VIII. ISSUES FOR DISCUSSION

1. Name some of the temptations facing kingdom leaders today. What specific situations might lead them to be proud and disobedient?

2. How can a kingdom leader "seek after God's own heart"? List specific ways a leader can learn the heart of God.

3. Compare the type of things that can be known about a person from observing his appearance with what can be known by trying his heart. Which is more indicative of real character?

4. List some of the more frightening adversaries faced by believers today. Discuss their physical and spiritual weapons. What specific things has God done to help us overcome them?

5. Why is it difficult to trust God's strategy and plan for our lives? Name some of the difficulties and how we can overcome them. What does it mean to say "the battle is the Lord's" in your life today?

1 Samuel 18:1–20:42

David and Jonathan

I. INTRODUCTION
Brian Piccolo

II. COMMENTARY
A verse-by-verse explanation of these chapters

III. CONCLUSION
Good for Our Health

An overview of the principles and applications from these chapters

IV. LIFE APPLICATION
What Friends Are For

Melding these chapters to life

V. PRAYER
Tying these chapters to life with God

VI. DEEPER DISCOVERIES
Historical, geographical, and grammatical enrichment of the commentary

VII. TEACHING OUTLINE
Suggested step-by-step group study of these chapters

VIII. ISSUES FOR DISCUSSION
Zeroing these chapters in on daily life

Q u o t e

"\
ll hearts are not traitorous; fidelity still lingers

among men: where godliness builds her house,

true friendship finds a rest."

C h a r l e s   H a d d o n   S p u r g e o n

BIOGRAPHICAL PROFILE: JONATHAN

- Eldest son of King Saul and Ahinoam (1 Sam. 14:49–50)
- Revealed exceptional courage in battle with Philistines at Micmash (1 Sam. 14:1–16)
- Had a close friendship with David (1 Sam. 18:1–4)
- Acknowledged David as the next anointed king (1 Sam. 23:16–18)
- Died in battle with Saul at Mt. Gilboa (1 Sam. 31:1–13)

ROYAL PROFILE: SAUL'S SPEAR

- At the beginning Saul and Jonathan were the only warriors who had a spear (1 Sam. 13:22)
- Saul's spear seems to have functioned like a scepter as sign of his kingship (1 Sam. 22:6; 26:7)
- Saul threw the same spear several times at David (1 Sam. 18:10–11; 19:10) and once at Jonathan (1 Sam. 20:33)
- David took the spear away from Saul (1 Sam. 26:2) and later returned it (1 Sam. 26:22)
- In his last battle, Saul, wounded and dying, leaned upon his spear (2 Sam. 1:6)

BIOGRAPHICAL PROFILE: MICHAL

- The youngest daughter of Saul (1 Sam. 14:49)

- Apparently the first wife of David (1 Sam. 18:27)
- David paid double the bride price required by Saul to marry her (1 Sam. 18:25–27).
- Helped David escape from Saul (1 Sam. 19:11–17)
- Criticized David for dancing before the ark of the covenant (2 Sam. 16:16–23)

I N   A   N U T S H E L L

avid has triumphed over the Philistine giant Goliath, and Israel has routed the Philistines and plundered their camp. Now David is presented to Saul as the hero of the day. Jonathan, Saul's son, becomes a true friend with David, and the two make a covenant. Saul gives David a high rank in his army but soon becomes jealous of his successes and seeks to kill him in envy. Even after David marries into Saul's family, Saul attempts to kill him. Jonathan seeks to mediate between his father and David, but in the end he must warn David of his father's desire to take his life. Jonathan reaffirms the covenant he made with David and sends him away in peace.

David and Jonathan

I. INTRODUCTION

Brian Piccolo

*I*n May 1970 Gale Sayers, the Chicago Bears' halfback, was given the George S. Halas award as the most courageous player in professional football at the Professional Football Writers annual dinner in New York. The six-foot, two-hundred-pound Sayers had been Rookie of the Year in 1965, scoring 22 touchdowns, a NFL record. But midway into the 1968 season Sayers suffered a ruptured cartilage and two torn ligaments in his right knee and was out for the rest of the season. After rehabilitation and physical therapy, Gale Sayers returned to the Bears lineup in 1969 and won a second rushing title. Later in 1970 Sayers would suffer an injury to his left knee that would effectively end his short football career. Nevertheless, he was elected to the College Football Hall of Fame, the Black Athlete's Hall of Fame, and even greater still, the Pro Football Hall of Fame.

But what amazed the professional football writers who attended that dinner in May 1970 was what Gale Sayers said as he accepted the Halas award and took the trophy. Sayers did not speak about himself; he spoke about his friend Brian Piccolo: "You flatter me by giving me this award, but I tell you here and now that I accept it for Brian Piccolo. Brian Piccolo is the man of courage who should receive the George S. Halas Award. I love Brian Piccolo and I'd like you to love him. Tonight, when you hit your knees, please ask God to love him too."

Brian Piccolo was Sayers's friend, and he was lying at home in bed, dying of cancer.

Brian Piccolo was signed by the Chicago Bears as a running back, and he played only four seasons in the overwhelming shadow of Gale Sayers. Sayers and Piccolo became roommates and fast friends. This deep friendship shattered racial boundaries and was the subject of the 1971 movie *Brian's Song* (and its 2001 remake) and Sayers's 1973 autobiography *I Am Third*. Piccolo died at the age of 26, a symbol of courage and a cherished friend.

The Bible records another amazing friendship, that of David and Jonathan. First Samuel 18:1 tells us that Jonathan's soul was "knit" or "bound" to the soul of David. David and Jonathan had a true friendship, godly in character and essence. Chapters 18–20 detail how this friendship developed and how it was tested and tried in the crucible of life.

II. COMMENTARY

David and Jonathan

MAIN IDEA: *Saul's jealousy of David's success as a warrior in his army drives him to try to kill David. But Saul's own son, Jonathan, befriends David and protects him from his father's rage.*

A Discovering a True Friend (18:1–30)

SUPPORTING IDEA: *Saul grows jealous of David when David is recognized by the people for his military exploits, and the king begins to plot against him. Jonathan, Saul's son, and David form a strong friendship.*

18:1–5. After defeating Goliath, David's life changed forever. Saul and the royal family would honor David with prestige, position, and possessions. In fact, David would even marry one of Saul's daughters. But David would also find a true friend in Jonathan, Saul's heir-apparent. Gene Getz calls the description offered in verse 1, "the best definition of true friendship I've ever read" (Getz, *David*, 74). The relationship of David and Jonathan provides a biblical model for godly friendship that is worthy of study and consideration.

Jonathan observed David's faith and courage in defeating Goliath. Both were young warriors, and both had trusted God for victory over the enemies of Israel. Now we learn that **Jonathan became one in spirit with David**. The Hebrew text actually tells us that the soul of Jonathan was "bound" or "chained" together with the soul of David. Jonathan **loved** David **as himself**. Saul is also said to have "loved" David (16:21). This was not an impure connection as some have suggested. The friendship of these two was pure and true and "focused on God and their deep love for Him" (Getz, *David*, 75).

From that day forward, Saul kept David with his royal servants (18:2). He sent him on special missions and **gave him a high rank in the army** (18:5). Jonathan also recognized David's abilities by doing two significant things. First, Jonathan made a personal covenant with David. This covenant would be very important for David's well-being later. Second, Jonathan sealed the covenant with royal gifts. Jonathan **took off** his **robe** and gave it to David. He also gave David his tunic, sword, bow, and belt. Jonathan honored David by giving to him the princely garments reserved for the heir to Saul's throne (Bergen, 199). "Here was a son of a king honoring a son of a shepherd!" (Getz, *David*, 79).

Perhaps Jonathan instinctively knew then what he would confess to later—that David would be king over Israel (23:17). David was successful in what he did for Saul because he "was a man under the control and direction of the Lord's Spirit" (Bergen, 200; cp. 16:13). Including David in the army of Israel not only satisfied the officers, but it also **pleased all the people** (18:5). As believers, we are called to follow Jonathan's example and honor one another above ourselves (Rom. 12:10).

18:6–12. It didn't take long for jealousy to rear its ugly head. It was quite natural for the Israelites to celebrate the victory over Goliath. The women rejoiced with **singing and dancing** (18:6). Probably a number of songs were composed to remember the defeat of the Philistines. Only a few lines of one of them is preserved in verse 7.

In good poetic parallelism, the song used a fixed word pair in common use in the ancient Near East. The terms *thousand* and *ten thousand* were understood to be synonyms (cp. Deut. 32:30; Ps. 91:7; Mic. 6:7). Neither Saul nor David literally killed that many Philistines. Instead, these are figurative terms intended to celebrate the stunning victory over the Philistine enemy. Both Saul and David were exalted in the song.

Saul should have known this. But the attribution of tens of thousands of the enemy killed to David angered Saul. The **refrain galled him** (18:8). Literally, this means that he considered it evil in his eyes. Saul remembered Samuel's prophecy that the Lord would give the kingdom to an anonymous neighbor who was better than he (Bergen, 201; cp. 15:28). No doubt this bothered Saul, so he **kept a jealous eye on David** (18:9). Bergen has pointed out that the verb translated "kept a jealous eye" was most likely deliberately used because there is a similar sounding word meaning "transgressed" (p. 201). Perhaps this wordplay was intended to inform the reader that from this point on, Saul intended to watch David like a hawk and do him evil.

One example of such attempted evil against David came the very next day (18:10). David was playing the harp for Saul as he usually did when **an evil spirit from God came forcefully upon Saul**. The text says that Saul was **prophesying in his house** (see "Deeper Discoveries"). The text also says that Saul had a spear in his hand. This may have been a symbol of his status as king. But the Lord was no longer with Saul, and he acted out of his own sinful fear. Saul said to himself, **I'll pin David to the wall** (18:11). He hurled the spear not once but twice at David. Both times David escaped harm. The Hebrew text says that Saul was afraid of the presence of David because he knew that **the LORD was with** him (18:12). Saul also knew that the Lord had left him. Saul's behavior is not that of a godly leader or a true friend. Jealousy is a dangerous and powerful temptation. Godly friends do not give in to jealous scheming.

18:13–30. Saul's behavior through the end of this chapter stands in stark contrast to the covenant loyalty exercised by Jonathan for his friend, David, in chapter 19. Here Saul attempted to use every means to bring about the downfall of David. But the reader understands why David had **great success** in everything he did. It is precisely **because the LORD was with him** (18:14). True friends reject such behavior as ungodly and sinful. Neither true friends nor godly leaders should act this way.

Saul tried three different ways to destroy David and build himself up. First, David was given **command over a thousand men** (18:13). While this was certainly an honor, it must be remembered that David was still young and inexperienced. Saul probably counted on David's defeat, and even death, on the battlefield. But when David enjoyed great success, Saul **was afraid of him** (18:15). The ESV translates this, "he stood in fearful awe of him." Contrast this with the reaction of Israel and Judah (18:16). They "loved" David. This is the same verb as that used to describe Jonathan's affection for David.

Second, Saul sought to honor David by offering his older daughter **Merab** to David in marriage. Normally, a suitor of the king's daughter would be required to provide a large dowry for the privilege of marrying into the royal family. Saul apparently waived the dowry, if David would serve him and **fight the battles of the LORD** (18:17). Saul put no time limit on the service. If David accepted, Saul could dictate what David would be required to do.

Saul's purpose was not to welcome David into his household, but to increase the amount of time David would have to spend on the battlefield to pay the bride price. Saul reasoned that the Philistines would do the work of killing David, and that he, Saul, would not need to **raise a hand against him** (18:18). But David refused on the ground of his family background. His origins were too humble to suppose that he could marry the king's oldest daughter (18:18). So when the time came for Merab to be given in marriage, she was wedded to someone else (18:19).

Saul attempted to destroy David the third time by offering another daughter in marriage to David. But this time a dangerous bride price was set. Saul learned that his daughter **Michal was in love with David** (18:20). This pleased Saul because he believed this would pose a double threat for David. First, Saul believed that Michal would be a snare to David. We are not told exactly how, but it is possible that Saul was counting on Michal's idolatrous inclinations to lead him astray spiritually from the Lord (Bergen, 204). Second, Saul saw the opportunity again to deliver David into the hand of the Philistines (18:21,25).

Saul manipulated the negotiations to require from David a bride price of a hundred Philistine foreskins (18:22–26). David accepted the challenge and succeeded so well that he paid double the price to Saul (18:27). Saul's plans failed. In fact, **when Saul realized that the LORD was with David and that his daughter Michal loved David**, he became even more afraid (18:28). From that day forward Saul regarded David as a enemy (18:29). God prospered David, and he became well known (18:30). God honors true friendships that are based on his principles. God also prospers kingdom leaders who follow after his own heart.

𝔹 Defending a True Friend (19:1–24)

> **SUPPORTING IDEA:** *Jonathan intercedes on David's behalf when Saul's jealousy and rage toward David grow stronger and stronger.*

19:1–7. Jonathan must have been shocked when Saul told him to **kill David**. At first Saul had tried to kill David by himself. When that didn't succeed, Saul tried by crafty design to obtain David's death by means of battle with the Philistines (Bergen, 206). Now Saul dropped all ruses and ordered all his servants and Jonathan explicitly to murder David (19:1).

But Jonathan had made a covenant with David and was a loyal friend. He **was very fond of David**, so he warned him that his father was seeking to kill him. Jonathan instructed David to **go into hiding** (19:2). His plan was to intercede with his father on David's behalf and to tell David what he found out (19:3). Jonathan had much to gain by David's death. With David out of the way, there would be no question about his right to the throne of Israel. But as a loyal friend Jonathan chose to speak **well of David** and to act as mediator to secure peace between Saul and David (19:4).

Jonathan offered his father three reasons to reconsider his plans against David (Bergen, 206). First, he argued that David was innocent. He had **not wronged** Saul. The one verb translated "wrong" three times in verses 4 and 5 in the NIV is actually the verb "sin." Saul should not "sin" against David because David had not "sinned" against Saul. Nothing David had done merited his death.

Second, Jonathan noted that what David did in reality benefited Saul and all Israel. David had defeated Goliath and the Philistines, a common enemy. Jonathan rightly attributed the victory to the Lord. Saul had seen it and was glad (19:5). Finally, Jonathan recognized that if his father killed David, he would sin against David and be guilty of shedding innocent blood.

Saul listened to his son and relented of his plan. In Jonathan's presence Saul took an oath: **As surely as the LORD lives, David will not be put to death** (19:6). Unfortunately, Saul's oath was short-lived. Saul had not kept other oaths (14:24,44). But for the time being Jonathan was able to bring David back to the royal household and his former status. This was the first time Jonathan went to bat for David. It would not be the last. Jonathan loyally supported David. He did so even when this meant going against the explicit command of his father, the king. Believers are called to model this type of faithful support for others.

19:8–17. Once again God used David to defeat the Philistines, the enemy of Israel (19:8), and once again an evil spirit came upon Saul while he was listening to David play the harp (19:9). Saul tried for the third time to pin David **to the wall with his spear** (19:10). David did not want to remain for a fourth attempt so he fled, intending to escape that night.

In his anger, Saul sent messengers to lie in wait for David at his house and **to kill him in the morning** (19:11). But like her brother, Michal loved David and **warned** him of the plot (cp. 19:2). What happened next is a classic act of subterfuge. Although some elements of the story point to less than perfect fidelity to the Lord on Michal's part, it does proves that she loved David. More importantly, the account shows that ultimately the Lord was with David and protected him.

First, Michal **let David down through a window** of their home, and David was able to escape (19:12). Then she put a teraphim (NIV **idol**) on the bed and made it look like David was lying there (19:13). She even put **some goats' hair at the head.** It is not clear where the idol in David's house came from. Perhaps the idol belonged to Michal and she trusted in the teraphim to save David. Maybe Saul recognized this flaw in Michal's life when he counted on her being a snare to David (18:21).

When the messengers came to capture David, Michal told them that he was ill (19:14). It was only after Saul sent the messengers back to bring David, bed and all, to the king that the hoax was revealed (19:15–16). When Saul confronted his daughter about the deception, Michal lied to him and made it sound like David had forced her to do it. Her lack of faith in the Lord eventually led to her downfall (cp. 2 Sam. 6:20–23).

Obviously, Michal loved David, but her actions showed that she was not altogether trusting in the Lord. Believers sometime make the same mistake. We don't resort to the use of idols and lies, but we do tend to trust in common sense, our own reason, or pop psychology to bluff our way through. These methods are all self-centered. Godly leadership trusts completely in the Lord and his deliverance.

19:18–24. David did not go very far when he fled from Saul at Gibeah. David went to Samuel at Ramah about three miles away. There he told Samuel everything that Saul had done to him (19:18). Perhaps as a precaution Samuel took David to **Naioth**. It is not clear exactly where or what Naioth was. Succeeding verses indicate that it was **at Ramah** (19:19,22,23). In Hebrew "naioth" means "habitations" or "dwellings." Given what follows in chapter 19, this appears to refer to a complex of houses or a religious compound where a company of prophets resided. In David's case, it served as place of refuge. The Lord would surely protect him there.

Three times Saul sent messengers to capture David, but each time the messengers saw Samuel and the prophets prophesying, the Spirit of God came upon them, and they also began to prophesy (19:20–21). Before these messengers could even look for David, they were captured by the Spirit and compelled to join the prophets. "Those who had entered into Naioth under the influence of the ruler of Israel now found themselves under the infinitely greater influence of the ruler of the universe" (Bergen, 210).

Without further options, Saul himself **left for Ramah** as a last resort (19:22). Perhaps he did not believe in the reports that David was at Naioth and that this was where his messengers had actually gone. At any rate he inquired of the people, stopping at **the great cistern at Secu**, concerning the whereabouts of Samuel and David. Having satisfied himself that Samuel and David were indeed at Naioth in Ramah, Saul headed in that direction.

What happened next has been called a true climatic tour de force. Unfortunately, the NIV translation hides somewhat the full impact of how "Israel's most powerful citizen was subjugated by the power of God" (Bergen, 210). The coming of God's Spirit upon Saul would precipitate five actions, ironically indicating that Saul was completely under God's control.

First, the **Spirit of God** came upon Saul while he was walking to Naioth (19:23). This happened to Saul's messengers only after they had arrived there, but Saul prophesied before he arrived while he walking along the road. God was reminding Saul that he could act whenever and wherever he chose. Second, when Saul arrived he stripped off his robes (19:24). Since God had rejected Saul as king (15:23,28), he would not be allowed to wear royal attire in his presence.

Third, Saul **prophesied in Samuel's presence**. Samuel had condemned Saul for rejecting the word of the Lord (15:23). Now Saul was forced to proclaim the same word that he had earlier rejected. Fourth, Saul fell naked before Samuel and all the other prophets that day and night. Lying naked in public was a great shame in the ancient Near East. Here was Israel's king debasing himself before God. Finally, the actions of Saul revived a proverb first coined when Saul was anointed king over Israel (10:11). There it indicated a positive change in Saul's life as the Lord's anointed. Here it is negative. At this point Saul is perceived as neither a genuine prophet nor a legitimate king. Believers must learn from this that God's will is immutable and irresistible. Godly leadership always seeks first the will of God.

Dedication for a True Friend (20:1–42)

> **SUPPORTING IDEA:** *Jonathan warns David to flee from his father's wrath.*

20:1–4. While Saul was still prophesying before Samuel, David made his escape from Naioth and came directly to Jonathan. Jonathan was David's direct link to the royal household. His questions to Jonathan reveal the extent of his emotions. David was upset and afraid.

David still felt that he must have committed some transgression or sinned in some way against Saul. To merit death, the crime must have been significant. David wanted Jonathan to tell him the truth (20:1). Instead, Jonathan denied that such a thing could be happening. After all, Jonathan had interceded on David's behalf and Saul had sworn an oath (19:6).

But David sensed differently. He too **took an oath**. David didn't doubt Jonathan's integrity; he just didn't trust Saul's motives. David revealed what Jonathan could not see. Saul had kept his determination to kill David from Jonathan because he knew his son would **be grieved**. David knew that there was **only a step** between him and death at the hands of Saul (19:3).

David needed to confirm Saul's motive. If Saul was determined to kill him, he must flee. But that would mean leaving his best friend and his wife. Jonathan responded to David's situation in love and faithful support. He was willing to do whatever it took, whatever David asked to get to the bottom of the problem.

In fact, the scene is more moving in the original Hebrew. Jonathan responded to David by saying, "Whatever your soul says, I will do for you" (20:4). Here was a true friend in need. Jonathan was willing to do whatever it took to help a friend regardless of the cost. This is the deepest expression of the love of one friend for another. Believers are not to count the cost when it comes to helping friends in dire circumstances. Jesus gave the ultimate sacrifice on the cross for our sins.

20:5–7. David put together a plan to confirm once and for all Saul's intentions toward him. David would **hide in the field** until Jonathan could ascertain Saul's true motives. Jonathan's part in the plan was more complicated. At the New Moon festival, Jonathan was to wait for his father to miss David (20:6). If Saul asked about David's whereabouts, Jonathan was to respond that David requested **permission** to attend an **annual sacrifice** for his clan in Bethlehem. Saul's response to Jonathan would reveal his intentions. If his answer was positive then David knew he was **safe**. But if Saul lost his temper, then David would know that Saul's intent was to kill him (20:7).

20:8–17. Then David reminded Jonathan of the covenant they had made together (20:8; cp. 18:3). Covenant terminology (cp. vv. 8,14–17) links together this section down to verse 17. Bergen argues that these verses form a thematic centerpiece to the story of Jonathan (Bergen, 215) for several reasons. Not only does Jonathan dominate this section by saying more than David, his actions also point to a turning point in the development of David's life. Jonathan came up with the plan to save David, and it was he who sent him away. This text also establishes the covenant between David's house and Jonathan's house so that Jonathan and his family would not be purged if David became king. Finally, this section implies that David was destined for greatness, a fact known by Jonathan.

David asked Jonathan to **show kindness** (*hesed*) to him, if by chance he was found guilty. If such was the case, David asked that Jonathan not hand him over to his father, but kill him himself. Jonathan's protest (20:9) assured David that he still had a friend and ally.

The last part of the plan to be settled was how David would be notified if Saul's response was negative (20:10). If Saul's response was positive, David could immediately come out of hiding. But if Saul was seeking to kill him, David could not risk showing himself. So Jonathan and David went out into the field to fix the plan.

But before finalizing the plan, Jonathan pledged his commitment by swearing an oath to David. He reassured David that he would carry out the plan and send David **away safely** if Saul desired to harm him (20:12–13). Jonathan also wanted reassurance that David would show him and his family unfailing kindness (*hesed*). Then Jonathan made David swear again by his love for him (**reaffirm his oath out of love**, v. 17). David would do this for Jonathan and his descendents.

20:18–23. Jonathan worked out a signal for David while he was hiding in the field. Jonathan would shoot three arrows into the air near to the side of a prominent stone heap and send a boy to retrieve the arrows. David's answer would come in the manner Jonathan spoke to the boy. If Jonathan gave one set of instructions, David was safe. But if he gave another set, David must flee. What is interesting is that Jonathan correctly recognized that the Lord would ordain which way the matter turned out. David, Jonathan, or Saul might have a hand in bringing the events to this point, but ultimately the decision belonged to the Lord. Before Jonathan left David in the field he gently reminded him that **the LORD is witness between you and me forever** (20:23). Their friendship was based on the Lord himself. He would preserve their friendship.

20:24–34. The stage is set for the New Moon festival. David was hiding in the field, and the king was sitting in his customary place by the wall, opposite Jonathan (20:24–25). Other dignitaries were there, but David's place was empty. On the first day Saul said nothing. Saul concluded that David, a devout man, must have been **ceremonially unclean** (20:26; cp. Lev. 7:20–21). But when David did not show up the second day, Saul asked Jonathan where David was. Notice, however, that Saul did not call David by his first name. He referred to him as the son of Jesse (20:27).

Following their prearranged plan, Jonathan related that David had asked permission to return to Bethlehem to his family for a special sacrifice (20:28–29). Saul's response was immediate and angry. It provoked a heated exchange between father and son, and it ended, unfortunately, in attempted murder (20:30–34). Saul's plunge into sinfulness was complete. He attempted to shame Jonathan into doing his bidding (Bergen, 218). This is not godly leadership, and this is not what a godly friend does to encourage and build up.

First, Saul attacked Jonathan personally. He called him the **son of a perverse and rebellious woman**. Second, Saul declared that Jonathan had chosen or **sided with** David to his personal shame. Third, Saul tried to instill guilt by suggesting that Jonathan had brought shame to **the mother who bore** him (lit. "to the shame of your mother's nakedness"). Fourth, Saul appealed to his pride and greed. Jonathan's kingdom would not be safe **as long as the son of Jesse lives on this earth**. Finally, when the shouting failed, Saul's anger revealed itself in physical abuse. He **hurled his spear at him to kill him**.

Jonathan tried to defend his friend. He wanted to know why David should **be put to death**. What had David done that caused Saul to want him exterminated? When Saul threw the spear at him, Jonathan knew that his father's true intent was to kill David. There was no question now. It was clear. In burning anger **Jonathan got up from the table** (20:34). He knew that he had to warn David, but it grieved his heart. He was truly sorry about **his father's shameful treatment of David**. As a good friend, Jonathan supported David. Saul, on the other hand, allowed selfish sin to destroy not only his relationship with David, but also more importantly, the relationship with his son. It is not appropriate for anyone to emulate Saul's behavior. In contrast, Jonathan is shown to be a godly friend.

20:35–42. The next morning Jonathan took a boy out to the field where he was to meet David. Jonathan instructed the boy to retrieve the arrows he shot into the air. So as the boy ran, Jonathan shot an arrow beyond him. Then loudly Jonathan called out the fatal question: **Isn't the arrow beyond you?** This was the signal to David that God had ordained for him to be a fugitive from Saul (20:38).

Jonathan's commands to the boy were intended for David, but the boy did not know this (20:39). Jonathan had the boy bring the arrows back quickly (20:38) and then sent him back to town with the weapons (20:40). This provided the opportunity for David and Jonathan with a private moment to bid each other farewell.

After the boy left, David got up from his hiding place and fell on his face to the ground (20:41). He bowed down with his face to the ground three times before Jonathan to acknowledge his covenant superiority. David did not forget his place here. Jonathan was a royal prince; David was not. It must have been a sad scene. They wept together, and **David wept the most**.

Jonathan gave a farewell speech (20:42). He reminded David of their mutual oath of friendship (20:17, 23). They swore to each other **in the name of the LORD**. The Ten Commandments warned about misusing this type of oath (Exod. 20:7; Deut. 5:11; Lev. 19:12). Jonathan was serious about their covenant of friendship. This was an eternal covenant. It included David and Jonathan and their **descendants forever**.

Neither of them knew what the future would hold, and neither of them knew if they would see each other again. As it turned out, the two would see each other only one more time (23:16–18) before Jonathan's death. David would grieve deeply over his friend's death (2 Sam. 1:17–27), but as he promised, he kept the covenant with Jonathan's descendants (2 Sam. 9:1–13).

Ultimately, Jonathan's friendship with David cost him much. He could have killed David several times, or at least turned him over to his father, Saul. But Jonathan's heart was knit together with David's. The two entered an everlasting covenant of friendship. Because Jonathan was a godly man, his friendship with David honored the Lord God of Israel. David was his friend regardless of the cost. Their friendship was based on love, integrity, and faithfulness.

MAIN IDEA REVIEW: *Saul's jealousy of David's success as a warrior in his army drives him to try to kill David. But Saul's own son, Jonathan, befriends David and protects him from his father's rage.*

III. CONCLUSION

Good for Our Health

A recent study by Australian scientists found that having friends around in old age can actually help people live longer. The team looked at how a range of social, health, and lifestyle factors affected the survival rates of more than 1,500 people over the age of 70. Individuals with the strongest network of friends and acquaintances were statistically more likely to be alive at the end of the study than those with the fewest. Friends are also more likely to encourage people to look after their health and to help reduce feelings of depression and anxiety at difficult times.

The Bible recognizes that godly friends help us grow spiritually as well. A godly friend "loves at all times" (Prov. 17:17), and a true friend will stick "closer than a brother" (Prov. 18:24). Even criticism from a Christian friend can keep us accountable (Prov. 27:6). If we stumble, the godly friend is there to help us up (Eccles. 4:10). Regardless of the circumstances, believers need to be godly friends honoring others above themselves (Rom. 12:10). The friendship of David and Jonathan is an example of what godly friendship should be. It was based on genuine honor, integrity, and faithfulness. If we could be this kind of friend to others, it would not be hard to win the world to Christ.

PRINCIPLES

- God sets the standards for true friendship.
- True friendship is based on mutual trust and faithfulness.
- Godly friendship is not self-centered and always seeks the best for others.
- Friends intercede with God on behalf of their friends.
- True friends love their friends as they love themselves.
- Godly friends remain faithful, no matter the cost.

APPLICATIONS

- Thank God for the model of true friendship shown by Jonathan and David.
- Pray that God will use you to be a true Christian friend to someone who needs one.
- Ask God for the strength to honor others above yourself.
- Seek to be loyal and faithful to your friends, no matter the cost.
- Ask God to give you the courage to lay your life on the line for a Christian brother or sister if necessary.
- Seek to be accountable to other Christian friends.
- Thank God for our Savior and Lord, Jesus Christ, the greatest of all friends.

IV. LIFE APPLICATION

What Friends Are For

I heard a story once about a teenage boy who lost all of his hair after radiation treatments and chemotherapy. On the way home from the hospital he worried about going back to school with a bald head. When he came home several friends surprised him with a welcome-home party. But what surprised the young man the most was not the party but that all of his friends had shaved their heads! His friends had sacrificed their hair to make him feel loved and less embarrassed.

This is the kind of godly friendship we need to offer the world. We need to go out of our way to invest in others, to share what true friendship is like. Jesus did this for us, and we are called to follow his example. He gave his life on the cross so that we might have life: "Greater love has no one than this, that he lay down his life for his friends" (John 15:13).

V. PRAYER

Gracious Father, teach us that true friendship begins with submission to your holy and perfect will. Help us be accountable in our friendships to you and to our Savior, Jesus Christ. Teach us the skills of godly friendship. Teach us how to honor, respect, and be faithful to our friends in order that they may see you in us. Give us the courage to befriend others who need to hear about the precious love that Jesus has for them. Help us to show others that Jesus is the perfect friend. In Jesus' name. Amen.

VI. DEEPER DISCOVERIES

A. Jonathan's Covenant (18:1–4)

Jonathan ratified his covenant by giving David his robe, tunic, sword, bow, and belt. This type of robe was also worn by Samuel (1 Sam. 28:14) and Saul (1 Sam. 24:5). It is possible that by giving these items to David, Jonathan was renouncing his claim to the throne and recognizing David as heir-apparent to the throne of Israel.

B. Bride Price (18:25)

Marital customs in the ancient Near East provided for a bride price paid by the suitor to the girl's parents. The bride price offered security for the wife in case the husband deserted her or died. The amount given would reflect the status of the bride. As a poor shepherd, David would not be able financially to enter into a royal marriage. Saul, however, set a test for David by connecting the bride price to a military victory instead.

C. Teraphim (19:13)

When Saul's men were waiting to capture David, his wife Michal helped him to escape through a window. Then in an effort to trick his pursuers, Michal laid an idol on the bed and covered it with garments and some goat's hair. *Teraphim*, the Hebrew word used here, occurs fourteen times in the Old Testament and refers to household or family idols. Their use was condemned by the Bible (Exod. 15:23; 2 Kgs. 23:24). Since they could be hidden under a saddle (Gen. 31:19), they were probably small. Thus far, full human-size *teraphim* have not been discovered by archaeologists. So it is possible that the idol used by Michal was in the shape of a head or a cultic mask.

D. Saul's Prophesying (19:23)

Saul prophesied five times during his career as king (10:10,11,13; 18:10; 19:23). Samuel predicted that Saul would do so and that he would be changed into a different person (10:6). People who knew Saul were astonished and asked, "Is Saul also among the prophets?" (10:11). This type of behavior was often equated with being mad (19:19–24; cp. Jer. 29:26). Apparently, Saul and the other men acted in a trancelike or ecstatic state. Music evidently helped in inducing this kind of behavior (18:10). Usually, this type of prophecy was a sign of the Spirit of God coming in power upon an individual (19:20). But in the case of Saul, an evil spirit from God was also apparently responsible for his prophesying (18:10). Bergen argues that this would identify Saul as a false prophet (cp. 1 Kgs. 22:21–23) who was not to be feared (Deut. 18:22; see Bergen, 201).

E. The New Moon Festival (20:5)

Ancient Israel followed a lunar calendar and marked the coming of the new moon as a festival day. All work was to cease (Amos 8:5) and sacrifices were offered (Num. 28:11–15). As the king, Saul may have required his soldiers and leaders to celebrate the festival with him (20:5; cp. Ezek. 45:17). Observance of the festival continued into postexilic times (Ezra 3:5; Neh. 10:33). David's request to return to his hometown of Bethlehem for an annual sacrifice is not attested elsewhere in the Old Testament.

VII. TEACHING OUTLINE

A. INTRODUCTION

1. Lead Story: Brian Piccolo
2. Context: After defeating the Philistine giant Goliath, David is presented to Saul as the hero of the day. Jonathan, Saul's son, becomes a true friend of David, and the two make a covenant. Saul gives David a high rank in his army, and offers him an opportunity to marry his daughter, Michal. Saul soon becomes jealous of David's success and seeks to kill him in envy. Even after David marries into Saul's family, Saul attempts to kill him. Jonathan seeks to mediate between his father and David, but must in the end warn David of his father's desire to seek his life. Jonathan reaffirms the covenant he made with David and sends him away in peace.
3. Transition: Saul's self-centered and disobedient rejection of the covenant had a negative impact on his personal and public relationships. Because he rejected God, God rejected him and took his spirit away from him. God expects kingdom leaders to model appropriate and godly relationships and friendships. Saul is unable to do this. Jonathan, on the other hand, develops an amazing friendship with David. First Samuel 18:1 tells us that Jonathan's soul was "knit" or "bound" to the soul of David. David and Jonathan possessed a true friendship, godly in character and essence. Chapters 18–20 detail how this friendship developed and how it was tested and tried in the crucible

of life. Kingdom leaders must learn to be godly in their friendships and relationships with others.

B. COMMENTARY

1. Discovering a True Friend (18:1–30)
2. Defending a True Friend (19:1–24)
3. Dedication for a True Friend (20:1–42)

C. CONCLUSION: WHAT FRIENDS ARE FOR

VIII. ISSUES FOR DISCUSSION

1. Name some of the ways Jonathan expressed his friendship for David. How can we show the same type of friendship to others?
2. What does 1 John 3:16 teach us about the character of Christian friendship?
3. Why are integrity and faithfulness important in friendship? Name some examples where integrity is crucial for a godly friendship.
4. What are the marks of true friendship? List some examples of true friendship mentioned in the Bible.
5. Where would you place yourself on a scale of 1 to 10 as a godly friend? List some specific steps you can take to be a better friend to others.
6. Is godly friendship limited to people within the church? List some ways God would expect us to befriend the lost in order to win them to Jesus.

1 Samuel 21:1–26:25

David, the Fugitive

"Fire is the test of gold; adversity, of strong men."

S e n e c a

GEOGRAPHICAL PROFILE: NOB

- Believed to be northeast of Jerusalem and south of Gibeah, but exact location is unknown
- Parts of the tabernacle appear to be relocated to Nob after the destruction of Shiloh
- The ephod (Exod. 28:6–14) and the table of the Presence (Exod. 25:23–30) are specifically mentioned in connection with Nob
- David went to inquire of the Lord here (1 Sam. 22:15)
- Doeg the Edomite, a servant of Saul, massacred the priests and the entire population of Nob (1 Sam. 22:18–19)

BIOGRAPHICAL PROFILE: AHIMELECH

- Son of Ahitub, the grandson of Phineas, and the great-grandson of Eli (1 Sam. 14:3)
- Priest at Nob and leader of more than 85 priests (1 Sam. 22:11,18)
- Helped David by giving him bread from the table of the Presence and Goliath's sword
- Murdered by Doeg the Edomite at the command of Saul (1 Sam. 22:18)

BIOGRAPHICAL PROFILE: ABIATHAR

- Son of Ahimelech and only priest to escape the massacre at Nob (1 Sam. 22:20)
- Brought the Ephod from Nob to David and served him as priest (1 Sam. 22:20–22; 23:6,9)

- Later, helped to bring the ark to Jerusalem and served as one of David's counselors (1 Chron. 15:11; 27:34)
- Supported Adonijah's bid for the throne and was expelled from office by Solomon, ending Eli's priestly line (1 Kings 1–2)

BIOGRAPHICAL PROFILE: ABIGAIL

- Wife of Nabal, a wealthy Calebite (1 Sam. 25:2)
- In contrast to her husband Nabal who was hard and evil, Abigail was intelligent and beautiful (1 Sam. 25:3)
- When Nabal insulted David, Abigail intervened on her own to bring gifts and food to David and his men (1 Sam. 25:18–19)
- Later after Nabal died, Abigail married David and bore him his second son (2 Sam. 3:3)
- David rescued her along with the rest of his family when they were captured by the Amalekites near Ziklag (1 Sam. 30:18)

1 Samuel 21:1–26:25

I N   A   N U T S H E L L

After determining that Saul does indeed desire to take his life, David becomes a fugitive and flees to Ahimelech the priest at Nob. Ahimelech gives David bread and the sword of Goliath and sends him on his way. Then David gathers a small band of men around him, and together they narrowly elude Saul's many pursuits. Saul slaughters Ahimelech and the priests at Nob for helping David. Only Abiathar, the son of Ahimelech, escapes and joins David. David also meets Abigail and eventually marries her. Saul continues to pursue David, but God enables him to flee each trap and remain faithful through every hardship.

David, the Fugitive

I. INTRODUCTION

The Prince of Preachers

*M*any Christians regard Charles Haddon Spurgeon (1834–1892) to be the "Prince of Preachers." He often preached to crowds of more than 5,000, and his sermons sold nearly 20,000 copies a week and were translated into 20 different languages. His collected sermons are still in print in more than 60 volumes. During his lifetime, Spurgeon was prolific in publishing more than 140 works of his own: commentaries, devotional books, hymn-books, and magazine articles. Spurgeon also founded an orphanage, several charitable and religious organizations, and a theological college. Even after more than a century, the legacy of Spurgeon's ministry still has a profound affect on pastors and Christians around the world.

But most people are not aware that Spurgeon's prolific ministry was accomplished under demanding circumstances and times of adversity. After giving birth to their twin sons, Spurgeon's wife Susannah became a virtual invalid and seldom heard her husband preach. Spurgeon himself suffered from gout, rheumatism, Bright's disease, and depression. Under these demanding circumstances, preaching often became a painful experience. These diseases eventually took his life at the age of 57.

In addition to his physical suffering, Spurgeon endured undeserved public ridicule and slander. Newspapers called him vulgar and colloquial. He was regarded as rude and rough; his ministry was dismissed as temporary. Probably the attacks by his fellow ministers were the most painful. Those on the left belittled him; those on the right doubted his salvation. In the great Downgrade Controversy, Spurgeon fought unsuccessfully for doctrinal integrity in the Baptist Union. Then, when he withdrew from the union, he was officially and publicly censured by it.

Still, throughout the pain and the adversity Spurgeon continued to preach. He remained faithful to his call, and his character was strengthened through the experience. His unwavering trust in God prevented him from caving in to the adversities he faced. Spurgeon believed God designed the afflictions of his life to help develop his character, to prepare him for the ministry that lay just ahead. In the end, the "Prince of Preachers" trusted that the ultimate victory over adversity and setbacks belonged to the sovereign Christ, the Prince of Peace.

In chapters 21–26 of 1 Samuel, David, alone and on the run, watched his privileged life in the court of Saul fall apart. The king who had first promoted him and made him a son-in-law now sought to kill him. God's hand was still upon David, but he must learn how to seek after the Lord's own heart in the bad times as well as the good. Each step in adversity and setbacks taught David godly character. The same God who directed Samuel to anoint David as king over Israel was with him as he fled from Saul's wrath. David's faithful response stands in stark contrast with Saul's evil designs. David's own experiences teach the believer that trusting God during difficult times not only builds character but also glorifies God.

II. COMMENTARY

David, the Fugitive

MAIN IDEA: *David goes on the run from Saul. He hides out with a group of sympathizers in deserts and caves to keep from being killed by the king. His years as a fugitive teach him to trust in the Lord as his ultimate protector.*

A David and the Priest (21:1–9)

SUPPORTING IDEA: *Ahimelech, a priest in the city of Nob, provides food for David and his hungry men.*

21:1–6. David had no choice but to flee from Saul's court. He realized that Saul's intent was to kill him. Saul's action against Jonathan had confirmed this (20:33). Bergen compares David's experience as a fugitive to the wilderness experience of Israel after their expulsion from Egypt (Bergen, 220). God had great things in store for David, but David had to learn how to remain faithful through hardship and adversity. Throughout this "school of hard knocks," David had to learn to live and relate by faith, trusting in God's purposes and will. He had to learn that God would make him king and bless him at the right time and the right place.

David left Saul's court and headed to **Nob**, a sanctuary where the sons of Aaron lived and where parts of the tabernacle appear to have been relocated. Nob was a small settlement probably located atop modern Mount Scopus. David had been there before (22:15). But this time, David unexpectedly came alone. This fact made **Ahimelech** nervous. David was vague in his requests and in response to Ahimelech's two questions.

David informed Ahimelech that the king had charged him **with a certain matter**. Supposedly, David had left his men at a special place and arrived alone because the king had said, **No one is to know anything about your mission and your instructions**. This statement can be understood in two distinct ways.

Note that David did not tell Ahimelech the name of the king who gave him this command. If the king was God, then David was not lying. He was following God's direction in fleeing Saul. In this case, David's statement was the truth, and he exercised a shrewd use of language.

On the other hand, it is possible that David may have lied to Ahimelech. While it is true that the Holy Spirit had fallen upon David (1 Sam 16:13), the Bible does not tell us that David was sinless. Gene Getz argues that David's action here indicated that he didn't trust God to protect and deliver him from Saul. Instead, David tried to take matters into his own hands, and the results were tragic (Getz, *David*, 90–91).

According to Getz, David hatched three schemes on his own without seeking God's will. The first was the concocted plan to have Jonathan find out Saul's true intentions toward him (1 Sam. 20:5–6). The second was the lie told to Ahimelech, and the third was David's feigned madness before Achish, king of Gath (21:10–11). It is true that David escaped physical injury in each case. But here he caused the tragic death of many innocent people. David recognized this later and acknowledged his responsibility to Abiathar (1 Sam. 22:22). It is possible that Psalm 34 contains David's heartfelt repentance for these sins. In this psalm David humbly confessed his faith and trust in God (Getz, *David*, 91–96).

David asked Ahimelech for **five loaves of bread**. The only bread on hand was the consecrated **bread of the Presence**. Normally, this bread was reserved for the priests. Evidently, Ahimelech could offer David some of this bread, providing that he and his men were ritually clean. David assured Ahimelech that he and his men had kept themselves from intimacy with women and that he and his men treated every mission as holy (21:5). So Ahimelech gave David **the consecrated bread** (21:6).

21:7–9. David was not the only servant of Saul at Nob that day. **Doeg the Edomite, Saul's head shepherd** was also there. Doeg had been **detained before the LORD** (21:7). We are not told why he was detained there, and his presence is noted without explanation. We will learn later that his presence was very important.

Ironically, David came to Nob lacking a weapon of any kind. David's excuse was that **the king's business was urgent** (21:8). The only weapon

Ahimelech had was the **sword of Goliath**. David may have placed the sword there as a gift of dedication (Lev. 27). David had used this very sword to cut off the head of Goliath. Now David needed the sword to fight for his life. Ahimelech offered the sword, and David took it.

At Nob, God provided David with food and a means for his protection. In times of adversity, it is easy to forget God's beneficent grace. If we lose a job or face an illness, we immediately worry about how we can provide for our families. But God is faithful. We need to learn to trust him in the bad times as well as the good. Difficult times can deepen our trust in God. Jesus gently reminds us not to worry about what we will eat or drink or wear. Instead, he calls us to seek God's kingdom and his righteousness first, "and all these things will be given to you" (Matt. 6:33).

B David and the Pagan King (21:10–22:5)

> **SUPPORTING IDEA:** *David escapes from Achish, a Philistine king, and hides from Saul in several different locations.*

21:10–15. David's flight from Saul took him to **Gath**, a Philistine city about 23 miles west of Nob. David ran all the way to enemy territory. Perhaps David did this to protect his family and friends. David must have felt that Saul was not above attacking his loved ones.

At first, David may have hoped that he would not be recognized in Gath. However, **the servants of Achish**, king of Gath, did recognize him. In fact, they knew the song the Israelites had sung about Saul and David: "**Saul has slain his thousands, and David his tens of thousands**" (21:11; cp. 18:7).

Technically, the servants of Achish had mistakenly identified David as **the king of the land**. Saul still ruled in Israel. But ironically, David had been anointed king, would become king, and would be the king who would defeat the Philistines. God was preparing him through these hardships to be king over the entire land, including the Philistine cities.

David paid attention to their words (lit. "put these words in his heart"). Since he was **very much afraid of Achish king of Gath**, David decided to take the initiative and **pretended to be insane** (lit. "change his judgment in their eyes"). He made marks on the door and drooled on his beard. The ruse worked. Achish declared David to be insane and chastised his servants for bringing him into his palace. In the ancient Near East, this type of insanity was considered to be the result of divine possession or affliction. Consequently, Achish did not regard David as a threat, and David was allowed to leave Gath.

Two other points of interest should be noted here. First, Bergen points out another irony in this situation. David had feigned insanity to conceal his sanity before the Philistines. Saul, on the other hand, had "surrounded himself with the trappings of sanity to cloak his insanity" (Bergen, 224).

On the other hand, Getz regards the act of feigning madness to be the last of three schemes hatched by David himself outside of God's will. Because of this David almost lost his life and had to resort to demeaning behavior to escape (Getz, *David*, 90–91). This was a far cry from the courageous young man who stood up to Goliath. David would need to move from fear to faith. He was confused and on the run, but he needed to trust God and turn to him. Perhaps David thought long and hard about this in the lonely cave of Adullam.

22:1–5. When David left Gath he turned east for the hill country of Judah. There he waited in the **cave of Adullam**. When his family heard the news, **they went down to him** (22:1). They certainly came to comfort David, but they may also have done this in fear of Saul. Soon there gathered around David all **who were in distress or in debt or discontented** (22:2). David's band of "outlaws" grew to 400 men, **and he became their leader**. These men were also outcasts from society.

David soon left the cave and went to **Mizpah** (lit. "watchtower") in **Moab**. Here he entreated the king of Moab to grant asylum to his **father and mother** until he knew God's will for his life (22:3). The king of Moab may have granted his request because of Ruth, David's Moabite great-grandmother (Ruth 4:13–22). David resided in a place identified only as **the stronghold** until the prophet **Gad** told him to go to Judah. David then left **and went to the forest of Hereth** (22:5).

Scholars are not sure about the location of the stronghold. Nevertheless, from this place David received a clear word from God. Scholars are also not sure when Gad joined David's band of followers. But God used this prophet to speak to David. The terse language underscores David's quick obedience. Apparently, the forest was west of the Dead Sea. Again, the location is uncertain. The implication is that God would protect and provide for David and his family there.

Trusting that God will provide for our families is a difficult thing to do in times of hardship and adversity. It takes faith to do this. When the Lord delivered David from the hand of Saul, he sang: "As for God, his way is perfect; the word of the LORD is flawless. He is a shield for all who take refuge in him. For who is God besides the LORD? And who is the Rock except our God?" (2 Sam. 22:31–32).

Years later, David would also sing of this trust and faith in God in many psalms. Over and over, David called for his people to put their trust in God. One example, among many, is Psalm 20:7: "Some trust in chariots and some in horses, but we trust in the name of the LORD our God."

Jesus also admonished his disciples not to let their hearts be troubled. He said, "Trust in God; trust also in me" (John 14:1). Our trust must be in the Lord. He will provide for our families.

C Saul and the Priests (22:6–23)

SUPPORTING IDEA: Saul slaughters Ahimelech and the other priest at Nob for providing food for David and his men.

22:6–10. One of the greatest tragedies in the history of the Israelite monarchy is recorded in this section. Saul's jealous personal vendetta against David escalated into the unjust murder of the faithful priests at Nob, their families, and the destruction of their possessions. Saul's sinful conduct stands in stark contrast to David's faith and trust in the Lord.

At first, Saul attempted to kill David alone. When Jonathan refused to help him, Saul turned his spear on him (20:33). Now Saul made a case for his kinsmen to join him in the hunt for David. Apparently, **all his officials** were from his own tribe because Saul addressed them as **men of Benjamin** (22:6). It is possible that Saul was trying to scare them by suggesting that if David became king, he would replace them as officials with members of his own tribe (Bergen, 227). If so, Saul was appealing to their desire for power and greed.

It is more likely that Saul had extensive conspiracy theories on his sick and sinful mind. The rhetorical questions in verses 7–8 suggest that Saul now believed all of his officials were against him. Saul wanted to know if the son of Jesse had promised them fields and vineyards and major rank in the military. Saul apparently believed that they had **all conspired against** him (22:8). This must be the case because none of them informed him about the **covenant** Jonathan had made with David. Saul actually thought that Jonathan had **incited** David **to lie in wait for** him (22:8). Perhaps Saul thought that Jonathan had hired David to kill him so Jonathan might have the throne.

These statements reveal Saul's distorted thinking. David was not lying in wait for him. David was in fact hiding from Saul's relentless pursuit. David was still a faithful servant of the king and would soon show this loyalty in his interaction with Saul. Saul's paranoia was a prelude to tragedy.

There must have been an awkward silence after Saul's ranting. Given Saul's treacherous behavior with his own son, we can understand why. **Doeg the Edomite**, Saul's head shepherd (21:7), spoke up and broke the silence by reporting what he had seen at Nob (22:9–10). Doeg claimed that he had witnessed Ahimelech do three things for David. Two of these, the gift of the bread and Goliath's sword, are recorded in 21:1–9. The third, that **Ahimelech inquired of the LORD for him** is noted for the first time (22:10). Ahimelech later confirmed this to be true (22:15).

This fact brings into clear contrast David's desire to know the will of God with Saul's own selfish rebellion from the will of God. David continued to be a man after God's own heart, while Saul followed his own desires.

22:11–19. Upon Doeg's testimony, Saul summoned Ahimelech son of Ahitub and his father's entire family (22:11). Acting as prosecutor, judge, and jury, Saul accused Ahimelech of conspiracy against him. Saul repeated the accusations of Doeg the Edomite to Ahimelech and then waited for his reply (22:13).

Bergen notes that Ahimelech defended his actions with four salient points (Bergen, 229). First, Ahimelech defended David by noting five things about his character (22:14). David was:

- Saul's servant,
- loyal,
- the king's son-in-law,
- the captain of Saul's bodyguard, and
- highly respected in Saul's household.

For Ahimelech it was impossible to conceive of David as a traitor who would rebel against Saul and seek to take his life. Second, David had come to have Ahimelech inquire of the Lord on many occasions. This was not the first time. Third, Ahimelech reminded Saul that he was the king's servant. Finally, Ahimelech protested that he knew **nothing at all about this whole affair** (22:15).

Despite his protestations, Saul passed judgment on Ahimelech. Saul's verdict was strongly worded and severe. Ahimelech would **surely die**, he and his family (22:16). Saul then ordered his bodyguards to carry out the sentence, but they refused to do so (22:17). Ironically, both the order and the refusal do not specifically mention Ahimelech and his family. Instead, Saul ordered his soldiers to execute the **priests of the LORD** (22:17).

Since David had been captain of the bodyguard, these men were his friends. They served with him and respected him. They were less likely to believe the accusations against him. But, even more so, like David, they were devout followers of the Lord. Consequently, the command to strike down the priests would be odious to them, so they refused.

Saul turned to a foreigner, perhaps a mercenary, **Doeg the Edomite**, to carry out the sentence. Doeg had no problem with the order, and **he killed eighty-five men who wore the linen ephod** (22:18). The carnage did not stop there. Apparently with Saul's approval, Doeg also traveled one hour's distance **to put to the sword** the citizens of Nob. This action of Doeg is reminiscent of the ban God placed on certain Canaanite cities as judgment during the conquest of the land. However, in this case, the call to destroy the city of Nob, its inhabitants, and its possessions did not come as a judgment from God as punishment for sin, but from a paranoid and jealous man who continued down a path of rebellion and sin against God and his divine will (22:19). Before his death, Saul would walk further down that road into the darkness of sin.

22:20–23. Saul did not succeed in obliterating the line of Ahimelech. Abiathar, **a son of Ahimelech, escaped and fled** to David (22:20). It must have been a very emotional moment when Abiathar told David that **Saul had killed the priests of the LORD** (22:21). What is stunningly different in the character of David is revealed in David's response to this tragic and sad news.

Instead of blaming Saul or others for this tragedy, David accepted responsibility for the death of Abiathar's **whole family** (22:22). David recognized that Doeg the Edomite would tell Saul, and he did nothing to prevent it. Consequently, David comforted Abiathar and invited him to stay with him where he would **be safe** (22:23). David reminded Abiathar that **the man who is seeking your life is seeking mine also**. Abiathar accepted David's offer and later helped David inquire of the Lord.

The superscription to Psalm 52 states that David composed this poem to remind him of the fateful day when Doeg the Edomite told Saul that David had sought help from Ahimelech. The contrast between David and Doeg is clear. Doeg trusted in his great wealth and "grew strong by destroying others" (Ps. 52:7). David, on the other hand, decided to "trust in God's unfailing love" (52:8). Even in the midst of tragedy, David let God sustain him. David did not seek revenge. He knew that God had said, "It is mine to avenge; I will repay" (Deut. 32:35). David trusted God to avenge the house of Ahimelech.

It is easy for us to seek revenge and desire vindication, especially when we consider ourselves to be innocent and persecuted for no cause. Paul experienced persecution and harassment. But in quoting this same passage, he reminded believers to leave the act of revenge to God (Rom. 12:19). Even when the desire for revenge is strong, we must allow God to sustain us.

D David and the Judahites (23:1–29)

SUPPORTING IDEA: *David rescues the city of Keilah from the Philistines and eludes capture while hiding in the territory of the Ziphites.*

23:1–13. Chapter 23 records David's interaction with two different groups living in the territory of Judah. Verses 1–13 explain how David rescued the city of Keilah from Philistine hands, and verses 19–29 describe the attempt of the Ziphites to turn David over to Saul. Between these two experiences, David received a last visit from Jonathan, the son of Saul. Jonathan encouraged David and renewed the covenant the two had made earlier (20:16).

In all three cases, the emphasis of the text is on communication. David always sought divine direction, but Saul placed his trust in human intelligence. David's success reveals that in times of adversity we must seek the will of God; He will direct us in all our ways (Ps. 119:35; Jer. 10:23; 2 Tim. 3:5).

While David was encamped with his men in the forest of Hereth, word came to him that the Philistines had attacked the walled city of **Keilah** in the Shephelah region of Judah. David immediately **inquired of the LORD** (23:2). David's heart desired to deliver his people from the hands of the enemy, but he did not dare make a move until he had sought God's leadership in the matter.

The Lord's answer was positive. God told David to **attack the Philistines and save Keilah**. His men were a little less than convinced. They were afraid of Saul in Judah; **how much more** would they be afraid of the well-trained and equipped army of the Philistines! So David inquired again, and the Lord assured David that he would **give the Philistines into** his **hand** (23:4). As a result, David and his men attacked and **inflicted heavy losses on the Philistines and saved the people of Keilah** (23:5). God had given David the victory over a larger and better-equipped army.

At this point, the text notes briefly that Abiathar the son of Ahimelech had **brought the ephod down with him** when he fled to David at Keilah (23:6). This note is very important because it grounds David's future actions in the sure communication with God offered by an officially sanctioned priest according to the Torah. This may have been the same ephod mentioned earlier by Ahimelech (21:9). From this point on David will have the proper means to seek God's will for him and his people.

In like fashion (the Hebrew text uses similar words), **Saul was told that David had gone to Keilah** (23:7). Ironically, Saul thought that this was God's doing in handing David over to him. But Saul did not inquire of the Lord, nor after destroying the priests at Nob did he have a means to do so. Saul believed that when David entered a walled city, he became a prisoner waiting to be caught. As a result Saul called out his troops and headed for Keilah.

Then David heard about Saul's plot to trap him in Keilah. What David did next became an important habit. He asked Abiathar to bring the ephod so he might inquire of the Lord before he took action (23:9). David asked two essential questions (23:11): **Will the citizens of Keilah surrender me to him?** and **will Saul come down, as your servant has heard?**

God answered the second question first. Saul would come down. Then David asked again about the citizens of Keilah (23:12). God revealed that in order to lift the siege of the city, the citizens of Keilah would turn David and his men over to Saul.

Perhaps David remembered what Saul had done to the priests and citizens of Nob, and he did not want that to happen to Keilah. David may also have recognized that he could not place his trust in walled cities and fortifications. David, too, may have wanted to be a diplomat and not spoil his relationship with the people he saved. His compassion for them outweighed his desire for security. In an effort to avoid bloodshed, David and his men left Keilah (23:13). They were now 600 in strength, and they moved **from place to place** to avoid Saul. When Saul was told **that David had escaped from Keilah**, he did not bother to go there.

23:14–18. While David managed to elude the grasp of Saul by staying in the desert strongholds and the desert of Ziph (23:14), Jonathan found him at Horesh, an otherwise unknown place. Jonathan's purpose was to help David **find strength in God** (23:16). Jonathan encouraged him not to be afraid. Jonathan knew that David would be king over Israel and that Saul would not be able to **lay a hand on** him (23:17). The two of them "cut" a covenant in the presence of the Lord, and Jonathan departed for home. Jonathan would not help his father hunt down David (23:18). Jonathan's presence was surely a blessing to David. Godly friends are important sources of encouragement during times of hardship and adversity.

23:19–29. Apparently, the **Ziphites** had been watching David in the stronghold at **Horesh** (23:19). Horesh is said to be located on the hill of Hakilah south of Jeshimon. Jeshimon is the name given to the barren eastern part of the mountains of Judah stretching toward the Dead Sea. This area was full of caves and thus was an ideal hideout for fugitives and outlaws. The Ziphites were connected with the family of Caleb (1 Chron. 2:42) and therefore associated with the tribe of Judah.

The Ziphites actually went to Saul at Gibeah to encourage him to come into their territory to seize David. They went so far as to promise that they would be **responsible for handing him over to the king** (23:20). Perhaps there was some conflict between David and the Ziphites. They did appear to be eager to hand him over to Saul.

Saul basically told them to go back and **make further preparation** for his coming. Saul may not have believed that they could deliver David, so he directed the Ziphites to become spies. He knew David was **very crafty** (23:22). Saul wanted **definite information**. He wanted a list of hiding places. When the Ziphites produced such intelligence, Saul bragged that he would go with them and **track him down among all the clans of Judah** (23:23).

The Ziphites' plans began to work. Saul was able to track David into **the Desert of Maon** (23:24–25). At the high point of the drama Saul was able to follow on **one side of the mountain** while David and his men were on the other side, trying to elude capture. It appears that Saul and his forces were closing in to take David (23:26).

But God would not be mocked. He would not allow David to be taken by Saul. In the nick of time, a messenger arrived to report that the Philistines had attacked and were **raiding the land** (23:27). Reluctantly, **Saul broke off his pursuit of David** (23:28). In commemoration of this deliverance, they named the place **Sela Hammahlekoth** ("the Promontory of the Parting" or "the Rock of Escape," cp. Bergen, 237). Saul returned to fight the Philistines, and David went north to live in the caves and strongholds of En Gedi (23:29).

Direct conflict with Saul had been averted. More would come. The Ziphites had come close to making the capture of David possible. They would not do so again. Again David spoke about his feelings in composing Psalm 54:

> Save me, O God, by your name; vindicate me by your might.
> Hear my prayer, O God; listen to the words of my mouth.
> Strangers are attacking me; ruthless men seek my life—
> men without regard for God. Selah
> Surely God is my help; the Lord is the one who sustains me.
> Let evil recoil on those who slander me; in your faithfulness destroy them.

I will sacrifice a freewill offering to you;
I will praise your name, O LORD, for it is good.
For he has delivered me from all my troubles,
and my eyes have looked in triumph on my foes.

Even when others attack us, we can echo the words of David. The Lord will sustain us. He will help us. He will deliver us from all our troubles. God will vindicate us by his might.

𝔼 David and the Anointed King (24:1–22)

SUPPORTING IDEA: *David refuses to kill Saul when he has a good opportunity to do so.*

24:1–7. This chapter records the first of two separate times when God delivered Saul into the hands of David. It is powerful narrative because it represents the rejection by David of the very action that would free him. Theologically, it confirms David's desire to see things God's way and to be submissive to his will. David dared to let God guide him, even if it appeared to be giving up a golden opportunity. Through it all, David recognized a higher principle than revenge. Be faithful to follow God's guidance, and God will eventually vindicate his servants (24:12).

When the Philistine threat passed, Saul enlisted the aid of 3,000 **chosen** soldiers from all Israel. He was told that David was near En Gedi, and he set out to catch David and his men near what was called **the Crags of the Wild Goats** (24:1–2). Somewhere in the vicinity, Saul spotted a cave and decided to **relieve himself** there. It turns out that David and his men were hiding in the back of that same cave. The scene is set for some type of confrontation.

David's men echoed the advice of the world. Kill Saul and your worries will be over! They hid their advice in a prophecy supposedly given directly from the Lord to David: **I will give your enemy into your hands for you to deal with as you wish** (24:4). The trouble is that this prophecy is not recorded anywhere in any biblical text associated with David. Bergen (p. 239) suggests that it is either a false prophecy (cp. 1 Kgs. 22:11–16), or that it is genuine and refers to some pagan enemy of Israel, but is misapplied here to Saul (24:5).

Instead of taking the opportunity to catch Saul off guard and kill him, David crept up behind him and cut off the corner of the king's robe. Saul was not aware that David had done this, and David crawled back to his men with the prized possession. After doing this David's behavior is surprising. He was conscience-stricken (24:5; lit. "David's heart struck him"). David realized what he had done.

According to Bergen (p. 239), David's act symbolically attacked Saul's claim to the kingship. First, in taking the corner of the robe, David was implying the transfer of power from Saul to himself. Secondly, by removing the corner David was most likely making Saul's robe, the obvious symbol of his kingship, noncompliant with God's law of the tassels (Num. 15:37–41; Deut. 22:12). David recognized that he had struck a blow not just at Saul, but also at the Lord. The Lord had placed Saul in this position, and the Lord would remove him. Saul was the **anointed of the LORD** (24:6). Literally this means the "messiah" of the Lord. Raising his hand against Saul meant rebelling against the Lord. Saul left the cave not knowing what had happened.

24:8–15. An unprecedented dialogue takes place between David and Saul from this point to the end of the chapter. David began the interaction by calling to Saul outside the cave (24:8). David used 114 Hebrew words to speak his heart. Saul responded in verses 16–22 with 67 Hebrew words. The length of the statements made by David and Saul point to their theological value. They should be studied carefully. Only the high points can be discussed here.

David not only addressed the king with proper respect (**my Lord the king**); he also responded to Saul's position by bowing and prostrating himself before him. David revealed by these acts his deference to Saul. Saul was still the king in David's eyes. Then David began to present his case before Saul.

Unidentified men had poisoned Saul's mind with the idea that David wanted to harm the king (24:9). David's own action in the cave proved this wrong. When he had the chance to kill Saul (as some of his men urged him do), he did not do so. The proof was in the piece of Saul's robe that David held in his hand (24:11).

David protested that he was **not guilty of wrongdoing and rebellion**. Saul was hunting him down without justification. In an oath David called upon the Lord to judge between Saul and himself. David called upon the Lord to avenge him of the evil Saul was afflicting upon him, but David would not touch Saul because he was the Lord's anointed (24:12–15). David's passionate plea touched the cold heart of the king

24:16–22. Saul responded to David with a broken heart. **He wept aloud** (24:16). He confessed that David was displaying correct and righteous behavior in response to his dogged determination to hunt him down (24:17). Perhaps Saul's near brush with death awakened him to the sinfulness of his actions. The piece of his robe was evidence of David's loyalty and faithfulness (24:18). Then Saul confessed to what Jonathan had said his father already knew (cp. 23:17). David would **surely be king**. The kingdom would be established in David's hands.

Saul asked David to swear that he would not destroy his descendents or wipe out his name from his father's family (24: 21). This is what typically happened in the ancient Near East. A new king would turn on the family of his predecessor and destroy any claimants to the throne. Then he would systematically remove all references to the previous king. There would be no memorials or mourning. David quickly gave his oath in response to Saul's request, and the two departed (24:22).

Note that Saul went home, but David and his men **went up to the stronghold**. Saul may have responded to David's plea, but his temperament and character were unstable. David recognized that he could not return to the court of Saul, and that he probably ought not to trust him either. This suspicion was later proven to be correct.

During times of adversity, there will be those who attack us. They will slander us and seek to destroy our reputation. Again, David is said to have composed psalms on this occasion. Psalm 57 states that David created this song when he hid in the cave from Saul. David asked God for mercy "for in you my soul takes refuge." David also declared his trust in the Lord when he said, "I will take refuge in the shadow of your wings until the disaster has passed" (Ps. 57:1). Psalm 142 notes that David composed it "when he was in the cave." In this psalm David also cried for mercy and declared to God, "You are my refuge, my portion in the land of the living." Through all of this David sought God's direction and guidance.

F David and Abigail (25:1–44)

SUPPORTING IDEA: David is prevented by Abigail from taking revenge against Nabal for his lack of hospitality.

25:1. Before moving on to David's next experience as a fugitive, the narrator stops to tell us that Samuel died. **All Israel assembled and mourned for him** (25:1). This may have included David. Perhaps under the circumstances Saul might have allowed David to attend the funeral without hostilities. Samuel's death marked the end of the era of the judges in Israelite history.

The NIV follows the Greek Septuagint translation in stating that **David moved down into the Desert of Maon**. This is one of the last places where

David was located earlier (23:25). It was the home of Nabal, a character in the next account (25:2). However, the Hebrew text identifies the desert as that of Paran, and other translations stay with this location.

25:2–13. Regardless of where David was hiding, the narrative of 1 Samuel turns its attention on a **certain man in Maon** (25:2). Before we learn his name, the text tells us that he was wealthy and that he was shearing sheep in Carmel, a region not far from Maon. The man's name was Nabal, which means "fool," and his wife's name was Abigail (25:3). Abigail was **intelligent and beautiful**, but Nabal was **surly and mean** (lit. "hard and evil"). Nabal was also a Calebite, meaning he was from the tribe of Judah. In essence, Nabal was a kinsman of David.

When David heard that Nabal was shearing sheep, he sent ten young men to greet Nabal in David's name (25:5). Sheep shearing was done twice a year. It was a festive occasion, and food and supplies were abundant. David sent the young men with salutations and wishes of good will. David and his men had watched over Nabal's men when they were shepherding the flock at Carmel. They did not mistreat them, and nothing of theirs was stolen or missing (25:7). David then asked for a gift in return. He did not specify the kind or the amount of the gift (25:8).

Nabal rejected David's request in scathing terms (25:10). David's men were forced to return empty handed. David was infuriated with Nabal's negative response. His response was simple: **Put on your swords!** (25:13). Four hundred of his men marched with David to punish Nabal. David's intent is recorded in 25:22. He planned to take vengeance on Nabal and not allow even one male of his family to live. David had allowed his anger to get the best of him. In times of stress and hardship, it is easy to let our anger loose. Rather then trust God to provide for him and his men, David was focused on revenge.

25:14–31. While David and his men were preparing to teach Nabal a lesson, a concerned servant alerted **Abigail**, Nabal's wife, to the alarming situation (25:14). David was right. He and his men had treated Nabal's servants well. They protected them, did not mistreat them, and nothing was missing. The shepherd described David and his men as **a wall around** them **all the time** (25:16). Nabal had hurled insults at David's messengers. Now the servant was afraid that Nabal's rude actions spelled disaster for him and his entire household (25:17).

Abigail grasped the seriousness of the situation and lost no time in responding. She gathered together a large gift (25:18). It was not enough to feed all of David's men, but it was a start. She set off to intercept David with the gift. She did not tell Nabal what she was doing (25:19). She met David as he and his men were descending down a mountain ravine. David had just invoked an oath about the revenge he was about to take (25:22).

Abigail's initial moments with David were filled with deference and respect, just the opposite of Nabal's response to David's men. It was extremely unusual for a woman to initiate this type of transaction in the ancient Near East. Abigail's response was wise and astute.

First, Abigail presented herself as David's servant. She deflected David's attention from Nabal by requesting that the blame for the bad treatment of David's men fall on her (25:24). Nabal, she said, was **just like his name**, a Fool! And making a wordplay on his name, she stated that **folly goes with him**. Abigail had not seen David's men, and the implication was that if she had, they would not have been sent away empty handed (25:25). Second, she gently suggested to David that the Lord had enabled her to meet David at just that crucial moment to keep David **from bloodshed and from avenging** himself. She urged David to accept her gift instead of taking the lives of her family and household. Third, Abigail took the blame for her husband's offense on herself and asked David to forgive her (25:28).

Finally, Abigail summed up the central theme of David's trials in the wilderness. Unlike Saul, David would be given a lasting dynasty because he fought the Lord's battles. But in order to fight the Lord's battle, David must be pure and free from wrongdoing or unrighteousness as long as he lived. Because David was faithful to seek after the Lord, the Lord God himself would make his life secure.

Even if someone intent on taking his life pursued David, they would fail. The Lord would **hurl away as from the pocket of a sling** the lives of David's enemies (25:29). Therefore, when the Lord made him king over all Israel, David did not need to have on his conscience **the staggering burden of needless bloodshed** or of having avenged himself against Nabal (25:31). Abigail also requested that David would remember her when the Lord had granted him success.

In essence, Abigail reminded David that the Lord would protect him. Since God would do this, there was no need for personal revenge. Consequently, in the midst of adversity God expects righteous behavior. Jesus taught the disciples to go beyond the idea of "an eye for an eye and a tooth for a tooth." He expects us to love our enemies instead (Matt. 5:38–48). God expects pure motives and righteous behavior out of us in the midst of hardships and trials.

25:32–44. Abigail's intervention surprised David. But he also learned from her wisdom. He viewed her coming as a messenger from the Lord, the God of Israel. Her good judgment kept him from bloodshed and revenge (25:33). David accepted her gift and sent her home in peace. David granted her request (25:34).

Abigail returned home to find Nabal throwing a grand party fit for a king. He had been drinking, and she held her tongue until the morning (25:36). When Abigail did tell him what had happened, Nabal had a heart attack and **he became like a stone**. The Lord struck Nabal ten days later and he died (25:38).

David soon heard that Nabal had died. He understood that it was the Lord's judgment on Nabal for treating him with contempt (25:39). David sent word to Abigail requesting that she become his wife. Abigail accepted and became David's wife (25:42). David had earlier married Ahinoam as well. While David was a fugitive, Saul gave Michal, his first wife, to another man (25:44).

G David and the Scepter (26:1–25)

> **SUPPORTING IDEA:** *David again refuses to kill Saul, whom he referred to as "the Lord's anointed," when he could easily do so.*

26:1–7. Even though the Ziphites were kinsmen of David, that did not stop them from aiding Saul in his treacherous attacks on him. Again, they went to Saul at Gibeah with intelligence that David was hiding on **the hill of Hakilah** (26:1; cp. 23:19). Once again Saul took a unit of troops and set out for the **Desert of Ziph** to capture David. Saul made his camp by the road to the hill of Hakilah, and David remained **in the desert** (26:3). David had sent out scouts to confirm Saul's arrival.

Instead of hiding in a cave, this time David scouted out Saul's position in the camp (26:5). Apparently, it was late in the day and David could see where Saul and Abner, the commander of the army, were bedding down for the night. David returned to his mighty men and enlisted the aid of **Ahimelech** the Hittite and **Abishai**, Joab's brother, to go and steal into the camp silently at night. Both men quietly made their way past the guards and through the personal bodyguards of Saul. Finally, they made it to the very spot where Saul and Abner were sleeping (26:7).

26:8–16. Saul was sleeping inside the camp with his spear stuck in the ground at his head. This was the spear that Saul had used to try to kill David and Jonathan. It was a type of scepter, a symbol of his royalty. Again, David's men wanted to kill Saul. Abishai volunteered to run Saul through with his spear (26:8). But David would not allow it. David had learned his lesson about trusting God in difficult times.

David's reply to Abishai summarizes the theme of the narrative in this part of 1 Samuel. Saul was the Lord's anointed (Heb. "messiah"). No one could touch him and **be guiltless** (26:9). It was the Lord's place to **strike him**. Either Saul would die of natural causes or he would die in battle. David would leave the vindication to God. He would not **lay a hand on the Lord's anointed** (26:11). David instructed his men to take only the water jug and Saul's spear.

God had put Saul's army into a deep sleep, so David and his men were able to cross **over to the other side**. David stopped on the top of a hill some distance away. There was a wide enough distance so Saul's army could not reach him (26:13). At this point, David stopped and called out to **Abner**, the commander of Saul's army.

In a masterful act of chastisement, David called out to Abner to wake him and chide him for falling asleep instead of guarding his master. David was correct. Abner and his men deserved death for falling asleep on the watch. It was their job to secure the area for the king. Someone could come into the camp, just as David had done. But unlike David, they might have taken the life of Saul. To prove that he had been in the camp, David challenged Abner to find **the king's spear and the water jug that were near his head** (26:16).

26:17–25. The noise awakened Saul, and he recognized David's voice. David was given the chance once again to plead his case before Saul (cp. 1 Sam. 24). This time, however, there was no doubt that Abner and the rest of Saul's army heard him as well. David asked again why the king was pursuing him. He wanted to know what he had done to incur the wrath of the king (26:18).

David was concerned about the motive behind the pursuit. If the Lord **incited** Saul against him, then David volunteered to bring an offering to the Lord. If, however, mere men had incited Saul, then David swore that they may **be cursed before the Lord** (26:19). These were the men who had deprived David of his inheritance. They had sent the king of Israel out to look for a flea (26:20).

Saul again confessed that he had sinned in chasing David. David again spared his life. Saul declared that he would not try to harm him again (26:21). The king acknowledged in front of the whole army of Israel that he was a fool.

Taking Saul's spear is another symbolic act of transferring the kingdom from Saul to David. Saul used this spear like a scepter. It was a symbol of his royal status and his reign. Taking it from Saul signified David's growing power and his claim to the throne. Returning the spear also carried symbolic significance. David reminded Saul that **the LORD rewards every man for his righteousness and faithfulness** (26:23).

Because David valued the life of Saul and did not kill him, so David humbly trusted the Lord to value his life and to deliver him from all trouble. David was giving notice to Saul. He did not expect him to repay the kindness that he had shown to Saul. He was warning Saul that God would deliver him. So if Saul again attacked David, Saul needed to know that he would have to fight the Lord (26:24). Then Saul blessed David and affirmed his future triumphs. The two parted ways, and Saul returned home to Gibeah.

David learned to seek vindication from the Lord. He had the opportunity to destroy Saul, his bitter enemy. But he did not. He recognized that God rewards us for our righteousness and faithfulness. Jesus reminded us that we should seek God's kingdom and his righteousness (Matt. 6:33) and not worry about the trials and difficulties we face in life. As disciples of our Lord Jesus Christ, God expects us to live faithfully before him, regardless of our circumstances. Paul encouraged us to be content in whatever state we are in (Phil. 4:11). He also warned us that whatever we sow, we also reap (Gal. 6:7). Faithful living in times of difficulty and hardship develops the kind of character that pleases God.

MAIN IDEA REVIEW: *David goes on the run from Saul. He hides out with a group of sympathizers in deserts and caves to keep from being killed by the king. David's years as a fugitive teach him to trust in the Lord as his ultimate protector.*

III. CONCLUSION

When the Rain Falls

Henry Wadsworth Longfellow (1807–1882) once penned the phrase, "Into each life some rain must fall." The statement is painfully true because each one of us faces difficulty and adversity at some time in our lives. For some only a little rain falls; for others it pours. We struggle to manage our own problems, and we admire those who have survived greater hardships.

One motivational speakers bureau lists 39 speakers under the category of overcoming adversity. Some of these are survivors of cancer, tragic accidents, or horrible crimes. Others are former POW's, terrorist victims, or individuals who suffer from disabling diseases. The initial circumstances of each speaker are different, but each one looked adversity in the face and walked away with a deeper appreciation for life and a stronger character. We marvel at their courage and their will to survive and make it through.

Before David could become the Lord's chosen king, he needed to have "some rain" fall into his life. God meant for David's experiences as a fugitive to teach him how to face adversity and hardship head-on. God did not leave David alone. He gathered a group of mighty men around him. God also gave David Abiathar as a priest and Abigail as a wife to help support him. God's purpose was to build in David a godly character so he would trust him and honor his will.

While adversity is sometimes very painful, God can help us develop our character through hardships and difficult times. In the Beatitudes, Jesus taught that believers would be blessed when they are "persecuted because of righteousness." When people insult us or lie about us, we are to rejoice because our reward is in heaven (Matt. 5:10–12). James told us to "consider it pure joy" when we "face trials of many kinds." The testing of our faith through adversity builds perseverance, and faithful perseverance builds godly character (James 1:2–4).

Peter reminds us that we may suffer grief in different kinds of trials. But these hardships and difficulties come in order to prove our faith genuine and to give "praise, glory and honor" to Jesus (1 Peter 1:6–7). If we remain faithful in suffering, we will be "counted worthy of the kingdom of God" (2 Thess. 1:5). God will surely vindicate those who suffer for him (2 Tim. 1:6–7). Right now, though, all we can do is hold on to Jesus. This holding on gets us through.

PRINCIPLES

- Adversity and hardships are part of life.
- Believers may suffer through many difficult times in their walk with Christ.
- Adversity and hardship are not always the results of individual sin.
- God does not send adversity just to punish us.
- Christ Jesus suffered on the cross for us and is an example for us to follow.
- Even though God seems to be hidden and far removed from us during difficult times, he is right beside us.

- Faithful reliance on God through times of difficulty builds godly character.

APPLICATIONS

- During difficult times constantly seek God's presence through prayer and Bible study.
- Always trust God's purpose for allowing you to face hardships and adversity.
- Ask God to show you clearly what he wants you to learn through difficult times.
- Remember that times of adversity can help build your faith through perseverance.
- Thank God for the difficult times and the opportunity to rely completely on him.
- Thank God that Jesus suffered on the cross for you and that you are counted worthy to suffer for his name.
- Remember that unjust suffering never justifies personal revenge; God will vindicate his faithful children.
- Rejoice that God has allowed us to be counted worthy of his kingdom.

IV. LIFE APPLICATION

Helping Others Survive Adversity

At the age of 76, Bill Marshall spends much of his time counseling serious burn victims at the Burn Center of Johns Hopkins Hospital, in Baltimore, Maryland. Marshall is able to connect with burn patients because of his own personal trauma. Twenty years ago, Marshall was one of only a few workers allowed to service a one-of-a-kind brass and iron furnace at the Sparrows Point plant of Bethlehem Steel. But one day after servicing it, and following standard operating procedure, Marshall threw the breaker to restart the furnace. In an instant, over 6,800 volts of electricity snaked down his left arm and ignited his body.

The fire melted his safety glasses to the side of his face, and 78 percent of his body was covered with third degree burns. The doctors gave him 24 hours to live. Instead, Marshall survived. For three months, he underwent painful skin graft surgeries to reconstruct his legs, torso, arms, neck, and face. Physical therapy was also long and difficult.

Bill Marshall certainly doesn't look like he did 20 years ago, but this Baptist deacon survived through the adversity. Marshall has given his testimony in church about the accident. But God also uses him to encourage and help burn victims in other ways.

Marshall visits the Burn Center once a week and more often when called in. He visits new and recovering patients. He lets them ask questions about their appearance, physical therapy, and how others will treat them after they "recover." Sometimes, he just sits next to their beds, reminding them that someone cares. He helped start a burn victim support group and is an active member.

Marshall doesn't want fanfare; he just wants to help others make it through the burdens of being a burn victim. Paul reminds us to help "carry each other's burdens" (Gal. 6:2). We can help others in times of pain and hardship, even if it is just sitting there to remind them that God cares and we care. In this way we honor Christ.

V. PRAYER

Heavenly Father, our souls cry out in pain and grief during times of trial and adversity. Give us strength to hold on to you and make it through. Remind us that our trust in you during hardships builds godly character. Teach us what we need to learn to help others in times of pain and grief. Thank you that Jesus was obedient and suffered for us on the cross. Help us to follow his example, knowing that we will be counted worthy of your kingdom. May our faithful response to suffering be a witness to bring others to a saving faith in Christ. In his name we pray. Amen.

VI. DEEPER DISCOVERIES

A. The Bread of the Presence (21:6)

According to Leviticus 24:5–9, twelve loaves of freshly baked bread were to be put on the table of the Presence in the tabernacle every Sabbath to symbolize the 12 tribes of Israel. The old loaves were to be eaten by the priests as part of their regular provision. Apparently, Ahimelech could offer the bread to David and his men in an emergency. However, David and his men had to be ritually clean.

B. The Ephod (21:9)

The ephod was a type of garment worn by the high priest as he ministered in the holy of holies in the tabernacle (Exod. 28:4–40; 35:27; 39:2–30).

Over the ephod the high priest wore a breastplate in which the Urim and Thummim were carried (Exod. 28:16). Ordinary priests and other functionaries wore linen ephods (1 Sam. 2:28; 14:3; 22:18), as did Samuel and David (1 Sam. 2:18; 2 Sam. 6:14). During his escape from Nob, Abiathar may have rescued this particular ephod. On two occasions David had Abiathar bring the ephod that he might inquire of the Lord (1 Sam. 23:9; 30:7). For David, at least, the ephod represented the presence and authority of the Lord.

C. David's Insanity (21:13–15)

When the servants of Achish, the Philistine king, recognized him, David realized that his life was in jeopardy. He responded by feigning insanity. In the ancient Near East, this type of insanity was considered to be the result of divine possession or affliction. The verbal root used three times in verses 14–15 to describe David's actions is actually the same as that used to identify a type of ecstatic prophetic behavior (1 Kgs. 9:11; Hos. 9:7; Jer. 29:26). Since this type of behavior was associated with the presence of God, the individuals so afflicted were ignored and allowed to live. David was counting on this.

D. The Massacre at Nob (22:16–23)

Saul's officers refused to follow his orders to massacre the priests at Nob because in the ancient Near East such action would be considered blasphemy against the deity worshiped there. Touching the priests or entering the sanctuary would be regarded as sacrilege and desecration. The reign of a king giving that order would be rejected by the deity. Doeg the Edomite was willing to carry out the order. He massacred not only the priest but also the entire population of Nob. Tragically, Saul's action cut himself off from the very place and people he needed to continue to be in contact with the Lord.

E. The Lord's Anointed (24:6; 26:8–11)

Even though his men advised it, David refused to kill Saul. This was because David considered Saul to be the "Lord's anointed" or the "Lord's Messiah." For David, the anointing of Saul as king over Israel was an act of God, and only God could take it from him. The king was under the protection of the deity. Political assassination was, therefore, an act against God. In refusing to kill Saul, David validated the Lord's original intent in anointing Saul. Saul's fate would be in God's hands.

VII. TEACHING OUTLINE

A. INTRODUCTION

1. Lead Story: The Prince of Preachers

2. Context: Because Saul had attempted on several occasions to kill him, David becomes a fugitive and flees to Nob where parts of the tabernacle were relocated after the destruction of Shiloh. Ahimelech the priest gives David the sword of Goliath and the bread of the Presence. Then David arrives at the Philistine city of Gath where he is recognized as an enemy. David feigns insanity to escape. Events turn tragic as Saul orders the massacre of the priests and the citizens of Nob for helping David. Saul relentlessly pursues him, but instead of taking revenge on Saul, David spares his life twice. A bright spot in David's career occurs when he meets Abigail. She wisely prevents David from taking revenge on Nabal, her ungrateful husband. When Nabal dies, Abigail marries David and gives him a son.

3. Transition: David went from being a hero in the court of Israel to a wanted fugitive almost overnight. His future had been bright. After all, Samuel had anointed him to be the next king over Israel. He had even married a princess, the daughter of the king. A prince was to be treated according to his royal status and not as a dead dog (1 Sam. 24:14). Now adversity and hardship became his constant companions. God did intend for David to have a glorious future. He would be king, and God would make a covenant especially with him so that the Prince of Peace would come from his family line. But before this happened David had to learn to trust God in the afflictions of life as well as the blessings. Chapters 21–26 describe the lessons David needed to learn in order to trust God in difficult times. David's faithful response to adversity developed in him the type of godly character he needed to rule over Israel and to be a man after God's own heart.

B. COMMENTARY

1. David and the Priest (21:1–9)
2. David and the Pagan King (21:10–22:5)
3. Saul and the Priests (22:6–23)

4. David and the Judahites (23:1–29)
5. David and the Anointed King (24:1–22)
6. David and Abigail (25:1–44)
7. David and the Scepter (26:1–25)

C. CONCLUSION: HELPING OTHERS SURVIVE ADVERSITY

VIII. ISSUES FOR DISCUSSION

1. List some of the physical, emotional, and spiritual hardships David faced in the wilderness in his flight from Saul. What are some types of adversity believers face today?
2. David relied on Gad and Abiathar to reveal God's will in times of difficulty. Where can the Christian go to find the comfort and direction of God in these types of circumstances?
3. The Ziphites, David's fellow tribesmen, were ready to hand him over to Saul. According to Psalm 54, David did not retaliate against the traitors. Instead, he trusted God to exact vengeance. As believers, how are we supposed to act toward those who betray us?
4. When Nabal attacked his character, David almost gave in to a vengeful spirit. Abigail helped David respond in an appropriate way. Christians are often tempted in the same way. What specific steps could we take to avoid giving in to the temptation of wanting revenge?
5. Saul was pursuing David in order to kill him. Although David had the right to defend himself, he chose not to kill Saul when the opportunity to do so arose. Sometimes, we work with or serve unjust or ungodly leaders, employers, or bosses. They may not be out to take our lives like Saul, but they do often make us miserable. How should the Christian respond to people like this? How could a believer be a witness to a person like Saul?

1 Samuel 27:1–31:13

The Death of Saul and Jonathan

- I. **INTRODUCTION**
  "I Am a Battleship"

- II. **COMMENTARY**
  A verse-by-verse explanation of these chapters

- III. **CONCLUSION**
  Jabesh Gilead

  An overview of the principles and applications from these chapters

- IV. **LIFE APPLICATION**
  God Is Still Good, All the Time

  Melding these chapters to life

- V. **PRAYER**
  Tying these chapters to life with God

- VI. **DEEPER DISCOVERIES**
  Historical, geographical, and grammatical enrichment of the commentary

- VII. **TEACHING OUTLINE**
  Suggested step-by-step group study of these chapters

- VIII. **ISSUES FOR DISCUSSION**
  Zeroing these chapters in on daily life

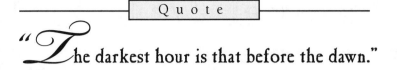

Quote

"*The* darkest hour is that before the dawn."

English Proverb

GEOGRAPHICAL PROFILE: ZIKLAG

- A city situated in the Negev, but the exact location is unknown
- Most likely candidate is Tell esh-Shari'a about fifteen miles southeast of Gaza
- A city within the inheritance of the tribe of Judah and given to Simeon (Josh. 19:5)
- Apparently taken by the Philistines in the time of the judges
- Achish of Gath gave the city to David as a base of operations
- Ziklag belonged to the kings of Judah since that time (cp. Neh. 11:28)

ETHNIC PROFILE: THE AMALEKITES

- The descendents of Amalek, grandson of Esau (Gen 36:12,16)
- A nomadic tribe that attacked the Israelites after the exodus (Exod. 17:8–13)
- Because of their atrocities, God commanded that the tribe be placed under the ban and destroyed (Deut. 25:17–19)
- Samuel commanded Saul to destroy them, but he disobeyed and did not (1 Sam. 15:2–3)
- David pursued the Amalekites after they attacked Ziklag and carried away his family and the families of his men (1 Sam. 30:1–20)

GEOGRAPHICAL PROFILE: MOUNT GILBOA

- A mountain on the eastern side of the Plain of Esdraelon
- Usually identified with modern Jebel Fuqus about seven miles west of Beth Shan

- Saul and the Israelites encamped here against the Philistines (1 Sam. 28:4)
- Saul and his sons died here when the Philistines defeated Israel (1 Sam. 31:1–8)

GEOGRAPHICAL PROFILE: BETH SHAN (BETH SHEAN)

- A fortified city on the crossroad of the Jezreel and Jordan Valleys
- Identified with modern Tell el-Husn next to the Harod stream
- The bodies of Saul and his sons were hung on the walls of this city because a temple to Ashtaroth was located here (1 Sam. 31:10)
- Valiant men from Jabesh Gilead rescued the bodies and disposed of them in Jabesh (1 Sam. 31:1–13)
- Rebuilt in the Hellenistic period and renamed Scythopolis, the site became one of the cities of the Decapolis

1 Samuel 27:1–31:13

IN A NUTSHELL

In the last chapters of 1 Samuel, David becomes a Philistine mercenary in order to resist Saul's wrath. While serving Achish, king of Gath, David is able to attack and defeat several enemies of Judah, including the Amalekites. Saul spirals out of control and desperately tries to find out what God will do by consulting the witch of Endor. He asks that she bring up the ghost of Samuel. Angry at being disturbed, Samuel declares that the Lord has already taken the kingdom from Saul. In addition, Saul and his sons will die on the battlefield the next day. The last chapter ends with the death of Saul on Mount Gilboa.

The Death of Saul
and Jonathan

I. INTRODUCTION

"I Am a Battleship"

American naval officer Frank Koch tells about a profound experience he once had on board a battleship. The following quote was first published in *Proceedings*, the magazine of the Naval Institute. It can be found in other books and many Web sites.

> Two battleships assigned to the training squadron had been at sea on maneuvers in heavy weather for several days. I was serving on the lead battleship and was on watch on the bridge as night fell. The visibility was poor with patchy fog, so the captain remained on the bridge keeping an eye on all activities. Shortly after dark, the lookout on the wing of the bridge reported, "Light, bearing on the starboard bow."
>
> "Is it steady or moving astern?" the captain called out.
>
> The lookout replied, "Steady, captain," which meant we were on a dangerous collision course with that ship.
>
> The captain then called to the signalman, "Signal that ship: We are on a collision course, advise you change course 20 degrees."
>
> Back came the signal, "Advisable for you to change course 20 degrees."
>
> The captain said, "Send, I'm a captain, change course 20 degrees."
>
> "I'm a seaman second class," came the reply. "You had better change course 20 degrees." By that time the captain was furious. He spat out, "Send, I'm a battleship. Change course 20 degrees."
>
> Back came the flashing light, "I'm a lighthouse."
>
> We changed course.

Many different people use this quote to say many different things. For many years the battleship was the most formidable naval war vessel in the world. It weighed 50,000 tons and was at least 300 yards long. It carried a large crew and massive armament. The battleship's large guns could lob a one-ton shell more than 20 miles to hit its target. Battleships were not to be toyed with. In this story the captain intrigues us most of all. He was certainly stubborn and aware of his important position as commander of the battleship. He was proud and self-assured. Nothing could make him turn away.

Except for a lighthouse. It had no weapons. It was often a humble structure and had only a skeleton crew. Yet, something as large and awesome as a battleship was no match for the lighthouse. If the captain did not learn, if he was not teachable, then disaster would result in the ensuing collision. That's often the way we are. We swell in pride and significance, and then marvel at our abilities and power to accomplish our self-centered will. We forget that God is the lighthouse. We are the ones who need to correct our course.

In the last chapters of 1 Samuel, David and Saul were on a collision course with God. Circumstances are bleak. The fog was everywhere. Both men needed to hear God and understand his direction. One had determined a long time before that he would not change his course. Saul collided with God and lost his sons, his kingdom, and his life. David, on the other hand, learned to seek God's will and changed his course. But before God would make David king over Israel, life would become very dark.

II. COMMENTARY

The Death of Saul and Jonathan

MAIN IDEA: *David becomes a mercenary in the army of Achish, a Philistine king, while Saul continues his downward spiral toward the Lord's judgment. The book of 1 Samuel comes to a conclusion with the death of Saul and his sons at the hands of the Philistines.*

A The Flight of David (27:1–28:2)

SUPPORTING IDEA: *David and his men become mercenary soldiers in the army of the Philistine king, Achish of Gath. This gives them protection from Saul's forces.*

27:1–7. Apparently David really didn't get it. God had delivered him from Saul and many other enemies. Samuel, God's appointed prophet, had anointed him king over Israel. What's more, David had just confessed his faith in the Lord with an oath (26:24). Now he doubted that God would protect him. He seemed to wallow in self-pity and doubt.

David's logic was good. He had spared Saul's life twice, but he didn't trust Saul. He reasoned that Saul would be so persistent that he would eventually catch him at a weak point and destroy him (27:1). But this contradicted what God had promised (Getz, *David*, 136). Nevertheless, David decided to go to the one place where Saul could not hunt him down. That one place was Philistine territory.

So David took his men and **went over to Achish . . . king of Gath** (27:2). He had been to Gath once before (21:10–15). At that time, he had feigned madness in order to protect himself. But now he pledged to serve a pagan king with a clear mind. David's plan worked. When Saul heard that David had fled to the Philistines, he no longer searched for him (27:4).

But what was David thinking? He was going to serve a king who worshiped idols and did not recognize the Lord. He was going to live in a land where they served idols and shunned the name of the Lord. As a servant, would he not be required to bow down to the pagan king's god? Would he not have to recognize the king's god and offer sacrifices to him?

Surely, David recognized this. He may have lived with Achish in Gath for more than a year (27:7). Then he appealed to Achish to give him **one of the country towns** controlled by Gath (27:5). David could live there without the snooping eyes of the king. Achish gave him **Ziklag**, a city south of Gath on the edge of the Negev. Ziklag was within the inheritance of the tribe of Judah, but it had not been conquered by the Israelites. Later, the Philistines captured it. After David arrived there, the city remained in the control of **the kings of Judah** (27:6) from that time on.

27:8–12. In order to keep up the charade and avoid attacking Israel, David and his men fought **the Geshurites, the Girzites and the Amalekites** (27:8). These were enemies of Judah, but not necessarily of Philistia. So when Achish inquired into his affairs, David lied about the battles. He told Achish that he had attacked Judahite settlements in the Negev (27:10). David knew that in order to cover his tracks he had to kill anyone who could **inform** on him (27:11). Achish believed David, and he thought David was becoming **so odious to his people** that he would be his **servant forever** (27:12).

28:1–2. David was so successful as a warrior that Achish informed him that he would have to accompany the Philistine forces in a battle **against Israel** (28:1). David's answer was vague and a bit arrogant. Now, he replied to Achish, **you will see for yourself what your servant can do**. But what would he do? What did he mean by these words? He couldn't hide in the reserves in the rear of the fighting units. In response to David's boast, Achish made him his **bodyguard for life** (28:2). David and his men would now have to go wherever Achish commanded.

David's plan to escape Saul by fleeing to the land of the Philistines had created an unthinkable problem. He was now required to fight against his own people. This was a lose-lose situation. David could fight with the Philistines against Israel. If he did so, he would become the enemy of God's people, the very people the Lord had anointed him to rule. He could turn on Achish and fight for the Israelites. But attempting this would almost mean suicide. There would be no escape to the Israelite side because Saul would surely capture him or cut him down. In a masterful stroke of the pen, the narrator leaves the reader in suspense about the outcome of this problem.

David's self-pity and doubt had created a grave dilemma. He may have thought that his life was getting better. He had pulled the wool over the eyes of Achish. He had his own city. Saul had stopped hunting him, and many warriors defected to him at Ziklag, including some of Saul's own kinsmen (1 Chron. 12:1–22). David may have been gaining prestige in the eyes of Achish and disgruntled Israelites, but in the eyes of God "he was sinking deeper and deeper into the mire of sin and walking farther and farther out of His will" (Getz, *David*, 141). David killed innocent people, and he lied to cover it up.

Perhaps this is why God refused to let David build the temple in Jerusalem. David was a man who had "shed much blood" (1 Chron. 22:8; cp. 28:3). This sin would lead David into a crisis of loyalty (28:1–2; 29:1–11) and family (30:1–31). It is hard to believe that this is the same David who wrote: "My salvation and my honor depend on God; he is my mighty rock, my refuge. Trust in him at all times, O people; pour out your hearts to him, for God is our refuge" (Ps. 62:7–8).

Ⓑ The Folly of Saul (28:3–25)

SUPPORTING IDEA: *Through a medium Saul calls up the spirit of the deceased Samuel to ask his advice on how to proceed against the Philistines. Samuel tells him that he is destined to die in a forthcoming battle.*

28:3–6. Before we return to David's dilemma, the narrator brings us back to Israel to consider the state of Saul's heart and mind. This was certainly the darkest moment in Saul's life. He was rejected and judged by God for his sin and rebellion.

After the death of Samuel, Saul had exercised pious judgment in expelling **the mediums and spiritists from the land** (28:3). The Torah prohibited any Israelite from seeking their services. The Lord had said, "I will set my face against the person who turns to mediums and spiritists to prostitute himself by following them" (Lev. 20:6). Trying to speak to the dead through these individuals was blatant idolatry and a capital offense.

We also learn that Saul mustered the Israelite forces on Gilboa south of Shunem where the Philistines set up camp. When Saul took a look at the Philistine army, **terror filled his heart** (28:5). The sight scared him so much that he immediately **inquired of the LORD** (28:6). He looked for an answer **by dreams or Urim or prophets**, but the Lord did not answer. He was left alone, totally rejected. This was what Samuel had warned him about. Saul had turned his back on God; now God apparently turned his back on Saul.

This must have been the darkest point in Saul's life. His response is significant. The king could have repented, confessed his sin, and come before God with a broken heart. But he did not. Instead, Saul chose to violate one of the most serious prohibitions in the Old Testament. The book of 1 Chronicles declares that Saul "was unfaithful to the LORD; he did not keep the word of the LORD and even consulted a medium for guidance, and did not inquire of the LORD" (1 Chron. 10:13–14). Because of this, a just and righteous God judged him and punished him accordingly.

The book of James commands, "Come near to God and he will come near to you" (4:8). We must never conclude that it is too late to come back to God. The Lord is a holy and righteous God, and he cannot bear sin. He will indeed punish sinners. But he is also a loving God who is willing to forgive us if we repent and turn back to him (1 John 1:9).

28:7–14. When Saul did not receive an answer from the Lord, he chose to seek guidance from a medium or spiritist. He asked his attendants to find a woman who was a medium so he could **go and inquire of her** (28:7). They told him there was a medium in **Endor**, and Saul set off to see her.

Saul's desperation in the matter is shown by several facts. He **disguised himself** by taking off his royal regalia and putting on other clothes. He also went at night, and he took only two men as bodyguards. Since Endor was above and east of the Philistine camp, he had to make it through enemy lines to consult the medium (28:8).

Despite Saul's request to consult a spirit and bring up the one he named, the woman suspected this intrusion to be a trap. Ironically, without knowing who he was, she protested that Saul had cut off the mediums and spiritists from the land (28:9). Tragically, however, Saul swore an oath that she would **not be punished for this** (28:10). Saul "invoked the Lord to grant immunity to one who broke the Lord's command" (Bergen, 266). The oath was blasphemy. It turned the Lord against the king.

Saul's oath was sufficient for the medium, and she asked Saul whom she should bring up. Saul requested **Samuel** (28:11). When the woman saw Samuel, she knew the identity of Saul. She thought Saul had deceived her.

Saul, however, quieted her and asked what she saw. The medium then described the spirit coming out of the ground as an old man wearing a robe. Saul surmised it to be Samuel, and **he bowed down and prostrated himself with his face to the ground** (28:14).

Did the medium actually bring up Samuel? More than half a dozen interpretations have been offered to explain how this event happened (cp. Bergen, 267, n. 150). The text does seem to imply that mediums had the ability to communicate with the dead. The Old Testament prohibited doing so because it offered supernatural guidance from a source other than the Lord. It is reasonable to suggest that this medium was not able to conjure up Samuel's spirit by her skill alone. This was a unique act of God to permit Saul to have one more audience with Samuel. Samuel served once again as a prophet bringing the word of God to a desperate and rebellious king.

28:15–25. Samuel demanded of Saul the reason for disturbing him (28:15). Saul responded by confessing that he was **in great distress**. The Philistines were attacking, and God was not answering Saul's inquiries **either by prophets or by dreams**. Saul wanted Samuel to tell him what to do.

Samuel did not tell Saul what to do. Instead, he reiterated the Lord's judgment against him (1 Sam. 15:22–29). Saul had continually disobeyed the Lord. He did not destroy the Amalekites (28:18). As a result, the Lord had **torn the kingdom** out of his hands and given it to David. The Lord would hand over Saul and Israel to the pagan Philistines. The Israelite army would be defeated in battle, and Saul and his sons would die. As Samuel put it, **tomorrow you and your sons will be with me** (28:19).

The news was too much for Saul to bear. He had not eaten anything that day and night (28:20). The medium urged him to let her prepare a meal for him. Initially, he refused. But at the urging of the medium and his men, Saul gave in. The woman quickly butchered a fattened calf, baked bread without yeast, and set the meal before Saul and his men (28:24). After eating and resting, Saul and his men left the woman's house the same night to return to the Israelite lines.

You can learn a lot about a person by noting where he turns for help in a time of trouble. Saul violated one of the most serious prohibitions in the Old Testament. He attempted by necromancy to learn the plans of God. Saul attempted to use an illicit way of manipulating the deity through magic. Saul was inconsistent in his actions. He banned the mediums and spiritists from the land, as he rightly should. But he also killed all of the priests who could use the Urim and Thummin to inquire of the Lord. He had listened to

Samuel, but then he did what he wanted, often carrying out only a portion of the Lord's command. Saul did not nurture his relationship with God.

God expects believers to seek him in every situation and circumstance. He is a holy and righteous God. He has declared that his Spirit would not contend with man forever (Gen. 6:3). God is compassionate and gracious, but he will not leave the guilty unpunished (Exod. 33:6–7). Those who seek to follow the Lord Jesus Christ must not seek guidance in magic, witches, mediums, or spiritists. Our trust must be in the Lord alone. David would learn this lesson in a painful way.

C The Predicament of David (29:1–11)

> **SUPPORTING IDEA:** Fortunately for David, the Philistines refuse to let him and his men join them in a battle against the Israelite army.

29:1–5. The narrative now moves the clock back a few days and returns to the events last portrayed in 28:1–2. The Philistines mustered their forces at **Aphek** by the Yarkon River on the coastal plain. The Israelites encamped in the Jezreel Valley.

David and his men marched **at the rear with Achish** as his bodyguard (29:2). As the Philistine **units of hundreds and thousands** pulled out and headed for the Jezreel Valley, the commanders of the Philistines noticed David and asked Achish about **these Hebrews** (29:3). In response to their question, Achish defended David's presence by pointing out David's strained relationship with Saul. David had been **an officer of Saul king of Israel**, but now he had served Achish for over a year. Achish had **found no fault in him**.

Achish's word was not good enough for the other Philistine commanders. They were extremely **angry with him**. Perhaps they could see what Achish could not. David's presence posed a risk that they did not want to take. In order to please Saul and seek to regain the favor of his former master, David might turn against them in battle (29:4). A similar thing had happened before with Hebrew mercenaries (1 Sam. 14:21). In addition, David was after all a famous hero the Israelites had sung about: "**Saul has slain his thousands, and David his tens of thousands**" (29:5). They concluded that David must not go with them. Achish must send him and his men back to Ziklag.

29:6–11. What Achish said to David suggests two things (29:6). First, it hints that Achish was frustrated with the Philistine rulers. He may have hoped that David's expertise in battle would win him a good share of the Israelite spoils. Second, Achish seemed to think that David would be disappointed by the news. It is interesting that Achish, a pagan king, swore to David by the life of the Lord that he did not agree with the other commanders. Note that Achish called upon the Hebrew God to confirm his sincerity. But the Philistine rulers did not approve of David, so Achish had no choice but to order David to **turn back and go in peace** (29:7). It is also ironic that Achish's relationship with David provides a significant contrast to Saul's treatment of David (Bergen, 272).

Of course, David protested the decision with three questions (29:8). David asked for an explanation: **what have I done?** David claimed to have been faithful to Achish from the first day he arrived in Gath. However, the last question was vague. David wanted to go and **fight against the enemies of my lord the king**. Notice that David did not specify which king. Achish would assume that David meant him, but in the context, it is possible to believe that David meant his real king, Saul, and the army of Israel. David's response implies that David would have turned on the Philistines (Arnold, 387).

Achish again tried to pacify David. He heaped compliments on him, even calling him an angel of God (29:9). The theme that God's hidden hand was on David so that he prospered in everything he did is clear here. Achish certainly benefited by this. Nevertheless, Achish prohibited David from arguing his case before the other generals, and he commanded him to **leave in the morning as soon as it is light** (29:10). David and his men did as Achish commanded and headed back to Ziklag.

The command of Achish to return to Ziklag was providential for two reasons. First, David found out that the Amalekites had attacked his home and carried away his own family, the families of his men, and all their possessions. Had he gone into battle, all this would have been lost (Arnold, 387). Moreover, the attack of the Amalekites proved to be a major wake-up call for David in his relationship with the Lord.

But second, God spared David from a difficult situation. David's questions in verse 8 only feigned shock and disappointment. By fleeing to the Philistines, David ran the risk of being ordered to fight against his own people, Israel. David did not ask the Lord if he should go to the Philistines. And now, he found himself in a mess of his own creation (Getz, *David*, 142). Achish, on the other hand, became an instrument of God's deliverance from this worst-case scenario. Even though Achish was a pagan king, God used him to enable David to escape from this trap. Through this unexpected grace, David was able to avoid conflict with both Saul and the Philistines.

Although David lapsed in his trust for God to protect him from Saul, God did not abandon him. David still loved the Lord and desired to do his will. He would exercise this kind of faith in the fight against the Amalekites. But God still remained faithful. Paul recognized this in his letter to the Romans. He reminded us "that in all things God works for the good of those who love him, who have been called according to his purpose" (Rom. 8:28). We may not see his hand clearly, but God always surprises us with unexpected grace.

The Triumph of David (30:1–31)

> **SUPPORTING IDEA:** *David and his men rescue the people of Ziklag who had been captured by the Amalekites.*

30:1–6. David must have breathed a sigh of relief as he and his men set off for the long journey back to Ziklag. Miraculously, David and his band were not required to go to battle against the Israelites. They may have joked and laughed along the way. Hopefully, David recognized that God had helped him get out of this predicament. But God was still building his character, and David had more difficult circumstances to face.

While David and his troops marched north to join the Philistines in preparation for battle, **the Amalekites**, the other great enemy of the Israelites, had raided the Negev and Ziklag. They **attacked Ziklag and burned it** (30:1). The Amalekites did not kill the inhabitants of the city. Instead, they carried them off captive, **both young and old**, including the women (30:3).

When David and his men reached the city, their merry attitude changed to sorrow. They witnessed what the Amalekites had done and realized that **their wives and sons and daughters** had all been taken captive. They **wept aloud until they had no strength left to weep** (30:4). They did not know if their families were dead or alive. This included David's two wives, Ahinoam and Abigail (30:5).

But the situation went from bad to worse. David was surrounded by trouble. David was distressed because the people began to talk about **stoning him** (30:6). This was the first time David's leadership was questioned. The soul of all of the people (**each one was bitter in spirit**) became bitter.

The fact that David's followers were resentful is understandable. Naturally, when they thought about what their families were going through as prisoners of the Amalekites, they began to grieve. There appeared to be no hope of rescue. David must have reached a low point in his life. He was in fact responsible for the tragedy.

The contrast between Saul's leadership and that of David is clearly shown in what David did next. David had not sought the Lord's help before he fled to Philistia, and that decision was partly to blame for the dilemma they were now facing. But this time David turned to the Lord. While the others were beside themselves with grief, **David found strength in the LORD his God** (30:6). The verb translated by the NIV as "found strength" actually conveys a reflexive idea. That is, "David strengthened himself" in the Lord. According to Arnold, this statement emphasizes the personal faith of David, as well as illustrating the synergistic nature of faith (Arnold, 389). "Faith requires a human response, but it is enabled by God (cf. Eph. 2:8)." In his greatest moment of crisis, David looked to God. He did not seek solace in himself or other human advisors. He sought a personal relationship with God and found the strength to lead from this empowerment.

30:7–25. David's response to the tragedy underscores his desire to rely completely on the Lord. He called for Abiathar the priest to bring the ephod, and he used this as he **inquired of the LORD** (30:8). David posed two questions to the Lord. The first was whether he should pursue the Amalekite raiding party. The second was if he would overtake them. The Lord answered that David should pursue them and that, yes, he would overtake them.

So David and 600 of his fighting men followed the trail of the raiding party. They must have marched on double time because when they reached **the Besor Ravine** 200 of the men were **too exhausted to cross the ravine**. Consequently, only 400 continued the pursuit (30:10).

David's troops **found an Egyptian in a field**. He had taken no food or water for three days (30:12), so David gave him **water to drink and food to eat**. This man had been a slave of an Amalekite. When he became ill, his master had abandoned him. In response to David's initial questions, the Egyptian revealed that he had been with the Amalekites when they raided Ziklag (30:13–14). Then David asked if the Egyptian could lead him **down to this raiding party**.

Before he would do so, the Egyptian asked for David to swear that he would not kill him or hand him over to his master. Apparently David obliged the slave because he did lead David and his men to the raiding party (30:16). The Amalekites were **eating, drinking and reveling** because of the great amount of plunder they had taken in battle.

David and his men attacked and fought the Amalekites for more than 24 hours. Four hundred young men fled on camels, but none of the rest escaped (30:17). Amazingly, David recovered everything that had been taken by the Amalekites. **Nothing was missing**. The wives and families of his men were restored. David also rescued his own two wives. The flocks and herds were driven back toward Ziklag. His men called it **David's plunder** (30:18–20). This was an amazing miracle. David's stature rose as the leader of his band. David had sought the Lord's will on the matter, and God had given him the victory.

David also revealed the nature of his character when they arrived back at the Besor Ravine. The 200 exhausted men who were left behind came out to meet David and the returning troops. They were naturally excited to be reunited with their wives and families. But all the evil and worthless men sought to deny the 200 any share in the plunder (30:21–22).

David would have none of this. The Lord, after all, had given the plunder to them. The Lord had protected them and given them the victory. Consequently, the spoils must be distributed in a way that honored the Lord. Thus David made a ruling that became **a statute and ordinance for Israel**. This principle of equality was practiced throughout his reign: **The share of the man who stayed with the supplies is to be the same as that of him who went down to the battle** (30:24).

30:26–31. From the Egyptian slave David had learned that part of the spoils had come from settlements and territories in Judah. So when he returned to Ziklag, David sent some of the plunder to the elders of Judah. The narrator specifically identified these elders as the friends of David. He then listed 14 sites or clan territories that received a gift. We learn from verse 31 that David sent gifts to all the other places where he **and his men had roamed**. This suggests that these towns and settlements had most likely sheltered David and supported him during his fugitive days in Judah.

Why did David do this? Several reasons have been suggested. First, we have already noted that David knew some of the plunder had come from territories in Judah. David may have been trying to return the items to their original owners. Second, David may have wanted to establish a network of treaties whereby David would be allowed to move his troops in and out of Judahite territory. David may have decided to leave Ziklag and his Philistine overlords as soon as possible, and he needed a secure place to hide from Saul. David had not yet heard that Saul and Jonathan had been killed.

Bergen argues for another reason. In verse 26 David sent a blessing or **present from the plunder of the LORD's enemies**. This suggests that the gift was an announcement of David's messianic status. David had been anointed king over Israel (1 Sam. 16:12–13). But now he was confirming this by his messianic deeds. The Lord's anointed would be expected to fight the Lord's enemies. Bergen proposes that the presence of the phrase "the Lord's enemies" instead of "the Amalekites" provides the key to the interpretation of the passage.

David's defeat of the Amalekites was theological in nature. He did not fight the Amalekites for secular reasons, for plunder, or for vengeance. David did so because God had commanded it. That is, this battle was "the fulfillment of ancient Torah mandates and fulfillment of timeless prophecies" (Bergen, 280). The Messiah would fight the Lord's battles and obtain the victory.

Some of the verses penned by David in Psalm 21 seem appropriate for this moment in his life: "O LORD, the king rejoices in your strength. How great is his joy in the victories you give! . . . For the king trusts in the LORD; through the unfailing love of the Most High he will not be shaken."

As David had learned to trust in the Lord, so also must believers trust in him today. Our Messiah encouraged us not to let our "hearts be troubled." Jesus commanded us to trust in God and trust in him (John 14:1). When we do trust in God and seek his will for our lives, we will find that there is true victory in Jesus.

⬛ The Tragedy of Saul (31:1–13)

SUPPORTING IDEA: *Saul and his sons die on Mount Gilboa in a battle against the Philistines. This paves the way for David to assume the kingship of Israel.*

31:1–6. Chapter 31 records the tragic events surrounding the death of Israel's first anointed king. Saul died in battle against the Philistines, the great enemies of Israel (cp. 1 Sam. 9:6). Saul was terror-stricken before the Philistines (1 Sam. 28:5). This fear led him to consult the medium of Endor. The medium conjured up the dead Samuel, who told Saul that he would die the next day on the battlefield (1 Sam. 28:16–19). All of this became a pre-scription for failure.

In quick succession we learn that the **Philistines** routed the **Israelites**. They fled before the Philistine army, and many died on Mount Gilboa (31:1). Among those slain were the sons of Saul, **Jonathan, Abinadab, and Malki-Shua** (31:2). The battle raged fiercely around Saul, and the Philistine archers **wounded him critically.**

Since death was always preferable to capture where the Philistines were concerned (Arnold, 399), Saul commanded his armor bearer to draw his sword and run him through (31:4). Saul knew that the pagan Philistines would probably torture him. However, the armor bearer was terrified and refused to do so. So **Saul took his own sword and fell on it.** When the armor bearer saw what Saul had done and that he was dead, he also fell on his sword and died beside his master. In one verse, we learn the somber news. Saul, his sons, his armor bearer, and all his men **died together that same day** (31:6).

31:7–10. As a response to Saul's death, the Israelites along the Jezreel Valley and across the Jordan River abandoned their towns. The victorious Philistines **came and occupied them**, leaving them in control of Israelite territory (31:7). Since the spoils belonged to the victors, the Philistines came the next day **to strip the dead**. They found the bodies of Saul and his sons fallen on Mount Gilboa (31:8).

The Philistines desecrated Saul's body by decapitating it and hanging his body on the wall of Beth Shan. Saul's defeat and death became the occasion for proclamation of glad tidings in the temple of the Philistine idols and among their people (31:9–10). Saul's armor was placed in the temple of the Ashtoreths that may have been in Beth Shan. The book of Chronicles records that Saul's head was also hung up in the temple of Dagon (1 Chron. 10:10).

31:11–13. While most of the Israelites in the region fled the Philistines in fear, the good **people of Jabesh Gilead** heard the news of the desecration of the body of Saul and decided to do something about it (31:11). Their courageous and valiant men traveled all night through treacherous terrain, seeking to avoid the Philistines. When they reached **Beth Shan**, they took the bodies of Saul and his sons down from the wall and carried them back to Jabesh (31:12). There in Jabesh, they burned their bones and buried them in peace **under a tamarisk tree**. These gracious people mourned for Saul and his sons for **seven days**. The people of Jabesh Gilead had never forgotten how Saul had rescued them from the Ammonites (1 Sam. 11). They repaid Saul's kindness with heroic loyalty.

With the death of Saul the contrast between David and Saul comes to a climax. In chapter 30, David rescued Ziklag and the lives of everyone associated with him from the hands of another great enemy of Israel, the Amalekites. But now at the end of chapter 31, Saul and everyone associated with him lay dead on the battlefield against the Philistines (Arnold, 400). David would be promised an everlasting dynasty (2 Sam. 7:10–13), but Saul's house was destroyed (1 Chron. 10:6).

> **MAIN IDEA REVIEW:** *David becomes a mercernary in the army of Achish, a Philistine king, while Saul continues his downward spiral toward the Lord's judgment. The book of 1 Samuel comes to a conclusion with the death of Saul and his sons at the hands of the Philistines.*

III. CONCLUSION

Jabesh Gilead

On a photo trip to Jordan, G. B. Howell Jr., the editor of *Biblical Illustrator,* and I once found ourselves lost on the north side of the Wadi Yabis looking for Tell Abu-Kharaz, the most likely site of Jabesh Gilead. The fact that our driver did not speak English made matters worse. What we eventually found was an isolated hill about two miles up from the Jordan River and ten miles southeast of Beth Shan.

When we climbed the tell we found no markers or memorials to attest to the loyalty and faithfulness of the men of Jabesh-Gilead to Saul. These men had risked life and limb to rescue the bodies of Saul and his sons from the wall at Beth Shan. This feat required a treacherous journey by night down the wadi, across the Jordan River, and up to Beth Shan. The return trip was even harder because they carried the lifeless bodies with them. The men of Jabesh Gilead cremated the bodies and buried them with honor in their small city. The remains of Saul and his sons stayed there until David ordered them exhumed and reburied in the tomb of Saul's father, Kish (2 Sam. 21:1–14). David commended the people of Jabesh Gilead for their courage and loyalty (2 Sam. 2:5–7). The tell is the only piece of evidence outside of the Bible that remains to remind us of this gracious act of faithfulness.

God does not always erect gaudy markers or memorials to his faithful care and blessings in our lives. In fact, God's hand is so well hidden that sometimes we think that God has deserted us or doesn't care. Many people believe in a distant God. They suppose that God is not active in the world at all. But when we take an honest look back at our lives, we can see how God has worked in and through the hardships and adversity. We see clear indicators of how God has blessed us and sometimes judged us. We see how he has helped us grow and mature in our faith through all kinds of circumstances. The Lord is trustworthy. He provides unexpected grace, and he gives us the victory through Jesus Christ.

PRINCIPLES

- The Lord delights to bless his people.
- The Lord is trustworthy in all circumstances.
- The Lord rejects idolatry and is jealous when we seek help from other sources.

- When we least expect it, God will bless us with his grace.
- True and lasting victory comes from the Lord.
- The sovereign Lord has a right to judge and exact punishment for rebellion.

APPLICATIONS

- Seek God's will and direction for your life constantly, not just in times of great adversity.
- Make study of the Scripture and prayer priorities in your life.
- Find and join a church that takes prayer seriously.
- Trust the Lord for victory and success.
- Thank God when he chastises you for rebellion and sin.
- Acknowledge that God has the right to judge us.
- Examine your motives constantly to make sure that your decisions are not based on any other source than the Lord.
- Thank God for the grace offered to us through our Savior Jesus Christ.
- Take the time to tell others about the wonderful grace of the Lord.

IV. LIFE APPLICATION

God Is Still Good, All the Time

"God is still good, all the time." That's what Robert Rogers says, even after that fateful night in August of 2003. Rogers and his wife Melissa were traveling home to Liberty, Missouri, from a wedding in Wichita, Kansas. Their four children, Mekenah, Zachary, Nicholas, and their newly adopted daughter Alenah, were sound asleep in the back seats of their minivan. Zachary and Alenah were special-needs children. As Roberts puts it, he and Melissa were hopelessly in love with Jesus, each other, and their precious children.

It was raining hard, and they began to run into water flowing across I–35. A flash flood suddenly washed the minivan off the highway and into a raging river six feet deep and hundreds of feet wide. As the van began to sink under the water, Rogers kicked out the driver's window. Robert, Melissa, and Mekenah were instantly swept out of the car. The three youngest were still buckled in their car seats. Robert began to drown under the rushing water, and then, somehow God pulled him above the rapids and to shore. Robert was the only survivor.

The news of the loss devastated the local community. Zachary had been a preschool buddy of my youngest son. But through the grief, Robert Rogers found peace in God's arms. He said, "In the worst moment of my life, God's presence was the sweetest it's ever been." Rogers believes that he survived to tell others of the hope God can give through tragedy. He went on to found Mighty in the Land ministries and to give his testimony through word and song to many. Today, he is married and the father of a brand new son. Robert is willing to go wherever he is needed to encourage families to cherish the precious moments they have with one another. He continues to tell others that there is peace in Jesus, and that "God is still good, all the time."

Even when our days are at their darkest, even when our lives are at their lowest ebb, the Lord is still present. He has not forgotten us. He has not abandoned us. We can find the peace that Jesus gives to us (John 14:27), the peace that transcends all understanding that will guard our hearts and our minds in Christ Jesus (Phil. 4:7). God is still good, all the time.

V. PRAYER

Our gracious Lord, help us to thank you for the many blessings you have given to us. Remind us to examine carefully how you have worked in and through times of difficulties and hardships in our lives, as well as times of peace and stability. Help us to trust you completely and to look to you for grace and victory. Even when life seems dark, teach us to trust your sovereign will. Give us the strength to finish the race by looking to Jesus. In his name. Amen.

VI. DEEPER DISCOVERIES

A. Mediums and Spiritists (28:3)

In the ancient Near East, mediums and spiritists used a variety of methods to attempt to ascertain the will of the gods and to predict the future. These individuals were condemned because they sought knowledge and power from spirits and not from the Lord. The Old Testament worldview held that the Lord was the sole source of power and authority in the universe. Any other view was considered idolatry.

B. Consulting the Dead in the Ancient Near East (28:8–11)

Consulting the spirits of the dead in order to determine the future, or necromancy, was practiced throughout the ancient Near East. As part of the popular religion of Canaan, mediums and spiritists would call up a "familiar" spirit or attempt to raise a ghost. Incantations and rituals would be performed at night, usually over a specially dug ritual pit, and with a food or blood offering. The spirits that appeared usually were seen only by the medium and "communicated" through them with the client.

C. Cutting Off the Head and Exposing the Corpse (31:9–10)

To decapitate or dismember a corpse and leave it unburied was the ultimate disgrace that a victim's family or nation could endure. In the popular religion of the ancient Near East, the proper burial of a corpse was necessary to the individual's peace and repose in the afterlife. Impalement of a foe's body on a wall was common during this period and was used as a tactic to terrorize and shame the enemy. This is why the men of Jabesh-Gilead marched through the night to rescue the bodies of Saul and his sons. The Assyrian king Ashurbanipal is reported to have hung the head of a conquered enemy in a tree in his garden.

VII. TEACHING OUTLINE

A. INTRODUCTION

1. Lead Story: "I Am a Battleship"
2. Context: After playing a cat-and-mouse game with Saul, David loses hope and decides to flee to the land of Philistia. Saul cannot hunt him there and leaves him alone. David and his men also serve Achish of Gath, eventually becoming his personal bodyguards. Achish gives him the city of Ziklag on the edge of the Negev for his headquarters. David is able to attack the enemies of Judah while deceiving Achish into thinking that the spoils came from Judah. But soon the time comes when Achish orders David to fight with him against Israel, and David marches north with the Philistine army. In the meantime Saul is terrified by the Philistine army and visits the medium of Endor in order to ask the dead spirit of Samuel what he should do. Samuel reveals that Saul and his sons will die the next day in battle, and a shaken Saul returns to his troops. In a surprise move, the other Philistine leaders refuse to allow David to join the upcoming battle, and Achish sends David and his men back to Ziklag. David returns

with his men to find that an Amalekite raiding party has captured their wives and families. David pursues the Amalekites, defeats them, and rescues the captured families. During this time, Saul's sons die in battle, and he is critically wounded by the Philistine archers and falls on his sword and dies.

3. Transition: The five chapters studied here document David's sojourn in the land of Philistia. They end with an account of the tragic death of Saul and his sons on Mount Gilboa. God was not yet ready for David to be king over Israel, so the Lord's anointed must learn several more hard lessons. Both David and Saul needed to experience the truth that the Lord blesses his faithful servants and judges those who rebel against him. David needed to trust the Lord in all circumstances. Saul must learn that the Lord is a jealous god. David needed God's unexpected grace, and he needed to learn to seek the Lord's guidance and direction in the face of the Amalekite raid. In the last chapter of 1 Samuel, the rebellious Saul would meet his Maker face to face. These were difficult lessons. By the end of 1 Samuel, the reign of Saul—the first individual to be anointed king over Israel—came to a tragic end. The reign of David, the second to be anointed king over Israel, was yet to begin.

B. COMMENTARY

1. The Flight of David (27:1–28:2)
2. The Folly of Saul (28:3–25)
3. The Predicament of David (29:1–11)
4. The Triumph of David (30:1–31)
5. The Tragedy of Saul (31:1–13)

C. CONCLUSION: GOD IS STILL GOOD, ALL THE TIME

VIII. ISSUES FOR DISCUSSION

1. In many circumstances God brings about unexpected grace. List some of the ways people in your group have experienced this type of grace.

2. Self-pity and self-centeredness often lead a person to make decisions without seeking God's direction and guidance. What are some of the ways we can avoid this?

3. When Abiathar fled from Saul, he brought an ephod into David's camp. This ritual garment was used several times by David to inquire of the Lord. Name some specific steps we can take today to ascertain God's will and direction for our lives.

4. Where does our modern culture encourage us to seek help and advice? Describe some of the subtle pressures we face to follow the ways of the world.

5. Mediums and spiritists claim to be able to consult departed loved ones. What do you think about this claim? What does the Bible say about consulting these individuals?

6. Some people believe that God is not interested in what happens in our world. The tragic death of Saul suggests that God does judge those who rebel against him. As believers we trust in the compassionate grace and forgiveness of Jesus our Lord. Does this mean that God will not judge the rebellious in our world? Name some of the ways the Bible suggests that God will judge the world in righteousness.

2 Samuel 1:1–4:12

David, King of Judah

*"*Adversity is the diamond dust with which

heaven polishes its jewels."

R o b e r t   L e i g h t o n

BIOGRAPHICAL PROFILE: ABNER

- Son of Ner the Benjaminite
- Uncle of King Saul
- Top military officer in King Saul's army
- Man responsible for making Saul's son Ish-Bosheth king following Saul's death
- Murdered by King David's top military officer, Joab

BIOGRAPHICAL PROFILE: ISH-BOSHETH

- Fourth son of King Saul
- Also known as Ishvi (1 Sam. 14:49) and Esh-baal (1 Chron. 8:33)
- Became king of Israel and a rival to King David after his father died fighting the Philistines
- Murdered by Baanah and Rechab

GEOGRAPHICAL PROFILE: HEBRON

- An ancient city located in the Negev 19 miles south of Jerusalem
- Nearest city to where Abraham buried his wife Sarah
- Given to Caleb as a reward for his faith-filled work as an Israelite spy during Israel's wilderness wanderings (Josh. 14:9–13)
- Became a city of refuge where people guilty of manslaughter but not murder could reside (Josh. 20:7)
- Used by King David as his first capital city

2 Samuel 1:1–4:12

2 Samuel 1:1–4:12

IN A NUTSHELL

As civil war breaks out in Israel, David seeks God's leadership in difficult times and uses God-given resources to take control of the nation. David acts wisely to lead his people to national unity through a seven-and-one-half-year period marked by a lengthy civil war and the murders of key Israelite leaders.

David, King of Judah

I. INTRODUCTION

From Store Clerk to Super Bowl Champion

*N*o one who knew Kurt Warner in the early 1990s at the University of Northern Iowa would have predicted that he would be picked as the most valuable player of Super Bowl XXXIV less than ten years later. But he was. On January 30, 2000, quarterback Kurt Warner completed 24 passes for 414 yards and two touchdowns, leading the St. Louis Rams to their first-ever Super Bowl championship.

Though Kurt played on Northern Iowa's varsity football squad for four years, he did not become a starter there until his senior year. In his final year at the university his true talent for football began to sparkle, however, as he was named the Gateway Conference player of the year. Warner tried out after graduation for a position with the Green Bay Packers, but was cut from the team before the regular season began. Needing income, he got a job stocking shelves at a grocery store. It seemed his hopes for a professional football career were over.

But his dreams did not die. Looking for something connected with professional football, Warner signed a contract in 1995 with the Iowa Barnstormers, an Arena League football team. He continued to play with that team through the 1997 season, twice being named as the first team all-Arena League quarterback.

His talents caught the attention of the St. Louis Rams in 1998, and they gave him a contract, assigning him to play in NFL Europe with the Amsterdam Admirals to gain playing experience and skill. Returning to the United States for the 1999 season, he was the Rams' third-string quarterback until both those ahead of him, Trent Green and Paul Justin, were injured. The Rams' head coach Dick Vermeil just wanted Warner to help the team win a game or two until Trent Green could get healthy. But Warner was determined to do more than that. He led the team to a 13–3 record and the Super Bowl championship, with a 23–16 victory over the Tennessee Titans.

Immediately after the Super Bowl victory Warner was asked the question by ABC reporter Mike Tirico, "First things first: did you say anything before you guys went out for that play?" Warner's immediate response was, "First things first: I gotta give the glory to my Lord and Savior up above. Thank you, Jesus!" Kurt Warner understood that the Lord was the true reason he overcame every obstacle to achieve great success.

II. COMMENTARY

David, King of Judah

MAIN IDEA: *As civil war breaks out in Israel, David seeks God's leadership and uses God-given resources to take control of the nation.*

A David Leads Israel in Mourning (1:1–27)

SUPPORTING IDEA: *After learning of the deaths of Saul and Jonathan, David executes Saul's killer and mourns the deaths of Israel's leaders in an eloquent lament.*

1:1–10. Flush with victory over the Amalekites, David and his men were now back in their hometown of Ziklag. It was a bittersweet moment for the men, however. On the one hand, they were enjoying a time of happy reunion with their recently rescued wives and children (see 1 Sam. 30:18–19). On the other hand, they were having to deal with the fact that the Amalekites had destroyed their homes when they burned Ziklag to the ground (1 Sam. 30:1).

At this complex moment in David's life a stranger came into his camp and bowed down before him, displaying symbols of grief—torn clothes and dust on his head. Realizing that the man must have critical information about the battles fought in the north between Saul and the Philistines, David asked him for details. He knew that acquaintances of his were dead as a result of the conflict in Gilboa, but were they from Philistia or Israel?

David's hopes fell when the messenger, an **Amalekite** (v. 8), claimed to have come from the Israelite camp. He stated that many of the troops had fallen and were dead, including **Saul and his son Jonathan**. This report, if true, would be devastating. David pressed the man for more details. He painted a vivid account of Saul's last moments, complete with convincing details such as Saul's possession of a spear (cp. 1 Sam. 13:22; 18:10–11; 19:9–10; 22:6; 26:7–22). The Amalekite indicated that he was personally responsible for delivering the death blow to Saul, but that it was done for compassionate reasons, since Saul was already mortally wounded. Any lingering doubts about Saul's death were removed when the Amalekite showed David the **crown** that was on Saul's **head** and the **armband** that was on his **arm**.

1:11–16. Shaken to the core by the news, David and his men suspended their personal victory celebration and tore their clothes in anguish. Weeping and denying themselves food until sundown, the group mourned a national tragedy—the deaths of King Saul, crown prince Jonathan, and uncounted numbers of the Lord's people.

David then acted to right the wrong as nearly as he could. The man had admitted to killing the Lord's anointed, an act that involved the unwarranted shedding of human blood and defiance of the Lord; therefore he must himself be killed (Exod. 21:23–25; Lev. 24:19–21; Deut. 19:21). The fact that Saul's killer was also an Amalekite made it doubly necessary for him to be killed (Exod. 17:15–16; Deut. 25:17–19; 1 Sam. 15:17–18). David ordered one of his men to execute the Amalekite.

1:17–27. The climax of this opening chapter is David's Song of the Bow, a lament composed by David to mourn the death of Saul, Israel's king and David's father-in-law, and Jonathan, Israel's crown prince who was also David's brother-in-law and best friend. This song is a lasting tribute to Saul and Jonathan, remembering key contributions these people made to the nation of Israel. At the same time the song is a tribute to the character of David. It shows David rising above all the vicious attacks that Saul had mounted against him.

The theme of the song is repeated three times in the emotion-laden phrase, **How the mighty have fallen!** Saul and Jonathan are remembered as the **glory** of **Israel** (v. 19) who were heroic in battle (v. 22), being swifter than eagles and stronger than lions (v. 23) in defending their nation. They were loved by their countrymen (v. 23), in part because Saul had created conditions that enabled the women of Israel to be clothed with luxurious garments and adorned with gold ornaments (v. 24).

On the personal level David mourned especially for his beloved friend Jonathan, whose love for David was **more wonderful than that of women** (v. 26). David did not suggest that a homosexual relationship had existed between the two of them. Rather, he reflected the social realities of ancient Israel. Women were not men's social peers, and men would never be expected to have women—even their own wives—as best friends or close confidants. Wives were partners in sexual fulfillment, procreation, and child-rearing, but a man's closest friends were other men.

B David Is Anointed King of Judah (2:1–7)

> **SUPPORTING IDEA:** David is anointed king over Judah, and he establishes Hebron as his capital city. He also begins efforts to gain control over all Israel.

2:1. With Saul and Jonathan now dead, it was appropriate that David, the man anointed by Samuel as Saul's successor (1 Sam. 16:12–13), return to

Israel to claim the throne. First, however, it was necessary to confirm the Lord's will in the matter. This was probably accomplished with the assistance of Abiathar using the Urim and Thummin contained in the ephod (1 Sam. 23:9–12; 30:7–8; Exod. 28:30). Under the Lord's direction David returned to **Hebron**, a prominent city in southern Israel.

Hebron was an especially good choice for at least three reasons: (1) it was a city of refuge (Josh. 20:7), (2) it was located in the tribal territory of Judah, and (3) it was a Levitical city. As a city of refuge, Hebron was a place where someone falsely accused of murder could find protection. This would help David, since he had been wrongly accused of crimes against Saul and his family (2 Sam. 16:7–8). As a city in Judah it was where David's support was strongest, since he himself was a Judahite. As a Levitical city reserved for Aaronic priests, it was populated by people who viewed David as a king who would protect them (1 Sam. 22:11–23).

2:2–4a. David, his two wives, and his soldiers—altogether a group that must have numbered more than a thousand (1 Sam. 30:9,22)—came to Hebron. However, because the group was so large, David's soldiers and their families stayed in the villages that surrounded the main city. Once David himself was settled in Hebron, his kinsmen **the men of Judah** anointed him as king. For the next seven years David would reign as king over his tribe even as he extended his claim to include all Israel.

2:4b–7. As the Lord's anointed and Judah's king, David's task was to extend his dominion over the entire nation of Israel. His first efforts were directed at **Jabesh Gilead**, a village in the eastern tribal territory of Manasseh. The inhabitants of this city had demonstrated the greatest loyalty to Saul and his family by retrieving the remains of the royal family members and giving them an honorable burial (1 Sam. 31:11–13). If David could win their support, it would be easier to gain the support of the rest of the nation. So he sent messengers to Jabesh Gilead to commend them with God's blessing, and to inform them that he had become the new leader over **Judah**.

Ⓒ Opposition to David Arises in Israel (2:8–3:5)

SUPPORTING IDEA: *The house of Saul reasserts its claim over Israel by installing Saul's son Ish-Bosheth as king. Ish-Bosheth's forces, under the direction of Abner, battle David's troops in the heartlands of Israel at Gibeon.*

2:8–11. David's control over the land of Israel was not uncontested. Besides the dominating presence of the Philistines over Israel's central regions, Saul's surviving relatives continued to stake their claim over the land as well. The dominant member of Saul's clan was his cousin **Abner**, Israel's top military commander during Saul's lifetime (1 Sam. 14:50). Apparently in David's fifth year as king over Judah, Abner made a major move to reassert his clan's leadership over **all Israel**. He moved Saul's only surviving son **Ish-Bosheth** across the Jordan River to **Mahanaim**—far away from the Philistines and David—and made him king over **Gilead**, **Ashuri**, **Jezreel**, **Ephraim**, and **Benjamin**. From that location Ish-Bosheth would rule for a period of **two years**. By contrast David's time as king over Judah amounted to **seven years and six months**.

2:12–16. To establish Ish-Bosheth's right to rule Israel, it was necessary for **Abner** to project military force. His efforts to do so began **at the pool of Gibeon**, within Saul's tribal territory of Benjamin. Aware of Abner's troop movements, David's general, **Joab**, responded immediately by taking David's soldiers—perhaps 600 men—out to encounter the opposing general. Gibeon was a religious center and a city where priests lived. It is possible that Joab went out to meet Abner because he feared that Saul's former general would try to wipe out priests of the Lord for supporting David, just as Saul had once done (1 Sam. 22:11–19).

The war between the house of David and the house of Saul began in an unlikely fashion—a contest between 24 men, a dozen from either side. Perhaps the hope had been initially that war could be avoided if both sides accepted the outcome of this small-scale conflict. However, the competition ended indecisively, as each man **grabbed his opponent by the head and thrust his sword into his opponent's side**, leaving no survivors. This tragic event was memorialized in the name given to the site where it took place, Field of Blades (or Field of Hostilities).

2:17–23. Vengeful passions flared, giving way to a **battle** that was **very fierce** between the forces of David and those who supported Saul's descendants. But David's men gained the upper hand in the conflict, forcing Abner and his men to retreat. Doggedly pursuing Abner was Joab's fleet-footed brother, **Asahel**. However, any showdown between the experienced fighter, Abner, and young Asahel would be a mismatch in Abner's favor. Besides his superior skills on the battlefield, Abner also carried superior weapons, including a spear. Undaunted, Asahel continued to follow after Abner. Not desiring to take the life of General Joab's brother, **Abner** encouraged the younger fighter to take whatever weapon he could obtain from some other soldier to make any encounter between them a fairer fight.

When Asahel refused to do that, Abner **warned Asahel** to **stop chasing** him, all to no avail. Asahel's superior speed soon brought him within striking distance of his opponent. Still Abner did not wish to kill his pursuer. In a defensive act, he used the blunt end of his spear to strike Asahel in the **stomach**. The spear perforated his body, and he **fell . . . and died on the spot**.

2:24–28. Undaunted—indeed motivated—by their brother's death, **Joab** and **Abishai** pursued **Abner**. They chased him as far as **the hill of Ammah**, an unknown location in the general vicinity of **Gibeon**. Abner and his forces were reinforced with local Benjamite militiamen, and together the group took their stand at the top of the hill. Though he and his men had the positional advantage, Abner did not wish to continue the fight as long as there was any chance for peace.

Abner attempted to end the fight by calling out three thoughtful questions to his adversary, Joab. He urged Joab to consider the long-term consequences of an Israelite civil war. Such a conflict would cause **brothers**—fellow Israelites—to kill each other and would result in **bitterness**. Whereas Abner's spear had struck Asahel in the stomach, his words struck Joab in the heart. So David's general **blew the trumpet**, signaling his troops to stop their advance. The day ended with a truce as Joab's forces **no longer pursued Israel**.

2:29–32. With the coming of darkness Abner and his men made their way eastward and downward **through the Arabah**. Then they made a dangerous nighttime crossing of **the Jordan** River and found their way back to Ish-Bosheth's capital city of **Mahanaim**. Joab and his troops, on the other hand, traveled southward to Bethlehem, where they buried **Asahel in his father's tomb**. From there they returned to David's capital city, **Hebron**. The casualty count for the day was high, given the relatively small size of the forces involved. David's forces lost 20 men—three percent of the 600 men David was said to have not long before (1 Sam. 30:9). However, his losses were dwarfed by the losses on the other side. Together, **the Benjamites and Abner's men** lost 360 fighters.

3:1. The conflict between **the house of Saul and the house of David** was not settled in a single battle. Rather, it was long and drawn out, apparently taking approximately two years to be settled. Nevertheless, the engagement described in 2:12–28 was characteristic of the general course of the war. As the number of battles between the groups mounted, **David** grew **stronger**, while **the house of Saul** grew **weaker**.

3:2–5. It was accepted practice for a king like David to have a harem (Deut. 17:17), even though this practice clearly departed from God's ideal of heterosexual monogamy (Gen. 1:27; 2:22–24; 1 Tim. 3:2; Titus 1:6). Harems served the practical purpose of increasing the likelihood that a male heir would be produced to succeed his father on the throne. The list found here provides the names of the six wives that David had during the Hebron phase of his kingship. Of the six women listed, four of them are not listed anywhere else in Scripture

The sons listed here are presented in the order of their birth, indicating the order in which David's sons were eligible to succeed him as king. This information provides background information useful in understanding the events associated with the stories of Amnon and Absalom in 2 Samuel 13–18, as well as the intrigues of Adonijah and Solomon in 1 Kings 1 and 2.

The list presented here differs slightly from the parallel list in 1 Chronicles 3:1–3. David's second-born son is named Kileab here, but in 1 Chronicles 3:1 he is named Daniel. Two possible explanations may be given for this discrepancy: (1) these may be two different names for the same person, as in the case of Solomon/Jedidiah (2 Sam. 12:24–25); (2) Chileab died in his childhood, and Abigail's second son Daniel was allowed to assume his brother's position in the order of succession.

Ⓓ Division Arises in Israel's Leadership (3:6–16)

SUPPORTING IDEA: *King Ish-Bosheth alienates General Abner, the power behind his throne, by accusing him of raping a member of Saul's harem. In turn Abner withdraws his support for Ish-Bosheth and takes steps to make David king of all Israel.*

3:6–7. As the two-year **war** between **the house of Saul and the house of David** progressed, it became apparent that the real power behind **Ish-Bosheth's** throne was **Abner**. Ish-Bosheth had become king because of Abner's efforts (2:8–9), and it was because of Abner's efforts that he remained in power (2:12–13). As people understood this and looked to him for leadership, Abner acquired even more power in the house of Saul. Ish-Bosheth was uncomfortable with this state of affairs, and he accused Abner of the vilest of deeds. One of the most brazen means of asserting one's claim to the throne was to have sexual relations with members of the former king's harem (2 Sam. 16:21–22), and Ish-Bosheth was convinced that his uncle had done just that.

3:8–11. Abner was **very angry** that the one living family member he had done the most to help would accuse him of such an act of disloyalty. Some commentators believe that Abner was actually guilty of wrongdoing with Rizpah, yet the logic of the situation makes it seem unlikely that anything unseemly occurred. If Abner was trying to make himself king, why did he go to David and offer to help him become king? Furthermore, the author of

1 and 2 Samuel never portrays Abner as performing any immoral or evil act. To the contrary, he is elsewhere seen to be a peacemaker (2:25–27) who served Saul faithfully (1 Sam. 20:25; 26:5) and worked diligently in behalf of David and the Lord's will (3:17–19).

If Ish-Bosheth was wrongly accusing Abner of disloyalty, then the writer of 2 Samuel was drawing an unflattering parallel between King Saul and the son who succeeded him. Both wrongly accused their most loyal and helpful military officer of treason. Perhaps it was Ish-Bosheth's troubling similarity to his father that ultimately drove Abner to support David. Whatever the reason, Abner vowed before God that he would **transfer the kingdom from the house of Saul** and establish the throne of David **over Israel and Judah**.

3:12–16. True to the terms of his vow, **Abner** initiated contact with David for the purpose of handing **all Israel** over to him. He requested that David make a covenant with him, a request to which David was favorably disposed. However, since David was the stronger party in the agreement, he would be the one to dictate the terms of the arrangement. As proof of Abner's good faith he must bring the **daughter of Saul**, who was also David's first wife, back to him. The most powerful member of the house of Saul had once taken **Michal** from David (1 Sam. 25:44), even though she had been legitimately acquired through the acquisition of **a hundred Philistine foreskins**, so it was appropriate that the leading member of the clan return her. The return of Michal to David's harem would strengthen his claim on Israel's throne, since it would clearly position him within the family of Saul, the previous king of all Israel.

Even though David had negotiated with Abner about Michal's return, it was appropriate for him to convey the formal demand to King Ish-Bosheth, who was little more than a pawn in the political power play. Undoubtedly guided by the hand of Abner, Ish-Bosheth sent someone to take her away **from her husband, Paltiel** [also known as Palti, 1 Sam. 25:44] **son of Laish**. The tragic human face of power politics is shown as this episode ends, with Paltiel following the group taking Michal back to David, **weeping . . . all the way**. He turned back only when Israel's top general, **Abner**, ordered him to do so.

Ⓔ Joab Murders Abner (3:17–39)

> **SUPPORTING IDEA:** *Joab takes matters into his own hands and murders Abner, even though Abner has pledged loyalty to David.*

3:17–19a. Having met David's demand to return his legitimate first wife, Abner then met with **the elders of Israel**, the powerful group that had been responsible for establishing Israel's first king (1 Sam. 8:4–5). Abner's words to this council show that this group had previously wanted David to be king; perhaps they had considered this option shortly after Saul's death. It was now appropriate for them to make David king of all Israel, Abner told them, because the Lord had chosen to use his **servant David** to save Israel from **the hand of the Philistines** and the power of all her enemies. This prophecy about David had not been previously revealed, though a similar one was known regarding Saul (1 Sam. 9:16). The text does not indicate the elder's response to Abner's proposal, but 2 Samuel 5:3 makes clear that his words achieved their intended effect.

Abner's final task in helping David become king over all Israel may have been the hardest of all. He had to convince members of the tribe of Benjamin, to which King Ish-Bosheth belonged, that they should change their loyalty from Ish-Bosheth to David, formerly the most wanted outlaw in the land. How he did this is unknown, but the fact is that because of Abner **the whole house of Benjamin** was agreeable to supporting David as their king.

3:19b–21. After his diplomatic successes Abner went to **Hebron** to inform David of the good news. He took along **twenty men**—many of whom were undoubtedly soldiers—to accompany him during his journey into the heartlands of those who were opposed to Ish-Bosheth's kingship.

David was delighted with Abner's visit, since he understood its implications for his career and for the nation. He treated Abner as an important visiting dignitary, hosting **a feast** for **him and his men**. Before leaving, Abner laid out for David the plan for transferring the kingship of all Israel into his hands. The two-step plan called for Abner to **assemble all Israel** together to meet with David, and then for the assembled body to **make a compact** with its new king. When this had been done, David would finally **rule over all** he desired—the land of Israel from Dan to Beersheba. After this cordial meeting, Abner was sent away **in peace**.

3:22–25. Shortly after David had dismissed Abner, **Joab returned from a raid** in which he had plundered goods from nearby enemies. Such raids were essential for David's government, since they financed his governmental operations and also cleared out groups that threatened the stability of the nation of Judah.

When David's top military commander learned that the highest-ranking military officer in Ish-Bosheth's army had just concluded a peaceful visit with David and that David had sent him away in peace, he became enraged. He refused to believe that Abner had defected and was now working to establish peaceful means by which David would gain control over all Israel.

Instead, he was convinced that Abner had actually come to **deceive** David and to spy on him. Having sized up David's defenses and fooled him about his true intentions, Abner would thus be in a position to destroy David and his forces.

3:26–27. Joab took matters into his own hands. Sending a delegation of men two miles northwest of Hebron to Sirah, Joab used false pretenses to have Abner return to David's capital city. Then, as Ish-Bosheth's general entered through the gateway, Joab **took him aside** into one of the alcoves in the **gateway**. There in the shady recesses of that structure he **stabbed** Abner and killed him. In this way Joab exacted personal revenge for the death of **Asahel** (see 2:23).

3:28–30. When David learned about Joab's vengeful act, he was infuriated. Whether or not Joab committed murder might be arguable, since Abner had indeed killed Asahel (Gen. 9:6). But what Joab had done was wrong, since the killing was committed within a city of refuge (Josh. 20:1–9). While David would not impose the death penalty on Joab at this time, he would later determine that Joab had committed murder and thus sentence him to die for the crime (1 Kgs. 2:5–6).

David distanced himself from Joab by declaring that the king and his kingdom would be **forever innocent before the** LORD in the matter of Abner's death. On the other hand, David pronounced a curse on Joab, calling for the blood of Abner to be upon Joab's head, with fateful consequences for Joab's entire clan. The plagues and disabilities David invoked upon future generations of Joab's family are reflective of the list of penalties associated with disobedience of God (Lev. 27:16, 25–26; Deut. 28:17–18, 21–22, 25). The Bible makes clear that Joab did not act independently in his efforts to kill Abner. Joab's brother, **Abishai**, was also deeply involved in the deed; perhaps he was the one who had met Abner at the well of Sirah and invited him to return to Hebron.

3:31–34. Abner was buried on the day of his death. The body was placed on a bier and carried to the burial site. His death had precipitated a national crisis that threatened to derail any hopes for a reunification of Israel. David's response to Abner's death was of utmost importance; a sensitive and sympathetic handling of the tragedy could prevent a meltdown of the reunification process. Aware of this, David acted quickly. He joined Abner's funeral procession, positioning himself behind the **bier**. But he would not be the only member of his government mourning the loss of the northern general. David also required **Joab and all the people with him** to **tear** their **clothes** and **put on sackcloth** as outward expressions of grief.

David had Abner buried with honor in the capital city of **Hebron**. Furthermore, the king publicly humbled himself by weeping **aloud at Abner's tomb**. To add dignity to the situation David drew from his reservoir of creativity and musical talent to compose and sing **a lament for Abner**. David bewailed the fact that Abner had died under tragic circumstances, an innocent man victimized by criminals. The king's efforts struck an emotional chord with all who attended the funeral, so that when David was done **all the people wept over him**.

3:35–39. Fasting was a practice in the Old Testament world often associated with grief caused by tragic loss of life (Judg. 20:26; 1 Sam. 31:13; 2 Sam. 1:12). Though many people expected David to rejoice over the death of his former enemy, the king continued to defy the expectations of his onlookers by fasting until sunset on the day of Abner's death. This act did not go unnoticed. In fact, **all the people took note** of what David did, and it **pleased them**. His sincere grief and self-denial also convinced his own troops and **all Israel**—those who were not yet under his authority—that David had played **no part in the murder of Abner**.

F Rechab and Baanah Murder Ish-Bosheth (4:1–12)

SUPPORTING IDEA: *Rechab and Baanah murder King Ish-Bosheth, and they are executed for their crime by David.*

4:1–3. When **Ish-Bosheth** learned of Abner's untimely death, he **lost courage**. Though Abner was now dead, Ish-Bosheth still had other military commanders. Among them were **Baanah** and **Rechab**, whose job it was to lead **raiding bands** against Israel's enemies. Those military excursions had helped to finance the kingdom's expenses and played an invaluable role in supporting the government. These two men were Benjaminites and should have been loyal to Ish-Bosheth; in reality, however, they were treacherous scoundrels who would soon betray him.

4:4. Among Ish-Bosheth's relatives was a nephew named **Mephibosheth**, the only **son** of Ish-Bosheth's brother, **Jonathan**. Mephibosheth, also known as Merib-baal (see 1 Chron. 8:34; 9:40), was **lame in both feet** due to a tragic accident during his early childhood. At the time of his father's death (1 Sam. 31:2) there was a very real fear that the Philistines would continue their advances southward from Mount Gilboa to Israel's then-capital city of Gibeah. Members of the royal family were evacuated from the area to preserve an heir to the throne. As Mephibosheth's nurse **picked him up and fled** she fell, with the result that he **became crippled**. This childhood injury afflicted him for the rest of his life (2 Sam. 9:3; 19:26).

4:5–7. After one of their raids, the trusted military leaders **Baanah** and **Rechab** came to Ish-Bosheth's house in Mahanaim on the pretext of getting some **wheat**. They came to the royal residence during **the heat of the day**— following the noon meal at the time of day when many people, including the king, were taking their siesta. At this unguarded moment the two men entered the king's bedroom, **stabbed him in the stomach**, and **killed him**. Baanah and Rechab's motive for murdering Ish-Bosheth became clear when they beheaded him, then transported his severed head by **night** on the desolate **way of the Arabah** to Ish-Bosheth's rival. They were hoping for David to reward them for helping to clear his way to the throne of all Israel.

The repetition of the genealogy and hometown of these two men (see v. 2) accomplished two purposes: (1) it reinforced the fact that the men who killed Saul's son were Benjaminites, members of Ish-Bosheth's own tribe, and (2) it underscored the fact that both David and the Gibeonites, a non-Israelite group that had reasons to take unauthorized revenge on Saul's family (2 Sam. 21:1–6), were not involved in Ish-Bosheth's death.

4:8–12. Baanah and Rechab mistook David's perception of Ish-Bosheth and his father, Saul. They believed that David wanted to take vengeance **against Saul and his offspring** and that he considered Ish-Bosheth an **enemy**. David did not consider Ish-Bosheth an enemy; rather, he understood him to be **an innocent man**. If David had wanted to take vengeance on Saul, he would have done it years before when he had opportunity to do so (1 Sam. 23:3–4; 26:7–11).

David ordered his soldiers to kill Rechab and Baanah. By this action he was enforcing the covenantal law of God (Num. 35:31) and fulfilling his responsibility as king over God's covenant people. By cutting off the **hands and feet** of Baanah and Rechab David was dishonoring their corpses, particularly the parts most instrumental in committing the crime. Hanging their remains identified them as cursed individuals under the judgment of God (Deut. 21:22–23).

> **MAIN IDEA REVIEW:** *As civil war breaks out in Israel, David seeks God's leadership and uses God-given resources to take control of the nation.*

III. CONCLUSION

Cromwell's Conquering Faith

In the early 1600s Oliver Cromwell was a wealthy landowner in the English shire of Essex and a member of Parliament. He was also a man with problems; he suffered from severe depression and had a dispute with other landowners in his area that ultimately caused him to sell his property and move to another part of England.

Though raised in the Puritan tradition, his faith did not play a central role in his life until he was almost 40. In 1638 Cromwell had a Christian conversion experience that changed his life. As he wrote in a letter that year, he had been "the chief of sinners," but because of God's work in his life had become part of "the congregation of the firstborn." From that point on his desire to do the work of God would motivate his life.

Cromwell's faith was put to the test in 1640 when King Charles I reconvened Parliament to try to raise money to fight the Scottish Presbyterians. Scotland had resisted the king's attempt to force it to follow the practices of the Church of England. Cromwell and other Puritans disagreed with the king's religious and military intentions and refused to grant him his wishes. When in 1642 King Charles I attempted to arrest five Puritan members of Parliament for treason, the stage was set for a civil war in England that pitted the king, his wealthy supporters, and the Anglican clergy against the Parliament, the Puritans, and their supporters among the nation's merchants.

Oliver Cromwell joined the parliamentary army and recruited a troop of cavalrymen to serve under him. Though never formally trained in the art of warfare, he and his troops gained valuable experience in a series of battles over the next year and a half.

A turning point in Cromwell's career occurred on July 2, 1644, at the battle of Marston Moor. This battle revealed not only Cromwell's battlefield skills but also his deep Christian faith. In the conflict Cromwell led his cavalrymen to a smashing defeat of horsemen led by Charles I's son, Prince Rupert. Then, seeing that the parliamentary army's infantrymen were in trouble in the same battle, he redirected his horsemen to come to their aid. As a result of his efforts, the king's forces experienced total defeat. Charles I lost his army, and Queen Henrietta Maria was forced to flee to France. Later Cromwell went on to become the lord protector of England, Scotland, and Ireland.

In a letter shortly after the battle, Cromwell expressed his deep Christian faith. He wrote, "Truly England and the Church of God have had a great favor from the Lord, in this great victory given unto us, such as the like never was since this War began. . . . Give glory, all glory, to God." Oliver Cromwell faced many trials in his military and political career, but God carried him through them all. He eventually became one of England's most famous leaders.

PRINCIPLES

- It is appropriate for God's people to honor those who have died defending their country.
- Nations need strong leadership from godly people during times of national tragedy.
- Diplomacy and negotiation are always preferable to violence in healing a divided nation.
- Crimes committed in the name of political gain must be punished as sternly as those committed for other reasons.

APPLICATIONS

- Write a note to the family of a recently deceased friend or acquaintance. Express your appreciation for the life this person lived, and include a word of encouragement based on God's Word.
- Help your church or home Bible study group develop an outreach to families in your community who have a family member in the military on assignment outside the United States.
- Make a list of the political leaders of your nation, state, and community. During the next week pray each day that God will help and protect them as they face difficult circumstances.
- Direct your Sunday school class or home Bible study group to have a special prayer for the nation's military and its leaders. Pray that God will give them great wisdom, skill, and success in defending our nation.

IV. LIFE APPLICATION

Race Car Revenge

In 1979 the noted NASCAR driver Richard Petty was in a slump. He had lost 45 races in a row. However, the losing streak ended at the Daytona 500 that year in a most unexpected way. On the last lap of the race Petty was in third place, more than half a lap behind leader Donnie Allison and Cale Yarborough. Before that final lap could be completed, however, Yarborough attempted to make a "slingshot" pass around Allison. Allison refused to let him by, forcing Yarborough's car to drive partially onto the muddy infield grass. Yarborough lost control of his car and bumped Allison.

The two leaders then began deliberately bumping each other, with the result that they locked together and crashed against the outside wall. Their cars ended up in the infield grass and never crossed the finish line. As a result, Richard Petty won. Because of their desire for revenge, both Donnie Allison and Cale Yarborough lost the opportunity to win the race.

Allison and Yarborough could have learned a lesson about revenge from Joab in this section of 2 Samuel. Joab's raging anger against Abner caused him to destroy not only Abner's career but later his own as well. By contrast, David forgave Saul for the vengeful acts committed against him and left revenge in God's hands. The Lord's words, "It is mine to avenge, I will repay" (Deut. 32:35), are just as applicable today as they were in David's time.

V. PRAYER

Lord, we want to do great things for you, to fulfill your perfect plan for our lives. Grant us the strength and endurance to persevere, the sensitivity, patience, and wisdom necessary to work effectively with others, and the commitment to justice needed to maintain personal integrity. In Jesus' name. Amen.

VI. DEEPER DISCOVERIES

A. Who Actually Killed Saul? (1:5–10)

The Bible suggests that three different individuals or groups delivered mortal wounds to King Saul: the Philistines, Saul himself, and an unnamed Amalekite. The first deadly blows were delivered by Philistine bowmen as they mounted an attack on Saul's position on the heights of Mount Gilboa (1 Sam. 31:3). Saul knew that his death was imminent and that Philistine chariots were rapidly approaching. Wishing to deny the enemy an opportunity to torture him and then deal the final death blow, Saul tried to kill himself by falling on his own sword (1 Sam. 31:4). However, it seems that he was too weak or wounded to take his own life (2 Sam. 1:6,9). Thus, when he saw the Amalekite nearby he pleaded with him to deliver the killing blow. The Amalekite did so, and thus became the final person involved in Saul's death.

B. Why Did Israelites Tear Their Clothes When Someone Died? (1:11)

A custom in Israel was for people to tear their clothing as an outward expression of grief. The grief could be caused by the death of a loved one (2 Sam. 1:11; 13:31) or by some other distressing circumstance (Gen. 37:29,34; 44:13; Num. 14:6; Judg. 11:35). The Bible never explains why it was done, but the custom seems to have been borrowed from surrounding cultures (see Job 1:20).

Scholars suspect that in ancient pagan cultures the practice began in an effort to help people close to a death or tragedy disguise themselves. They apparently believed that an evil spirit or god had caused the trouble and that it would attack them if it recognized them. Thus, the survivors would tear their clothes. They might also throw dirt on their heads and perhaps even cut themselves.

We have no reason to suspect that the Israelites believed they were protecting themselves from demonic forces by tearing their garments any more than we suspect Christians of secret paganism by having a Christmas tree in their house at Christmastime.

VII. TEACHING OUTLINE

A. INTRODUCTION

1. Lead Story: From Store Clerk to Super Bowl Champion
2. Context: During a time of national chaos following the death of Israel's first king, Saul, David returned to the land to provide leadership for God's people. Starting with the tribal territory of Judah, David used both military means and peaceful negotiations to expand his control over the land.
3. Transition: Effective leadership requires an array of qualities coming together in one person. Among those qualities are courage, faith,

wisdom, integrity, and the ability to act decisively. God blessed the nation of Israel by providing it with that rare individual, David, who had all the qualities needed to help it through a difficult period in its history.

B. COMMENTARY

1. David Leads Israel in Mourning (1:1–27)
2. David Is Anointed King of Judah (2:1–7)
3. Opposition to David Arises in Israel (2:8–3:5)
4. Division Arises in Israel's Leadership (3:6–16)
5. Joab Murders Abner (3:17–39)
6. Rechab and Baanah Murder Ish-Bosheth (4:1–12)

C. CONCLUSION: RACE CAR REVENGE

VIII. ISSUES FOR DISCUSSION

1. Was it right for David to kill the Amalekite, since the Amalekite had just assisted Saul in taking his own life?
2. David tore his clothes, fasted, and composed a song to show his respect for friends who had died. What are appropriate ways for Christians today to remember those who die?
3. Joab killed Abner out of revenge. Do you have someone you would like to take revenge against? What does the Bible say about how you should treat that person?

2 Samuel 5:1–6:23

David, King of All Israel

"*A* leader, once convinced that a particular course of

action is the right one, must be undaunted when the going

gets tough."

R o n a l d   R e a g a n

BIOGRAPHICAL PROFILE: UZZAH

- The son of Abinadab
- From Baalah of Judah
- One of two men who helped to guide the cart carrying the ark of God from Baalah to Jerusalem
- Died when he touched the ark to steady it after the oxen stumbled

BIOGRAPHICAL PROFILE: MICHAL

- Youngest daughter of King Saul
- Given as a wife to David when he killed 200 Philistines
- Helped David avoid being murdered by her father
- Taken away from David by her father, given to Paltiel as a wife
- Given back to David as a wife by Abner
- Died childless

GEOGRAPHICAL PROFILE: CITY OF DAVID

- Originally a Jebusite city located on the border between the tribal territories of Judah and Benjamin
- Originally named Jerusalem; also known as Jebus (Judg. 19:10), Salem (Ps. 76:2), and Zion (2 Sam. 5:7)
- Captured by King David, renamed after him
- Located on the southeastern hill of old Jerusalem

2 Samuel 5:1–6:23

IN A NUTSHELL

As king over all Israel, David took three steps to stabilize and take control of the nation. First, he established a new capital city in a more central location. Second, he defeated Israel's biggest foe, the Philistines. Finally, he moved the ark of God to Jerusalem.

David, King of
All Israel

I. INTRODUCTION

A New Way Down the Hill

*J*ean-Claude Killy was born into a family of skiers and began skiing at age three. From his earliest days he showed real promise as a skier, and by the time he was eighteen in 1961 he was a senior member of the French national ski team. Killy trained hard on the slopes with his fellow team members during the day and then ran sprints and lifted weights in the evenings. But since the other team members did the same thing, Killy was unable to gain an advantage over his peers.

Jean-Claude soon realized that to become the leading member of the team he would have to try ski-racing techniques never before used by others. Instead of skiing downhill with his legs together, he spread them apart for greater stability; instead of leaning forward, he leaned backward as he went. Killy's innovations, combined with his talent and hard work, enabled him to become the most famous and successful skier of the 1960s. In 1966–1967 and then again in 1967–1968, he won the World Cup trophies. In the 1968 Winter Olympics held at Grenoble, Switzerland, Killy climaxed his career by winning three gold medals—in the downhill, slalom, and giant slalom events.

What created the winning edge in Killy's life? His willingness to confront the challenges that others had met before him, but to do it in new and creative ways. In doing this Killy was following the example of King David. Many centuries before the famous French skier's career began, David attempted an often-tried feat—the conquest of the Jebusite city popularly known as Jerusalem—but in a new way. When David combined innovative ingenuity with God-given skill and determination, God gave him a great victory.

224

II. COMMENTARY

David, King of All Israel

> **MAIN IDEA:** *The citizens of all Israel make David their king. He accepts his expanded role and acts immediately to unify and strengthen the nation. David succeeds by conquering Jerusalem, moving the capital city into northern territory, working peacefully with the king of Tyre, striking major blows against the Philistines, and moving the ark of the covenant to Jerusalem.*

A The Israelites Anoint David as King (5:1–5)

> **SUPPORTING IDEA:** *Following the deaths of Ish-Bosheth and Abner, the Israelites come to David at Hebron and ceremonially anoint him as king over the entire land. In doing so they are accepting God's chosen leader for their nation.*

5:1–2. The deaths of Ish-Bosheth and Abner created a crisis of leadership for the tribes of Israel outside of Judah. It did not take **all the tribes of Israel** long to conclude that David was the person to fill their need for competent leadership. Representatives from each of these tribes came to David at **Hebron** to express their acceptance of him. In their request to have him be their king, they first identified with him, noting that the Israelites and David shared a common family heritage—they were his **own flesh and blood**. Second, they noted that in earlier days David had provided them with capable leadership during their **military campaigns**. Finally, they confessed that the Lord had set David apart as the one to shepherd his **people Israel**, serving as their ruler.

5:3. Accepting their request, David **made a compact** (lit. "cut a covenant") with **all the elders of Israel** in David's capital city of **Hebron**. There he was anointed, probably by one of the priests living in Hebron. For the first time in his life David was now king over all Israel.

5:4–5. In all David ruled over some or all of the 12 tribes of Israel for slightly more than **forty years**. For the first **seven years and six months** he reigned over only the citizens of his own tribe, Judah. However, for the next **thirty-three years**, until his death at age 70, David **reigned over all Israel**.

B David Conquers Jerusalem (5:6–8)

> **SUPPORTING IDEA:** *In his first recorded act as king over all Israel, David leads his men to victory against the Jebusites, capturing the city of Jerusalem.*

5:6–8. As recorded in Scripture, David's first act as king over all Israel was to lead **his men** out of Hebron to **Jerusalem**. This city was apparently the main city of the **Jebusites**. Undaunted by the presence of Israelite forces outside their city walls, the Jebusites taunted them. They declared that the Israelites would not get into their stronghold. Furthermore, the city was so secure that **even the blind and the lame** could **ward** them **off**.

In one of the truly remarkable feats in the history of Israelite warfare, David **captured the fortress of Zion**. The account is very brief, with the result that the reader focuses on the end result of David's feat. The meaning of the name "Zion" is unknown; perhaps it was the Jebusite term for the citadel located within the walls of Jerusalem.

Many details of how David achieved this victory are not revealed. Even the method he used remains a subject of scholarly debate, mainly because of uncertainty about the meaning of the key term in verse 8 (Heb. *tsinnôr*). While most scholars accept the translation **water shaft**—perhaps a reference to the forty-nine-foot-long "Warren's tunnel" discovered by archaeologists in Jerusalem—other suggestions include "gutter" (KJV), "grappling iron" (NEB), and "dagger" (LXX).

David's statement, **The blind and lame will not enter the palace**, should not be taken literally to mean that anyone with a vision problem or a mobility problem would be barred from David's palace or the Lord's house in Jerusalem. After all, David invited lame Mephibosheth to live in the royal palace and to dine daily with the king (2 Sam. 9:13). This statement is better understood to mean that any remaining Jebusites would be banned from the royal palace or Zion.

C David Enlarges Jerusalem (5:9–12)

> **SUPPORTING IDEA:** *David enlarges the capital city and builds a palace there, aided by contributions from his newfound ally, Hiram of Tyre. It becomes evident that the Lord has established David as king in Jerusalem and blessed him abundantly.*

5:9. After conquering the Jebusites, David acted quickly to establish the newly acquired real estate as the national capital. Though Israel had defeated the Jebusites of Jerusalem on previous occasions, they had never succeeded in holding the city itself (Josh. 10:23–26; Judg. 1:8,21). Following an Israelite custom, David renamed the conquered city after himself (Num. 32:41–42; 2 Sam. 12:28).

Now that Jerusalem had become the capital of a large nation, it was necessary to enlarge the city. That was something of a challenge, since it was situated atop a narrow, finger-shaped hill. To maximize the city's usable land, David apparently constructed a series of **supporting terraces** around the edge of the hilltop, filling the area with dirt to create more level land on which to build.

5:10–11. Because **the Lord God Almighty was with him**, David's successes continued to mount. From the earliest days of his career in public service, the Lord was with him (1 Sam. 16:18). As the Lord's presence continued to abide in his life, David became **more and more powerful**.

Proof of David's impressive power in the arena of regional politics came from his neighbor to the northwest, King **Hiram . . . of Tyre**. In an apparent effort to curry the favor of David, whom Hiram perceived to be a brilliant military and political leader, a delegation was sent from Tyre that included political representatives and craftsmen. Hiram also provided David with a generous gift of **cedar logs**, Tyre's most valuable natural resource. These logs would have been especially prized for their value as beams in the construction of large, flat-roofed public buildings. In fact, Hiram's **carpenters and stonemasons** used these logs, along with limestone quarried a few miles west of Jerusalem, to build **a palace for David**. Some scholars believe that David's palace was constructed by Hiram's men during the latter part of David's reign.

5:12. David was impressed with the royal palace made for him by the Tyrian craftsmen. But the main effect of this gift was to deepen his conviction that **the LORD had established him as king over Israel**. David also recognized that God had a greater purpose in blessing him; God did it **for the sake of his people Israel**. David had been blessed so that he in turn could be a blessing to the nation.

🄳 David Acquires More Wives and Sons (5:13–16)

SUPPORTING IDEA: *As a sign of his increasing power as king over Israel, David takes more wives, and he fathers many sons after he moves to Jerusalem.*

5:13–16. Further evidence that David was increasing in power is the fact that he took **more concubines and wives** after he settled in **Jerusalem**. Besides the six sons whom David fathered in Hebron (2 Sam. 3:2–5), the writer of 2 Samuel lists 12 additional sons here and notes that daughters were also born to him. Parallel lists of sons born to David in Jerusalem include 13 names (1 Chron. 3:5–8; 14:4–6). First Chronicles 3:9 indicates that David also fathered sons by his concubines, though none of the names of those sons are supplied.

ⓔ David Defeats the Philistines at Baal Perazim (5:17–21)

> **SUPPORTING IDEA:** *God leads David to a convincing victory against the Philistines early in his kingship over Israel. Following God's leadership, David attacks and defeats them at Baal Perazim.*

5:17–18. David had once lived in Gath under the protection of a Philistine king (1 Sam. 27:1–12). When he was king of Judah in Hebron the **Philistines** still considered him something of an ally, since he was also at war with Israel's king. But when the Philistines heard that **David had been anointed king over Israel**, they knew that the one whom they had formerly counted as an ally was now their enemy. They came looking for David. He eluded them by going down to the **stronghold**—probably a reference to Zion, though it could be a southern desert location. The Philistines countered by bringing their forces to **the Valley of Rephaim**, a site about a mile from Jerusalem.

5:19–21. David did not attempt to fight the Philistines in his own strength; he looked to the Lord for leadership. It is probable that a priest helped him as he **inquired of the LORD**, just as priests had helped him in times past (1 Sam. 22:15; 23:2–6; 30:8). The Lord gave guidance to David, probably by means of the priest's Urim and Thummin (Exod. 28:30; 1 Sam. 28:6).

Obedient to the Lord's word, David went to **Baal Perazim**, a location somewhere in the Valley of Rephaim, where he defeated the Philistines. Rather than taking credit for the victory, however, David confessed that it was the Lord who had **broken out against** his **enemies**. He named that place Baal Perazim, "The Lord Bursts Out." The magnitude of Israel's victory against the Philistines is apparent in the fact that the Philistines **abandoned their idols** on the battleground. The king and his men carried them off, probably to destroy them (Num. 33:52; Deut. 7:5; 12:3).

F David Defeats the Philistines a Second Time in the Valley of Rephaim (5:22–25)

SUPPORTING IDEA: *Following the Lord's guidance, David defeats the Philistines a second time in the Valley of Rephaim. So successful is he that he strikes them down all the way to Gezer.*

5:22–24. Undeterred by David's previous success against them, the **Philistines came up** to fight again in the Valley of Rephaim. This strategic location enabled them to easily mount an attack against David and his forces in Jerusalem. Once again David **inquired of the LORD** on how best to confront the enemy.

God rewarded David's inquiry with a remarkable answer. Not only was David assured that the Lord himself would **strike the Philistine army**—thereby assuring the Israelites of victory—but he also provided David with a battle plan. The Israelite forces were to **circle around behind** the Philistines, thus cutting off their escape route back to Philistine territory. David and his men were then to prepare to fight **in front of the balsam trees**. The Lord would assist the Israelites by producing **the sound of marching** in the tops of the balsam trees. This sound would be interpreted by the Philistines as supernatural forces advancing in behalf of Israel and would strike fear in their hearts.

5:25. David did exactly **as the LORD commanded him**. This places him alongside heroic men of faith who had gone before him: Noah (Gen. 6:22; 7:9, 16), Abraham (Gen. 21:4), and Moses and Aaron (Exod. 7:6,10,20). The king was successful, striking down the Philistines **all the way from Gibeon to Gezer**, a distance of more than 20 miles.

G The Priests Improperly Move the Ark of God (6:1–11)

SUPPORTING IDEA: *David moves the ark of the covenant away from Baalah of Judah, apparently to protect it from the Philistines. He plans to move it to Jerusalem; however, the ark is transported in a forbidden way, and as a result an attending priest dies on the journey. Fearful of more acts of judgment, David halts the procession and has the ark taken to the house of Obed-Edom.*

6:1–2. After David's victories against the Philistines and his acquisition of the idols they had abandoned (5:21), it was virtually guaranteed that the Philistines would retaliate. An easy target for them would have been the ark of the covenant, located just nine miles north of Jerusalem in the village of **Baalah of Judah**, known elsewhere in Scripture as Kiriath Jearim. This location had probably served as the ark's home since the time when the Philistines had returned it to Israel after Eli's death (1 Sam. 7:1).

In an apparent effort to protect the ark of the covenant, David **brought together out of Israel chosen men**, a force numbering about **thirty thousand**, to secure the ark by moving it inside Jerusalem's protective walls. The ark, built during the days of Moses more than 400 years earlier (Exod. 25:10–22; 37:1–9), was the most sacred object of Israelite religion. It was the very throne of **the LORD Almighty** (Num. 23:21; 1 Sam. 12:12; Ps. 24:8).

6:3–5. David provided **a new cart** on which it would be transported **from the house of Abinadab** to Jerusalem. The chosen means for transferring God's sacred throne to the capital city violated divine regulations. God had directed that the ark was to be carried on the shoulders of Levites from the clan of Kohath (Exod. 37:5; Num. 4:5–6, 15). The text makes no mention of whether Uzzah and Ahio were priests. But the name Uzzah does appear in a priestly genealogy (1 Chron. 6:29), and his ancestor Eleazar had been consecrated for the task of guarding the ark (1 Sam. 7:1). Both men acted as guardians of the ark during the procession. David and the **whole house of Israel** celebrated as the ark made its way southward to Jerusalem. Festive music filled the air as the procession went down the road.

6:6–7. As the cart moved over the road, the oxen stumbled. To protect the ark, **Uzzah reached out** and grabbed it. This act was a violation of God's command not to touch the ark, and the penalty for breaking it was death (Num. 4:15). This **irreverent act** produced immediate consequences: God struck Uzzah down, so that **he died beside the ark of God**.

6:8–9. David was both angry and afraid (v. 9) **because the LORD's wrath had broken out against Uzzah**. The priests' mistreatment of the ark had brought down divine wrath on the Israelites and caused their king to wonder how the ark of the Lord could ever be transported to the royal city of Jerusalem. To memorialize the tragedy—and perhaps to serve as a warning for other priests who might dare to break the Lord's law—David named the location of Uzzah's sinful act **Perez Uzzah**, meaning "Uzzah's breach" or possibly "The outbreak against Uzzah."

6:10–11. God's act of judgment led David to set aside his plan—at least for a time— to bring **the ark of the LORD** to Jerusalem. Perhaps he feared that some future priestly breach might bring fatal judgment against Israel's new capital. So instead of continuing the procession to Jerusalem, David took the ark to **the house of Obed-Edom the Gittite**. Obed-Edom was a Levite who would later become a gatekeeper for the temple in Jerusalem (1 Chron. 15:18). For a period of **three months** the ark remained in the house of Obed-Edom. During all this time, **the Lord blessed him and his entire household.**

▣ The Ark Enters Jerusalem (6:12–19)

SUPPORTING IDEA: *David brings the ark of the Lord from Obed-Edom's house to Jerusalem, taking care to do so in accordance with God's guidelines. Dressed as a priest, David leads the joyous procession. Once the ark is inside the city, sacrifices are offered and generous gifts of food are provided for everyone in attendance.*

6:12–13. When David received a report that the Lord had **blessed the household of Obed-Edom** because of the ark of God, he decided to make a second attempt to bring it to **the City of David.** The king was confident that if the ark could be a source of blessing for one family, then it could become a source of blessing for an entire city and the nation it represented. Thus the event was a cause for **rejoicing.**

The question was, How could the ark be moved properly? The answer was to move it in accordance with divine guidelines. It must be carried on the shoulders of Levites from the clan of Kohath, being transported with poles to avoid touching the sacred object itself (Num. 4:6,15). These guidelines were implicitly followed, since the text notes that men **were carrying the ark of the Lord.** As a symbolic dedication of the entire journey from the house of Obed-Edom to Jerusalem, David had the men stop after they had carried the ark **six steps** so that **a bull and a fattened calf**—very costly sacrifices—could be made to God. This "Sabbath rest" symbolically sanctified the remainder of the undertaking (Gen. 2:2–3).

6:14–15. David had prepared himself for the joyous occasion by putting on **a linen ephod,** a garment generally associated with the priesthood (Exod. 28:4; Lev. 8:7; 1 Sam. 2:28). This may suggest that he considered himself a priest of the Lord in the order of Melchizedek (see Ps. 110:4). Perhaps he received this title when he conquered Jerusalem, the city the priest Melchizedek had once governed (Gen. 14:18). The ten-mile journey was marked with celebrative sacred dance (Exod. 15:20; Pss. 30:11; 149:3; 150:4), with David himself leading the way. The **entire house of Israel** rejoiced with **shouts** and **the sound of trumpets,** probably sacred trumpets blown by the priests (Num. 10:2; Josh. 6:4).

6:16. David's hopes were realized as the **ark of the Lord** entered the city of Jerusalem. The king was ecstatic as it made its way down the streets of the capital city, and he expressed his joy by **leaping and dancing** before the

Lord. Michal, David's first wife and the daughter of King Saul, was not part of this significant event, even though other women were (v. 19). Not only was she physically absent from the group, she was emotionally and spiritually distant as well. Her resentment toward her husband—perhaps because of the fact that he had taken her back after Saul had forced her to live in an adulterous relationship with another man (1 Sam. 25:44)—caused her to despise **him in her heart** as she watched him in the processional.

6:17–19. In anticipation of this day, David had **pitched** a **tent** for the ark of the covenant. This structure probably resembled the one prescribed in Exodus 26:1–37. The procession reached the end of its journey as the ark was **set . . . in its place** inside the tent.

With the ark now properly situated in its new home, David offered sacrifices consisting of burnt offerings and fellowship offerings. Then he **blessed the people in the name of the LORD** Almighty and gave a food gift to **each person** in attendance. The **bread**, **dates**, and **raisins** would have helped to sustain the people as they returned to their homes after the celebration.

∎ David Confronts Opposition in His Own Home (6:20–23)

> **SUPPORTING IDEA:** *David's first wife, Michal the daughter of King Saul, criticizes David for his conduct during the processional into Jerusalem. David responds that he behaved as he did "before the Lord" and that others would honor him for it even if she didn't.*

6:20–22. David returned to his household following the celebration to **bless his household**, even as he had blessed the public assembly. But before he could enter his residence, his wife **Michal** came out to meet him. She began to berate him, accusing him of **disrobing in the sight of the slave girls of his servants**—an apparent reference to David's enthusiastic leaping and dancing. Did David actually expose himself in public? It seems highly unlikely. The text never confirms the accuracy of Michal's accusation, and if David were dressed as a priest, he would have worn a linen undergarment beneath the priestly ephod (Exod. 28:42–43).

David responded to Michal by saying that his actions were done **before the LORD**, not people. And the Lord had accepted him; he had placed his seal of approval on David by appointing him **ruler over the LORD's people Israel**. Though he was king, David was willing to **be humiliated in** his **own eyes** in his attempts to honor God. Michal might not appreciate David's public worship of God, but the **slave girls** would hold him **in honor** for what he had done.

6:23. This verse contains the last mention of Michal in the so-called "Deuteronomic History" extending from Joshua through 2 Kings. The fact that **Michal daughter of Saul** died childless would have been understood in either of two ways by the original Israelite audience. It could indicate that David dissociated himself from Michal from this point onward, or it could express the fact that God had placed a curse on her womb because of her spiritual rebellion (Deut. 28:18).

> **MAIN IDEA REVIEW:** *The citizens of all Israel make David their king. He accepts his expanded role and acts immediately to unify and strengthen the nation. David succeeds by conquering Jerusalem, moving the capital city into northern territory, working peacefully with the king of Tyre, striking major blows against the Philistines, and moving the ark of the covenant to Jerusalem.*

III. CONCLUSION

Listening Slowly

Charles Swindoll, the noted pastor, writer, and chancellor of Dallas Theological Seminary, tells of a time in his life when he had an especially busy schedule. With a demanding professional agenda, his home life suffered. If he was able to come home to eat at all, meal times would be rushed, conversations short, and tensions elevated. During one such appearance at home, his younger daughter Colleen wanted to tell him about something important that had happened at school that day. In his book *Stress Fractures* Swindoll describes what happened next. "She began hurriedly, 'Daddy, I want to tell you somethin' and I'll tell you really fast.' Suddenly realizing her frustration, I answered, 'Honey, you can tell me—and you don't have to tell me really fast. Tell me slowly.' I'll never forget her answer: 'Then listen slowly.'"

When faced with the difficult prospect of fighting a Philistine army on the march in the heartlands of Israel, David took the time to "listen slowly" to God. By listening carefully to the Lord, David found guidance that helped him turn a dangerous situation into a dynamic success for his country. In your trials in life, are you taking the time to "listen slowly" to God? He's still speaking today, and his words will make all the difference in your situation.

PRINCIPLES

- True success in life requires God's enablement and the support of key people.
- Ingenuity and determination are required to accomplish God's work in the world.
- Success in life comes from following God's direction in life.
- God will judge those who disobey him.
- Being a godly leader does not insure that one's family will also be godly.

APPLICATIONS

- Write down the greatest challenge you face in your life today. Ask God to help you discover new ways to deal with that challenge.
- Set aside an additional five minutes in your prayer time today. Instead of rushing through your prayer requests, use the additional time to rephrase your requests and to listen for answers from God.
- Pray today for the leaders of the Christian churches in your community. Pray that God will help them observe his guidelines for living.
- Each day this week pray for the spiritual health of your spouse. If you are unmarried, pray for the spiritual well-being of other members of your family.

IV. LIFE APPLICATION

The Mischievous Mate

John Wesley, the great Christian theologian, preacher, and reformer, was one of the most influential personalities in eighteenth-century England. Due in part to his busy career he waited until he was 48 years old to marry. In January 1751 Wesley married Molly Vazeille, a widow whom he greatly admired for her "indefatigable industry . . . exact frugality . . . [and] uncommon neatness and cleanness both in person . . . clothes and all things around."

However, within a month of the wedding it became apparent that the marriage would be a difficult one. When John was away speaking Molly would write him only infrequently. Later, she agreed for a time to travel with him and help out in benevolent ministries among the poor. However, she stopped doing this when she found her husband's schedule to be too exhausting. John encouraged her to be obedient to him and to continue traveling with him, but she refused. Frustrated with her husband's long periods away from home, she became increasingly resentful and angry.

After a time she expressed her frustration in hurtful ways. On one occasion she destroyed some of her husband's writings. She also began criticizing him publicly and on several occasions accused him of adultery.

When Wesley was 68 years old, his wife Molly left him, though she returned three years later. The time spent apart from each other did not restore harmony to their marriage, however. The couple eventually separated, never to see each other again. To his wife Wesley later wrote, "You have . . . increased the number of rebels, deists, [and] atheists, and weakened the hands of those that love and fear God. If you were to live a thousand years twice told, you could not undo the mischief which you have done."

Like King David, John Wesley experienced hurt and pain from a wife who was not supportive of his God-given calling. One of the most important vocations in life—and yet one easily overlooked in today's secular society—is to be the loving and supportive spouse of a person who is called into full-time service to God.

V. PRAYER

Lord, grant us the courage, ingenuity, and determination of David. Grant us also the other resources we need to meet life's daily challenges, but especially a step-by-step obedience to you that keeps us in close fellowship with you. Only in fellowship with you do we experience real success. In Jesus' name. Amen.

VI. DEEPER DISCOVERIES

A. David, the Shepherd of Israel (5:2)

One of the most powerful leadership images in the ancient Near East was that of the shepherd. Shepherds were to provide guidance for their animals, taking them over the best paths to the best places for food and water. Shepherds were also to provide protection, placing their own lives at risk if necessary to protect those under their authority. The qualities that made a man a good shepherd over flocks of livestock also made him a good leader over the people of their nation.

Before David became king he proved himself as a good shepherd. He stayed with the flock even when others had gone on to other things (1 Sam. 16:11). He attacked wild animals that threatened the flocks under his care (1 Sam. 17:34–36). Through these actions David provided convincing evidence that he had the character and qualities necessary to lead the people of God. He also served as a forerunner of the ultimate Good Shepherd, Jesus Christ (John 10:11,14).

B. Michal, a True Daughter of Saul (6:20–23)

King Saul is portrayed in the Bible as a person who disobeyed God. His failure to obey cost him his kingship (1 Sam. 16:19–23) and his dynasty (1 Sam. 13:11–14). He also had an idol/teraphim in his palace complex (1 Sam. 19:13), killed a city full of innocent priests (1 Sam. 22:6–23), and consulted a spirit to try to learn about future events (1 Sam. 28:7–19). His daughter Michal seems to have followed his spiritual example. While other women were attending a festival to honor the Lord, she stayed home. Other women were impressed with David's enthusiastic faith in God, but Michal was disgusted. Michal was a true daughter of Saul.

VII. TEACHING OUTLINE

A. INTRODUCTION

1. Lead Story: Finding a New Way Down the Hill
2. Context: David's fitness to serve as the leader of all Israel became apparent as he used his creativity and military skill to conquer Jerusalem and make it the nation's new capital. Turning back a Philistine challenge on the battlefield by carefully following the Lord's instructions, David provided the nation with stability. His efforts to strengthen the nation by uniting Israel's political and religious centers took a giant step forward as the ark of God was brought to Jerusalem.
3. Transition: Effective leadership often requires creative thinking. Just as Jean-Claude Killy came to dominate the world of competitive skiing in the 1960s through his athletic innovations, so King David brought military success to Israel through his creative strategies on the battlefield.

B. COMMENTARY

1. The Israelites Anoint David as King (5:1–5)
2. David Conquers Jerusalem (5:6–8)
3. David Enlarges Jerusalem (5:9–12)
4. David Acquires More Wives and Sons (5:13–16)
5. David Defeats the Philistines at Baal Perazim (5:17–21)
6. David Defeats the Philistines a Second Time in the Valley of Rephaim (5:22–25)
7. The Priests Improperly Move the Ark of God (6:1–11)
8. The Ark Enters Jerusalem (6:12–19)
9. David Confronts Opposition in His Own Home (6:20–23)

C. CONCLUSION: THE MISCHIEVOUS MATE

VIII. ISSUES FOR DISCUSSION

1. In what ways should modern political leaders be like shepherds?
2. Should military leaders openly seek God's help in war today? Why or why not?
3. Does God bring judgment against religious leaders who sin against him? In what way?
4. How important is the support of a pastor's wife in the pastor's ministry? What should a pastor do if his wife does not support his ministry?

2 Samuel 7:1–29

God's Covenant with David

I. **INTRODUCTION**
Generosity Fit for a King

II. **COMMENTARY**
A verse-by-verse explanation of this chapter

III. **CONCLUSION**
God's Word Changed Everything
An overview of the principles and applications from this chapter

IV. **LIFE APPLICATION**
Awestruck yet Satisfied
Melding this chapter to life

V. **PRAYER**
Tying this chapter to life with God

VI. **DEEPER DISCOVERIES**
Historical, geographical, and grammatical enrichment of the commentary

VII. **TEACHING OUTLINE**
Suggested step-by-step group study of this chapter

VIII. **ISSUES FOR DISCUSSION**
Zeroing this chapter in on daily life

Quote

"*Oh*, that I could dedicate my all to God. This is all the

return I can make Him."

D a v i d   B r a i n e r d

2 Samuel 7:1–29

BIOGRAPHICAL PROFILE: NATHAN

- A prophet during the reigns of David and Solomon
- Initially encouraged David to build a temple to the Lord (2 Sam. 7:2–3)
- Revealed to David God's covenant of kingship with the family line of David (2 Sam. 7:11–17)
- Announced God's judgment against David for his sins against Uriah and Bathsheba (2 Sam. 12:7–14)
- Helped install Solomon as David's successor (1 Kgs. 1:11–40)
- Recorded events in the kingships of David and Solomon (1 Chron. 29:29; 2 Chron. 9:29)

I N   A   N U T S H E L L

In his zeal for God, David expressed his desire to build a luxurious temple for the Lord. After initially encouraging him to do this, the prophet Nathan received a revelation from God indicating that David must not do this. Instead God would build a dynastic "house" for David so that his family line would be the only legitimate rulers over Israel forever. From David would come One who would reign as king over the Lord's people forever. David responded with wonder, gratitude, and faith to the Lord's promise.

God's Covenant
with David

I. INTRODUCTION

Generosity Fit for a King

 *A*lexander the Great is recognized as the most successful conqueror of the ancient world. Born in 356 B.C. in Pella, Macedonia, he was the son of King Philip II of Macedon. His life was a privileged one. Reflective of this is the fact that he was tutored by the famous Greek philosopher Aristotle.

When his father was assassinated at the wedding of one of his daughters in 336 B.C., Alexander was proclaimed king of Macedon at age 20. From that time until his death in 323 B.C., Alexander would earn the title "the Great" by achieving an unequaled series of military conquests that took him from the Greek peninsula to the regions of modern Turkey, Pakistan, Afghanistan, India, Iran, Iraq, Syria, Lebanon, Israel, and Egypt. Besides spreading Greek culture and philosophy in a process known as hellenization, Alexander also acquired some new practices as well. From the Persians he acquired the practice of using gold coins to pay the mercenaries and other soldiers in his army, instead of the bronze coins that the Greeks had used.

During one of Alexander's military campaigns he met a beggar by the roadside. The shabbily dressed, hungry man asked for alms from the great monarch as he passed by. Alexander surprised those traveling with him when he threw the man several gold coins. Afterward, one of them asked the king about the incident: "Sir, copper coins would adequately meet a beggar's need. Why give him gold?" The king responded in royal fashion: "Copper coins would suit a beggar's need, but gold coins suit Alexander's giving." This report about Alexander the Great may or may not be true, but it is consistent with his other acts of lavish giving that historians can confirm.

One event of generosity in history that can be confirmed is the Lord's amazing gift of an eternal covenant with David recorded in 2 Samuel 7. God's promises to David not only blessed the nation of Israel for centuries, but they also bless us today through the work of David's ultimate royal descendant, King Jesus.

II. COMMENTARY

God's Covenant with David

> **MAIN IDEA:** *David desires to build the Lord a temple in Jerusalem. But God informs David through the prophet Nathan that he will not build the structure. Instead, God will build David a "house"—a dynasty—establishing his family line as the only one authorized to provide royal leadership for God's people, Israel. David responds to God's gracious gift with wonder and faith.*

A David Desires to Build the Lord a Temple (7:1–3)

> **SUPPORTING IDEA:** *David expresses concern over the fact that he is living in a luxurious residence while the ark of the covenant remains in a tent. The prophet Nathan encourages him to do what he thinks is right in changing this situation.*

7:1–2. Some time after David was **settled in his palace** and the Lord had **given him rest from all his enemies**, the king had a conversation with the prophet Nathan. David indicated that he was uncomfortable with the fact that the earthly throne of the Lord of the universe was relegated to **a tent** while he, a servant of the Lord, was **living in a palace of cedar**. David wanted to eliminate the disparity by building a sacred temple for God.

7:3. Nathan assumed that since the Lord was with David (1 Sam. 16:13; 18:12, 28), the king's thoughts in this matter must have been inspired by God. So he advised David to **go ahead** and carry out **whatever** he had in mind.

B God Declines David's Offer to Build a House for Him (7:4–7)

> **SUPPORTING IDEA:** *The Lord reveals to the prophet Nathan that he did not direct David to build him a temple.*

7:4–7. The same night, after Nathan had spoken with David, **the word of the LORD** came to the prophet with a response to the king's concerns. Scholars have noted that God's words to Nathan here constitute the theological centerpiece of Joshua through 2 Kings. The 197 Hebrew words in God's revelation to Nathan provide the primary justification for David's family line ruling over Old Testament Israel for more than 400 years, and they lay the foundation for the coming of the Messiah.

God's answer began in an affirming way as the Lord called David **my servant**, an acknowledgment of the king's relationship with God. The message then provided what must have seemed at first to be a dose of bad news.

Though phrased as a rhetorical question, the meaning was clear: David would not be the **one to build** an earthly **house** for the Lord **to dwell in** (see 1 Chron. 17:4). But Israel's king should not take this rejection personally. God had never **dwelt in a house** from the day he brought Israel out of Egypt right up until David's day. What's more, the Lord had never asked *any* of Israel's rulers to build him **a house of cedar**.

C God Promises to Bless David and Provide a Home for His People Israel (7:8–11a)

> **SUPPORTING IDEA:** *In a promise reminiscent of the one made centuries earlier to Abraham, God promises to make David's name great. Furthermore, he promises to protect his people Israel and to give them a home of their own.*

7:8–9. Through the prophet Nathan the Lord reminded David that he had guided the king's career from its humble beginnings to the present. Referring to himself as **the LORD Almighty**, a name that emphasizes God's power over all the forces of the universe, the Lord affirmed that he was the one who took David **from the pasture and from following the flock** to make him ruler over Israel. David's successes resulted from the fact that God had been with him **wherever** he had **gone**. God, and not David's sword, had **cut off** all his enemies from before him. And that same God would catapult David into the ranks of the great patriarch Abraham, making his name great, like the names of the **greatest men of the earth** (see Gen. 12:2).

7:10–11a. Not only would the Lord bestow blessings on David, he would also bless David's nation. True to the promise God gave to the patriarch Abraham generations earlier (Gen. 12:7; 13:14–15; 15:18–21), God would **provide a place** for his people Israel, planting them in the land so they could have **a home of their own**. With land would come justice and freedom from foreign oppressors. People would not oppress them any more. As this happened the Lord himself would give David rest from all his enemies.

D God Announces that he Will "Build a House" for David (7:11b–17)

> **SUPPORTING IDEA:** *God promises to establish a dynasty through David; from his descendants would come Israel's rulers. One of David's offspring would build a house for God, and God would establish the throne of his kingdom forever.*

7:11b–13. The heart of God's covenantal promises to David began at this point as the Lord declared that he would **establish a house**—that is, a dynasty—for David. Thus, after David's days on earth were over, the Lord would **raise up** one of David's **offspring** to succeed him. David's destiny thus contrasts sharply with that of King Saul, whose family line was virtually wiped out by the Philistines, traitorous Israelite soldiers, and the Gibeonites (1 Sam. 31:2; 2 Sam. 4:5–6; 21:8–9). God would **establish** the **kingdom** of David's son on the earth. Though David was denied the privilege of building a temple for God, his son Solomon would build a **house** to honor God's **name** (1 Kgs. 6:1).

7:14–16. The favored son of David would be granted a unique relationship with the Lord. God would be his **father**, and David's heir would be counted as the Lord's **son**. This concept is expressed later in two psalms (Pss. 2:7; 89:27) and reflects the understanding that David's royal descendant would have a unique relationship with God. Christian interpretation—based on Jesus' own self-understanding (Luke 22:70; John 10:36)—views this verse as a key prophecy relating to Jesus (Rom. 1:4; 2 Cor. 1:19; Heb. 4:14).

On the one hand, David's son would be the recipient of privileges not accessible to other Israelites. On the other hand, as God's adopted son, he would also be disciplined by God. The Lord would **punish** him when he did wrong (Heb. 12:7). God would make these punishments painful and humiliating, using **floggings** inflicted by **the rod of men**. Even so, God's fatherly love would **never be taken away** from this one, with the result that David's dynasty would not end as Saul's had. David's house and his kingdom—that is, Israel—would **endure forever** before the Lord. The concluding sentence in verse 16 restates (see v. 13) God's remarkable promise that David's **throne** would be established forever (1 Kgs. 9:5; Ps. 89:4,29,36; 132:12; Isa. 9:7; 16:5), thus confirming its certainty. These divine commitments would be celebrated in song by the Israelites (Ps. 89:4,35–36); their ultimate fulfillment would occur in Jesus Christ (Luke 1:32–33; Heb. 1:8).

7:17. Nathan spoke all these words and **this entire revelation** to David. They were arguably the most significant words God had spoken since the revelation at Mount Sinai; they would change the landscape of Israelite politics and ignite messianic hopes that would energize the people of God through the end of the biblical period. Nathan's words may have been given to the king in both an oral and written form (1 Chron. 29:29; 2 Chron. 9:29).

E David Expresses His Appreciation for God's Gracious Promises (7:18–29)

SUPPORTING IDEA: *David responds to God's promises with eloquent expressions of praise and faith.*

7:18–19. David's first reaction to Nathan's prophetic message might have been one of anger. After all, God had rejected the king's plan to build him a temple. However, as David learned of God's gracious gift that he was giving—one unparalleled since the days of Abraham (Genesis 12; 15)—he was overwhelmed with gratitude and wonder. Seeking a place of communion with God, David went into the sacred tent housing the ark of the covenant and **sat before the LORD**, and began speaking with him. This is the only time in the Old Testament where a person is said to have sat down in the presence of God.

David began his response to God just as the Lord had begun his to David—with a question: **Who am I . . . that you have brought me this far?** David was the undisputed king of Israel and the nation's greatest military hero. Yet no human achievement could justify the greatness of God's gifts to him. The Lord had transformed a small country shepherd boy into the most powerful man in Israelite society. And as if that **were not enough**, he had also promised the brightest possible **future** for the house of his servant David. None of these divine workings reflected God's **usual way of dealing with man**.

7:20–21. David provided a thoughtful response to the question he had raised in verse 18. It was not because of David or his family that God had bestowed favors on him. The real reason the king had been so blessed was that God might be glorified. It was **for the sake of** God's **word** that God had **done this great thing** and then made it known to David. That is, God was honoring the promise he had made hundreds of years earlier in the days of the patriarch Jacob. As promised, "the scepter will not depart from Judah" (Gen. 49:10). What amazed David was that God had chosen his family out of all the families of Judah for this honor.

7:22–24. The grandeur of the promise-keeping God caused David to marvel at how great the Lord is. In all the universe there is **no one** like him. Just as the Lord is without equal, so his people are uniquely favored. Israel stands apart from other nations because God has selected it for special treatment. Israel is **the one nation on earth** that God went out to **redeem as a people for himself**. Thus they were **established** as God's very own **forever**. This special treatment in Israel's behalf was given to them for the same reason that special treatment had been given to David—so God could **make a name for himself** before all the other nations of the earth.

7:25–29. David began the conclusion to his prayer of gratitude with a bold command. He ordered God to **keep forever** the promise he had made about his servant, the promise to **build a house**—i.e., a dynasty—for David. In addition, the king asked God to **bless the house** of his servant, that it might **continue forever** in his sight. David's courage to make these brash requests rested squarely on the word of God. The king knew that God's **words are trustworthy.** And since the Lord had revealed that he would build a house for him and that it would last forever (v. 16), the king found the courage to make these requests.

> **MAIN IDEA REVIEW:** *David desires to build the Lord a temple in Jerusalem. But God informs David through the prophet Nathan that he will not build the structure. Instead, God will build David a "house"—a dynasty—establishing his family line as the only one authorized to provide royal leadership for God's people, Israel. David responds to God's gracious gift with wonder and faith.*

III. CONCLUSION

God's Word Changed Everything

In the 1970s Southern Baptists began the process of producing an updated hymnal to replace the denomination's standard song book, one that had been in use since 1956. Committees composed of professional musicians, theologians, and other members of the denomination were called together to carry out the task. Their assignment was to sort through thousands of Christians hymns to find the ones most suited to Southern Baptist worship in the current generation.

One of the committees was asked to consider "I Come to the Garden," a hymn that had been very popular in the early twentieth century but had been excluded from the 1956 book. The words of the hymn's first verse and chorus are:

> I come to the garden alone,
> While the dew is still on the roses;
> And the voice I hear, falling on my ear,
> The Son of God discloses.
> And He walks with me, and He talks with me,
> And He tells me I am His own,
> And the joy we share as we tarry there,
> None other has ever known.

As the group began the discussion of the hymn, the musicians weighed in first. Their opinion: the score was not impressive. Next the theologians gave their opinion: the text was too self-centered. At this point, the fate of this "unimpressive," "self-centered" song seemed certain: it would be kept out of the new hymnal.

However, before a vote could be taken Russell Dilday, president of Southwestern Baptist Theological Seminary, quoted the words of the Twenty-third Psalm to the group: "The Lord is my shepherd, I shall not want. He leadeth me beside the still waters. He maketh me lie down in green pastures. He restoreth my soul. . . ." This brief, beloved psalm contained *seventeen* "self-centered" references.

Without further discussion "I Come to the Garden" was voted into the hymnal. As in the case of Nathan the prophet so many years earlier, when God's Word entered the situation, human courses of action were changed. God's Word made the difference.

PRINCIPLES

- A natural and healthy part of devout faith in the Lord is the desire to give him gifts that require great sacrifice.
- God's spokespersons should always be careful to listen for the word of the Lord before announcing his will for another person.
- God's spokespersons must faithfully pass along the Word of God to the intended recipients.
- The appropriate responses to blessings from God are thanksgiving and faith-filled acceptance of them.

APPLICATIONS

- Search the Bible for promises God has made that apply to your life as a Christian.
- Make a list of those promises that God has made to you.
- Go through the list and meditate on how you should respond to these promises.
- Find a psalm that expresses thanks to God for his blessings. During your private prayer time read that psalm aloud to the Lord as an expression of your thankfulness for his blessings.

IV. LIFE APPLICATION

Awestruck yet Satisfied

Perhaps the most famous Southern Baptist musician of the twentieth century was B. B. McKinney. He served on the music faculty at Southwestern Baptist Theological Seminary, became the first music editor of the Baptist Sunday School Board, and the first secretary (director) of the Southern Baptist Convention's church music department. He started composing Christian music in 1915 and throughout his career was responsible for authoring the words and music to about 180 hymns, the tunes for 185, and the texts for an additional sixteen.

One Saturday afternoon during his tenure at Southwestern Seminary, McKinney began reflecting on what God had done for him throughout history—his work as Savior, comforter, and friend. On that afternoon God's work in his life seemed immensely satisfying—more than it ever had before. At the same time, he felt equally dissatisfied with his own life. Motivated by these two conflicting streams of emotion, McKinney was moved to write one of the best-known hymns of his career, "Satisfied with Jesus." First published in 1926, the hymn has been included in every major hymnal published by Southern Baptists since that time.

As in the case of King David thousands of years ago, when B. B. McKinney took time to ponder the greatness of God's work in his life, the deepest pools of emotion in his soul began to stir. In 2 Samuel 7 David was moved to express one of the most eloquent prayers of wonder and faith in the Old Testament; McKinney's soul expressed itself in memorable music and poetry. Both men gave testimony to the presence of two vital ingredients in the life of a mature person of faith—a sense of unworthiness before God and love and devotion to the God who graciously loves and saves anyway.

V. PRAYER

Lord, like David we have built ourselves palaces of cedar while giving you nothing but a small tent within our lives. Forgive us for this. At the same time, we are awestruck at the magnificence of the gifts you have graciously given to us. Thank you for fulfilling the promises made to David so many years before. Thank you for being the One whose throne is established forever. We are especially moved by the gift of salvation provided for us through your death and resurrection. In Jesus' name. Amen.

VI. DEEPER DISCOVERIES

A. In What Locations Had the Ark Resided in a Tent? (7:6)

The ark of the covenant resided in a tent for more than 485 years, from the time the Israelites were at Mount Sinai (Exod. 40:21) until Solomon placed it in the newly dedicated temple (1 Kgs. 8:3–6), about 960 B.C. In its journey from Sinai to Jerusalem, the ark traveled to several locations throughout the land of Israel. Locations would have included Gilgal (Josh. 5:1–10), Shechem (Josh. 8:30–35), Bethel (Judg. 20:26), Shiloh (1 Sam. 3:3), and Kiriath Jearim/Baalah (1 Sam. 6:21; 2 Sam. 6:2).

VII. TEACHING OUTLINE

A. INTRODUCTION

1. Lead Story: Generosity Fit for a King
2. Context: King David fought many battles in behalf of God and Israel throughout his career. Over a period of several years he succeeded in bringing peace to the region. At the same time David had not neglected building up the nation's infrastructure; he strengthened the defenses of Jerusalem and constructed administrative buildings within the city.
3. Transition: Now that these two vital tasks had been accomplished, David turned his attention to a third challenge. He wanted to create a permanent structure for the worship of the Lord in Jerusalem, one which would replace the tent in which the ark of the covenant resided at that time.

B. COMMENTARY

1. David Desires to Build the Lord a Temple (7:1)
2. God Declines David's Offer to Build a House for him (7:4–7)
3. God Promises to Bless David and Provide a Home for His People Israel (7:8–11a)
4. God Announces that He Will "Build a House" for David (7:11b–17)
5. David Expresses His Appreciation for God's Gracious Promises (7:18–29)

C. CONCLUSION: AWESTRUCK YET SATISFIED

VIII. ISSUES FOR DISCUSSION

1. Is it okay for us to delay attempting to do great things for God until other tasks in life are finished?
2. Does God speak through other Christians today to tell us what his will is for us? Has this ever happened to you?
3. Have you thought about doing some extraordinary thing for God? If you have, did you share your idea with another Christian? What did he tell you? Did you ever actually do it?

2 Samuel 8:1–10:19

The Battles of David

I. **INTRODUCTION**
A "Stone Wall" of Faith

II. **COMMENTARY**
A verse-by-verse explanation of these chapters

III. **CONCLUSION**
The Price of Sacrifice
An overview of the principles and applications from these chapters

IV. **LIFE APPLICATION**
Be Kind to the Honeyguide
Melding these chapters to life

V. **PRAYER**
Tying these chapters to life with God

VI. **DEEPER DISCOVERIES**
Historical, geographical, and grammatical enrichment of the commentary

VII. **TEACHING OUTLINE**
Suggested step-by-step group study of these chapters

VIII. **ISSUES FOR DISCUSSION**
Zeroing these chapters in on daily life.

Q u o t e

"*W*ith God we will gain the victory, and he will trample down our enemies."

King David, after defeating the Aramean cities of

Naharaim and Zobah (Ps. 60:12)

BIOGRAPHICAL PROFILE: MEPHIBOSHETH

- Son of Jonathan
- Grandson of King Saul
- Injured his feet in infancy when a nurse dropped him (2 Sam. 4:4)
- Lived in exile east of the Jordan River following Saul's death (2 Sam. 9:4)
- Became King David's permanent guest at the royal court (2 Sam. 9:7)
- Accused of attempting to usurp David's throne, but denied it (2 Sam. 16:3; 19:26–27)

BIOGRAPHICAL PROFILE: HADADEZER

- King of Aramean city-state of Zobah during King David's era
- Was defeated by King David when David reasserted control over the western portions of the Euphrates River (2 Sam. 8:3–4)
- Sent troops to fight with Ammon against Israel, again defeated by David (2 Sam. 10:16–19)

GEOGRAPHICAL PROFILE: ARAM ZOBAH

- An Aramean city-state located in what is modern Syria
- Exact location is unknown; probably northeast of modern Damascus

---

- Israel had fought against it during the reign of King Saul (1 Sam. 14:47)
- In King David's day, Hadadezer was its king
- Went to war against Israel twice in David's time

GEOGRAPHICAL PROFILE: AMMON

- Semitic kingdom located east of the Jordan River
- Rabbah Ammon (modern Amman) was its capital city
- Lived in enmity with Israel since the days of Moses (Deut. 23:3)
- Jephthah, Saul, and David led military campaigns against Ammon (Judg. 11:4–33; 1 Sam. 11:6–11; 2 Sam. 10:1–12:31)

2 Samuel 8:1–10:19

IN A NUTSHELL

God demonstrates his special blessing on King David by helping him achieve a stunning array of military victories over his enemies on every side. Throughout his career David defeats the Philistines, Moabites, Arameans, Amalekites, and Edomites. David demonstrates his fitness to serve as God's appointed leader over his people by caring for Mephibosheth, thus fulfilling a sacred vow made to Jonathan and Saul.

The Battles of David

I. INTRODUCTION

A "Stone Wall" of Faith

*P*erhaps the second most famous Confederate general during the Civil War was Thomas Jonathan Jackson. Born in 1824 in Clarksburg, Virginia, Thomas was the third of four children born to Jonathan and Julia Jackson. Thomas's father and oldest sister died of typhoid when he was just two. His mother remarried, but Thomas's poverty-stricken stepfather disliked his stepchildren. During his seventh year of life his mother died, and the boy and his surviving siblings were sent away to be raised by uncles.

In 1842 Jackson was accepted into West Point Military Academy. Graduating seventeenth in his class in 1846, he spent the next two years serving as a lieutenant in the Mexican War. He remained in the U.S. Army until 1851, when he accepted a teaching position at Virginia Military Institute. A committed Christian, Jackson and his wife Mary organized a series of Sunday schools for blacks through their local Presbyterian church in 1855. The two of them served as Sunday school teachers for the blacks. Many of his students thought him to be overly pious and rigid in the expression of his faith, and they often made fun of him.

When the southern states seceded from the Union, Jackson did not support the effort. But when Virginia governor John Letcher ordered him to take command of five regiments of the Virginia infantry in 1861 to fight against the North, he did so. Given the rank of brigadier general, Jackson led his troops so effectively in the first battle of Bull Run in July of that year that his troops stood their ground against the Union forces "like a stone wall." From that point on, the general would be known as "Stonewall" Jackson.

During the next two years Stonewall Jackson distinguished himself as the most brilliant tactician in the Civil War and one of the greatest in American military history. He led his troops to victories at Front Royal, Winchester, Cross Keys, Port Republic, Bull Run, Antietam, and Fredricksburg.

At the same time, Stonewall Jackson was also known as one of the most outspoken Christians in the Confederate army. After one of his victories he noted, "Without God's blessing I look for no success, and for every success my prayer is, that all glory may be given to him to whom it is properly due." One of his fellow officers once asked him how he was able to stay so calm in the midst of battle. Jackson replied, "Captain, my religious belief teaches me to feel as safe in battle as in bed. God has fixed the time for my death. I do not concern myself about that, but to always be ready, no matter when it may overtake me." Stonewall Jackson died of pneumonia on May 10, 1863, a complication resulting from being shot three times in the arm by members of a North Carolina regiment in a "friendly fire" incident.

Throughout his distinguished military career Stonewall Jackson understood the truth that David knew during his lifetime: every victory is won with the Lord's help, and he alone deserves the praise for each one.

II. COMMENTARY

The Battles of David

> **MAIN IDEA:** *The Lord gives David victory over all the enemies of Israel. David acts faithfully by caring for Mephibosheth.*

David Defeats Several Enemies (8:1–14)

> **SUPPORTING IDEA:** *In keeping with God's covenant of blessing with David, the king leads Israel to victory against the Philistines, Moabites, Zobah, Aram, Edom, Ammon, and Amalek.*

8:1–2. In the course of time (lit. "after thus") after God had established his covenant with David, the Lord made good on his promise to grant Israel peace and security (7:10). God worked through David to bring about military blessings for the land. Since the days of Samson no enemy had posed a greater threat to Israel than the Philistines. They had dealt Israel major defeats during the days of Eli and Saul (1 Samuel 4; 31), but the situation changed under David's administration. He **defeated the Philistines** and **subdued them**. He also took **Metheg Ammah** from their control. The exact meaning of the phrase "Metheg Ammah" is unclear. The parallel passage in 1 Chronicles 18:1 substitutes the phrase "Gath and its surrounding villages," suggesting that it was a technical term for that prominent Philistine city.

Another of Israel's historic enemies was Moab. David also virtually eliminated this traditional enemy of Israel as a threat when he defeated them and disposed of large numbers of prisoners. In an unparalleled act of judgment on an enemy, David made the captured Moabite fighters **lie down on the ground**, then measured them off with a **length of cord**. Every two lengths of them were **put to death**, but the third length of warriors was allowed to live. This action, however unthinkable it might seem today, served the dual purpose of reducing the ranks of Moab's fighters to a nonthreatening minimum, while at the same time insuring that Moabite men would be able to produce tribute that would benefit the Israelites.

8:3–8. After David had diminished Israel's most serious threats to the west and east, he turned his attention to the north. The Lord had given Israel the land from the river of Egypt to the Euphrates River (Gen. 15:18), and apparently Saul had tried to help Israel lay claim to the region (1 Sam. 14:47). Here David showed himself to be the man after God's heart by helping Israel reclaim possession of God's promise.

David had to fight **Hadadezer** son of Rehob, king of Zobah, **when he went to restore his control along the Euphrates River**. David and his forces were amazingly successful in battle, as he captured **a thousand** of Hadadezer's **chariots, seven thousand charioteers**, and **twenty thousand foot soldiers**. Resisting the opportunity to reshape Israel's military forces into a chariot- and cavalry-based militia, David hamstrung all but a hundred of the **chariot horses**. This was in keeping with God's command, which prohibited Israel's kings from acquiring large numbers of horses (Deut. 17:16). From Hadadezer's top military officials David took their **gold shields**, and from two of the towns that were under Hadadezer's control David took a great quantity of **bronze**. The bronze was useful for fashioning military weapons.

Hadadezer's allies, the **Arameans of Damascus**, came to help him fend off David's attack. The move proved to be disastrous, as David struck down **twenty-two thousand** of them. The Arameans were so badly defeated that the Israelites were able to put **garrisons** in Damascus. They were forced to make annual payments of **tribute**—essentially heavy taxes—to David's kingdom.

8:9–12. David's dramatic success in the north produced a secondary benefit. It intimidated one of Israel's would-be adversaries, and caused them to pursue friendly relations with their southern neighbor. **Tou** [Heb. "Toi"] **king of Hamath** sent a high-level delegation led by his son **Joram** (known elsewhere as Hadoram; 1 Chron. 18:10) to David and presented him with articles of **silver and gold and bronze**.

Although David may have been tempted to enrich himself with these gifts, to do so would have caused him to violate one of God's laws (Deut. 17:17). David chose instead to dedicate these **articles** to the LORD. This practice involved him giving custody of these objects to the Levites, so that they could be used for holy purposes. These metals, like those taken from **Edom and Moab, the Ammonites and the Philistines, and Amalek**, were used later in Solomon's time to build the magnificent temple of the Lord.

8:13–14. David's international reputation increased still further after he succeeded in striking down **eighteen thousand Edomites** in the valley of Salt. Contrary to the NIV's reading here, which is based on 1 Chronicles 18:12, the Hebrew text indicates that David defeated the Arameans in this locale. "Edomites" is certainly a logical reading, since the valley of Salt is located in traditionally Edomite territory. However, it is possible that the Arameans, whose home territory was far to the north, had previously taken control of the trade route that ran through Edom in an effort to gain more wealth for themselves. Either way, David put **garrisons throughout Edom**, and he succeeded in making **all the Edomites** subject to him.

8:15–18. The Old Testament repeatedly states that God is righteous and just (Ps. 36:6; Isa. 5:16; Jer. 9:24), and he expects his people to display these same qualities (Ps. 106:3; Prov. 21:3). David proved himself to be a man after God's own heart (1 Sam. 13:14; Acts 13:22) by doing what was **just and right for all his people**.

A key to David's success in leading his people with justice and righteousness was the team of people that surrounded him. Administrators in both the military and religious dimensions of government are listed here. Heading up Israel's army throughout most of David's administration was his nephew **Joab** son of Zeruiah. **Benaiah** son of Jehoiada was over **the Kerethites and Pelethites**. The Kerethites and Pelethites are mentioned only in connection with King David's administration, and they probably functioned as David's personal bodyguard. **Zadok** and **Ahimelech**, both direct descendants of Israel's first high priest, were the nation's highest-ranking spiritual leaders. The family line of Abiathar/Ahimelech would eventually be banned from serving in Jerusalem because of their support of Adonijah in his unsuccessful attempt to make himself king of Israel at the end of David's life.

Though the NIV states that **David's sons were royal advisers** (based on 1 Chron. 18:17), the Hebrew here states that they were "priests." Perhaps they were granted that status because David considered males in his family line to be priests in the order of Melchizedek (Ps. 110:4).

Jehoshaphat was **recorder**, a position that would have put him in charge of keeping the archives of royal records and correspondence, as well as disseminating royal commands. Assisting him in the task was **Seraiah** the **secretary**.

𝕭 David Fulfills a Promise Made to Jonathan (9:1–13)

SUPPORTING IDEA: *David demonstrates his loyalty to his brother-in-law and best friend Jonathan by providing for Jonathan's son Mephibosheth.*

9:1–5. At this point in his career David had stabilized conditions for his nation in the international arena and reigned in Jerusalem as the undisputed king over Israel. Under these favorable circumstances, it was appropriate for David to fulfill commitments he had made to key members of the former ruling family. He had previously made pacts with his best friend and brother-in-law, Jonathan, and with his father-in-law, King Saul. In those agreements he had promised to maintain loyalty toward Jonathan's family (1 Sam. 20:15–17) and not to cut off Saul's descendants (1 Sam. 24:21). Now it was time to make good on these commitments.

David made a search to find out if **anyone** was **still left of the house of Saul** to whom he could show kindness for **Jonathan's sake**. At that time the foremost authority on Saul's family was a servant of Saul's household named **Ziba**, the well-to-do manager of the former king's estate. From Ziba, who lived only a few miles north of Jerusalem in the village of Gibeah, David learned there was **still a son of Jonathan**, an individual who was crippled in both feet due to an injury sustained in childhood (2 Sam. 4:4).

Jonathan's son was not living anywhere near his family estate at the time. Instead, he was living in exile east of the Jordan River. He was staying in that relatively remote area at **the house of Makir** son of Ammiel in Lo Debar. Makir would later provide vital assistance to David as well (17:27–29). When David learned the whereabouts of Mephibosheth, also known as Merib-Baal (1 Chron. 8:34; 9:40), he had him brought from Lo Debar.

9:6–7. When **Mephibosheth** arrived in Jerusalem, he was brought before David, the one who had once warred against Mephibosheth's uncle, Ish-Bosheth. The experience was probably a frightening one for him, and he approached David with respect and humility. He **bowed down** and declared himself David's **servant**, but the king set his mind at ease by making him three noble promises.

First, the king would show Mephibosheth **kindness** for the sake of his **father Jonathan**. Second, David would make him rich: he would restore **all the land** that belonged to his **grandfather Saul**. Finally, he would extend to Mephibosheth the high privilege of living at the royal palace. As David had once eaten at King Saul's table (1 Sam. 20:5), so now Mephibosheth would **always eat** at David's **table**.

9:8–12. Mephibosheth continued to express his sense of unworthiness in David's presence as once again he referred to himself as a **servant** and then called himself **a dead dog**—an uncomplimentary phrase used elsewhere as an insult or in self-deprecation (1 Sam. 24:14; 2 Sam. 16:9). He was amazed that Israel's most powerful citizen would extend such privileges to the lame grandson of a man who had tried repeatedly to kill David.

Ignoring Mephibosheth's words, David started the process of making good on his promise. Ziba, along with his fifteen sons and twenty servants, would work for Mephibosheth. They were to **farm the land** for him and **bring in the crops**, so Mephibosheth would be provided for. David himself would serve as the permanent host and caretaker for Mephibosheth, who would henceforth always eat at the king's table just like **one of the king's sons**. This arrangement allowed David to keep his promises to Jonathan and Saul, and it helped him keep his eye on the key heir to the throne of King Saul.

The apparent losers in David's decision were **Ziba** and all the members of his household, who would now have to turn over all the income of Saul's estate to another, and become the servants of Mephibosheth. But Ziba had no choice in the matter. He agreed to **whatever . . . the king** commanded **his servant to do**. Later, however, he would find a way to get back some of that property for himself (2 Sam. 16:1–4; 19:29). The infant **Mica**, known elsewhere as Micah (1 Chron. 8:34–35), would grow up to produce four sons, thus preserving the family line of David's best friend, Jonathan.

C David Conquers the Ammonites and Arameans (10:1–19)

> **SUPPORTING IDEA:** *David leads his people to victory against Israel's enemies to the north and east. This happens after the Ammonites humiliate a group of Israelite ambassadors and then mass troops from Ammon and Aram against David's forces.*

10:1–2. In the course of time (lit. "after these things") following David's act of loyalty to Jonathan and Saul, the Ammonite king Nahash died. The Ammonites had become allies of Israel following their defeat by Saul (1 Sam. 11:1–11), and David wished to show his respectful appreciation to Nahash for his submission and cooperation. So he sent a delegation to **express his sympathy to Hanun**, who was Nahash's son and the new king of Ammon.

10:3–5. The Ammonite nobles misinterpreted David's intentions in sending representatives to the Ammonite head of state. They convinced their inexperienced king, Hanun, that David had sent them to the capital city of Rabbah to **explore the city and spy it out and overthrow it.** Hanun seized David's men and ordered that they be humiliated. He **shaved off half of each man's beard, cut off their garments in the middle of the buttocks, and sent them away,** thus exposing them to public shame. In addition to this, the cutting of the beard and removal of the tassels at the corners of the garments caused the men to be in violation of the law of God (Lev. 19:27; Num. 15:38; Deut. 22:12).

When David was told about how his ambassadors had been **humiliated,** he immediately responded with concern for their welfare. To help the men avoid further humiliation, he directed them to **stay at Jericho**—the first Israelite city west of the Jordan River on the road leading to Jerusalem—until their beards had grown back.

10:6–8. The Ammonites soon realized that their disgusting actions had caused them to become **a stench in David's nostrils.** They also presumed that these actions would precipitate an armed response from David. So they hired **twenty thousand Aramean foot soldiers** from the Aramean city-states of Beth Rehob and Zobah, as well **a thousand men** from Maacah and **twelve thousand men** from Tob. The Arameans may have done this in order to provoke a war with David, hoping to break free from treaty obligations that had been imposed on them by Israel.

When David learned of the Ammonites' extensive military preparations, he ordered **Joab** to march to Rabbah Ammon with the **entire army of fighting men.** Even so, the Israelites found themselves at a great disadvantage when they arrived, because the enemy had already positioned itself for the battle. The Ammonites came out of their fortified city and **drew up in battle formation** at the entrance to their **city gate.** The mercenary forces from Aram were **by themselves in the open country,** poised for a classic two-front battle designed to wipe the Israelites out.

10:9–12. Joab discovered how perilous the situation was for his troops when he saw that there were **battle lines in front of him and behind him.** So he selected some of the best troops in Israel and **deployed them against the Arameans.** Perhaps he thought the Arameans would be easier to defeat, since they were not defending their own soil. By attacking them with Israel's finest soldiers, the Aramean threat could be quickly eliminated, and Israel would then be free to use all of its army against the Ammonites.

Joab then put the rest of the men under the command of **Abishai his brother** and deployed them **against the Ammonites**. The two groups were separated with the understanding that if the Arameans proved too strong for Joab's fighters, then Abishai's troops would withdraw from the Ammonites and rescue him. And if the Ammonites were too strong for Abishai, then Joab's troops would come to rescue him.

10:13–14. Joab and his troops advanced to **fight the Arameans** in the open fields surrounding Rabbah Ammon. As the Israelites charged, the mercenary Aramean troops fled before them. Joab's success against the Arameans did not go unnoticed by the Ammonite troops that were situated near the top of the hill on which Rabbah was situated. When they saw that the Arameans were fleeing, they retreated from Abishai and went inside their fortified capital city. Having diminished the threat of an invasion of Ammonites and Arameans, Joab returned to Israelite territory across the Jordan River, soon arriving back in **Jerusalem**.

10:15–18. After the Arameans saw that they had been disgracefully **routed by Israel**, they **regrouped**. They stood to gain much from a victory over David, since they were forced to bring annual tribute payments to David due to a previous defeat (8:6). The Aramean king **Hadadezer** made diplomatic arrangements to have additional Arameans brought from beyond the Euphrates River to create a formidable force against Israel's army. Hadadezer's capable general, Shobach, then led the Aramean troops to **Helam**, a city about 30 miles east of the Sea of Galilee.

When David learned about this, he responded with massive force. He gathered together the military reserves of **all Israel**, crossed the Jordan River, and went to **Helam**. The Arameans were ready for him as they **formed their battles lines** to attack their foe. But they were no match for David. The Israelite forces turned the encounter into a bloody massacre as they killed **seven hundred . . . charioteers** and an additional **forty thousand** foot soldiers.

10:19. The outcome of the battle could not have been more disastrous for Hadadezer. In addition to the huge loss of life, all the kings who had been his vassals now **made peace with the Israelites and became subject to them**.

MAIN IDEA REVIEW: *The Lord gives David victory over all the enemies of Israel. David acts faithfully by caring for Mephibosheth.*

III. CONCLUSION

The Price of Sacrifice

The Vietnam War was an extremely difficult military turbulence for the United States. It created much conflict within American society; it also created heroes who will be remembered with honor in the annals of American military history.

One such hero was created February 10, 1970, during a nighttime ambush operation in the Phuoc Long province of Vietnam. Twenty-one-year-old John Baca, a Specialist Fourth Class serving with the 1st Cavalry Division of the U.S. Army, was part of a nine-man patrol on duty when an enemy attack began. Another patrol from his unit moved forward to respond to the enemy, but they came under heavy fire and needed help. Baca led his patrol to a firing position in his patrol's defensive perimeter. As the men prepared to engage the enemy, a fragmentation grenade suddenly landed in the midst of their position. Reacting instantly, Baca removed his helmet and placed it on top of the unexploded grenade. Then he covered the helmet with his own body. Baca was injured, but the eight other members of his patrol were saved. For his "conspicuous gallantry and intrepidity in action at the risk of his life above and beyond the call of duty," John Baca received the Congressional Medal of Honor on June 15, 1971.

Many years before the Vietnam War, David and Jonathan had established a covenant of loyalty with each other. David promised to provide lifetime care for Jonathan's family if the need ever arose. In this section of Scripture, King David demonstrated the sterling nature of his character and his willingness to sacrifice for a comrade, no matter what the price.

PRINCIPLES

- True success in life comes from the Lord, even though it may be achieved through much human effort.
- Giving God a portion of one's material gains in life is always appropriate.
- Fulfilling a commitment made to another person is a great virtue and reflects God's nature.
- Bringing shame or humiliation on others will lead to conflict.
- Teamwork is needed when confronting big challenges.

APPLICATIONS

- Make a list of the three most important people in your life. Beside each name list the three most important commitments you have made to them.
- Using the list you have just made, pray that God will help you have both the will and the resources to fulfill the commitments you have made to these people.
- During a quiet time this week ask God to bring to mind family members or work associates you have accidentally or purposely insulted or humiliated. Ask the Lord to forgive you for hurting these people. Then ask the offended people to forgive you.
- Make a list of major challenges confronting family members or work associates who are close to you. Consider ways you could help them face the challenges they confront.

IV. LIFE APPLICATION

Be Kind to the Honeyguide

The story is told in Zulu society of a greedy man named Gingile who wanted some honey. He knew that the easiest way to get what he wanted was to follow the flight of a honeyguide bird. This bird, which loves to eat beeswax and honeybee larvae, has the uncanny ability to locate trees with beehives hidden inside their trunks. It welcomes hunters who help it get the wax and insects and who will lead them to the hidden hives.

Gingile followed a honeyguide bird named Ngede to a wild fig tree. When Ngede stopped there, the Zulu hunter carefully climbed the tree. Sure enough, a large beehive was in its trunk. Gingile built a fire and placed a smoking stick in the hollow trunk of the tree to drive away the bees. After the bees left, the hunter took a large amount of honey and beeswax from the trunk, but he gave none of it to the bird that had been so helpful to him.

After that honey had all been eaten, Gingile wanted more. Once again he found Ngede the honeyguide bird and followed it on its daily flight through field and forest. Ngede knew what greedy Gingile was doing and remembered how the hunter had wronged him before. So on this day the bird carefully selected another tree for Gingile to climb. When the bird stopped in a particular tree, the man eagerly climbed it, not realizing that a leopard was resting on a branch above. The leopard slashed the hunter and knocked him to the ground. This Zulu hunter paid a hefty price for having wronged the helpful bird.

Like Gingile the Zulu warrior, Hanun's mistreatment of those who were kind to him led to a disastrous confrontation that created scars—in Hanun's case, great damage to his nation. He learned the hard way the importance of treating others right.

V. PRAYER

Lord, teach us how to work together with other Christians to overcome those threats in life that would overwhelm us and hinder your work in the world. Thank you for being faithful in fulfilling the commitments you have made to us. Help us take seriously the commitments and promises we have made to others. In Jesus' name. Amen.

VI. DEEPER DISCOVERIES

A. Dogs in Ancient Israel (9:8)

When Mephibosheth wished to display proper humility before King David, he called himself "a dead dog." The attitude that ancient Israelites had toward dogs was very different from that of modern Americans. In our culture dogs are often considered beloved members of the family—perfect pets for the kids and loyal companions for the elderly. But in the culture of ancient Israel, dogs were despised. Packs of wild dogs would attack flocks of sheep and goats, destroying families' sources of milk, meat, and fiber. In addition, dog packs threatened the safety of people in the streets of unwalled villages throughout the land.

B. The Importance of a Man's Beard in Ancient Israel (10:4)

In ancient Israel every adult male was expected to have a full beard. Men were forbidden from trimming the edges of their beards (Lev. 19:27). The only exceptions to this were in connection with a religious vow (Num. 6:9), for medical evaluation (Lev. 13:33), or during a time of distress or mourning (Ezra 9:3; Job 1:20). To forcefully shave a man's beard—or worse, to shave only half of it—was considered a supreme insult. To insult an ambassador in this way was considered an affront to the nation they represented, and thus an act of war.

VII. TEACHING OUTLINE

A. INTRODUCTION

1. Lead Story: A "Stone Wall" of Faith
2. Context: These chapters serve as the logical sequence to the previous unit of material; in chapter 7 the Lord declared King David to be the founder of the family line through whom he would lead and bless the nation of Israel. Chapters 8–10 demonstrate the wisdom of God's decision by portraying David as the king who led Israel to victory against every enemy and embodied the highest ideals in his conduct as he carefully followed God's laws.
3. Transition: The great Civil War general Stonewall Jackson, like many other prominent leaders throughout history, recognized that success on the battlefield and in other areas of life is ultimately the work of God. In this he placed himself in the tradition of King David, who won great victories but also recognized the Lord as the true source of his success in leading the nation of Israel.

B. COMMENTARY

1. David Defeats Several Enemies (8:1–14)
2. David Fulfills a Promise Made to Jonathan (9:1–13)
3. David Conquers the Ammonites and Arameans (10:1–19)

C. CONCLUSION: THE PRICE OF SACRIFICE

VIII. ISSUES FOR DISCUSSION

1. In what ways did Israel's treatment of conquered nations differ from America's treatment of nations it helped to defeat in war? Were David's actions meant to set a precedent for future nations to follow?
2. David dedicated to God the gold, silver, and bronze that he acquired from the nations he conquered. What should we give to God from the gains we experience in life?
3. David fulfilled a commitment to his best friend Jonathan by taking care of Jonathan's son Mephibosheth after Jonathan died. If you have younger children, have you arranged for someone to care for them if

you and your spouse were to die? If so, why did you choose that person?

4. What challenges is your church facing that require a team effort? What should your role be in helping your church face those challenges?

2 Samuel 11:1–12:31

The Great Sin of David

I. **INTRODUCTION**
Written on the Heart

II. **COMMENTARY**
A verse-by-verse explanation of these chapters

III. **CONCLUSION**
Pesky Prophet, Powerful Politician,
Painful Truth
An overview of the principles and applications from
these chapters

IV. **LIFE APPLICATION**
When God Answers with a No
Melding these chapters to life

V. **PRAYER**
Tying these chapters to life with God

VI. **DEEPER DISCOVERIES**
Historical, geographical, and grammatical enrichment of the commentary

VII. **TEACHING OUTLINE**
Suggested step-by-step group study of these chapters

VIII. **ISSUES FOR DISCUSSION**
Zeroing these chapters in on daily life

*"O*miserable man, what a deformed monster has sin

made you! God made you 'little lower than the angels'; sin

has made you little better than the devils."

J o s e p h   A l l e i n e

BIOGRAPHICAL PROFILE: BATHSHEBA

- Wife of Uriah the Hittite
- Granddaughter of Ahithophel, King David's most trusted advisor (2 Sam. 23:34)
- Became pregnant in an adulterous relationship with King David
- Became David's wife after her husband died in battle
- Bore David a total of four sons: Shammua, Shobab, Nathan, and Solomon (1 Chron. 3:5)
- Chided by her son, King Solomon, for assisting Adonijah in an attempted coup (1 Kgs. 2:13–25)

BIOGRAPHICAL PROFILE: URIAH

- A Hittite (non-Israelite) by birth
- First husband of Bathsheba
- Served with distinction in Israel's army under King David
- A member of the "Thirty," King David's most honored group of soldiers (2 Sam. 23:39)
- Upon orders of David, he was deliberately killed in battle with Ammon in order to hide David's sin of adultery

2 Samuel 11:1–12:31

IN A NUTSHELL

*K*ing David sins against God and compromises his leadership role by committing adultery with Bathsheba, the wife of Uriah, one of the king's most honored soldiers. He then arranges for Uriah to be killed in a battle with the Ammonites. With Uriah now dead, David marries Bathsheba. Through the prophet Nathan, God confronts David with his sin and announces a series of catastrophic judgments against the king's family. David repents of his sin, but the child born out of adultery to David and Bathsheba dies. Later, the Ammonites are defeated by Israel.

The Great Sin of David

I. INTRODUCTION

Written on the Heart

*G*rantley Morris once observed, "Fire brings comforting warmth, or destruction, depending on whether it is under control. Likewise sexual passion enriches or impoverishes, heals or harms, depending on how it is controlled." Human history chronicles that fire's comforting warmth and cruel destruction.

Proof of the universal threat that adultery posed to individuals and society is found throughout the written history of humanity. For example, the Code of Hammurabi, a law code originating in ancient Mesopotamia around 1750 B.C.—about three hundred years before the law of Moses—declared that any man caught in the act of adultery was to be tied up and thrown in the Euphrates River (law 129).

Adultery laws have long been a part of the American legal landscape, though the laws have varied from state to state. In Michigan being convicted of adultery could potentially result in life imprisonment. In Maryland adultery is punishable by a ten-dollar fine.

The virtually universal presence of adultery laws in human society points to the fact that God has written anti-adultery laws on the human heart. God made human beings in his image. He makes commitments to others and faithfully keeps them. David's sin with Bathsheba was against her and her husband, but fundamentally it was against God, whose command he violated.

II. COMMENTARY

The Great Sin of David

> **MAIN IDEA:** *King David sins against God and abuses his role as Israel's leader by committing adultery with Bathsheba and then arranging for her husband Uriah to be killed. God judges David for his sins, and lasting consequences result for his family. After seeking and receiving God's forgiveness, David leads Israel to complete the conquest of Ammon.*

▲ David Commits Adultery with Bathsheba (11:1–5)

SUPPORTING IDEA: *While Joab and the army of Israel are besieging Ammon, David commits adultery with Bathsheba, the wife of one of his most honored soldiers.*

11:1. In the spring, at the time when kings go off to war, David decided to teach the Ammonites a lesson. Spring was an ideal time to go to war, since the enemy's wheat fields were full of ripe grain. Thanks to Israel's recent victories over the Ammonites' allies to the north (10:13–19), the Aramean threat had been eliminated. Thus, David was free to focus Israel's military assets on his rebellious former ally to the east. To carry out this task David sent out **Joab . . . with the king's men**—perhaps a term for David's elite soldiers, such as the Thirty (23:24–39) or the Kerethites and Pelethites—and **the whole Israelite army**, that is, the citizen soldiers who had been temporarily conscripted to support the current military operation.

Under Joab's leadership David's fighting force **destroyed the Ammonites**. When the defeated remnant of Ammonite forces retreated behind the walls of their capital city of Rabbah, David ordered his men to lay siege to the city, dooming its citizens to die from starvation and disease.

11:2–3. One evening while the army was besieging Rabbah, David **got up from his bed** and walked on the flat roof of his palace. Sturdy, flat rooftops were regularly used in the ancient Near East as outdoor living space, something like patios or decks are used today; they could even be used as sleeping places on warm evenings (1 Sam. 9:25). From the vantage point of the rooftop of the palace—probably the structure located on the highest ground within the city—David **saw a woman bathing**. Houses had no indoor plumbing, and the law of Moses required Israelites to wash after certain bodily discharges (Lev. 15:13,16,18); Bathsheba was probably bathing to end her ritual uncleanness following the completion of her regular menstrual cycle (Lev. 15:19).

When David saw that she was **very beautiful**, he sent a servant to **find out about her**. Though David had already acquired a considerable harem, he was always ready to enlarge it. His servant returned with the news that the woman was **Bathsheba**, the wife of **Uriah the Hittite**, one of his most honored soldiers (23:39).

11:4–5. Once David learned that Bathsheba was married, any further pursuit of her amounted to committing adultery with her in his heart (Matt. 5:28). However, David also knew that he had ordered her husband to be away from Jerusalem on military assignment and that the woman was alone. David used these circumstances to pursue a sinful course of action; the king sent messengers to summon Bathsheba to his palace. She **came to him**, and **he slept** [lit. "laid down"—a biblical euphemism for engaging in sexual intercourse] **with her**. Afterward, the woman went back home. Hidden from both David and Bathsheba at the time was the fact that **the woman** had **conceived.**

Not long after David violated Bathsheba—probably within a month of the event—Bathsheba knew the truth of what had happened during her time with David. The fact that he was sexually intimate with her immediately after she had ritually **purified herself** from her menstrual uncleanness through the act of bathing could mean only one thing—David was the father of the child. Bathsheba sent word to the king: **I am pregnant.**

B David Summons Uriah Back to Jerusalem (11:6–8)

SUPPORTING IDEA: *David has Uriah sent back to Jerusalem in hopes of covering up his adulterous affair with Bathsheba.*

11:6. David devised a plan to hide his sin with Bathsheba—he would temporarily reunite the woman with her husband. As long as Uriah spent even a single night with his wife at this time, David could quash any ugly rumors that might be started by David's servants or Bathsheba's friends. David ordered his field commander **Joab** to send back to Jerusalem **Uriah the Hittite**.

11:7–8. Uriah was almost certainly bewildered by what he heard from David once he arrived. All David wanted was a report of **how the soldiers were** and **how the war was going**. Even more surprising was the fact that the king ordered him to go to his house and **wash** his **feet**—that is, enjoy a time of refreshment. To reinforce the point, **a gift from the king was sent after him**. The gift probably consisted of food and wine from the royal table.

C Uriah Frustrates David's Scheme (11:9–13)

SUPPORTING IDEA: *David tries to humiliate Uriah and then gets him drunk in order to make him sleep with his wife. However, Uriah disobeys the king in order to remain loyal to God and his fellow soldiers.*

11:9–10. In spite of David's order, Uriah **did not go down to his house**. Instead, he went out to sleep on his mat in the palace area among David's **servants**. When David was informed of Uriah's actions the next day, he summoned the soldier to explain his actions. David did not condemn Uriah for disobeying the royal order. Instead he mounted an attack on Uriah's manhood: **Haven't you just come from a distance? Why didn't you go home?** In other words, "What kind of a weirdo are you that you refused to spend a night with your wife after being away from her for so long?"

11:11. Uriah's noble answer deflected David's malicious words: **The ark**—and, by extension, the Lord, since the ark was his throne (6:2)—and the soldiers of Israel and Judah were **staying in tents**, that is, living away from urban comforts and from their wives. Thus for Uriah to go to his house and **eat and drink and lie with** his **wife** would be for him to break solidarity with his comrades in arms. But far more serious than that, if he had sexual relations with his wife he would become ceremonially unclean (Lev. 15:16). David required his men to be ceremonially clean during military operations (1 Sam. 21:5). If Uriah violated this rule, he risked possible death, and could even cause God to bring defeat to Israel's army (Josh. 7:1–12). As a loyal soldier and a faithful follower of the Lord, Uriah would **not do such a thing**.

11:12–13. By this time David was desperate. He came up with another plan to make Uriah spend the night with his wife. If he could get Uriah drunk, then perhaps he would forget his obligations to God and his fellow soldiers. The king ordered Uriah to stay in Jerusalem **one more day**. Then **at David's invitation**, he ate and drank with the king, and **David made him drunk**. However, not even alcohol could pry Uriah away from his commitments. Instead of going home to his beautiful wife, **Uriah went out to sleep on his mat among his master's servants**.

Ⓓ David Has Uriah Killed (11:14–17)

> **SUPPORTING IDEA:** *David orders Joab to have Uriah killed in battle against the Ammonites. Joab follows David's orders, and Uriah dies while attacking a city.*

11:14–15. David wrote a letter to Joab the next morning with a deadly plan. As the king planned it, Joab was to put Uriah in **the front line** where **the fighting** was the fiercest. Then Joab was to have the other troops **withdraw from him** so he would be **struck down and die**. In this way Uriah's death would look like a fatal tactical error on the part of Joab and a heroic defensive act by the Ammonites. David then sent Uriah's own death warrant **with Uriah**. He would not have known what he was carrying, however, since the order was sealed with a royal clay seal.

11:16–17. Joab and his men were encamped around Ammon's capital city of Rabbah. Joab had the city **under siege**, so there was no need to attack the city directly. All the Israelites would have had to do was make sure no one entered the city, and its residents would slowly starve or die of plague.

However, Joab stationed Uriah at a place where he knew **the strongest defenders were** and then apparently had his soldiers provoke an attack. The men of the city came out and **fought against Joab**. In the encounter some of the men in David's army fell, including **Uriah the Hittite**. David's insidious plan had worked to perfection.

E David Responds to Uriah's Death (11:18–26)

SUPPORTING IDEA: *Joab reports Uriah's death to David. The king responds by sending a message of encouragement to Joab and taking Uriah's widow into his harem.*

11:18–21. General Joab regularly sent couriers back to Jerusalem to keep David informed about the situation in Ammon. The news being carried by the messenger on this day was not good. The king's top military commander had committed a tactical blunder. He had gotten too **close to the city** to fight safely, and as a result one of David's best soldiers had died. In passing along to David a **full account of the battle**, the messenger was warned that the king's anger might **flare up**. In the event that David became provoked at Joab's failure, the messenger was to let David know that his servant **Uriah the Hittite** was among the battlefield casualties.

11:22–25. After making the trek to Jerusalem, the messenger **told David everything Joab had sent him to say**. The most complete description of the events leading to Uriah's death are presented in the servant's account. According to the servant, Ammonite defenders came out from Rabbah to attack the Israelites. In response, Israel's forces **drove them back to the entrance to the city gate**. In the process, Ammonite archers stationed on top of the wall killed some of the king's men, one of whom was **Uriah the Hittite**.

David took the news philosophically. Rather than exploding in anger, he calmly played the role of a pastoral counselor. David urged Joab to accept the fact that **the sword** of battle—or in this case, the arrow—**devours** people indiscriminately, sometimes taking the lives of even the best fighters. Joab should not be **upset** by this unhappy reality; instead, he should take encouragement from the fact that David still had confidence in his general and wanted him to **press the attack against the city and destroy it**.

11:26–27. If David's response to the news of Uriah's death was one of calm acceptance, Bathsheba's was one of sorrow; **she mourned** for her dead husband. After her mourning time was over, David had her **brought to his house** and **she became his wife**. It seems that David was playing the role of a substitute *go'el*—a kinsman-redeemer (Deut. 25:5–6; Ruth 3:1–4:6)—by taking on the obligation to care for a widow who had no close adult male relatives within her former husband's family. David seems to have fulfilled this role with Abigail, the wife of Nabal, on a previous occasion (1 Sam. 25:39–42).

One of the obligations associated with the role of the go'el was helping the woman bear a child (Deut. 25:6). From a worldly perspective, this new situation was perfect. Now it was David's duty to get Bathsheba pregnant! And indeed, the scheme worked perfectly. Bathsheba **bore him a son**. But what seemed so right from a worldly point of view was totally wrong from God's perspective. The thing David had done **displeased the LORD**, and David would soon pay dearly for his sin.

F The Lord Rebukes David for His Sin (12:1–14)

> **SUPPORTING IDEA:** *The Lord sends Nathan the prophet to David to confront him with his sin. When David hears the prophet's words, he repents of his sin and the Lord forgives him. Nevertheless, David is informed that as a result of his sin his son will die.*

12:1–4. Though David had tried to conceal his sin with Bathsheba from people, he was unable to hide it from the Lord. And the all-knowing Lord, who oversees human actions with perfect justice, sent **Nathan** the prophet to confront the king with his sin.

Nathan did not directly condemn David for his sin. Instead, he let David condemn himself. The prophet played the role of an advocate for a person who was in need of justice. He told about **two men** in a certain town, **one rich and the other poor**. The rich man was a shepherd—like David—who owned a **large number of sheep**. The poor man had nothing except **one little ewe lamb**, who was **like a daughter to him**. The rich man took the lamb that belonged to the poor man, killed it, and served it to a guest for dinner.

12:5–6. Before Nathan could finish the tale David interrupted him and pronounced judgment against the man. Burning with **anger**, David reacted first with his emotions—**the man who did this deserves to die!**—and then with his head. The rich man must pay for that lamb **four times over**—the penalty prescribed in the law of Moses for a lamb that was stolen and killed (Exod. 22:1).

12:7–12. Nathan confronted David with his sin by equating him with the wicked man of the story: **You are the man**. Nathan then delivered a three-part oracle of judgment against David consisting of (1) a description of God's gracious dealings with David in the past (vv. 7b–8), (2) a listing of David's relevant sins (v. 9), and (3) a declaration of God's resulting judgments (v. 10). All of these statements were designed to convince David of the seriousness of his sin and to drive him to repentance.

In the first part of the judgment oracle, the Lord reminded David of the blessings he had given the young man from Bethlehem. A lowly shepherd boy was anointed **king over Israel**. God had protected David, delivering him from **the hand of Saul**. David had received both material blessings—his **master's house**—and sexual pleasures—his **master's wives**, that is, Saul's harem. Beyond all that, the Lord had made David ruler over **the house of Israel and Judah**, so that the anointed youth did indeed become king.

The second part of Nathan's judgment dealt with David's sins. The starting point for David's wrongdoing was the fact that he had despised **the word of the LORD**. David knew what God had said about murder and adultery, yet he rejected God's commands. The instrument used to murder Uriah was **the sword of the Ammonites**, but it was actually David who **struck down Uriah the Hittite** because he cooked up the scheme and issued the orders designed to get Uriah killed. All this was carried out so David could take Uriah's **wife** to be his **own**.

The final part of God's word through the prophet was a declaration of judgment against the king. Because of David's sins against God, Uriah, and Bathsheba, David would pay a lifelong price. **The sword** of God's judgment would **never depart** from David's **house**. Indeed, soon after this violence and death wracked the royal family. Furthermore, the sexual sin that David had committed in secret would bring about a public **calamity** upon the king. God would give some of David's own **wives**—members of his harem—to one who was **close to** David, and this person would **lie with** David's **wives** in broad daylight **before all Israel** (see 16:21–22).

12:13–14. When confronted with his sin, David showed himself to be a man "after God's heart" (1 Sam. 13:14; Acts 13:22). Rather than deny his sin, he admitted that he had **sinned against the LORD** (see Psalm 51). And true to his word (Exod. 34:7), the Lord forgave the sinful king. No sin was too great for God to forgive. Then the Lord did something unexpected. He commuted David's death sentence. Both murder and adultery were sins that required the death of the sinner (Gen. 9:6; Exod 21:12; Lev. 20:10; Deut. 22:22), yet in this case God chose to allow David to live. Why? Only because of divine grace. But David's sin would bring about some immediate consequences: **the son** born to David and Bathsheba would **die**.

G David Loses One Son and Conceives Another (12:15–25)

SUPPORTING IDEA: *As a result of David's sin, the infant son he had conceived in adultery dies. Some time afterward, David and Bathsheba conceive another son, Solomon.*

12:15–17. God's promised judgment followed soon after Nathan had made the pronouncement against the king. The Lord **struck** the newborn **child that Uriah's wife had borne to David**, and he became ill. Trouble within David's family drove him to prayer, and the king **pleaded** with God for the child. The king also **fasted**, spent time in his house away from his public duties, and spent the nights **lying on the ground**. Lying on the ground was an expression of self-abasement in ancient Israel that was not fitting for a king. The elders of David's household—probably his counselors— **stood beside him to get him up from the ground**. But David refused to give up his acts of humility just as he also rebuffed the elders' attempts to get him to eat.

12:18–19. On the **seventh day** of its life **the child died**. This is especially significant because it meant that the infant boy was never circumcised, and thus never became a part of the covenant community (Gen. 17:12; Lev. 12:3). The fact that the boy was never circumcised may also explain why no name is given to him in Scripture (see Luke 1:59–62).

David's servants were **afraid to tell him** that the child was dead, being concerned that he might **do something desperate** (Heb. *ra'ah*, "bad"). As they debated among themselves whether to tell him, David noticed that his servants were **whispering among themselves**. The king immediately realized the child was dead, yet he wished to hear the word from the servants directly: **Is the child dead?** The servants had no choice but to affirm that the infant had indeed died.

12:20–23. David surprised everyone by his reaction to the news of the child's death. After having lain on the ground for several days in an act of self-abasement, the king now **got up**. He had gone through the valley of the shadow of death (Ps. 23:4) in his house as he witnessed his child lose its struggle for life. But in that time of crisis the Lord had been with him. And the Lord would continue to be with him even after the child's death. Now David would move on and would do so in fellowship with the One who had sustained him in his darkest hour.

David would begin a new chapter in his relationship with God. Accordingly he **washed, put on lotions**, and **changed his clothes** in preparation for a time with God in God's house. When David entered **the house of the LORD**, he worshiped the One who was his strength and fortress (Pss. 18:1; 22:19; 59:16–17). Afterward the king returned home, had his servants serve him **food**, and **he ate**. David's actions following the death of his son mystified his servants. Normally people who had just lost a loved one might be expected to throw dust on their heads (Job 2:12) and fast (2 Sam. 1:12), not wash and eat.

David provided a theological explanation for his actions. He knew that the Lord was **gracious** (see Exod. 34:6) and could have **let the child live**. But the gracious God let the child die. And though God had separated David from his child for a time, he could look forward to a time when he would **go to him**. Furthermore, David could worship God, confident that the Lord would be with him every step of the way leading to that coming reunion.

12:24–25. Grieving outside of the narrative limelight in this ordeal was the infant's mother, Bathsheba, who had now experienced the death of two family members within the space of a year. Her new husband, David, who had brought so much grief to her life through his sin, now tried to become her greatest earthly comforter. As he **comforted** her, the king **went to her and lay with her**. As a result, she conceived and **gave birth to a son**.

The parents gave the newborn son a name that surely expressed their hopes for the future—**Solomon**. The name (Heb. *shlomo*) is a derivative of the word *shalom*, a term that means "peace," "restoration," and "wholeness." Sharp contrasts exist between David and Bathsheba's first and second sons. Whereas the Lord took the first son's life, **the LORD loved** Solomon. The first son died without receiving a name; this one was given a name from God delivered through **Nathan the prophet**. The name **Jedidiah** means "Beloved of Yahweh" and is related to the name "David." Its connection to his father's name hints at the fact that Solomon/Jedidiah would become the successor to his father David.

⊞ David Conquers and Subjugates the Ammonites (12:26–31)

> **SUPPORTING IDEA:** *Joab besieges the Ammonite capital city of Rabbah, permitting David to capture and plunder the city. David then makes the defeated Ammonites serve the Israelites.*

12:26–27. After using a lengthy siege against the Ammonites' capital city, Joab moved on to the next phase of the conquest. He **fought against Rabbah**, pressing an attack against the weakened defenders. The account suggests that he first **captured** the district in the city that contained **the royal citadel**. Then he captured the city's **water supply**. With the palace complex and water supply now in Israelite hands, the rest of the city was set to fall to Israel as well.

12:28–30. Now that the slowest and hardest part of the conquest of Rabbah was completed, Joab sent messengers to David informing him of the progress and directing him to **muster the rest of the troops** and finish the task of besieging and capturing the city. David's presence on the battlefield would insure that he would be given due credit for the conquest. Otherwise, Joab would be the one to **take the city**, and would memorialize his achievement by naming the city after himself (see Num. 32:42). David followed Joab's instructions. Leading the entire army to Rabbah, a distance of more than 40 miles, David then **attacked and captured it**.

To demonstrate his control over the city and the Ammonite nation, David took **the crown from the head of their king**—an amazing headpiece containing 75 pounds of gold, besides precious stones—and had it placed on his own head. Then he stripped the city of its wealth, taking **a great quantity of plunder** back to Jerusalem. This wealth was dedicated to the Lord and set aside for the construction of the temple in Jerusalem (see 8:11–12; 1 Chron. 29:2–5).

12:31. As a final assertion of power over the citizens of Rabbah, David consigned them to labor with **saws and with iron picks and axes**. Others he put to work making bricks. What David did to the residents of Ammon's capital city he did to **all the Ammonite towns**. The lumber, cut stones, and bricks produced by the Ammonites were probably used to build Israelite fortresses and settlements throughout the land. When the Ammonite towns were under Israelite control, **David and his entire army** returned triumphantly to **Jerusalem**. The conquest of the Ammonites is narratively the last recorded conquest of a foreign nation in King David's illustrious military career.

> **MAIN IDEA REVIEW:** *King David sins against God and abuses his role as Israel's leader by committing adultery with Bathsheba and then arranging for her husband Uriah to be killed. God judges David for his sins, and lasting consequences result for his family. After seeking and receiving God's forgiveness, David leads Israel to complete the conquest of Ammon.*

III. CONCLUSION

Pesky Prophet, Powerful Politician, Painful Truth

Agnes Bojaxhiu, known to the world as "Mother Teresa," was a Roman Catholic nun who won the Nobel Prize in 1979 for her selfless work among the poor in Calcutta, India. She founded the Catholic order of the Sisters of

Charity and ministered to "the poorest of the poor"—orphans, widows, people infected with leprosy, tuberculosis, and AIDS—in India from 1929 until her death in 1997.

On February 3, 1994, Mother Teresa was given the opportunity to address the National Prayer Breakfast in Washington, D.C. Attending the event was then-president Bill Clinton and his wife Hillary. The tiny, soft-spoken woman, a mere four feet, ten inches in height, spoke like a giant with her words before the group on that day.

Those who attended were captivated as she spoke of the poor in the world. Then they were stunned as she addressed the topic of abortion, especially since the pro-abortion president and vice president of the United States were sitting at the head table. As she addressed the topic, Mother Teresa noted: "By abortion, the mother does not learn to love, but kills even her own child to solve her problems. And by abortion, the father is told that he does not have to take any responsibility at all for the child he has brought into the world." She then added a silent indictment of the president of the United States and his nation: "Any country that accepts abortion is not teaching the people to love, but to use any violence to get what they want. That is why the greatest destroyer of love and peace is abortion."

As the frail nun returned to her seat, the entire audience rose and gave her a sustained standing ovation. Well, almost the entire audience. President Clinton, his wife, and Vice President Gore remained seated as others stood to recognize her. Mother Teresa had used her opportunity to confront the president of the United States with the truth of God, regardless of how unwelcome the words may have been to powerful politicians. In so doing she stood on that day in the tradition of the great prophet Nathan as he spoke the word of God to King David.

PRINCIPLES

- Being godly does not make a person immune from temptation or incapable of sinning; even godly people are capable of great sin.
- Trying to hide one sin with another only makes a problem worse.
- God can expose even the best-hidden sin: "be sure that your sin will find you out" (Num. 32:23:).
- Sin's negative consequences always outweigh its positive pleasures.
- God forgives confessed sin, though he may not remove many of its consequences.

- We should fully accept God's answer to our prayers, even when the answer is *no*.

APPLICATIONS

- During a time alone with God, confess out loud a secret sin you have committed. Ask God to forgive you for it.
- Go to a mature Christian leader or trusted Christian friend and confess that secret sin to him. Ask him for advice on how to deal with the consequences of that sin.
- Bring to mind a specific, difficult situation in your past when you prayed but God answered with a *no*. Evaluate how you feel about the situation now. If you are still bitter about it, ask God to help you accept the outcome and find something positive in it.

IV. LIFE APPLICATION

When God Answers with a *No*

In 1989 Don Piper was a Baptist pastor in the south Texas town of Alvin. After attending a church-growth conference at the Trinity Pines Conference Center near Lake Livingston outside of Houston, Don headed for home. He never made it; an eighteen-wheeler collided head-on with his vehicle on a two-lane bridge, running nine of its wheels over the driver's side of Piper's car. Piper was apparently killed instantly, and his body was horribly mangled in the process.

Clearing the wreck off the bridge took hours. Because Piper was obviously dead, no early effort was made to remove his body from the wreck. However, a pastor named Dick Onerecker entered the wrecked vehicle some ninety minutes after the accident, prayed for him, and Piper returned to life! Don Piper had spent the previous hour-and-a-half at the entrance to heaven, surrounded by departed Christian family members, friends, and former teachers. But now he was back in his mutilated body.

When emergency response personnel learned from Onerecker that Piper was alive, they cut him out of the car and rushed him to the hospital. Over the next several years Piper underwent 34 major surgeries and endured incredibly painful procedures designed to rebuild his broken body. During this period of time Piper experienced almost unending pain. Heaven had been so pleasant and life in his tortured body was so painful.

During this phase of his life Piper wanted to die. He prayed several times that God would take him away from the pain and back to heaven. But God said *no*. Piper didn't understand at the time why God said *no* to his prayerful request. But like King David many years before when David prayed for his sick son, Piper accepted God's answer.

Ultimately, God's disappointing *no* became a great blessing for Piper. Out of miraculous experience many people have become Christians; countless others have had their faith in God strengthened. Today, Piper is known to many as the "Minister of Hope."

V. PRAYER

Lord, give us hearts to confess our sins and seek your forgiveness when we do sin. Thank you for taking away the worst of the consequences of our sin through the atoning death of Christ, and give us the grace to live with the consequences that remain. In Jesus' name. Amen.

VI. DEEPER DISCOVERIES

A. Why Did David Get Uriah Drunk? (11:12–13)

Ironically, David might have used his knowledge of the Bible when he devised a plan to get Uriah drunk. Lot, the father of the Ammonites, was coerced into sexual misbehavior when his daughters made him drunk (Gen. 19:32–38), and his shameful activity resulted in the birth of a child. David, who would have been familiar with that event from his knowledge of the books of the law, may have used that disgusting chapter in Genesis as a guide in planning his own scheme against Uriah.

B. Ancient Israelite Mourning Customs (12:20–23)

The death of a loved one in ancient Israel was marked in many different ways by those who were left behind. Commonly practiced mourning customs included weeping (Jer. 22:10; Ezek. 24:17; Joel 1:8; Zech. 12:10); wailing—that is, expressing a mournful, high-pitched cry (Jer. 6:26); rolling in dust or ashes (Ezek. 27:30; Jer. 6:26); changing one's diet for a period of time (Jer. 16:5; Ezek. 24:17); cutting one's hair or body (Lev. 19:28; Deut. 14:1; Mic. 1:16); and wearing different clothes—either putting on sackcloth or, in the case of a woman who had lost her spouse, wearing clothes that identified her as a widow (Gen. 38:14; Jer. 6:26; 49:3).

VII. TEACHING OUTLINE

A. INTRODUCTION

1. Lead Story: Written on the Heart
2. Context: After God had established the covenant of blessing with David and had given him victory over all his enemies, David rebelled against the Lord by committing adultery with Bathsheba and bringing about the death of her husband. These events confirm the sad truth that all people are sinners. At the same time, they demonstrate the importance of confession. God forgives even the darkest of sins, though he may not remove all of sin's consequences.
3. Transition: God is absolutely faithful in the commitments he makes to his people. Because all people are made in God's image, the demand for faithfulness in our relationships with others is also written on our hearts. Even pagan cultures throughout history have had laws against adultery. When David committed adultery he sinned by violating not only the law of Moses but also the demands of God written on his heart.

B. COMMENTARY

1. David Commits Adultery with Bathsheba (11:1–5)
2. David Summons Uriah Back to Jerusalem (11:6–8)
3. Uriah Frustrates David's Scheme (11:9–13)
4. David Has Uriah Killed (11:14–17)
5. David Responds to Uriah's Death (11:18–26)
6. The Lord Rebukes David for His Sin (12:1–14)
7. David Loses One Son and Conceives Another (12:15–25)
8. David Conquers and Subjugates the Ammonites (12:26–31)

C. CONCLUSION: WHEN GOD ANSWERS WITH A *NO*

VIII. ISSUES FOR DISCUSSION

1. Even though David was called a man after God's heart (Acts 13:22), he committed the sins of adultery and murder. What could he have done to avoid committing these sins?

2. What are some practical steps that Christians should take to avoid sexual temptation?

3. Nathan confronted David, the most powerful politician in his nation, with his sin. How should Christians today deal with politicians who commit grave personal sins?

4. Solomon, Israel's next king after David, was born to David and Bathsheba after David confessed his sin. What, if anything, does this say about God's forgiveness?

2 Samuel 13:1–14:33

Troubles in David's House

"*S*in is ... a lit fuse on a stick of dynamite [that] will unleash an explosion I can't stop."

Bryan Mondok

BIOGRAPHICAL PROFILE: AMNON

- Firstborn son of King David and Ahinoam
- Raped his half-sister Tamar
- Murdered by his half-brother Absalom

BIOGRAPHICAL PROFILE: TAMAR

- Daughter of King David and Maacah
- Noted for her beauty
- Raped by her half-brother Amnon
- Lived under the protection of her brother Absalom after Amnon's act
- Never married

BIOGRAPHICAL PROFILE: ABSALOM

- Son of King David and Maacah
- Grandson of Talmai, king of Geshur
- Brother of Tamar
- Considered very handsome
- Murdered Amnon to avenge the rape of his sister Tamar
- Lived in exile with his grandfather Talmai, king of Geshur
- Led an unsuccessful coup against his father David
- Killed by Joab

GEOGRAPHICAL PROFILE: GESHUR

- Aramean city-state northeast of the Sea of Galilee
- Located between Bashan and Hermon
- Talmai, father-in-law of David, was once its king
- City to which Absalom fled after killing Amnon

2 Samuel 13:1–14:33

IN A NUTSHELL

The prophesied punishment for David's sin extends to his household. His firstborn son Amnon rapes his half-sister Tamar. In revenge, Tamar's brother Absalom murders Amnon. After fleeing to Geshur and living in exile there for several years, Absalom returns to Jerusalem and is temporarily reconciled with his father David.

Troubles in David's House

I. INTRODUCTION

Like Father, Like Son

*C*armine "The Snake" Persico was born in 1933 in Brooklyn, New York, the son of a soldier in the Genovese crime family, a notorious mafia gang. In his youth he was encouraged by his father to become involved in crime, and he led a group of thugs. By the time he was 17 he was put on trial for murder, but before he could be convicted his brother confessed to the crime.

In his early twenties he became a capo, a divisional leader, in the Colombo crime family of the Mafia. His responsibilities were those of an enforcer—a hit man—and a loan shark. During this time he was shot in the face by a rival gang, but lived. Throughout his career he was shot more than 20 times, but he managed to survive each time. As a result he acquired the nickname "Immortal." Through a series of gangland murders, Carmine was able to become the godfather of the Colombo family. In 1986 Carmine was convicted of murder and racketeering and was sentenced to 100 years in prison.

When he was 21 Carmine fathered a son named Alphonse. Though Alphonse "Little Allie Boy" Persico was given a college education, he was encouraged by his father to become a member of the Colombo crime family. This he did, and he became deeply involved in underworld activities. As a result he was put on trial with his father in 1986 and convicted of racketeering. Released from prison in 1993, Alphonse followed his father in serving as a capo for the Colombo family. In 1999 he became the acting head of the Colombo family, but he was convicted a year later of illegal possession of guns and sent back to prison. In 2001, on the day he was due to be released from prison, he was charged with racketeering, loan sharking, and money laundering. Due to a plea bargain he was sentenced to an additional 13 years in prison.

The lives of Carmine and Alphonse Persico serve as eloquent testimonies to the power of a father to influence his sons. Following his father's example, Carmine not only became involved in a life of crime, but exceeded his father in this dark endeavor. Carmine also set an example that led to his own son's downfall. Alphonse became an imitator of his father's example and so shared his father's fate.

The Persico family was not the first to demonstrate the powerful effect that fathers' examples can have on their sons. In these chapters of 2 Samuel, we see that David's sexual misbehavior provided a pattern that would be imitated by his oldest son, with tragic results.

II. COMMENTARY

Trouble in David's House

MAIN IDEA: *David's firstborn son Amnon falls in love with his half-sister Tamar. Unable to seduce her, he rapes her instead, thereby condemning Tamar to a life without marriage. Tamar's half-brother Absalom avenges his sister's rape by murdering Amnon. Afterward Absalom flees to Geshur, where he lives until Joab is able to secure permission for him to return to Jerusalem. After an additional two years, Absalom is restored to his father's favor.*

A Amnon Rapes His Half-Sister Tamar (13:1–20)

SUPPORTING IDEA: *David's firstborn son Amnon becomes infatuated with his half-sister Tamar. Following a scheme suggested to him by his cousin Jonadab, he succeeds in forcing himself upon her. Afterward he despises her. Rejected and disgraced, Tamar goes to live under the protection of her brother Absalom.*

13:1–2. After the prophet Nathan had pronounced God's judgment against David, the divine curse began its deadly work in David's household. **Amnon son of David fell in love** with his beautiful half-sister **Tamar**. Since the law forbade sexual relations between a man and his half-sister (Lev. 18:11; 20:17; Deut. 27:22), Amnon had a choice to make. He could obey God and "get over" his emotional attraction to Tamar, or he could reject God and pursue his passions. Amnon chose the latter.

Amnon's pent-up passions grew, and he became **frustrated to the point of illness**. However, he was unable to fulfill his sinful lusts because his virtuous half-sister was a **virgin**, just as the law of Moses required her to be (Deut. 22:13–21). Thus, it seemed **impossible** for him to **do anything to her**.

13:3–5. Amnon had a wicked **friend**, who was also a cousin—**Jonadab son of Shimeah**. Jonadab was a **very shrewd** [lit. "very wise"] **man**. However, his "wisdom" was "earthly, unspiritual, of the devil" (James 3:15). When Jonadab learned why Amnon looked **haggard morning after morning**

because of lovesickness, he devised a crafty plan to help him achieve his sinful objective. Amnon was to lie in his **bed** and **pretend to be ill**. His father would come to check on him. When he did, Amnon was to ask David to have Tamar fix him some food and feed it to him in his bedroom. The plan would provide Amnon with the perfect opportunity to fulfill his fantasy with his half-sister.

13:6–10. Jonadab's sinister plan could not have worked better. When Amnon **lay down and pretended to be ill**, his father left the palace and came to see him. Amnon repeated the lines given to him by Jonadab, with the result that Tamar went to **the house of her brother**. She had brought some bread dough along with her, and she **made the bread in his sight**. After she had baked it, she served him the bread. However, **he refused to eat** it. Instead, Amnon ordered everyone except his half-sister out of the house. Then he ordered her to bring the food into his bedroom.

13:11–14. In the privacy of the bedroom Amnon gave full expression to his lustful intentions. Instead of accepting the medicinal bread prepared by Tamar, he **grabbed** the one who had prepared it. Then, in spite of the three-fold prohibition in the law (Lev. 18:11; 20:17; Deut. 27:22), he ordered his half-**sister** to **come to bed** with him.

Tamar refused her brother's order. She asked him to consider the effects his actions would have on her life: it would humiliate her—that is, force her to live as a shamed woman in a world where honor was more important than life. Tamar also reminded him that his request was completely contrary to Israelite customs; it **should not be done** in Israel. In addition, she noted that his actions, if carried out, would brand him as **one of the wicked fools** in Israel. But Amnon rejected her wise counsel and refused to listen to her impassioned pleas. Using his brute strength, Amnon **raped** his half-sister.

13:15. As soon as he had spent his passions, an entirely new set of emotions took over. Amnon's lust-driven "love" turned to **intense hatred**. Perhaps because of shame and a realization of the inevitable consequences of his actions, Amnon now **hated** Tamar **more than he had loved her**. He immediately ordered her to **get up and get out**—as though getting rid of her would undo the deed and its effects.

13:16–20. Tamar understood the devastating implications of Amnon's actions toward her. Now that she had lost her virginity, she could never become the wife of one of the rich and desirable men whom her father would have arranged for her to marry. Her only possible marriage partner was now Amnon (Deut. 22:28–29). If he refused to fulfill his duty, it would be a **greater wrong** than what he had already done to her.

Amnon **refused to listen** to her. Instead he ordered a slave to remove her from the building. Wearing for the last time the **garment the virgin daughters of the king wore**, Tamar expressed her grief by tearing the garment and putting **ashes** on her head. Then putting her hand on her head and **weeping** loudly as she went, she returned to her quarters. Tamar's older brother Absalom seems to have played the leading role in providing consolation and support to Tamar during this tragic phase of her life. He spoke words of comfort to her and provided her with a place to live—something she would never be able to obtain from a husband, due to Amnon's insidious actions.

B Absalom Murders His Half-Brother Amnon (13:21–33)

> **SUPPORTING IDEA:** *Two years after Amnon's crime, Tamar's brother Absalom takes revenge on Amnon by having him killed at a party in the countryside. Initial reports of the event lead David to believe that Absalom has killed all of David's sons, but such is not the case—only Amnon has been killed.*

13:21–22. When David learned about crown prince Amnon's actions, **he was furious**. Such behavior was inexcusable for a person who was in line to become the next king of Israel. Nevertheless, legally there was little David could do to rectify the situation. According to the law (Deut. 22:29), he could fine his son fifty shekels of silver (probably not a large sum for Israel's future king) or he could force Amnon to marry Tamar, thereby creating even more tension in the young pair's relationship. The Scriptures are silent regarding any actions that David might have taken against his son. But one thing is clear—David's treatment of the situation did not suit Absalom. Absalom was enraged to the point of committing murder, but he hid his true feelings toward Amnon. Instead, it seems, Absalom quietly plotted Amnon's death and bided his time.

13:23–27. Two years passed before Absalom put his murderous plan into action. Probably during the fall sheepshearing, while Absalom was in Jerusalem and his **sheepshearers** were at **Baal Hazor near the border of Ephraim**, Absalom announced that he was throwing a party for the men of the royal family. All the king's sons as well as King David were invited to Baal Hazor to celebrate the end of the annual sheepshearing event.

Absalom selected a time for the celebration when his father would be unable to attend. Thus, when his father turned down the invitation and indicated he **should not go**, Absalom was not surprised. He proceeded to ask that Amnon, who was next in line to become king, be present at the party instead, probably as a substitute for David himself. The king ordered his sons to attend the event because **Absalom urged him**.

13:28–29. Absalom was mimicking the plot hatched by Amnon that had led to his sister's devastation. The parallels are so close that it seems Absalom was deliberately trying to give Amnon a taste of his own medicine. Before any of the guests arrived, Absalom **ordered his men**—slaves who were loyal to him and probably hated Amnon as much as he did—to participate in the act of revenge with him. After the crown prince was **in high spirits from drinking wine**, they were to follow his command to **strike Amnon down**.

The celebrative event proceeded as planned. Then at just the right moment Absalom's men did to Amnon **what Absalom had ordered**. Panic ensued, and all the king's surviving sons **mounted their mules and fled**. The men apparently scattered, and most took indirect routes back to Jerusalem, perhaps because they feared Absalom's men would try to kill them also.

13:30–33. One of the sons' attendants arrived back at Jerusalem first. However, panic and haste in escaping the attack had caused him to misinterpret the true nature of what was going on. Thus, he wrongly informed David that **Absalom** had **struck down all the king's sons**.

David and his men **tore** their **clothes**, and David also **lay down on the ground** in an expression of profound grief. The prophet Nathan's prophetic words of deadly judgment against the house of David (12:10) undoubtedly filled everyone's thoughts. However, the king's nephew, Jonadab son of Shimeah, who may have been in attendance at the event, knew better. He was a cousin to both Amnon and Absalom and was well informed of the murderous grudge that Absalom harbored. Jonadab's report that **only Amnon is dead** gave the royal court its first accurate information about what had happened at Baal Hazor.

C Absalom Flees to Geshur (13:34–39)

> **SUPPORTING IDEA:** *Following Absalom's murder of Amnon, Absalom leaves Israel to live in exile with his grandfather Talmai, king of Geshur. He remains in Geshur for three years.*

13:34–37. Confirmation that Jonadab's report was accurate came when **the man standing watch** in Jerusalem **looked up and saw many people on the road west of him, coming down the side of the hill**. The fact that the group came down the western road leading from Horonaim and not from the northeast—Baal Hazor's location relative to Jerusalem—suggests that the men had taken a roundabout way home to try to avoid Absalom's men.

As the group drew nearer, Jonadab was able to confirm to David that all but Amnon of **the king's sons** had survived. Those who returned were **wailing loudly** as they entered David's presence. Their powerful expressions of emotion, evoked by witnessing the cold-blooded murder of their oldest brother, spilled over into the royal court. David and **all his servants** also **wept very bitterly**.

Absalom knew it would not be safe for him to return to Jerusalem after he had killed Amnon. So he **fled**, heading about 80 miles northeast to his maternal grandfather, **Talmai son of Ammihud, the king of Geshur**. Absalom's absence from Jerusalem meant that David had effectively lost two sons as a result of the Baal Hazor incident. This double loss grieved David deeply, but he **mourned** especially for his murdered son **every day**.

13:38–39. For a period of **three years** Absalom lived in exile outside of Israel in **Geshur**. While those years must have been difficult for Absalom, they were painful for David as well. After a period of time the king was sufficiently **consoled concerning Amnon's death**, and he wanted to begin the reconciliation process with his errant son Absalom. And with this, the stage was set for the most violent phase of God's judgment against the house of David.

Joab Seeks to Bring Absalom Back to Jerusalem (14:1–24)

> **SUPPORTING IDEA:** *Joab uses his influence with the king to persuade him to let Absalom return to Jerusalem.*

14:1–3. **Joab** son of David's aunt **Zeruiah** was one of the small circle of people who had been with David continuously from his early days up to the present. He had been with his cousin through bad times and good, and he knew David almost as well as David knew himself. He knew the mental anguish the king had endured over the past three years following Amnon's death, and he knew that the king's heart **longed for Absalom** to return to Jerusalem. But he also knew that David himself would never take the initiative to reconcile with his son. So Joab devised a bold plan to help the king and his son get what both of them wanted.

Joab enlisted the help of **a wise woman** from the village of **Tekoa**, located about ten miles south of Jerusalem. She was apparently known for her intelligence as well as her communication skills. Joab asked her to perform before King David and to deliver a monologue that had been composed by Joab himself.

14:4–11. On a day when King David was functioning in his role as the supreme judge of the land (1 Kgs. 3:16–28; Prov. 20:8; 31:9; Jer. 21:12), this **woman from Tekoa** went to the king. She approached him by following the courtly customs of the day, putting **her face to the ground**, and then requesting his help. David asked her what was **troubling** her, and she presented her case. She was **a widow** who once **had two sons**. However, as in the case of Cain and Abel (Gen.4), the brothers were alone in a field when one brother **struck the other** and **killed him**. Vengeance-seeking relatives within the clan had demanded that she **hand over the one** who had killed his brother. If the clan members succeeded in doing this, they would take away the woman's only surviving family member, leaving her **husband neither name nor descendant**.

Perhaps David remembered how God had dealt with Cain when he feared for his life following Abel's murder. God had spared Cain's life (Gen. 4:15) in response to a plea, so David would spare the murderer's life in the present situation. The king issued **an order** in the woman's **behalf** that would protect the young man's life. Though some might complain that all murderers must die (Gen. 9:6) and therefore the woman's son must also be killed, David took responsibility for his decision and promised on oath that **not one hair** of the woman's living **son** would **fall to the ground**.

14:12–17. Then the woman began to reveal the true purpose of her visit to the king. David's refusal to permit Absalom, his oldest living son and therefore the next in line to become king after David, was an action that worked **against** the best interests of **the people of God**. Although David permitted the woman's hypothetical son to return to live among his clan members, he had **not brought back** his own **banished son**. The story of Cain had demonstrated that God doesn't just try to remove people from fellowship with him; instead he **devises ways so that a banished person may not remain estranged from him**.

14:18–20. Behind the woman's pleas David perceived **the hand of Joab**. It seems apparent that Absalom had been a much-discussed topic among the royal advisors in Jerusalem, and that Joab had advised David to permit him to return. However, for parts of three years David had resisted not only the recommendations of others, but his own inclinations as well. The king's question to the woman about Joab produced a direct answer: **Yes, it was . . . Joab** who had instructed her to do her performance, and it was he also who had put in her mouth all the words she had spoken to the king. David had not asked for the reason behind Joab's actions, but the woman volunteered it anyway; it was **to change the present situation**.

14:21–24. Turning his attention away from the woman of Tekoa, the king now spoke directly to Joab. He ordered his top general to **bring back the young man Absalom**. Joab bowed down to pay honor to David and **blessed the king** for his gracious ruling. By thanking David for granting **his servant's request**, Joab acknowledged that it was he who had engineered the encounter between David and the woman from Tekoa.

Joab then made the eighty-plus miles journey to **Geshur** to inform Absalom of the good news. He **brought Absalom back** to the royal city of Jerusalem. Even so, full restoration between David and his son had not yet occurred. David was not yet ready to let a man who had committed fratricide be given the right to become Israel's next king. Thus although Absalom **went to his own house** and resumed his role as Tamar's protector (13:20), he was not permitted to **see the face of the king**.

E Absalom Is Restored to David (14:25–33)

SUPPORTING IDEA: *Absalom, a handsome man with four children, lives for two years in Jerusalem without being reconciled with his father. Deeply frustrated by this, Absalom forces Joab to negotiate a reconciliation with David. Finally, Absalom's broken relationship with his father is restored.*

14:25–27. Physically, Absalom was a remarkable specimen. In fact, no man in all Israel was as **handsome** and **highly praised** as he. In addition, he had remarkable facial hair. Every year he would get a haircut—probably a head shave—something that was not usually done in Israel unless one had taken a Nazirite vow (Num. 6:18) or was entering a state of ceremonial cleanness for religious purposes (Lev. 14:8–9; Num. 8:7). The fact that he was cutting his hair because it was **too heavy for him** trivialized and secularized the act. At the same time the mention of his extraordinary hair connects him with Esau and Samson, two characters who also lived troubled lives. The **hair of his head** weighed **two hundred shekels** by the royal standard—about five pounds.

14:28–30. For **two years** Absalom lived in virtual internal exile in Jerusalem **without seeing the king's face**. Although he was David's oldest living son and by birth order next in line to become Israel's king, he was not even allowed to eat at the royal table, much less be considered for the throne after his father's death. The situation became intolerable for Absalom, so he decided to enlist the help of Joab to change the situation. Yet when he **sent for Joab**, he **refused to come**. Even after summoning Joab **a second time**, David's top general refused to pay Absalom a visit. So Absalom took a drastic step to insure that Joab would meet with him face to face. He ordered **his servants**—some of whom may have also been involved in the plot to kill Amnon (13:28–29)—to go to Joab's barley field and **set it on fire**.

14:31–33. When Joab found out about the damage done to his crop, he quickly learned that Absalom was responsible. According to the law, anyone responsible for burning another man's grain field had to pay the landowner for the destroyed crop (Exod. 22:6). Thus, Joab went to **Absalom's house** to settle the issue. In the course of the discussion, Joab asked Absalom to explain what motivated him to commit this senseless act.

Absalom's answer came in the form of a request—that Joab would go to **the king** to ask for an opportunity for Absalom to see his father the king's **face**. Being forced to live in Jerusalem but without royal status had been more frustrating than living as an exile in **Geshur**. Joab told David what Absalom had asked. David's wall of stubborn resistance to full reconciliation was broken. The king **summoned Absalom**, and for the first time in five years he saw the face of his oldest living son. Absalom **came in and bowed down . . . before the king**. David then **kissed** Absalom, symbolizing his full acceptance of the wayward son. Absalom was now restored to his position of privilege within the royal family.

> **MAIN IDEA REVIEW:** *David's firstborn son Amnon falls in love with his half-sister Tamar. Unable to seduce her, he rapes her instead, thereby condemning Tamar to a life without marriage. Tamar's half-brother Absalom avenges his sister's rape by murdering Amnon. Afterward Absalom flees to Geshur, where he lives until Joab is able to secure permission for him to return to Jerusalem. After an additional two years, Absalom is restored to his father's favor.*

III. CONCLUSION

The High Price of Lust

Steven D. Green, a former private first class in the United States Army, was serving in Mahmoudiya, Iraq, in 2006 when he saw Abeer Qasim Hamza, a pretty fourteen-year-old girl, among the Iraqi people. He decided he wanted to be intimate with her. After some consideration he decided the only way he could carry out his desires was to enter her house, kill the rest of her family, and then carry out his lustful actions. Enlisting the help of four other soldiers in his unit in planning the crime, the group carried out the plan on March 12, 2006, with all of them participating in some way. Then, in order to make sure that no Iraqi would reveal their secret, Green also killed the young girl the men had just assaulted.

Word spread quickly among the citizens of Mahmoudiya, and outrage inflamed the community. Within a month three members of Green's platoon had been brutally killed by Iraqis. A video released by al Qaeda stated that these killings occurred as partial revenge for the rape and murder of the Iraqi girl. Citizens in the area said that al Qaeda vowed to repay the Americans ten to one for what the soldiers had done.

This horrific series of events echoes many of the events in the story of Amnon and Absalom. It reminds us that vengeance is an enduring part of the human landscape and that it always produces casualties and unforeseen consequences. It also reminds us of the wisdom of God's declaration, "It is mine to avenge, I will repay" (Deut. 32:35).

PRINCIPLES

- A father's sinful ways may establish patterns for sinful actions in the lives of his children.
- Lust and love can be easily confused. Lust differs from love in that it is selfish and insensitive to the other person.
- A man who destroys a woman's life for the sake of selfish pleasure will be despised forever.
- Some of sin's most serious consequences may not become apparent until many years after the sin has been committed.
- Personal vengeance injures two people—the one who first did wrong and the one who avenges.
- Sometimes healing a broken relationship requires the help of a mediator who has credibility with both offended parties.
- The time needed to heal a damaged relationship is greater than the time it takes to damage it.

APPLICATIONS

- Seek an accountability partner who will hold you accountable in your moral life by asking you pertinent questions about your personal conduct.
- If you harbor anger and resentment against someone because of something he has done to hurt you or a family member, write down that person's name. Ask God to help you develop a

forgiving attitude toward that person. Then write the words "I forgive" above that person's name.

- For the next seven days pray for a family member or Christian friend who has a painful, broken relationship with another member of his family. Ask God to help him be reconciled to his relative.

IV. LIFE APPLICATION

Wanted: A Father's Approval

Dale was the younger of two sons in a middle-class American household in the 1960s. Dale loved his father, but it seemed his father loved his older brother a lot more than he loved him. His older brother was a great athlete, excelling in both football and baseball. The father gave lots of time and attention to helping the older brother develop his athletic skills, but he didn't seem to spend much time with the younger one. Dale wasn't good at any sport and wasn't a great student, either. However, he did seem to have some musical talent, and he began playing a musical instrument. Beatings and verbal abuse were a common experience for Dale. As he tells it, it felt at times like his middle name was "Stupid."

When Dale was fifteen, his parents divorced. He chose to live with his mother because his father was violently abusive, unreliable, and an alcoholic. Throughout his high school years he played in the high school band and became first chair trumpet and an instrumental soloist. But he never saw his father at a single concert and never received a fatherly compliment for his achievements. This made him feel even more unloved, and he had no real contact with his father during those years.

Dale was in his twenties and married when he tried to reconnect with his father. By this time the father had remarried and lived 60 miles away. For five years Dale worked at trying to establish a good relationship with him, but each visit resulted in only more verbal abuse and criticism. After one particularly insulting outburst from his father, the relationship abruptly ended.

Fifteen years passed before Dale saw his father again. He learned from his brother that his father was dying. His brother also told him that his father wanted to talk with him before he died. Dale made a long journey to the hospital where he was told he could find his father. He scarcely recognized the man he found there. Awakening him gently, he asked his father if he knew who was standing over him.

"You're my second son," he replied.

"Do you know my name?" Dale asked.

"Dale," he said, and began to cry. Then he told his son he was sorry for all the things he had done to him. In the minutes that followed both men hugged and cried.

After several minutes they began to speak again. Dale's father said that he attended many of Dale's band performances but felt ashamed to tell him, because he had heard that Dale's stepfather was a better father than he. Then for the first time in Dale's life his father told him the words he had always wanted to hear: "I was proud of you, son."

"I've been looking for your approval all my life, Dad."

"You've got it, son."

Before the day ended, Dale's father was also reconciled to his heavenly Father. Dale prayed with his father for his sins to be forgiven through Christ. A week later Dale's father died.

This painful story that ended in reunion reminds us of the story of Absalom and David. Dale's desire to be restored to his father's good graces mirrors Absalom's desire to see David again. Likewise, his father's desire to see Dale echoes the emotion that drove David to see his son again.

V. PRAYER

Lord, too often our minds get filled with thoughts and desires that have no place in a healthy Christian life. Sometimes lustful thoughts crowd their way into our minds. Sometimes we waste our imaginations on angry, vengeful fantasies. Forgive us for squandering our God-given resources for such worthless pursuits. Create within us a mind that shuns evil and focuses only on pursuits worthy of Christians. Develop within us, one thought at a time, the mind of Christ. In Jesus' name. Amen.

VI. DEEPER DISCOVERIES

A. Amnon and Shechem (13:1–29)

The writer of 2 Samuel made a special effort to draw parallels between the tragic events of Amnon and Tamar and those involving Shechem and Dinah in the book of Genesis. In both instances the woman who was violated was the only named daughter of an important leader in the history of Israel. In both cases the women were unmarried. Both Amnon and Shechem were the sons of rulers, and both men "loved" the women they violated (Gen. 34:3; 2 Sam. 13:1). Both accounts referred to the men's actions as things that "should not be done" (Gen. 34:7; 2 Sam. 13:12). After the wicked deed became known to the male siblings of the violated women, they initially did nothing but devised a devious plan to kill the offender (Gen. 34:13–17; 2 Sam. 13:24–27). Ultimately, both men who had violated the women were killed by the girls' brothers (Gen. 34:26; 2 Sam. 13:29).

B. The Weight of Absalom's Hair (14:26)

According to the Bible, the hair that was cut off Absalom's head every year weighed two hundred shekels. The standard weight for a shekel was 11.5 grams; thus his hair would have weighed about five pounds.

How could anyone grow five pounds of hair in a single year? The Bible does not answer this question. However, it is possible that the extraordinary weight came about through additions that Absalom made to his hair. Absalom likely had gold beads or other adornments strung into his hair that were responsible for most of the weight. These "extras" would have made him a standout in any crowd, and may have been one of the reasons he was once considered the most handsome man in Israel (14:25).

VII. TEACHING OUTLINE

A. INTRODUCTION

1. Lead Story: Like Father, Like Son
2. Context: The prophet Nathan's solemn pronouncement of divine judgment proves to be correct. This section continues to trace the bitter progression of events that followed David's sin against Bathsheba and Uriah.
3. Transition: In the law of Moses, God said that the consequences of the father's sins would be visited on the sons (Exod. 34:7). These chapters prove the accuracy of that statement as two of David's sons imitated their father with tragic results: Amnon violated a woman who was not his wife, and Absalom killed a man who had not committed a capital crime.

B. COMMENTARY

1. Amnon Rapes His Half-Sister Tamar (13:1–20)
2. Absalom Murders His Half-Brother Amnon (13:21–33)
3. Absalom Flees to Geshur (13:34–39)

4. Joab Seeks to Bring Absalom Back to Jerusalem (14:1–24)
5. Absalom Is Restored to David (14:25–33)

C. CONCLUSION: WANTED: A FATHER'S APPROVAL

VIII. ISSUES FOR DISCUSSION

1. Many women in our society today have been sexually abused by family members. How does this abuse affect them? What should Christians do to help these women?
2. What efforts could David have taken to help defuse the situation between Amnon and Absalom before it turned deadly?
3. In the biblical accounts, David is never seen taking the initiative to heal the broken relationship between himself and his son Absalom; other people did the work to bring father and son together. Why do you think David did not try to reconnect with his son? What, if anything, should he have done differently?

2 Samuel 15:1–18:33

Absalom's Rebellion

Th' ambitious youth, too covetous of fame, Too full of angel's metal in his frame; Unwarily was led from virtue's ways; Made drunk with honour, and debauch'd with praise.

John Dryden, description of Absalom, from *Absalom and Achitophel*, lines 309–312

BIOGRAPHICAL PROFILE: AHITHOPHEL

- From Giloh, a village in Judah, south of Jerusalem
- Grandfather of Bathsheba
- Considered King David's wisest counselor
- Supported Absalom in the revolt against David
- Committed suicide when Absalom rejected his advice on how to attack David

BIOGRAPHICAL PROFILE: HUSHAI

- From Archi, a village on the border between Benjamin and Ephraim
- Counselor to King David
- Loyal to David, but joined Absalom's administration to misguide Absalom
- Provided Absalom with a military plan that saved David's life

BIOGRAPHICAL PROFILE: ITTAI

- Military leader from the Philistine city of Gath
- Served King David in Jerusalem
- Went into exile with David in Mahanaim
- Served as one of David's three top commanders in the struggle against Absalom

2 Samuel 15:1–18:33

IN A NUTSHELL

*A*fter being restored to his father's favor, Absalom positions himself to become Israel's next king by undermining the nation's confidence in David's administration. Declaring himself king four years later, Absalom and his followers then take over the capital city of Jerusalem. Meanwhile, David and his followers flee to Mahanaim, east of the Jordan River. There David receives assistance from some wealthy supporters. David's forces face and defeat Absalom's army in the Forest of Ephraim and kill Absalom.

Absalom's Rebellion

I. INTRODUCTION

The Fifth Column

*E*milio Mola Vidal was born in the Spanish colony of Cuba in 1887, where his father served as a military officer. Emilio decided to pursue a military career himself, so he entered the Infantry Academy of Toledo at age 20. He fought with distinction in the Spanish colonial war in Morocco and was awarded the Medalla Militar Individual for his efforts. By age 40 he was a brigadier general in the Spanish army. Three years later he was the nation's director of security.

But General Mola found himself in an awkward position. Socialists and left-wing politicians were in charge of Spain's government at the time, and Mola was a conservative. Troubled by the direction his government was taking, Mola and others decided to stage a revolution. Because of his organizational skills and experience, the general played a leading role in the revolt against his own government in 1936.

Emilio Mola's most memorable role in the war that ultimately led to the overthrow of the Spanish government was his attack on the capital city of Madrid in October 1937. From a rebel radio station Mola stated that four columns of troops would attack the city from the outside, and a "fifth column" of secret supporters living in Madrid would join in the attack when his army entered the city. The news that vicious undercover rebels were living throughout the nation's capital led to much anxiety and fear. Though Mola's attack on Madrid ultimately proved unsuccessful, many people in Madrid joined the infamous "fifth column."

King David faced a similar revolt in his day. Many people in David's government and in his own family disliked the way he was leading the nation. When crown prince Absalom initiated a revolution against his father, some of David's top government officials switched their allegiance to the upstart king. David found that administrators he had considered his most trusted supporters were in fact members of a "fifth column," and the results would be disastrous for all.

II. COMMENTARY

Absalom's Rebellion

MAIN IDEA: King David's oldest surviving son Absalom mounts a rebellion against his father in an effort to take over the throne of Israel. To survive, David flees Jerusalem and goes into exile in Mahanaim east of the Jordan River. David thwarts Absalom's plans to kill him with the covert assistance of an advisor and some priests who secretly remain loyal to him. Soldiers who support David fight against Absalom's forces and defeat them, killing Absalom in the process.

A Absalom Lays the Groundwork for a Rebellion Against David (15:1–6)

SUPPORTING IDEA: Over a period of four years, Absalom creates resentment for David and popular support for himself among the Israelites. In doing this he lays the groundwork for a coup that would make him king in place of his father.

15:1–4. After Absalom was restored to his father's good graces, he began carrying out a plan designed to make himself king in place of David. If Absalom wanted to take over the kingship of Israel, he needed to look like a king. Thus he took steps to establish a regal image. First he **provided himself with a chariot and horses**, trappings associated with powerful leaders in the ancient Near East. Then he gathered **fifty men to run ahead of him**. These individuals were probably armed, and they served as a massive bodyguard or a small militia to provide the perception of strength for Absalom.

One of the most important tasks of a king in Israel was providing justice for the citizens of the land (2 Sam. 14:4–11; 1 Kgs. 3:16–28; 7:7). To look like a king, therefore, it was necessary for Absalom to act as a **judge in the land**. However, his father was already Israel's supreme judge, and Israelites would regularly make their way to Jerusalem to seek justice from the king.

To keep the people from getting help from David, Absalom would **get up early** and stand by the side of the road **leading to the city gate**. Then before citizens could enter the royal city Absalom would listen to their complaints and tell them their **claims** were **valid and proper**. He would also foster discontentment toward the existing leadership by saying that there was **no representative of the king** to hear their problems. Lastly, Absalom gave the people an alternative to David—himself. If someone came to him for help, Absalom saw to it that he received **justice**.

15:5–6. Sometimes grateful citizens would express their appreciation to Absalom by trying to **bow down before him**. This traditional action symbolically indicated that they were accepting him as a respected person who was socially superior to them. But before a person could bow down Absalom would **take hold of him and kiss him**. Through this action Absalom was symbolically saying, "I'm not some egotistical, uncaring superior; I'm your friend and peer." This dramatic, unexpected act had a profound effect on those who experienced or witnessed it. Before long Absalom succeeded in stealing **the hearts** and loyalties of the **men of Israel**.

Ⓑ Absalom Declares Himself King over Israel (15:7–12)

> **SUPPORTING IDEA:** *After four years of preparation, Absalom initiates a coup against King David. Using the pretext of fulfilling a vow, he goes to Hebron, where he proclaims himself king.*

15:7–9. After Absalom had spent **four years** laying the groundwork for open revolt against his father, it was time to take the next step. Absalom would have himself proclaimed as a rival king to David. But to do this in Jerusalem would be suicidal; there were too many of David's supporters there. The city of Hebron was a much better location. It was 20 miles away from Jerusalem; it was a walled city that could be more easily defended; and it was already recognized as a capital city, since David had used it as his first capital.

Absalom used religion as a cover for his devious actions. As Israel's crown prince who was next in line to become king when David became incapacitated or grew too old to serve, Absalom might have been expected to stay in the capital city. In order to leave the city, therefore, he went to his father to request permission. His stated reason was a sham, but it sounded very pious: it was **to fulfill a vow** Absalom had **made to the LORD** while he was still living with his grandfather in **Geshur**. David encouraged him to **go in peace**.

15:10–12. Once in Hebron Absalom began to implement his plan. First he positioned **secret messengers** throughout the tribes of Israel. When they heard the **sound of . . . trumpets**—literally "rams' horns"—they were to announce that **Absalom** had become **king in Hebron**. Those who were already favorable to accepting him as king would welcome the news. Others would support him, suspecting that David had died and was being replaced by his heir-apparent.

An ingenious part of Absalom's plan was that he took **two hundred men from Jerusalem** with him to Hebron. No doubt many of these were key officials in David's government, since they had gone to Hebron **quite innocently**, knowing nothing about Absalom's coup. Now trapped in the walled city of Hebron, these loyal allies to David's cause were Absalom's hostages and thus unable to help their king.

Absalom realized that he would need help in plotting the course of his takeover. No one was a more respected counselor in all of Israel than **Ahithophel the Gilonite**. Once **David's counselor**, Ahithophel switched his loyalties to Absalom at the beginning of the rebellion. Perhaps he did so because of what David had done to his granddaughter Bathsheba (2 Sam. 11:3; 23:34) and her husband Uriah. Other key leaders in Israel joined with Ahithophel in supporting Absalom, so **the conspiracy gained strength**.

Ⓒ David Flees Jerusalem (15:13–16:14)

SUPPORTING IDEA: *When David learns what Absalom has done, he flees Jerusalem with a group of loyal supporters. But he leaves behind a small group of people loyal to him to care for his palace and to serve as spies.*

15:13–16. Among the last to be informed about Absalom's revolt was David himself. A messenger conveyed the news of the crisis to the king when he told him that **the hearts of the men of Israel** were with Absalom. Not only had Absalom laid claim to Israel's kingship; he also claimed the loyalties of most of its citizens as well.

Since David could not count on the support of the majority of his subjects, he knew he would have to abandon the capital city in order to survive. He ordered the officials still in Jerusalem to **flee** immediately in order to **escape from Absalom**. If they did not, then the city would be besieged and captured, and all its residents would be put to the **sword**. His officials declared their willingness to do whatever David wanted them to do.

The only members of his household that David left behind were **ten concubines**. Perhaps the king believed that taking these ten women along was too dangerous. They would slow his escape and increase his chances of being caught by Absalom. So he ordered them to remain in Jerusalem **to take care of the palace**. By having only women in the palace, David would communicate to Absalom that he was giving it to him without a fight; thus the structure could be taken without having to destroy it. In this way David hoped to preserve not just the palace, but all the capital city's government buildings.

15:17–22. After David and his group made it safely outside the city walls, the group **halted** for a short time. David used this occasion to determine exactly who was with him and then to organize their departure. Among those who went with him were **his men**—probably his personal bodyguards—and **the Kerethites and Pelethites**, as well as **six hundred Gittites**. These three groups were probably foreign mercenary fighters who were answerable only to David. Because they were not native Israelites, they would have been less inclined to get involved in Israelite politics. Thus they were indifferent about the matters Absalom had used to bring others into his camp.

Ittai the Gittite was probably the leader of the contingent of Philistines who had accompanied David back to Israel after the death of Saul (2 Sam. 2:1–3). David found it surprising that one who was **a foreigner** and **an exile** would display more loyalty to him than most Israelites did. The fact that Ittai was willing to **wander about** with him, even though David did not know where he was going, impressed the Israelite king and evoked a wish that the Lord would display **kindness and faithfulness** toward one who had been kind and faithful to David. The presence of the Gittite **families** with the group probably meant that more than a thousand Philistines were with David in his flight from Jerusalem.

15:23–29. Many of David's loyal supporters lived in or around Jerusalem. Though they did not accompany him in his flight from the city, they did provide moral support for him. As **all the people passed by** on their way eastward through **the Kidron Valley**, the loyalists **wept aloud**. David and his group, meanwhile, headed **toward the desert** in the vicinity of Jericho. Among David's staunchest supporters were **the Levites**, members of the priestly tribe who lived in and around Jerusalem. When David abandoned the capital city, the priestly leaders **Zadok** and **Abiathar** apparently directed the Levites to go with David, **carrying the ark of the covenant** with them. Abiathar, a direct descendant of Aaron, **offered sacrifices** on David's behalf as he made his way outside the royal city.

After the several hundred people in David's group had passed through Jerusalem's city gates and begun their ascent up the Mount of Olives, David had a crucial conversation with Zadok the priest. He asked Zadok to **go back to the city in peace**, accompanied by Abiathar, his **son Ahimaaz** and **Jonathan son of Abiathar**. These four men were to act as spies who would gather information from Absalom's group after they occupied Jerusalem and then **inform** David of Absalom's plans.

15:30–37. David **continued up the Mount of Olives**, overwhelmed by a flood of emotions. He had been stunned and disgraced with the news of his son's coup, grieved by the forced separation from his beloved city and those he had to leave behind, and intimidated by the knowledge that armed men were advancing from Hebron against him. The king wept as he went, with his **head . . . covered**, and he was **barefoot**. All the people with him shared his expression of grief, covering their heads and **weeping** as well.

David's anxieties multiplied when he learned that **Ahithophel** was **among the conspirators**, because Ahithophel had been David's chief advisor (1 Chron. 27:33). In this troubled moment, David the man of prayer (Ps. 109:4) prayed that the Lord would do the seemingly impossible—**turn Ahithophel's counsel into foolishness**.

No sooner had this prayer been expressed than who should appear but **Hushai the Arkite**, another of David's top advisors (1 Chron. 27:33). David knew that Hushai was on his side, because his **robe** was **torn** and **dust** was **on his head**. The fact that he met David on the road suggests that Hushai intended to accompany David into the wilderness. The king, however, had other plans for his trusted friend. He proposed that Hushai **return to the city** and request permission to join the camp of **Absalom**. If Absalom accepted Hushai into the inner circle of his counselors, perhaps the Lord could use him to frustrate **Ahithophel's advice**.

Even if Hushai did not succeed in persuading the upstart king to follow bad advice, Hushai would be able to serve as a listening ear to Absalom's plans. Then he could pass along anything he might **hear in the king's palace** to the priests **Zadok and Abiathar**. In turn, these priests could relay the information to their two sons, **Ahimaaz** and **Jonathan**, who would communicate it to David. Hushai agreed to the king's plan and arrived at Jerusalem just as Absalom was **entering the city**.

16:1–4. As David was descending the Mount of Olives he was met by **Ziba, the steward of Mephibosheth** and caretaker of King Saul's family estate (2 Sam. 9:1–11). On short notice Ziba had put together transportation and food resources for David's group and presented them as a gift to the king. Since Ziba was a former supporter of Saul—and therefore a possible enemy—why had he brought these supplies? And since Ziba was there, where was Ziba's **master's grandson**—the other key member of Saul's household?

Ziba had brought the small caravan of gifts for the benefit of **the king's household**, to provide them with transportation, food, and drink. Ziba also indicated that Mephibosheth was still in **Jerusalem**, because he hoped **Israel** would use this opportunity to **give** him **back** his **grandfather's kingdom**. Without probing further, David made a snap decision to disinherit Mephibosheth, giving **all that belonged to Mephibosheth** to Ziba. This decision would later be modified, as David came to doubt the truth of Ziba's statements about Mephibosheth (2 Sam. 19:24–30).

16:5–13. Not many miles down the road David and his group encountered a situation that confirmed the king's fears about the house of Saul. As the entourage entered the Benjamite village of Bahurim, a man from the same clan as Saul's family, **Shimei son of Gera**, came out to "greet" them. Shouting curses as they approached, Shimei pelted David and **all the king's officials** with stones.

Shimei accused the king of being a **scoundrel** and a **man of blood**, that is, a murderer—a charge likely based on the Philistine victory in which Saul and three of his sons died (1 Samuel 31) or the Gibeonite executions (2 Sam. 21:1–9). Furthermore, Shimei charged David with being a usurper who wrongly took over the kingdom after Saul's death. As Shimei interpreted it, the Lord himself was now bringing judgment against David by handing **the kingdom** over to his son **Absalom**.

David's cousin and military leader, **Abishai**, rose to the king's defense. Calling Shimei a **dead dog**, Abishai requested permission to **cut off his head**. However, David considered this course of action rash and quite possibly a revolt against God. In fact, in this moment of confusion and self-doubt David concluded that the Lord had told Shimei to utter a **curse** against him. Futhermore, the king believed a potential blessing could result from these outrageous actions being carried out against him. Shimei might overplay his role and verbally and physically injure David's group more than the Lord intended. If that happened, then the Lord would see David's **distress** and **repay** him **with good**.

16:14. Finally, David and all the people with him **arrived at their destination**. The day was one of the most difficult in David's life. Since sunrise that day he had learned of Absalom's murderous revolt, had hastily abandoned his beloved palace and capital city, was pelted with stones and condemned by an outspoken critic, and had hastily traveled more than 12 miles—much of it on foot—to escape death.

🄓 Absalom Rapes David's Concubines (16:15–23)

> **SUPPORTING IDEA:** *Hushai returns to Jerusalem, gains Absalom's confidence, and becomes an advisor to him. After entering the city Absalom follows Ahithophel's advice and rapes ten of David's concubines.*

16:15. This verse reminds the reader that Absalom had entered Jerusalem (15:37) and refocuses the story line on David's rebellious son. At the same time it indicates that **Ahithophel**, David's most valuable counselor before the revolt, was with Absalom.

16:16–19. Hushai, David's "friend"—as used here, a technical term that referred to an official position in Israelite government (1 Chron. 27:33)—**went to Absalom** as he was setting up his government in Jerusalem. Hushai's first recorded words in Absalom's presence are a remarkable example of his wisdom and cunning. On the one hand, **long live the king** sounds like an enthusiastic affirmation of the young king before whom Hushai stood; however, the discerning reader suspects that it is a secret expression of loyalty to David, Israel's only legitimate king. Hushai's words caught Absalom by surprise. He had always considered Hushai to be one of David's most loyal friends. His question, **Is this the love you show your friend?** is ironic, because Hushai's presence in Jerusalem was indeed an expression of his love for David.

Hushai's cool-headed response once again reveals his cunning: **The one chosen by the LORD, by these people, and by all the men of Israel—his I will be**. On three previous occasions the biblical writer indicated that David was chosen by the Lord (1 Sam. 16:1,12; 2 Sam. 6:21); Absalom was never said to be the Lord's chosen. Thus it seems that Hushai was once again secretly expressing allegiance to David, and that once again Absalom missed it. To increase the new king's confidence in him, Hushai pledged to **serve** Absalom just as he had served Absalom's father.

16:20–23. Though Absalom accepted Hushai as one of his counselors, he did not ask his advice about what to do first to assert his royal authority in Jerusalem. For that task he consulted Ahithophel, his most trusted advisor. Ahithophel's suggestion was brash and seductive: **Lie with your father's concubines whom he left to take care of the palace.** Only the king was permitted to have intimate relations with the royal harem; thus the counselor advised Absalom to perform an act that would make it clear to all who learned about it that Absalom was Israel's king. For Absalom to do this while King David was still alive would make him **a stench** in his **father's nostrils**. At the same time it would embolden everyone with him by making clear that he was committed to taking control of the land and getting rid of his father.

Absalom's followers **pitched a tent** for him on the roof of the very palace where David had lusted after Bathsheba, and it was there **he lay with his father's concubines in the sight of all Israel**. By taking another man's wife Absalom was now committing the same sin that had created so much grief for his father. By committing it ten times more than his father, he invited a catastrophic judgment against him that would dwarf what David had experienced.

E Hushai Misleads Absalom (17:1–14)

SUPPORTING IDEA: *Absalom consults Ahithophel and Hushai for advice on how to defeat David. Absalom rejects Ahithophel's plan in favor of Hushai's. Hushai then secretly passes word along to David, telling him how to avoid being defeated by Absalom.*

17:1–4. Now that Absalom had taken possession of Jerusalem and assembled a team of top-level advisors, the next order of business was to come up with a plan to defeat David and his forces. As Absalom's most trusted advisor, Ahithophel presented his plan first.

Ahithophel's plan consisted of four main points: (1) the assemblage of a large force—**twelve thousand men**; (2) a quick deployment—the group would set out that very night, when David's group was **weary and weak**; (3) extreme intimidation that would terrorize David's group and cause **all the people** with him to flee; and (4) a limited objective—**strike down only the king**. The plan was simple, quick, and relatively inexpensive. Because it would be carried out when David was distraught and his group was disorganized, it would almost certainly succeed. The plan **seemed good** to Absalom and to all the **elders of Israel** who had switched their loyalties to Absalom.

17:5–6. One of the most subtle but significant events of Israelite history took place immediately after Ahithophel's presentation: Absalom summoned **Hushai the Arkite** before the group so they could **hear** what counsel he would give in this matter. Hushai was asked to react to Ahithophel's plan and then present a better one, if he could.

17:7–10. Hushai began by rebuffing Ahithophel's advice. He gave four reasons for rejecting Ahithophel's proposed course of action. First, David and his men were fighters, **fierce as a wild bear robbed of her cubs**. Second, David was an experienced and savvy fighter who would know better than to **spend the night with the troops**. Thus, any attempt to kill him would end in complete failure. Third, David and his troops might anticipate an early attack by Absalom, in which case they could attack Absalom's troops first. Finally, false reports arising out of the "fog of war" and the strength of David's reputation as a fighter would circulate and cause **the bravest soldier** to **melt with fear.**

17:11–14. Having effectively discredited Ahithophel's proposal, Hushai now presented an alternative. His plan was as massive and heavy-handed as Hushai's was light and reactive. Instead of involving only a small force, **all**

Israel—with troops **as numerous as the sand on the seashore**—were to be gathered to Absalom. Instead of Ahithophel leading the troops, thus freeing up Absalom to tend to governmental business, Hushai's proposal required Absalom to spend a lot of time away from Jerusalem. Finally, instead of focusing on killing just David, the alternative plan called for wiping out David's entire army—an objective that would surely create untold heartache in Israel, as well as enduring resentment toward Absalom. Hushai even envisioned sieges and the violent destruction of entire Israelite cities, whose stones would be dragged **down to the valley**.

This ponderous plan was doomed to fail. It would give David and his men weeks to hide out, organize, and plan both offensive and defensive strategies, as well as give Israelite fence-sitters the opportunity to recommit themselves to David. Nevertheless, all the men of Israel who heard Hushai's presentation agreed that the advice of **Hushai** was **better** than that of **Ahithophel**. The biblical writer explains this surprising turn as the work of the Lord, who had determined to **bring disaster on Absalom**.

F David Goes to Mahanaim (17:15–29)

> **SUPPORTING IDEA:** *Jonathan and Ahimaaz give David information that has been secretly sent from Hushai. As a result, David and his group cross the Jordan River and go to Mahanaim. Once there, the group receives much-needed supplies from three wealthy supporters who live in the area.*

17:15–17. Even though Absalom and his attendants reacted favorably to his plan, Hushai knew that they could change their mind at any time and return to Ahithophel's proposal. Consequently, it was necessary for David to act as though Absalom's men would attack that very evening. With this in mind, Hushai hastily went to **Zadok and Abiathar** to inform them of what **Ahithophel** had advised Absalom to do. He then told them to **send a message** to David immediately, instructing **the king and all the people** to cross over the Jordan River that very night. This physical barrier separating the two groups would increase the likelihood that David's group could avoid capture and death.

These two priests made arrangements to pass the word to their sons **Jonathan and Ahimaaz**, who would in turn convey the message to David. But Zadok and Abiathar could not risk being seen leaving Jerusalem and going to **En Rogel** (lit. "Spring of the Spy") to speak with their sons. This task was given instead to **a servant girl**—one whose job it was to fetch water from the nearby spring.

17:18–20. As Jonathan and Ahimaaz were receiving the vital information from the servant girl, **a young man** who was loyal to Absalom saw them. He understood them to be loyalists who supported David, so he immediately went up the hill to Jerusalem to inform Absalom. Jonathan and Ahimaaz realized they were in danger, so they went to the house of a man in Bahurim who was loyal to David. Here they hid in a cistern (NIV, "well") in the man's **courtyard**. To help insure the messengers' safety, the man's wife spread a covering over the opening of the well and scattered grain over it. All this was done before any of Absalom's soldiers could get there, so **no one knew anything about it**.

As expected, Absalom's men came to the house seeking information about the two spies. Giving an answer similar to the one Rahab had given many years earlier (Josh. 2:4–5), the woman told Absalom's messengers the men had **crossed over the brook**—apparently suggesting that they had gone south.

17:21–22. When the coast was clear, Jonathan and Ahimaaz **climbed out of the well** and went eastward down to the Jordan River to **inform King David**. The king and the people with him proceeded to make their way across the Jordan. By daybreak, **no one was left who had not crossed**. God had again acted graciously on David's behalf.

17:23. The Hebrew grammar of this verse suggests that an important event was happening in another part of Israel at the same time as David and his group were fleeing east of the Jordan River: **Ahithophel** was abandoning Absalom. When he saw that his advice had been rejected, Ahithophel realized that Absalom's rebellion against David was doomed to fail. With failure would come the arrest and execution of all those who had supported Absalom, including Ahithophel. The wise counselor then tried to do the "rational" thing to respond to what he saw coming: **he put his house in order and . . . hanged himself**.

17:24–26. King David went to **Mahanaim**, the same city where Saul's son Ish-Bosheth had once ruled as king-in-exile (2 Sam. 2:8). Soon Absalom and a massive army **crossed the Jordan** to track him down and kill him. They camped north of Mahanaim in the **land of Gilead**. Absalom used a fellow Judahite, **Amasa** the son of Jether (or "Ithra"; see 1 Chron. 2:17), whose father was either an Israelite or an Ishmaelite (1 Chron. 2:17), to lead his troops. After Absalom's rebellion had been put down, David would also employ Amasa as a general (2 Sam. 19:13).

17:27–29. David and his group had successfully escaped Absalom's clutches and situated themselves in a walled city. However, they still faced grave danger. Besides the threat of an imminent attack from Absalom's troops, David's followers needed food and other basic supplies. David had some wealthy sympathizers in the region, **Shobi** and **Makir**, who supplied the group with needed resources. These benefactors provided David and his group with such practical resources as **bedding**, **bowls**, and **pottery**, as well as food. The provisions of food provided David's group with the physical strength needed to carry on the fight against the insurgents.

G David's Forces Kill Absalom (18:1–33)

SUPPORTING IDEA: *David's forces engage Absalom's army in the forest of Ephraim. In the battle Absalom has a freak accident that allows him to be caught and killed. With Absalom's death the revolt ends, though David grieves deeply when he learns about his son's death.*

18:1–5. Because David's situation had stabilized well before Absalom's troops arrived, he was in a position to organize his troops and get them ready for battle. First he **mustered the men**, counting them and looking them over to determine exactly what human resources were available to him. Then he organized them, appointing **commanders of thousands** and **commanders of hundreds**. Over the commanders of thousands he appointed three generals, each with equal authority: **Joab**, David's cousin on whom he had relied many times previously in times of battle; **Abishai**, Joab's brother; and **Ittai the Gittite**, a Philistine who had proven loyal to David.

David then announced his intention to **march out** with his army, and he attempted to take his place at their head. However, the soldiers commanded him not to go with them because he was too valuable to risk losing. His life was **worth ten thousand** of the common soldiers. Besides, he could serve a more important function by providing **support from the city** within the confines of its fortifications. David reluctantly submitted to the men's demand. Thus the king took his place **beside** the city **gate** while all his warriors marched out to battle. However, before they left, he issued one last command in the hearing of all the troops: **Be gentle with the young man Absalom for my sake.**

18:6–9. David understood the importance of creating and exploiting battlefield advantages. This was doubly important now, since Absalom had a much larger army than he did. To maximize the chances of victory, David positioned his forces in the **forest of Ephraim.** By deploying his men there, he made it impossible for Absalom's army to stay together to fight as a unified force. Thus the rebels were forced to fight only in small units, and to do so against an enemy that was well-hidden and prepared to strike before they could even be seen.

David's strategy worked perfectly. The enemy that came against his army was overwhelmed by a combination of the smaller army and the perils of **the forest**. Both armies were fully engaged with each other as the battle spread out over the countryside. The **casualties** among Absalom's troops that day were great—**twenty thousand men**.

Unlike David, Absalom had accompanied his army into the battle. In the course of the conflict, Absalom **happened to meet David's men**. Apparently he attempted to make a hasty retreat from them. In doing so his **head got caught** in a tree as the mule he was riding on went under the thick branches of **a large oak**. Possibly he was trapped by his long hair. The upstart king was left **hanging in midair**.

18:10–15. One of David's men saw Absalom in this helpless position and told his commander. Joab knew about the king's order not to kill Absalom, but he also believed that the only way to end the conflict that was tearing Israel apart was to kill the rival king. So Joab took three javelins and **plunged them into Absalom's heart**. Ten of Joab's armor-bearers followed their leader's example and also struck and killed David's son.

18:16–18. When Absalom died, the revolution died. Thus Joab **sounded the trumpet** (lit. "shophar"), signaling the troops to end their attack. Before sunset, Joab's men took Absalom down from the tree, **threw him into a big pit**, and **piled up a large heap of rocks over him**. In doing this they were following prevailing customs and obeying the guidelines of the law. People were expected to be buried the same day they died, and rebellious sons were to be stoned to death (Deut. 21:21). Even as the victors were burying Absalom, all the Israelites who had followed Absalom into battle **fled to their homes**.

Ironically, Absalom was memorialized with two rock "monuments." Both had a tragic dimension to them. This final one was a pile of rock that served as a silent condemnation of his rebellion. But before his death Absalom had erected a pillar in **the King's Valley** outside of Jerusalem as **a monument to himself**. It was constructed to serve as a reminder that he had no son to carry on the **memory** of his **name**. It became known as **Absalom's Monument**, a name that it held down to the days when this account was recorded in the Bible.

18:19–23. Now that the civil war was over, King David had to be informed about Absalom's death. **Ahimaaz**, who had earlier warned David to cross the Jordan River to flee Absalom, now wished to share with him the news that he need fear Absalom no longer. Ahimaaz apparently believed that David would be elated by news of his army's victory. But Joab knew that David would not welcome the news. So Joab sent **a Cushite**—a north African, who was probably one of his slaves—to tell the king what he had seen.

After the Cushite left, **Ahimaaz** again requested permission to carry news to David, but to do so **behind the Cushite**. Joab gave in and told him to **run**. But Ahimaaz's intention was to arrive at Mahanaim ahead of the Cushite, who was making his way up and down forested hills. Ahimaaz succeeded in doing just this by traveling **by way of the plain**—by taking the longer but smoother route next to the Jordan River.

18:24–27. The king, who had been compelled by his troops to stay away from the fighting, nervously sat in the entranceway to Mahanaim awaiting word about the battle's outcome. Assisting him in the task was a **watchman** who stood on the wall above Mahanaim's **gateway**, an ideal observation site, since Mahanaim was located on a hilltop. As the watchman observed the roads, in the distance he saw a man **running alone**, and he reported it to the king. David knew the messenger would have **good news**, since a defeat would have been marked by survivors being chased back to the fortified city in large numbers.

When the watchman reported **another man running alone** on the road, David became even more confident that **good news** awaited him. His expectations were raised still higher when the watchman informed him that the lead runner appeared to be **Ahimaaz son of Zadok.**

18:28–30. Ahimaaz's arrival brought the expected positive report: **All is well** (Heb. "Shalom"). After presenting that brief summary, Ahimaaz bowed before the king and continued his narrative. He began by giving **praise . . . to the LORD**, the source of Israel's success. Then he provided a slightly expanded account of the course of events, telling David that God had **delivered up the men** who had lifted their hands against him.

This news, while good, was of secondary interest to David. He wanted to know if **the young man Absalom** was **safe**. Ahimaaz avoided answering the king's question. Instead, he made an ambiguous observation: **I saw great confusion**. Frustrated at Ahimaaz's lack of information, David ordered him to **stand aside** and wait for the second messenger to arrive.

18:31–33. The Cushite messenger confirmed David's worst fears, but did so with remarkable tactfulness: **May the enemies of my lord the king . . . be like that young man.** However delicately phrased, the news stunned David, and he was deeply **shaken**. Seeking a place of solitude and isolation, he went up to the **room over the gateway** and wept. All the way up the stairs he repeated the mournful mantra, **My son, my son Absalom! If only I had died instead of you**! The Lord's curse of violent death announced by the prophet Nathan (2 Sam. 12:10) had struck David's family a second time (2 Sam. 13:28–29). A third would follow later (1 Kgs. 2:23–25).

> **MAIN IDEA REVIEW:** *King David's oldest surviving son Absalom mounts a rebellion against his father in an effort to take over the throne of Israel. To survive, David flees Jerusalem and goes into exile in Mahanaim east of the Jordan River. David thwarts Absalom's plans to kill him with the covert assistance of an advisor and some priests who secretly remain loyal to him. Soldiers who support David fight against Absalom's forces and defeat them, killing Absalom in the process.*

III. CONCLUSION

Heroes that Hid

Born in 1892, Corrie ten Boom was the youngest daughter of a Christian watchmaker in Haarlem, Holland. She grew up to become the first female watchmaker in her country. Corrie directed the Haarlem Girl's Club from 1921 till 1940 and founded a Christian organization for girls that at one time had thousands of members in Holland and Indonesia. Since she was single, Corrie lived in her parents' home.

Her life changed radically on May 10, 1940, when the German army, following Adolph Hitler's orders, invaded her country. Using their infamous Blitzkrieg tactics, the Germans conquered Holland in less than one week.

Corrie's family did not support Germany's actions. And when the occupying forces began oppressing the Jews, the ten Booms joined the Dutch underground to help Jews escape the grasp of Hitler's troops. As many as four Jews a night would secretly stay at the ten Boom's house as they surreptitiously made their way out of Holland to freedom. To hide these clandestine visitors when German soldiers entered the home, a tiny secret room was built into one corner of Corrie's third-story room. Only thirty inches wide, the hiding place had an all-but-invisible entrance in an adjoining bookshelf. Because of the ten Boom's efforts, hundreds of Jews were saved from slaughter by the Germans.

The courageous actions of Corrie ten Boom's family bring to mind the equally daring actions of the unnamed Israelite family that saved the lives of Jonathan and Ahimaaz on their journey to King David. The Lord has worked through the courageous actions of godly people throughout the ages to save innocent lives.

PRINCIPLES

- A person who can impress people with good looks and smooth words will not necessarily make a good leader.
- If you sin against a person, his relatives may turn against you.
- Hard times help you discover who your true friends are.
- Some people will pretend to be your friends for the sake of personal gain.
- A person who advises another to sin is a fool.

APPLICATIONS

- If you have been deeply hurt by a person who has betrayed you in the past, mention that person by name in prayer, asking God to forgive him for what he did to you. Then mentally visualize a picture of that person and tell him you forgive him for the wrong he did to you.
- As a Bible study group, identify someone who is going through a financial and emotional hardship. Collect goods or money from everyone in the group and then donate these to the person in need.
- To enhance your Christian testimony in the workplace, determine to listen carefully to your boss's directions and follow them exactly.

IV. LIFE APPLICATION

Israel's Bloodstained Monarchies

What was the most dangerous job in ancient Israel? It might have been that of being a king. While these chapters of 2 Samuel tell the tragic story of how Absalom tried to kill his father David, his attempt to kill a king was neither the first nor the last in Israel's history. The first to die at the hands of his own subjects was Saul's son Ish-Bosheth, who was murdered by two of his own soldiers around 1003 B.C., the seventh year of David's reign (2 Sam. 4:6–7).

Throughout its long history Israel had a total of 43 people who claimed the office of king. Of those, 15 were killed by others while in office. Thirteen of those kings—30 percent of the 43—were murdered by their fellow Israelites. Only two died at the hands of foreign invaders. Of the 13 who were killed by other Israelites, three of them were direct descendants of David. Ahaziah was killed by Jehu and his allies in 842 B.C. (2 Kgs. 9:27). Joash was killed in Jerusalem by two of his own servants in 796 B.C. (2 Kgs. 12:21). In 640 B.C. Amon was likewise killed by his servants, inside his own palace (2 Kgs. 21:23). The prophetic sword that Nathan proclaimed would pierce David's family did so for many generations beyond David's lifetime (2 Sam. 12:10). God's word proves true from generation to generation.

V. PRAYER

Lord, in our hard times life's pleasures seem few and far between. We experience anxiety, pain, and want; those we once counted on as sources of love and affirmation—family members and former friends—are now the ones who grieve us. The resources within our souls and checkbooks grow thin and we hurt. In these hard times, dear Lord, come to us with your healing, affirming presence. Restore us so our lives may become an ever more vibrant testimony to your grace and goodness. In Jesus' name. Amen.

VI. DEEPER DISCOVERIES

A. Why Did Men Kiss One Another in Old Testament Times? (15:5)

Kisses had three primary functions in the Semitic cultures of the Old Testament. They were used to express respect, familial affection, and romantic affection. Romantic kisses were exchanged only between adult men and women (Prov. 7:13; Song 1:2). A man might express familial affection for his children and grandchildren at a time of reunion or departure by kissing them (Gen. 31:55). Likewise, at a time of reunion or departure adult men could express familial affection in this manner (Gen. 29:13; 33:4; 45:15).

Men could also express acceptance and respect for one another (1 Sam. 20:41; 2 Sam. 19:39) by a kiss. Absalom's actions in 2 Samuel 15:5 were meant to convey his acceptance and respect of the men who came to Jerusalem seeking justice. Since Absalom was a prince, it would have been surprising for him to kiss someone of a lower social class, and his actions would have impressed the citizens of Israel who witnessed or experienced it.

B. Foreigners in David's Army (15:18)

During David's reign as king over Israel, three different non-Israelite groups are mentioned as providing military service for Israel: Kerethites, Pelethites, and a group of 600 Philistines from Gath. In addition, Uriah the Hittite was a non-Israelite. The Kerethites came from the Negev, a semidesert region close to both Judahite and Philistine settlements (1 Sam. 30:14). The Hittites were a non-Israelite group that had settled in Canaan. The region from which the Pelethites came is unknown, but the Philistines lived along the Mediterranean coast west of Judah. Before David became Israel's king, he spent time living in the Negev and in the Philistine city of Gath and would have been aware of the availability of these foreign soldiers.

Since no Kerethites, Pelethites, Gittites, or Hittites are mentioned as serving in Israel's army before or after the time of David, it seems that these men were personally recruited by him at some early point in his royal career. They may have helped David before he became king or while David was still at Hebron, helping him defeat the forces of Ish-Bosheth. Alternatively, David enlisted them as a personal militia—soldiers who would have been answerable only to the king and who would have had no reason to participate in a revolt against him.

VII. TEACHING OUTLINE

A. INTRODUCTION

1. Lead Story: The Fifth Column
2. Context: Nathan's prophetic declaration that a "sword would never depart" from David's house proved true as the king's oldest surviving son, Absalom, staged a bloody but unsuccessful coup against his father.
3. Transition: Even as General Mola led a revolt against his own government in 1936, so David's son Absalom led the nation in revolt against King David. In the chaos that followed, David was forced to deal with the consequences of his sins against Bathsheba and Uriah.

B. COMMENTARY

1. Absalom Lays the Groundwork for a Rebellion Against David (15:1–6)
2. Absalom Declares Himself King over Israel (15:7–12)

3. David Flees Jerusalem (15:13–16:14)
4. Absalom Rapes David's Concubines (16:15–23)
5. Hushai Misleads Absalom (17:1–14)
6. David Goes to Mahanaim (17:15–29)
7. David's Forces Kill Absalom (18:1–33)

C. CONCLUSION: ISRAEL'S BLOODSTAINED MONARCHIES

VIII. ISSUES FOR DISCUSSION

1. To what extent was Absalom's rebellion a result of poor parenting on David's part? What, if anything, could David have done differently?
2. David prayed that God would make Ahithophel give foolish advice to Absalom (15:31). When is it right for us to pray that our adversaries will perform poorly?
3. Hushai deceived Absalom, leading him to believe he had switched his loyalties. When, if ever, is it right to deceive others?
4. Joab disobeyed David's order by killing the man who would have killed David. Is it ever right to disobey a boss's order? If so, under what circumstances?

2 Samuel 19:1–20:26

The Return of the King

2 Samuel 19:1–20:26

Quote

"*I*t's not whether you get knocked down.

It's whether you get up."

Vince Lombardi

BIOGRAPHICAL PROFILE: KIMHAM

- Probably a relative of Barzillai the Gileadite
- Lived in Gilead during his early years
- Lived in Jerusalem at the royal palace following Absalom's defeat
- May have been given a piece of land—Geruth Kimham near Bethlehem—by David

BIOGRAPHICAL PROFILE: SHEBA

- Member of the tribe of Benjamin
- Led an unsuccessful rebellion against King David shortly after Absalom was defeated
- Beheaded by the citizens of Abel Beth Maacah

IN A NUTSHELL

*D*avid publicly mourns Absalom's death at first, but then follows Joab's advice and commends his troops for their victorious efforts. Then David, his troops, and their families return to Jerusalem. On the return journey David is reconciled to several people, but he witnesses the outbreak of rebellion led by Sheba the Benjamite. In the days that follow, David's troops put down this second revolt against the king's authority.

The Return of the King

I. INTRODUCTION

Gratitude for the Difference Makers

*B*eside a road in Pennsylvania's Valley Forge National Historical Park stands a larger-than-life bronze statue of Frederick Augustus von Steuben. This honor was accorded to Steuben, a German immigrant to the United States, because of the invaluable contributions he made to the American military efforts during the Revolutionary War. Steuben is remembered as America's most effective inspector general during the Revolutionary War.

An out-of-work Prussian military officer in 1776, Steuben traveled to Paris in 1777 to meet with Benjamin Franklin and gain employment in America's Continental Army. Franklin was impressed with the forty-six-year-old officer and sent him to General George Washington with a glowing recommendation. Franklin was convinced that, even though Steuben spoke no English, he could help the American army establish a training program that would prepare them to fight effectively against the British.

From February of 1778 until the end of the war, Steuben served in the American army as an unpaid general. Even as he learned to speak English he designed and led the daily activities that prepared the fledgling nation's soldiers to win the Revolutionary War against the British. In appreciation for his efforts, General Steuben was given a pension of $2,500 by Congress.

Steuben's efforts to assist America in her war for independence remind us of the assistance Barzillai provided David during his war against Absalom. Similarly, America's gratitude expressed toward Steuben brings to mind David's expression of gratitude toward Barzillai during the king's triumphant return to Jerusalem.

II. COMMENTARY

The Return of the King

> **MAIN IDEA:** *David deals appropriately with his friends and enemies to regain their confidence in him as their king.*

A David Conceals His Grief to Support His Victorious Troops (19:1–8)

SUPPORTING IDEA: *Joab warns David against neglecting his troops and continuing to mourn Absalom's death. David follows Joab's advice and expresses appreciation to the men who have saved his life.*

19:1–4. Devastated by the news of his son's death, King David continued **weeping and mourning** for Absalom. News of David's reaction reached the field commander, Joab, and the rest of the troops, and the report disturbed them. So instead of celebrating, **the victory** that day was **turned into mourning**. The troops had fought valiantly that day and won a major victory; however, they **stole into the city** of Mahanaim as though they had been routed and forced to **flee from battle**. Instead of hearing the sound of festive singing by the women, all they heard in the city was the king as he cried out for his dead son Absalom.

19:5–8. David's personal grief was out of control and in danger of destroying his newly salvaged kingship. He needed someone with a clear mind and a firm hand to put an end to his pity party. This job fell to Joab. Joab pointed out that, in a world where one's honor was more than one's life, David had brought shame on **all the men** who had just **saved** his **life** and the lives of his **sons and daughters** and his **wives and concubines**. The king had done this by showing more sympathy for those who hated him—Absalom in particular—than praise for those who loved him—his soldiers who had risked their lives on his behalf. Joab then warned David that if he did not go out and **encourage** his **men**, he could permanently alienate himself from those he needed most.

David followed Joab's advice. He hid his profound grief and went to the area where the king should greet his returning heroes, in the **gateway** of Mahanaim, his temporary capital city.

B David Journeys as Far as the Jordan River (19:9–15)

SUPPORTING IDEA: *Following the death of Absalom, his supporters switch their loyalties back to David. The men of Judah, David's own ancestral tribe, likewise affirm their support for the king. With these assurances of support, David leaves Mahanaim and travels back to the Jordan River.*

19:9–10. The men of Israel—the citizens of the tribal regions of Judah—had once anointed David's son **Absalom** as king in place of David. But now that their new king had **died in battle**, all their hopes of establishing a new direction for the country were gone. As the men of Israel weighed their options for national leadership, they remembered that David had **delivered** them **from the hand of the Philistines**. He had protected their lives and property, but they had driven him out of the country. Though not stated in the text at this point, they decided to bring David back as their king (see vv. 40–43).

19:11–13. Unlike the rest of Israel, David's own tribesmen, the Judahites, were not enthusiastic at first about accepting David back as their king; they had supported another Judahite—Absalom—as their king. But David had a plan to get them back on his side. He would send the priests **Zadok and Abiathar**, two of the most respected men in his government, to meet with **the elders of Judah** and win them over. David probably hoped to incite jealousy among his fellow tribesmen by having the priests tell the elders that the rest of the nation had already thrown their support behind David.

David provided a second motivation for having the tribe of Judah support him in his return as the nation's king. Amasa, a Judahite who had served as Absalom's general, would serve as the top military commander in David's revamped army. Having Amasa as David's highest profile military leader would make it easier for David to regain the loyalties of those soldiers who had previously followed Amasa in Absalom's army. In addition, it would punish Joab for his act of insubordination (18:5,14). Because Amasa was David's relative (2 Sam. 17:25; 1 Chron. 2:16), he was likely to remain loyal to David.

19:14–15. David's plan worked to perfection; he won over **all the men of Judah**, thus gaining their support. They signaled their support for him by inviting the king and all his men to come back to Jerusalem. Further proof came in a very practical form. As David arrived at the Jordan River, a large group of men from Judah came to Gilgal to **meet the king** and bring him and his entourage **across the Jordan**.

C David Gives Shimei a Temporary Reprieve (19:16–23)

SUPPORTING IDEA: *When David's most ardent opponent among the Benjamites begs him for mercy, the king graciously permits him to live.*

19:16–18. As David and his supporters were fleeing from Jerusalem, Shimei the Benjamite had met them with curses and insults (2 Sam. 16:5–8, 13). Now that David was returning victorious from his battle with Absalom, Shimei knew that his life was in peril. As one who had opposed David, he could expect only to be arrested and executed. Shimei decided to appeal directly to David for mercy. Though he was a Benjamite, he **hurried down**

with the men of Judah to meet the king. He was not alone among those who joined with David's tribesmen in greeting the king at the river. There were **a thousand** other **Benjamites**, including **Ziba**, the caretaker of Saul's estate (2 Sam. 9:9–10), and his household. Shimei **fell prostrate** before the king. This act of placing his face in the dirt before the feet of David symbolized his absolute submission to his authority.

19:19–20. Shimei admitted that he had done **wrong** and **sinned** on the day that the king left Jerusalem. In addition, he demonstrated his zeal to reestablish himself as a loyal supporter of David by being **the first of the whole house of Joseph**—that is, the first of all the non-Judahites—to meet David on his return to Jerusalem.

19:21–23. Among those who remembered Shimei and what he had done was **Abishai** son of Zeruiah, one of David's commanders (2 Sam. 18:2). Abishai had previously requested permission to kill Shimei (2 Sam.16:9). Abishai repeated his earlier suggestion that **Shimei be put to death** (2 Sam. 16:9). But as he had done before (16:10), David rejected his commander's suggestion. This day was a day for celebration, not a day for death. As David's kingship **over Israel** had been given a reprieve, so Shimei would be given a reprieve, even if it should prove only temporary (1 Kgs. 2:8–9). Thus the king **promised** Shimei that his life would be spared.

Ⓓ David Deals Equitably with Mephibosheth and Ziba (19:24–30)

SUPPORTING IDEA: *After listening to Mephibosheth's explanation of his behavior during Absalom's revolt, David restores to him a portion of Saul's estate.*

19:24. Mephibosheth, Saul's grandson, was next to appear before David in search of a gracious word from the king. Mephibosheth's appearance before the king was remarkable, but in an unexpected way. Normally one would appear before the king looking as clean and well manicured as possible. But the one who stood before David on this occasion had not taken care of his lame **feet** or **trimmed his mustache** or **washed his clothes** since the day David had left Jerusalem. Such neglect would have been interpreted by David as an expression of mourning on Mephibosheth's part.

19:25–28. Mephibosheth's appearance contrasted sharply with what David had expected, based on the report given by Ziba at the outbreak of the rebellion (2 Sam. 16:3). Throughout the entire ordeal David had believed that Mephibosheth was a traitor who had abandoned him during his hour of greatest need. Yet now Mephibosheth's actions and appearance gave evidence of unwavering loyalty. David asked him why he didn't go with him when he fled Jerusalem.

Starting with the obvious—that he was **lame**—Mephibosheth then suggested that he had been **betrayed** by his servant **Ziba**, who made it impossible for Mephibosheth to get on his **donkey** and **go with the king**. Mephibosheth also declared that Ziba had **slandered** him, providing David with false reports. Mephibosheth put his fate in David's hands. He realized that in the past the king had been kinder to him than he had expected. He expressed confidence that David would act as wisely as **an angel of God** in this situation.

19:29–30. Mephibosheth's actions, appearance, and words created uncertainty in David's mind about who was telling the truth—Ziba or Mephibosheth. The king had previously given Mephibosheth's property to Ziba (16:4). Yet in view of the evidence presented to him on this occasion, David changed his previous decision. The king issued an edict ordering Mephibosheth and Ziba to **divide the fields** of Saul's former estate evenly among themselves.

Ⓔ David Rewards the Family of Barzillai (19:31–40)

SUPPORTING IDEA: *David rewards the family of Barzillai for their kindnesses to him during Absalom's rebellion by allowing Kimham to live as a permanent guest in the royal court.*

19:31–33. David and his group had not left Mahanaim alone as they journeyed to the Jordan River on their way back to Jerusalem. Accompanying the group was eighty-year-old **Barzillai the Gileadite** to celebrate the king's victory and **to send him on his way** back to the royal palace. Barzillai, who was **a very wealthy man**, was one of the benefactors who had provided much-needed supplies and food for the king during his stay in Mahanaim (17:27–29). David wished to repay his generous supporter. He urged Barzillai to cross over the Jordan River with him and stay with him in Jerusalem. Barzillai would be given the "royal treatment" for the rest of his life in exchange for the favors he had extended to David.

19:34–37a. Barzillai gave several reasons why he could not accept the king's offer. He was **eighty years old**, and would probably not live many more years to enjoy the privilege. Besides, the lavish pleasures associated with the royal court would be wasted on him. He could no longer taste food, and his hearing had deteriorated to the point where he could no longer **hear the voices of men and women singers**. Barzillai also believed he would be **an added burden** to the king, who would feel obligated to take care of him.

Finally, Barzillai wished to die in his **own town**, near the tomb of his **father and mother**.

19:37b–40. Barzillai provided David with an alternative plan that would allow the king to express his appreciation to the gracious benefactor's family. He requested that David do for **Kimham**—apparently the elderly man's relative—**whatever** special things he might wish. David seized upon the suggestion and ordered that Kimham cross the Jordan River with him. Mirroring Barzillai's words, David declared that he would do for Kimham whatever pleased the elderly friend of the king.

A triumphant moment came for Barzillai as he **crossed over** the Jordan with David. That short trek represented the satisfying culmination of a multitude of risks he had taken in his efforts to save the king and his nation from certain disaster. Protecting the entourage as they made their way across the river were **all the troops of Judah** and **half the troops of Israel**. Kimham was among the other people who crossed the Jordan with the king. Biblical evidence suggests that David kept his commitment to take care of Kimham. The mention in Jeremiah 41:17 of a site near Bethlehem named Geruth Kimham ("The Hospitality of/accorded to Kimham") implies that David provided this friend with an estate not far from the king's own hometown.

🄵 Strife Breaks Out Between the Soldiers of Judah and Israel (19:41–43)

SUPPORTING IDEA: *David's return to Jerusalem is marred by a quarrel between the soldiers from Judah and those from ten of the other tribes of Israel.*

19:41–43. The day of David's return to Jerusalem had been a festive occasion marked by reconciliation between the king and his subjects. But all was not harmonious on that day. Bitter rivalries dating back to the early days of David's rise to the kingship (2 Sam. 2:14–17) resurfaced with the king's return. The **men of Israel** feared that the soldiers from David's own tribe were using this occasion to try to gain special favors. They complained that **the men of Judah** were trying to **steal the king away** from the rest of the nation.

Though the Bible does not record David's response to this complaint, it does state that the men of Judah answered the charge. First, they claimed a position of privilege for themselves. The king was **closely related** to them—more closely than he was to members of other Israelite tribes. Second, they had not enriched themselves from the experience. They had not **eaten any of** the king's provisions, nor had they **taken anything** from the royal group's possessions for themselves.

The northern army had two trump cards to play in this verbal poker game. First, they had a numerically **greater claim** on Israel's king than did Judah, since they represented **ten shares** (ten tribes), whereas Judah represented only one. Second, they had a chronologically superior claim on David, since they were **the first to speak of bringing back** the king. The soldiers of Judah disregarded these legitimate claims and buttressed their position through verbal force. Acting on the assumption that verbal might makes right, they **responded even more harshly** than did **the men of Israel**.

G Sheba Incites a Rebellion Against David (20:1–2)

SUPPORTING IDEA: *Sheba the Benjamite incites the non-Judahites to reject David as their king and follow him instead.*

20:1–2. Sheba son of Bicri, a member of the tribe of Benjamin, was present at the confrontation between the soldiers of Judah and those of the rest of Israel. Capitalizing on the intense anger generated by the conflict between the rival military groups present at David's return, Sheba used it to set off a second revolt against David. The writer of 2 Samuel refers to Sheba as a "son of Belial" (NIV, "troublemaker"), a phrase that elsewhere refers to people who reject authority and lack moral integrity (1 Sam. 2:12; 10:27; 25:17; 30:22).

Sheba called **all the men of Israel**—that is, those who were not members of the tribe of Judah—to take **no share** in the process of returning David as their king. Sheba urged **every man** to return to **his tent** instead. This call would later be repeated in a rebellion against another member of the Davidic dynasty (1 Kgs. 12:16). Thus the day that had started out so well for David spiraled off into chaos and danger.

H David Prepares for War Against Sheba (20:3–7)

SUPPORTING IDEA: *Faced with the threat of another challenge to his kingship, David first deals with essential matters in the capital city and then hastily rallies his troops for war against Sheba.*

20:3. David's first order of business after returning to his palace in Jerusalem was to deal with the problems created there by Absalom's rebellion. This required thoughtful attention to **the ten concubines** David had left to **take care of the palace**. Though they were technically part of David's harem, their status had been altered by Absalom's abuse of them (2 Sam. 16:22). To guarantee that the women would never again be subject to physical abuse, the women were placed in a house **under guard**. As was required of a husband, David **provided for them** (Exod. 21:10). However, because of the circumstances under which the women had been abused, David **did not** again **lie with them**. Perhaps he considered them to have been married to Absalom, so he treated them **as widows** of his son (Lev. 18:15).

20:4–7. David then turned his attention to the challenge to his authority posed by Sheba. He ordered **Amasa**, the former commander of Absalom's troops, to **summon** the men of **Judah**. The men were to report to Jerusalem and be ready for war **within three days**. David's appointment of Amasa as his top military officer was probably designed to help bring about a reconciliation between the king and Absalom's former supporters, as well as to punish Joab for his insubordination (2 Sam. 18:5,14).

David's hopes for a rapid response to Sheba's rebellion were jeopardized however when Amasa took too long to mobilize the troops. So David hastily appointed Amasa's cousin **Abishai** as commander of his army.

Joab Murders Amasa (20:8–13)

SUPPORTING IDEA: *Joab murders Amasa and assumes command of David's troops in pursuit of Sheba.*

20:8–10. After David's troops had traveled about seven miles from Jerusalem to **the great rock in Gibeon**, Amasa came to meet them. Joab stepped forward to greet him. Then Joab took Amasa **by the beard** as if to greet him with a kiss. But Joab's intentions were anything but peaceful. As he was kissing Amasa, he stabbed him to death him with his dagger. Then Joab and Abishai got down to the business of pursuing **Sheba**.

20:11–13. Joab was considered a heroic figure by many in the Israelite army, even though he had fallen out of favor with David. So when Joab reasserted himself as a leader by his bold action against Amasa, the soldiers followed Joab eagerly. An unnamed soldier called for the troops to **follow Joab**, and all the men set out in pursuit of Sheba.

Joab Puts Down Sheba's Rebellion (20:14–22)

SUPPORTING IDEA: *Joab and David's troops pursue Sheba to Abel Beth Maacah, where they lay siege to the city. The rebellion ends after Joab convinces the citizens of Abel Beth Maacah to execute Sheba.*

20:14–15. After Sheba convinced the Israelites to withdraw their support for David, he faced the more difficult task of motivating them to start another war against the king who had just defeated them. The Benjamite **passed through all the tribes of Israel** trying to rally them to his cause but apparently found little support. Finally Sheba came to the northern limits of Israelite settlements in the land. **Abel Beth Maacah** was located about 30 miles north of the Sea of Galilee. There in the **region of the Berites** Sheba was able to enlist men who **followed him** in his attempts to mount an armed revolt.

Meanwhile, David's forces under the leadership of Joab advanced into the region. Sheba and his small force were not prepared to fight the king's forces in the open fields, so they sought refuge in the walled city of Abel Beth Maacah. Joab and his troops placed the city under siege. A siege could be carried out either passively or actively. In a passive siege, the attacking troops sealed off all movement in and out of the city to starve the city's inhabitants into submission. An active siege involved attacks on the city's defenses. To end Sheba's rebellion quickly, Joab conducted an active siege. He directed his troops to build **a siege ramp** up to the city and begin **battering the wall**.

20:16–21. As the siege progressed and the walls of Abel Beth Maacah began to shake from the assault, a woman from the city told Joab that this city in Israel was renowned for the service it rendered to those who came seeking wise counsel. Its citizens were both **peaceful and faithful**. If Joab continued with the siege, he would destroy a city that was **a mother in Israel**—a city that had provided nurture and support for others.

Joab made clear that his quarrel was not with a city but a man—**Sheba son of Bicri**, who had rebelled against David. If the citizens of Abel Beth Maacah would **hand** him **over**, the troops would **withdraw from the city** without destroying it. She made the gruesome promise that Sheba's **head** would be **thrown** to him **from the wall**.

20:22. The people of the city agreed with this woman's plan, and they soon **cut off the head of Sheba** and threw it to Joab. This ended the rebellion, and David's army returned to Jerusalem.

Ⓚ David's Administrative Personnel (20:23–26)

SUPPORTING IDEA: *David maintains an effective governmental administration throughout his kingship.*

20:23. For the second time in the account of David's kingship (see 8:16–18) the biblical narrator lists key players in the royal administration. This list probably comes from a period near the end of David's life. Heading both lists is **Joab**, commander of **Israel's entire army**. Although David had tried to replace Joab as his chief military officer (19:13), Joab was able to retain the position by killing Amasa (20:10). **Benaiah** held the second most important military position. He was commander over the **Kerethites** and the **Pelethites**, probably foreign mercenaries who served as the king's personal bodyguard.

20:24–25a. Third in the list of David's key personnel was **Adoniram**, who was **in charge of forced labor**. He was responsible for procuring the services of non-Israelites for work projects. He continued in this position under King Solomon (1 Kgs. 4:6; 5:14). The task of recording vital information in the royal court and maintaining access to it was the responsibility of **Jehoshaphat**, who apparently held this position throughout David's entire reign (2 Sam. 8:16). These well-kept records probably served as one of the sources for the author of 1 and 2 Samuel. Assisting Jehoshaphat in this task was **Sheva** the **secretary**.

20:25b–26. Israel, like every other nation in the ancient Near East, made no attempt to draw a sharp line of division between government and religion. David highly valued God's guidance in his administration. Three of his most important officials were priests. **Zadok and Abiathar** were direct descendants of Aaron, and both served as the leading **priests** associated with the ark in Jerusalem. David's personal **priest** was **Ira the Jairite**, a person mentioned nowhere else in Scripture.

MAIN IDEA REVIEW: *David deals appropriately with his friends and enemies to regain their confidence in him as their king.*

III. CONCLUSION

Gerontology and the Bible

One of the many great things about the Bible is that it depicts human experience. For example, predictable changes occur as a person ages. Besides the obvious physical changes in outward appearance, significant physical changes occur in a person's body that affect the ability to perceive sensory stimulation. These tendencies increase with age. While approximately one-third of the people over age 65 have some hearing loss, three-fourths of those age 75–79 have this problem. Typically older people experience the greatest hearing loss in the higher frequency range. Hearing loss affects men more than it does women.

Taste is another sense affected by advancing age. By the time a person reaches age 70 he has only about half the taste buds he had as a young adult. Of the four primary taste sensations—sweet, sour, bitter, and salty—the one that becomes most degraded is sweetness. The ability to taste what is sour is also reduced.

The Bible accurately depicts these age-related realities in this section of 2 Samuel. As an eighty-year-old man, David's friend Barzillai was dealing with problems associated with advancing age. He admitted that he couldn't taste what he ate and drank. Furthermore, he had lost the ability to hear singers' voices.

PRINCIPLES

- One of the important traits of a good leader is his ability to express appreciation to those who help him achieve success.
- It is sometimes appropriate for an authority to lessen the punishment of an offender who shows genuine regret for the wrong he has done.
- What a person values in life tends to change as that person ages.
- Wise people use special opportunities to bless the next generation.
- It is important to stop problems early rather than letting them continue until they get worse.
- Situations in life may arise where there are no good choices; in such cases one must always choose the least evil alternative.

APPLICATIONS

- Make a list of three people who have helped you during critical times in your life. Beside their names write down what they did to help you. Pray a prayer of thanks to God for the assistance these people provided you. If any of them are still alive, write a note to them expressing your appreciation to them for what they did.
- Locate a shelter for abused women in your city or region. Then have your Sunday school class or Bible study group donate time or money to help that organization as a Christian witness to them.
- Lead your Sunday school class or Bible study group in prayer for those who are working to protect our country from those who would destroy it.

IV. LIFE APPLICATION

The Cost of Peace

Throughout Israelite history cities and nations were often called upon to make sacrifices in order to get an enemy to suspend their attack. Normally the price consisted of silver and gold. For example, when Tiglath-pileser led the Assyrian army against Jerusalem in 701 B.C., the Judahite king Hezekiah attempted to make the Assyrians withdraw by providing them with eleven tons of silver and one ton of gold (2 Kgs. 18:14). On other occasions an invading king might not leave until he had also taken hostages in addition to material wealth. Such was the case when Daniel, his friends, and about ten thousand others were carried off to Babylon by Nebuchadnezzar in 605 B.C.

When Joab launched an attack against Abel Beth Maacah, it was not for the purpose of conquering the city to bring it under Israelite control; the city was already a part of the nation. However, this walled city was acting as a hostile enemy by providing safe haven for the person who was a threat to David's kingship. Joab could have demanded that the city pay all costs associated with Israel's efforts to put down the revolt—a price tag that would have taken every bit of the citizens' wealth. He could have demanded that all the city leaders be arrested and handed over to him for execution because of their willingness to support the rebellion. Instead, he demanded only that Sheba be killed.

V. PRAYER

Lord, when we feel like retreating from the world because of emotional wounds we have received, teach us to look beyond ourselves. Help us to reach out to others and express appreciation to them for the good things they have done for us. Help us to look beyond our pain and find people who need a blessing. Then help us find a way to bless them. As we put our lives back together, help us to deal with important matters in the home and in the larger circle of our lives, even as you did for David so many years ago. In Jesus' name. Amen.

VI. DEEPER DISCOVERIES

A. Why Did David Sit in the Gateway? (18:24)

Within walled cities the gateway was a place of great importance. It was the most prominent location in the city, since everyone who entered or left the city had to pass through it. The area just inside the gateway was the largest open area within the city, because it was used as the marketplace where people sold goods to the crowds of people.

By claiming the most important spot in the city as his own, David was able to symbolically present himself as the most important man in the city—the king. Furthermore, because it was next to the largest open space within the city walls, the largest possible crowd of soldiers was able to gather in front of him to see him and listen to his remarks.

B. Why Is Jonathan's Son Called Mephibosheth in 2 Samuel and Merib-Baal in 1 Chronicles?

Throughout the book of 2 Samuel (4:4; 9:6; 16:1; 19:24) Jonathan's only named son is called Mephibosheth. In 1 Chronicles (8:34; 9:30), however, this same son is called Merib-Baal. The key difference in the two names is that the first name contains the Hebrew word "bosheth," which means "shame," whereas the second name contains the name of a pagan god, "Baal." The reason for the different spelling in 2 Samuel is probably the law found in Exodus 23:13 (see Josh. 23:7; Ps. 16:4): "Do not invoke the names of other gods; do not let them be heard on your lips."

VII. TEACHING OUTLINE

A. INTRODUCTION

1. Lead Story: Gratitude for the Difference Makers
2. Context: David expressed appreciation to his troops for defeating Absalom, then began his journey back to Jerusalem. At the Jordan River he encountered three key people, each of whom he treated with fairness and generosity. The king then reasserted his authority by tending to business in the palace and putting down a revolt in the land.
3. Transition: Both persons and nations are measured by the way they treats others. Following the Revolutionary War the United States provided the Prussian general Steuben with a generous pension for the invaluable service he provided to the colonies' military efforts. Similarly, King David rewarded Barzillai for the contributions he made to David's successful campaign to put down Absalom's rebellion.

B. COMMENTARY

1. David Conceals His Grief to Support His Victorious Troops (19:1–8)
2. David Journeys as Far as the Jordan River (19:9–15)
3. David Gives Shimei a Temporary Reprieve (19:16–23)
4. David Deals Equitably with Mephibosheth and Ziba (19:24–30)
5. David Rewards the Family of Barzillai (19:31–40)
6. Strife Breaks Out Between the Soldiers of Judah and Israel (19:41–43)
7. Sheba Incites a Rebellion Against David (20:1–2)
8. David Prepares for War Against Sheba (20:3–7)
9. Joab Murders Amasa (20:8–13)
10. Joab Puts Down Sheba's Rebellion (20:14–22)
11. David's Administrative Personnel (20:23–26)

C. CONCLUSION: THE COST OF PEACE

VIII. ISSUES FOR DISCUSSION

1. David grieved deeply over the loss of Absalom, yet he had to hide his grief enough to express appreciation to his troops for their valiant efforts. Have you ever had to pretend you weren't hurting on the inside? How well did it work?
2. David delayed instituting the death penalty against Shimei because Shimei showed regret for his wrongful actions. Was this an adequate reason to show leniency?
3. After listening to Mephibosheth explain why he didn't follow David into exile, the king changed the terms of the agreement he had made with Ziba. Was Mephibosheth telling the truth? Did David make a good decision?
4. The citizens of Abel Beth Maacah were given the difficult choice of executing a person or having their city attacked. Did they make the right choice? Why or why not?

2 Samuel 21:1–22:51

The Song of David

Quote

"*G*onna say it loud, gonna say it proud,

Hey! I, I love the Lord,

I, I love the Lord.

Come join the throng—ten million strong.

Come lift your voice and sing this victory song."

Lyrics to Petra's

"I Love the Lord"

BIOGRAPHICAL PROFILE: RIZPAH

- Daughter of Aiah
- One of Saul's concubines
- Mother of Armoni and Mephibosheth
- Suspected of having sexual relations with Abner following Saul's death
- Slept outdoors on sackcloth for six months near the unburied corpses of her two sons after they were ritually slain by the Gibeonites

BIOGRAPHICAL PROFILE: ELHANAN

- Israelite soldier from Bethlehem
- Son of Jaare-Oregim, also known as Jair (1 Chron. 20:5)
- Killed Lahmi the brother of Goliath (acc. to 1 Chron. 20:5) or possibly an individual named Goliath (see 2 Sam. 21:19)

2 Samuel 21:1–22:51

IN A NUTSHELL

*T*his section of 2 Samuel is part of an appendix to the book that extends from chapters 21 through 24. Chapter 21 depicts the exploits of King David and some of his greatest men. Chapter 22 is a theologically rich psalm that expresses the intensity and depth of David's relationship with God.

The Song of David

I. INTRODUCTION

A Mother's Sacrificial Love

Thirty-three-year-old Lorraine, already the mother of three girls, was excited to learn that she and her husband Martyn had conceived a fourth child—their first boy. But four months into the pregnancy, Lorraine began to experience stomach cramps. Medical tests revealed that she was suffering from advanced liver cancer.

The doctor informed her that she had to make a soul-wrenching choice. According to the oncologist, she could begin aggressive therapy immediately to arrest the cancer's growth, or she could delay it. If she started the chemotherapy treatments during the pregnancy, the cancer could probably be stopped, but the baby would die. Yet if she delayed receiving treatments until after the baby was born, the cancer would grow to the point where it would surely kill her.

Lorraine's decision? She would wait to receive any chemotherapy until the baby was far enough along to have a good chance of surviving. She scheduled a Caesarean section during the twenty-sixth week of the pregnancy. She went into premature labor during the twenty-fifth week, however, and on November 18, 2007, she gave birth to a healthy boy, whom she named Liam.

Immediately after the baby's birth she underwent aggressive treatment for her cancer. The chemotherapy was unable to arrest the cancer. But in the fragile, final four weeks of her life, she was able to hold tiny Liam several times. "Toward the end we knew things weren't going well, but she was overjoyed that she had given life to Liam," said her husband Martyn.

Lorraine's sacrificial love for her son reminds us of the love Rizpah had for her sons, Armoni and Mephibosheth. Rizpah, too, sacrificed her personal comfort to express her profound love for her two sons. She set an example of a mother's love at its most inspiring.

II. COMMENTARY

The Song of David

> **MAIN IDEA:** *Chapters 21–22 are the first half of the appendix section of 1 and 2 Samuel, and they reveal key details about David and his soldiers. David is depicted delivering his nation from famine through a difficult but wise ruling. David's soldiers are shown delivering the nation through their great heroism in battle against the Philistines. King David's great heart of faith is beautifully expressed in a song that resembles Psalm 18.*

David Ends a Drought by Granting Justice to the Gibeonites (21:1–9)

> **SUPPORTING IDEA:** *After learning that a three-year drought in Israel was caused by Saul's sin against the Gibeonites, David rectifies the matter by granting the Gibeonites the right to take revenge on the household of Saul.*

21:1. At an undisclosed point in David's thirty-three-year reign over all Israel, the nation experienced a crisis. There was a **famine** for **three successive years**. While a year-long famine was serious, it would not automatically have been interpreted as evidence of divine displeasure. However, a famine lasting three years could be understood as nothing other than a divine judgment against the nation. In an effort to determine the reason for God's wrath, **David sought the face of the LORD**. God revealed that it was on account of **Saul and his blood-stained house**. In particular, it was because Saul had **put the Gibeonites to death**.

21:2–6. When David learned that Saul in his **zeal for Israel and Judah** had tried to annihilate the Gibeonites even though the Israelites had sworn to spare them (Josh. 9:15), he summoned some representatives of the surviving **Gibeonites** to his palace. The God of justice required the king to act with justice toward these abused people, and David was determined to bring it about. He asked the Gibeonites how he could **make amends** so they could **bless the Lord's inheritance** and thus end the divine curse. The Gibeonites requested that **seven** of Saul's **descendants** be given to them to be killed and exposed **before the LORD at Gibeah of Saul**. David agreed to their request.

21:7–9. David, not the Gibeonites, selected which of Saul's descendants would pay the price for their forefather's crime. Because of a commitment the king had made to his best friend Jonathan (1 Sam. 20:42), he **spared**

Mephibosheth son of Jonathan. Of the seven who were chosen for execution, two were sons of Saul and five were his grandchildren. Because Armoni and Mephibosheth, Saul's two sons, were the offspring of a concubine, they were probably ineligible for kingship.

David handed these seven men over to the Gibeonites, who then performed a solemn execution in early spring, just as the **barley harvest** was beginning. Afterwards the bodies were **exposed . . . before the LORD**, that is, left unburied. This denial of an honorable burial marked these individuals as disgraced and under God's judgment.

B Rizpah and David Honor the House of Saul (21:10–14)

SUPPORTING IDEA: *Rizpah and David preserve the dignity of Saul's family by preserving the bones of deceased members of the family and providing them with an honorable burial in the tomb of Saul's father, Kish.*

21:10. Rizpah daughter of Aiah, one of Saul's widows, was the mother of two of the men who were ritually killed by the Gibeonites. In a unique act of love and loyalty to her beloved sons, Rizpah spread **sackcloth . . . on a rock**, where she remained for a period of about six months, extending from early spring until early fall. During that entire time she protected the bones of the bodies from desecration. Depriving herself of sleep during the long nights, Rizpah risked her life in the dark to keep **wild animals** away from the bones of her loved ones.

21:11–12. When the king was told about this remarkable act of family loyalty on the part of one of his father-in-law's concubines, he decided to reward it. He contacted the citizens of **Jabesh Gilead**, who had previously acted valiantly to preserve the honor of the house of Saul. The men of this town had retrieved the corpses of Saul and three of his sons **from the public square at Beth Shan** where the Philistines had hung them, then provided a dignified burial for them (1 Sam. 31:11–13). Wishing to honor Israel's first royal family further, David took the bones to a more central site to establish a more fitting resting place for these honored relics.

21:13–14. David then ordered that the bones of those seven relatives of Saul who had **been killed and exposed** be **gathered up** and provided with a dignified burial. In the concluding comment of this account, the biblical narrator suggests that God was pleased with the plan that David had worked out in behalf of the Gibeonites and Israel's first royal family. After the dignified burial that David provided for the remains of Israel's first royal family,

God answered prayer **in behalf of the land**. This is a clear indication that rain once again fell on Israel.

C Heroic Achievements by David's Soldiers (21:15–22)

> **SUPPORTING IDEA:** *David's soldiers proved their great skill in battle by defeating formidable Philistine opponents.*

21:15–17. The Philistines were Israel's most troublesome opponents from the days of Samson until the end of David's reign. Thus it is understandable that special honors were given to Israelite soldiers who defeated the Philistines' most formidable fighters. The heroic activity of **Abishai son of Zeruiah**, one of David's cousins and the man David entrusted with the task of putting down Sheba's rebellion (2 Sam. 20:6), is recorded here.

During a military encounter between the **Philistines and Israel**—probably one that occurred before Absalom's rebellion (2 Sam. 18:3–4)—David found himself in trouble. Exhausted and unable to escape from the enemy, he was confronted by **Ishbi-Benob**, one of the descendants of Rapha. This remarkable soldier had a spear with a bronze **spearhead** that weighed **three hundred shekels**—about eight pounds. Just when it seemed that David would be killed by him, Abishai came to his rescue, striking the Philistine down and killing him.

David's brush with death prompted his men to force the king to change his behavior. The king's life, metaphorically referred to as **the lamp of Israel**, was far too valuable to be put at risk on a battlefield. If David died it would be as if Israel's greatest light had been **extinguished**. Therefore his soldiers took an oath vowing that David would **never again** venture forth onto the battlefield.

21:18. The second of the four accounts describing Israelites killing descendants of Rapha involves the death of **Saph**, known elsewhere as Sippai (see 1 Chron 20:4). This task was accomplished by **Sibbecai the Hushathite**. For his efforts David recognized him as one of his honored fighting men (1 Chron. 11:29).

21:19. This verse is the most controversial one in this chapter, and perhaps in all of 2 Samuel. Here the claim is made that **Elhanan** [also known as Jair; see 1 Chron. 20:5] **killed Goliath the Gittite**. This statement seems to contradict the account of David killing Goliath that occurs in 1 Samuel 17. After all, in the accounts both Philistine opponents were named Goliath, both were from Gath, and both had spears described in identical ways.

Three different approaches have been taken by scholars in dealing with this issue. These passages are possibly (1) true contradictions, present in the original manuscripts, (2) true contradictions, introduced by a careless copyist in pre-Christian times, or (3) apparent contradictions that can be reconciled with each other. Rather than concluding that these two accounts of the death of Goliath contradict one another, it seems preferable to allow for the possibility that the original reading is preserved in 1 Chronicles 20:5, which states that Elhanan "killed Lahmi the brother of Goliath the Gittite." If the third option is chosen, then it can be hypothesized that: (1) Elhanan is a nickname for David, (2) there was more than one Gittite named Goliath, or (3) "Goliath" is a title and not a personal name.

21:20–22. The final account of an Israelite killing a descendant of **Rapha in Gath** involves David's nephew, **Jonathan son of Shimeah.** Jonathan achieved fame when he killed a huge Philistine with **six fingers on each hand and six toes on each foot.** A person with four extra digits was very unusual, and this would have made him seem especially formidable.

🄳 David Praises the Lord–I (22:1–4)

> **SUPPORTING IDEA:** As part of a lengthy psalm, David expresses praise to the Lord.

22:1. This verse introduces the longest stretch of text attributed directly to David within the books of 1 and 2 Samuel. They are the words of a song **David sang to the Lord** after he had delivered him from **the hand of all his enemies** and from **the hand of Saul.** Perhaps it was composed shortly after the rebellion led by Sheba had been put down.

A major part of the four-chapter-long appendix section of 2 Samuel (chs. 21–24) is a lightly edited form of Psalm 18, the longest psalm attributed to King David. Psalm 18 is the longest of the Davidic psalms in the Bible, and it expresses David's love for and triumphant faith in the Lord. A series of eight different metaphors found in these opening four verses depict David's many-sided view of God's role in his life. These eight images can be divided into two broad categories, those that are passive and those that are active.

22:2–3. Five of the images emphasize God's role as a protector and defender, a function David deeply appreciated during his military encounters. Twice in the passage David celebrates God as **my rock.** The Hebrew term translated "rock" refers to a massive outcropping, such as might be found on a mountainside. David had found protection in rocky caves on two occasions in the past (1 Sam. 22:1; 24:3; see Pss. 57:1; 142:1–4), and his reference to a rock

in whom I take refuge here may be based on the protection he experienced in those situations.

In addition to the Lord being David's rock of safety, he was also David's **fortress**, his **shield**, his **stronghold**, and his **refuge**. All of these images are expressed in a very personal way; each of the five is preceded by the word **my**. For David, God's help was intimate. Without denying that the Lord is the savior of the world, David celebrated the fact that God also acted in an intensely personal way; he had come to David and helped *him* in his times of need.

Three metaphors portray God's intervention on David's behalf in a more active way. They present the Lord as David's **deliverer**, the **horn** of David's **salvation**, and his **savior**. As David's deliverer and savior, God performed deeds that preserved David's life when enemies sought to kill him. David had seen God act on his behalf—as aggressively as a dangerous horned bull—to bring about his salvation in a time of great danger to **save** the king from **violent men**. An example of this was presented in 21:15–17.

22:4. Because of God's consistent help, David had confidence to **call to the LORD**, who **is worthy of praise**. With God's help in every case, David had been **saved** from his **enemies**.

🅴 The Lord Delivers David (22:5–20)

> **SUPPORTING IDEA:** *David had experienced much trouble in his life, but God had acted decisively to deliver him from every threat.*

22:5–7. In classic poetic fashion, Israel's psalmist-king described trials he had faced in life as **waves of death** that swirled about him. Israelite culture as a whole had little contact with large bodies of water, even though the land of Israel was bordered by the Mediterranean Sea and the Red Sea. The sea was considered a mysterious and often terrifying place. David suggested that his circumstances in life had been as life-threatening as the waters of a stormy sea.

Furthermore, in David's soul-wrenching times it was as if **the cords of the grave** had coiled around him. In the accompanying parallel line, David compared his troubles to **the snares of death**. Both images suggest that David faced certain death. However, when others might drown in despair David **called to the LORD**. His prayers were not in vain. God **heard** David's plea.

22:8–9. The living God not only heard His servant's cry; he responded to it. Because of the unjust threats against one of his saints, the Lord became **angry**. His wrath created a ripple of terror throughout all creation. The earth **trembled and quaked**, and heaven **shook**. The Lord's explosion of righteous anger changed the divine countenance. **Smoke** rose from his **nostrils** and **consuming fire** came out of his **mouth**. While these images are poetic and metaphorical in nature, they express the profound truth that the Lord is a being who feels our pain and responds powerfully in our time of need.

22:10–15. In David's time of need, God **parted** [lit. "stretched"] **the heavens and came down** to a place where his terrifying glory could be seen and his salvation experienced. The Lord's mysterious presence, though real, was shrouded from view with **dark clouds . . . under his feet**. Aloft in the heavens, God rode upon **cherubim**, powerful supernatural beings with wings. Cherubim are portrayed elsewhere in the Old Testament as God's attendants (Isa. 6:2–6).

The Lord **soared** on the **wings of the wind**. There he made **darkness** his temporary dwelling (Heb. *sukkot;* "booth," "tabernacle"; NIV, **canopy**) as he moved about in the **dark rain clouds of the sky**. God's power and glory were evident within the storm cloud, however, as **bolts of lightning** flashed, indicating the **brightness of his presence**. These awe-inspiring emanations from his presence were viewed by the biblical writer as **arrows** shot from the divine bow that **scattered** and **routed** the enemies of God (Exod. 9:23).

Equally intimidating was **the voice of the Most High**, metaphorically expressed as the thunder that resonated from the lightning flashes. Within ancient Near Eastern societies it was commonly believed that gods were present in the skies during times of war between nations. The sound of thunder emanating from clouds was taken as the voices of the gods. If the resounding thunder was believed to be the voice of an enemy's god, it could be enough to cause an enemy to flee. Such was the case when the Philistines attacked the Israelites during the days of Samuel (1 Sam. 7:10).

22:16–20. David's metaphor continues as he depicts the saving God delivering him from all dangers. The climactic saving act took place when the Lord caused the deadly waters to flee with **breath from his nostrils**. Once trapped in the **deep waters**, David was now rescued as the Lord reached down from on high and took hold of him. Israel's king had been rescued from his **powerful enemy**. Foes who were too strong for David were no match for the Lord.

F David Reveals the Reasons for His Deliverance (22:21–29)

> **SUPPORTING IDEA:** *David declares the reasons why God granted him deliverance, then makes six observations about how God treats people.*

22:21–25. In this portion of the psalm, David enumerated the reasons why God had blessed him. The purpose of this list was to help the listeners understand how they also could experience divine blessing. David made clear that the Lord responds to a person's choices in life, and that a person's choices will affect his relationship with the Lord. As a person chooses to follow God's ways, he will respond positively.

Another secret of David's success was that he took responsibility for his own behavior. He did not rely on others to force him to do the right thing; rather, he **kept** himself from **sin** and made the tough choices necessary to live **blameless** before God. And because of the **cleanness** of his motives and actions before God, the Lord rewarded him.

22:26–28. David used these three verses to identify positive and negative character traits in people and describe the divine response to each. God is not morally neutral in his treatment of human beings. Those who behave virtuously will find the Lord to be a source of blessing in their lives. Conversely, those who reject the way of virtue will experience God's judgment.

Within ancient Hebrew society the most desirable character trait was faithful, commitment-based love. David suggests that a **faithful** person—one who lives out that kind of love in their treatment of others—will experience God as One who acts with **faithful** love toward them. Likewise, the **blameless** man—literally, "a champion of (moral) perfections"— will experience God as the One who acts with perfect moral integrity. To one who acts in a **pure** way—that is, with moral refinement—God will reveal himself as one who is **pure**. Finally, the Lord acts to **save** those who are **humble**—literally, "afflicted people."

Just as surely as God acts with faithfulness, blamelessness, and purity and brings salvation to the godly, he comes in judgment to the wicked. As David noted, **to the crooked** the Lord shows himself **shrewd** (lit. "tortuous"). Similarly, God engineers circumstances to **bring . . . low** those who are **haughty**—that is, self-exalted.

22:29. In the final two verses of David's song, he affirmed what may be the most essential contribution that the Lord made to his life. Inwardly, David experienced the Lord as a **lamp**—a source of moral and intellectual illumination. God's presence turned **darkness into light** within his soul.

Ⓖ The Lord Delivers David Again (22:30–46)

> **SUPPORTING IDEA:** David glorifies the Lord by enumerating the many ways he received divine help on the battlefield.

22:30. This verse opens a section in David's song that continues the theme of divine deliverance found in vv. 5–20. In contrast to the previous verse, which emphasized the interior role the Lord played in David's life, this section emphasizes the Lord as the source of David's outward success. He experienced God's **help** in times of battle, and with that divine assistance he was able to **advance** against the enemy.

22:31–37. Praise for God's sufficiency is David's first note in this passage. Literally the passage states, "The [true] God, perfections [are] his way." That is, everything God does is done right and turns out right—**his way is perfect**. The guidance that God provided David in battle led him to victory. God's perfect leadership in times of war was matched by his perfect protection. The Lord served as a **shield** for all who had taken **refuge** in him. As David confessed, God is peerless; there is no **God besides the LORD**. Thus no other so-called god could deliver protection and victory in battle like the Lord. He alone is the **Rock** of protection for his people.

God supplied David with six different resources that enabled him to triumph over his enemies. First on his list was **strength**. In a life-threatening encounter with a powerful enemy, David needed energy equal to the demands of the moment, and he found what he needed in the Lord. Second, Israel's leader needed guidance, so the Lord, whose way is always perfect (v. 31) made David's way **perfect** as well.

Because of God's gracious enablement, David's feet were **like the feet of a deer**—fast and nimble. Thus David was able to **stand on the heights**—a location with significant tactical advantages during battle. To the resources of strength, agility, and speed that God supplied David, he added skill. David declared that God personally trained his **hands** for battle. Through the training, he gained not only skill but also strength as well. Because of God's help David declared he could **bend a bow of bronze**. Since Israelites used only bows of wood, David was probably using metaphorical language to express the truth that God enabled him to do extraordinary things.

Supplementing all these resources that God provided David was a **shield of victory**—literally, "the shield of your salvation." Although a military leader or king would sometimes be accompanied by a human shield-bearer onto the field of battle (1 Sam. 17:41), David had someone much greater—a divine shield-bearer. Israel's king marveled over the fact that the Lord himself stooped down to make that former shepherd **great**. God had supplied David with everything he needed for victory.

A final provision supplied by the Lord for David in battle was a broadened **path**. When on a journey kings might have slaves prepare a smooth path before them (Isa. 40:4), but in a field of battle such a luxury was unthinkable. However, God graciously supplied this for David so that his **ankles** did **not turn**.

22:38–43. With these divinely supplied provisions, David won an overwhelming victory over his enemies. He described the completeness of his victory using five different verbs: he **crushed** (Heb. *shamad;* lit. "destroyed") them, **crushed them completely** (Heb. *kalah;* lit. "brought to an end"), **destroyed** (Heb. *tsamat*) them, **beat them as fine as the dust** (Heb. *shahaq;* lit. "ground up"), and **pounded** (Heb. *daqaq;* lit., "powdered") them. David's use of such rich verbs to describe a single event emphasizes the completeness of his conquest.

And yet, David took little personal credit for his outstanding military achievements. Though it was certainly David's hand that wielded the sword against his enemies, it was God who **armed** him with **strength for battle**. And with that strength Israel's king **did not turn back** from pursuing his enemies. Because it was divinely supplied resources that enabled David to win the victories, he confessed to the Lord, **You made my adversaries bow at my feet**.

22:44–46. Throughout his long career as Israel's king David had faced many foes. Some of his most dangerous threats came not from outsiders but from his own **people**: fellow Israelites—Saul, Ish-Bosheth, and Sheba—and even family members—Absalom. But the Lord had faithfully **delivered** David from all the attacks. As David's battlefield reputation grew, so did his enemies' fear of him. Some of David's foes lost all heart to fight and came **trembling from their strongholds** before he could even mount an assault on their position. As they surrendered, these **foreigners** would approach him **cringing**, eager to obey him in hopes of saving their lives.

🔢 David Praises the Lord Again (22:47–51)

SUPPORTING IDEA: *As David concludes this psalm, he expresses praise to the Lord for the blessings God has bestowed upon him.*

22:47–49. The final section of this lengthy psalm gives rich expression to David's love and admiration for the Lord. Intertwined with the praise is a list of the blessings the king has received from his God.

David first celebrates what may be the most amazing truth in all the universe, expressing it with just two Hebrew words, "Yahweh lives!" (NIV, **The LORD lives!**) This brief sentence implicitly contains several weighty affirmations: first, that there is a God; second, that God is not just a force or power, but a living being; third, this living God has a name he has given himself, and therefore he has invited people to approach him in the context of a personal relationship. But the living God who relates to people is also one who protects them. For this David, who has experienced God as a **Rock** of safety and salvation, could do nothing but express **praise**.

22:51. David concludes this great psalm by confessing the source of his personal success: it was God who gave him **great victories**. The same God who had **anointed** him in the days of Samuel the prophet (1 Sam. 16:13) had also shown **unfailing kindness** to him throughout his career, helping David achieve unparalleled success. But the God who had anointed David to lead his people had also given Israel's greatest king the ultimate promise. The Lord would show unfailing kindness to his **descendants forever** (see 2 Sam. 7:11–16).

> **MAIN IDEA REVIEW:** *Chapters 21–22 are the first half of the appendix section of 1 and 2 Samuel, and they reveal key details about David and his soldiers. David is depicted delivering his nation from famine through a difficult but wise ruling. David's soldiers are shown delivering the nation through their great heroism in battle against the Philistines. King David's great heart of faith is beautifully expressed in a song that resembles Psalm 18.*

III. CONCLUSION

The Power of God in a Thunderstorm

In the predawn hours of August 6, 1945, three B-29s took off from the American air base located at Tinian in the West Pacific. One of these planes, the Enola Gay, carried the bomb that would forever change world and military history. After a six-hour flight the plane piloted by Colonel Paul Tibbetts arrived at the prescribed target location for his one-bomb payload—Hiroshima. At 8:15 a.m. local time the Enola Gay's bomb, nicknamed the Little Boy, was released, beginning a free-fall that lasted 57 seconds. Then at a height of 1,900 feet above the city the world's first atomic bomb was detonated. It created an explosion equivalent to the simultaneous detonation of approximately 13,000 tons of TNT. The bomb was responsible for the destruction of about 90 percent of Hiroshima's infrastructure and about 70,000 deaths initially, with as many as 200,000 people dying overall.

The power of that first atomic bomb is well documented. But what is not often realized is that a typical, well-developed thunderstorm releases even more power than the bomb dropped by the Enola Gay. As amazing as it seems, an ordinary summertime thunderstorm releases energy equivalent to twenty thousand tons of TNT—more than one and one-half times the amount produced by the Little Boy's explosion over Hiroshima.

Three thousand years ago David declared that the "dark rain clouds of the sky" gave witness to the power of God. The "lightning" that "blazed forth" was a powerful divine weapon; the voice of God was heard as the massive clouds "thundered from heaven." Through eyes of faith David saw what we so easily miss—the power of God is in the thunderstorm.

PRINCIPLES

- Sins you commit during your lifetime may have disastrous consequences long after you are gone.
- Even great warriors sometimes need a little help on the battlefield; no person is so great that he never needs the help of others.
- God is the ultimate source of a person's success.
- God provides resources to his followers that enable them to handle the difficulties they face in life.
- Prayer can bring about a happy ending to a hard time.

APPLICATIONS

- If you are going through a hard time right now, tell a trusted Christian friend about it. Then agree that both of you will pray about your situation every day for the next week.
- After God has brought you through a hard time in life, create an Internet blog describing your difficulty and how God got you through it.
- If someone in your Bible study group or church is going through a hard time, have at least five people in your group volunteer to show support for that person. If the person is discouraged, send cards expressing Christian encouragement. If the person is injured or sick, visit him or bring him a meal.

IV. LIFE APPLICATION

God Is My Trainer

Since the time he was a little boy Terry Rush had wanted to play professional baseball. As a little kid he made two vows—that he would never go to church, and that he would play baseball with the St. Louis Cardinals. As a little leaguer, he used to stuff dried marshmallows in his mouth to make it look like he was chewing tobacco the way pro baseball players did.

As a young man Terry never got the chance to play professional baseball. Ironically, he became a pastor instead! But he never lost his love for baseball, and he wanted to have a chance to improve his baseball skills. When in 1984 he learned that the St. Louis Cardinals were holding their first-ever Fantasy Baseball Camp in St. Petersburg, Florida, Terry felt as if he had to go. However, he couldn't possibly afford the trip. Amazingly, a family in the church gave him the gift of an all-expenses-paid trip to the camp. There for one week "The Preach" was trained in the finer points of baseball with such famous St. Louis Cardinal baseball players as Bob Gibson, Curt Flood, Mike Shannon, Tim McCarver, and Dal Maxvill. It was the experience of a lifetime.

Israel's great King David was also the nation's most famous warrior. Not only did David kill mighty Goliath, he led his nation to overwhelming victories over every enemy they ever fought. What was the secret of David's incredible success on the battlefield? He revealed the answer in the inspiring psalm found in this section: God was his trainer. "He [the Lord] trains my hands for battle," declared the king. As a result of the training he received from God's hand, David declared, "My arms can bend a bow of bronze." With God as David's trainer, success was assured.

V. PRAYER

Lord, it is good to praise you for the blessings you so graciously bring our way. You have protected us in times of trouble; you have been our companion in dark nights of distress and supported us when everyone else abandoned us. You have helped us find a way through our difficulties. As you have so generously given of your resources to assist us, may we also give to our Christian brothers and sisters in their hour of need. In Jesus' name. Amen.

VI. DEEPER DISCOVERIES

Does God Really Have Nostrils? (22:16)

The Bible teaches that God is spirit (John 4:24). As such, it is not at all clear that God has a form that looks like a human body. When David stated that a "blast of breath" came "from his [God's] nostrils," he was probably using a literary device known as an anthropomorphism. An anthropomorphism is a symbolic use of language in which God is described using human anatomical terms. Other anthropomorphisms include God's finger (Exod. 31:18), hand (2 Chron. 30:12), arm (Isa. 53:1), face (Gen. 33:10), mouth (2 Chron. 35:22), eye (Ps. 33:18), ear (Isa. 59:1), and feet (Exod. 24:10).

Because God is not a material being, David's reference to the blast of breath from God's nostrils is probably a poetic reference to a powerful wind sent by God.

VII. TEACHING OUTLINE

A. INTRODUCTION

1. Lead Story: A Mother's Sacrificial Love
2. Context: As the account of David's kingship over Israel draws to a close, David's role as a judge and the exploits of his greatest soldiers are recounted. The king's great hymn of praise to God for victory in battle follows these narratives.
3. Transition: Just as Lorraine sacrificed her personal welfare for the sake of her unborn son, so Rizpah gave of herself to preserve the dignity and memory of her sons.

B. COMMENTARY

1. David Ends a Drought by Granting Justice to the Gibeonites (21:1–9)
2. Rizpah and David Honor the House of Saul (21:10–14)
3. Heroic Achievements by David's Soldiers (21:15–22)
4. David Praises the Lord (22:1–4)
5. The Lord Delivers David (22:5–20)
6. David Reveals the Reasons for His Deliverance (22:21–29)
7. The Lord Delivers David Again (22:30–46)
8. David Praises the Lord Again (22:47–51)

C. CONCLUSION: THE POWER OF GOD IN A THUNDERSTORM

VIII. ISSUES FOR DISCUSSION

1. David authorized the Gibeonites to kill seven of Saul's descendants, even though he had promised not to wipe out Saul's descendants

(1 Sam. 24:21–22). Did he keep his promise to Saul? Did he do the right thing?

2. Rizpah exemplified self-sacrificing motherhood in her devotion to her sons. What sacrifices did your mother make on your behalf? What sacrifices are you making in behalf of your children?

3. Second Samuel 21:19 states that Elhanan killed Goliath, whereas 1 Samuel 17:50 says David killed Goliath; 1 Chronicles 20:5 says Elhanan killed Goliath's brother. How do you resolve the tensions in these texts?

4. Could David have written the lyrics recorded in 2 Samuel 22 if he hadn't experienced hard times in his life? Does God purposely let Christians go through hard times today? What can we gain from these?

2 Samuel 23:1–24:25

The Last Words of David

I. **INTRODUCTION**
Last Words of the Saints

II. **COMMENTARY**
A verse-by-verse explanation of these chapters

III. **CONCLUSION**
A Tiger in a Pit in Winter

IV. **LIFE APPLICATION**
Sacrifice for One's Nation
Melding these chapters to life

V. **PRAYER**
Tying these chapters to life with God

VI. **DEEPER DISCOVERIES**
Historical, geographical, and grammatical enrichment of the commentary

VII. **TEACHING OUTLINE**
Suggested step-by-step group study of these chapters

VIII. **ISSUES FOR DISCUSSION**
Zeroing these chapters in on daily life

Quote

"*T*he weal or woe of a people mainly depends on the qualifications of those rulers, by whom we are to be governed. ...It is indeed an honor which God puts upon some above others, when he takes them from among the people, and sets them up to rule over them, but it is for the peoples' sake."

Samuel Willard, The Character of a Good Ruler, 1694

BIOGRAPHICAL PROFILE: ABISHAI

- Son of King David's sister, Zeruiah
- Military commander in David's army
- Commander of special military group known as the Three
- Accompanied David during a secret nighttime visit to Saul's camp in the Judean desert
- Intervened to save David from Philistine attacker
- Killed three hundred men during a single battle
- Helped lead attack against Ammonites in Ammon
- Helped lead David's forces during Absalom's rebellion
- Helped put down Sheba's rebellion

BIOGRAPHICAL PROFILE: BENAIAH

- Son of Jehoiada the priest
- Commander of King David's personal bodyguard units, the Kerethites and Pelethites
- Killed two of Moab's best fighters in battle
- Killed a large, heavily armed Egyptian fighter using only a club

- Went into a pit on a snowy day and killed a lion
- Executed David's son Adonijah at Solomon's request
- Executed David's former commander Joab at Solomon's request

2 Samuel 23:1–24:25

IN A NUTSHELL

This section of 2 Samuel is part of an appendix to the book that extends from chapters 21 through 24. Chapter 23 presents King David's final oracle and lists his greatest soldiers, along with some of their accomplishments. Chapter 24 describes a divine judgment against Israel, including David's role in inciting it and bringing it to an end.

The Last Words of David

I. INTRODUCTION

Last Words of the Saints

In many cultures throughout the world and in various periods of history, death has been viewed as an inevitability that is to be prepared for throughout a lifetime and faced with dignity. Part of dying well involved leaving behind a legacy of good deeds and well-chosen last words. One's last words would often be the most remembered words of a person. A person who wished to die "properly" would try to formulate his last formally spoken words with great care.

Some saints chose to die with Scripture on their lips. Robert Murray McCheyne was a great Scottish preacher who helped bring about a spiritual awakening in Dundee, Scotland, in the early 1800s. Considered one of the most influential Scottish religious leaders of the nineteenth century, he died of typhoid at age twenty-nine, having been infected by sick members of his church whom he had gone to visit. McCheyne's last words were, "Be stedfast, unmoveable, always abounding in the work of the Lord, forasmuch as ye know that your labour is not in vain in the Lord," a quotation from 1 Corinthians 15:58.

Other Christians used their final words to testify to their faith in Jesus. The well-known seventeenth-century English Puritan John Owen was an author and eloquent preacher who had once been ordered to preach before Parliament. On his deathbed his final utterance was, "I am going to him whom my soul loveth, or rather who has loved me with an everlasting love, which is the sole ground of all my consolation."

Still others used their final opportunity to speak as a testimony to the reality of heaven. Philip W. Otterbein was a German evangelist in the late seventeenth and early eighteenth centuries who came to America and worked among the Mennonites. After an evangelistic career that spanned half a century, Otterbein died uttering these words: "The conflict is over and past. I begin to feel an unspeakable fulness of love and peace divine. Lay my head on my pillow and be still."

Within this final unit in 2 Samuel we have the last words of Israel's greatest and most influential king, David. This great man of God used his final words to declare both the secret of a king's success and the effect a successful leader of God's people has on their nation. What will you do with your final words?

II. COMMENTARY

The Last Words of David

MAIN IDEA: *A person who rules over others in righteousness is like the light of the morning at sunrise.*

 ### David's Final Oracle (23:1–7)

SUPPORTING IDEA: *David's final prophetic word describes the blessing of a righteous ruler, and affirms that David and his family line have been chosen by God to rule, whereas evil men have been cast aside.*

23:1. The opening verse of chapter 23 begins the second half of the appendix portion of 1 and 2 Samuel. Chapters 23–24 are a mirror-like reflection of the previous two chapters. Thus, the elements of chapters 21–22—David acting to end a divine judgment (21:1–9), David's soldiers and their exploits (21:10–22), and a divinely inspired poetic composition written by David (22:1–51)—are present in an inverted order in chapters 23–24—a divinely inspired poetic composition written by David (23:1–7), David's soldiers and their exploits (23:8–39), and David acting to end a divine judgment (24:1–25).

Entitled **The last words of David**, these words are not literally the final words to come from David's mouth, but rather the last **oracle of David**. Israel's greatest king is described in four different ways in the opening verse of this oracle. Humanly, he was the **son of Jesse**. More importantly, however, he was the man whose life was **exalted by the Most High**. In addition, he was a **man anointed by the God of Jacob**. Anointing involved having specially prepared olive oil poured on a person's head by an authorized representative of God. The oil symbolized the enabling presence of God coming upon an individual, marking and equipping him to carry out divinely commissioned tasks.

David's fourth designation was that of **Israel's singer of songs**. From the earliest period of David's recorded life story (1 Sam. 16:23) and throughout his career, David was Israel's most famous musician. Within the book of Psalms he is credited with composing 73 psalms—more than any other person.

23:2–4. David reveals the source of his oracle here: it is **the Spirit of the LORD** who spoke through the king. His words were not his own; instead, God's **word** was on his **tongue**. What the God of Israel revealed to David was the ideal character and ultimate effect of a godly leader. As **the Rock**, or secure refuge, of Israel declared, a proper leader for God's people is one who **rules over men in righteousness**, that is, who exercises authority in a manner that is consistent with God's values and guidelines. Furthermore, a God-pleasing leader is of necessity one who **rules in the fear of God**, that is, with the highest degree of respect for God's power and authority.

One who leads while living in submission to the leadership of God is like the **light of morning at sunrise on a cloudless morning**. This image suggests that a leader who follows God helps bring about opportunities for growth and blessing for his subjects. This concept is reinforced when David compared the ideal leader to **the brightness after rain that brings the grass from the earth**. This metaphor suggests that proper leaders help create an environment in which their subjects can flourish.

23:5. Having described the qualities and benefits of proper leaders, David now affirmed that his own family line had these essential qualities. Through God's grace David's **house** was **right with God**, that is, David and his descendants sought to rule in righteousness and the fear of God. Graciously God made with David **an everlasting covenant**—a promise of blessing that would endure throughout the generations. And because it was a covenant established by God, it was **arranged and secured in every part**. Like many other ancient kings, David hoped that God would allow him to have a long and prosperous reign and that his descendants would continue to provide leadership for the nation. Thanks to the promises the Lord had given him, David possessed the confidence that God would **bring to fruition** his salvation and grant him his **every desire**.

23:6–7. In contrast to David, who sought to please God in every way, there were also **evil men** present in his society. But such men would not experience God's blessing. Instead, they would **be cast aside like thorns**. Just as thorns can bring pain to those who touch them, so it is with the wicked.

𝔹 David's Most Heroic Soldiers (23:8–39)

SUPPORTING IDEA: *Many soldiers in the Israelite army performed heroic acts on the field of battle. These men were honored by King David by being appointed to elite military units.*

23:8–12. These verses begin a 32-verse unit that names David's **mighty men**, the king's most honored soldiers. Within the symmetrically structured appendix section of 2 Samuel the 32 verses correspond to 2 Samuel 21:15–22. These initial five verses of this section describe David's most elite soldiers, a group known as **the Three**.

First among the Three was **Josheb-Basshebeth**, the **chief** of the Three. Elsewhere in Scripture he is known as Jashobeam (1 Chron. 11:11) and possibly Adino the Eznite (see the Masoretic Text's reading of 23:8). He earned this prestigious position when he performed the remarkable feat of raising his **spear against eight hundred men, whom he killed in one encounter.**

Second among the Three was **Eleazar** son of Dodai the Ahohite. While with David in an encounter with the Philistines, he found himself in a precarious position. The **men of Israel retreated**, leaving him alone in battle. But he stood his ground and fought the enemy. Eleazar **struck down the Philistines** until his hand grew tired and **froze to the sword**. Humanly speaking, Eleazar was the hero of the day, but the ultimate source of his triumph was **the LORD**, who brought about **a great victory** that day.

The third member of Israel's most prestigious military group was **Shammah**. As was the case with Eleazar, Shammah distinguished himself by standing his ground in battle against the Philistines when the rest of Israel's troops fled. This act of courage, strength and skill not only earned Shammah great honor, but it brought credit to God as well. Israel understood that it was the Lord who brought about **a great victory**.

23:13–17. Perhaps the noblest deed of the three mighty men took place **during harvest time** one year while David was oppressed by **a band of Philistines** in the valley of Rephaim. This incident may have occurred before David became king (1 Sam. 22:1) or soon after he conquered Jerusalem (2 Sam. 5:17). Either way, David was virtually trapped in **the stronghold** of **the cave of Adullam** within the Judean wilderness.

The cave would not have had an internal water supply, and David **longed for water**. In his thirst he happened to express the wish for someone to get him **a drink . . . from the well . . . near . . . Bethlehem**, his boyhood home. Taking this as a cue from their commander, the three mighty men **broke through the Philistine lines**, traveled approximately 12 miles, and drew water from the well just outside the city near the gate of Bethlehem. Then the three retraced their steps, carrying the water back to David.

Rather than gulping the water down, David **refused** to drink it. Instead, he **poured it out** on the ground **before the LORD**. By denying himself the pleasure of quenching his thirst with the water from Bethlehem, David chose to present it as an extravagant gift to God. It represented the **blood** of the men who **went at the risk of their lives**. Such a precious liquid belonged only to the Lord.

23:18–23. Two additional soldiers worthy of special recognition within David's administration were **Abishai** and **Benaiah**. Both of these individuals were mentioned previously in the books of 1 and 2 Samuel. Because of their outstanding feats these men became as **famous as the three mighty men** and were **held in greater honor than the Three**, though neither of them actually entered that circle of honor.

Abishai had played important roles in several previous narratives in 1 and 2 Samuel. Added to these activities is the heroic deed recorded here. While fighting an unnamed enemy Abishai **raised his spear against three hundred men, whom he killed**. For this achievement David made him **commander** of the Three.

Benaiah earned the reputation of being a valiant fighter through a series of exploits. Listed here are three of them. First, he struck down **two of Moab's best men**. Like David (1 Sam. 17:34–36), he also successfully engaged a dangerous wild animal. Benaiah went down into **a pit** (or cistern) **on a snowy day and killed a lion**. Finally, he struck down a huge **Egyptian** using **a club**. For these reasons David placed him in charge of his **bodyguard**.

23:24–39. The final section of chapter 23 is devoted to honoring **the Thirty**, another group of distinguished soldiers in David's army. Though not as highly honored as the Three, these men earned a place of distinction in Israel through their military prowess. This group is called the Thirty, yet more than 30 individuals were apparently included in this group. The NIV's listing contains 30 elements, though one of these is **the sons of Jashen**, thus making the total number of individuals at least 31. Verse 39 states that there were **thirty-seven in all**, though this number may have included the Three, as well as Abishai and Benaiah.

One of the reasons why more than 30 individuals were included in this group may be because the list includes people from different periods of David's kingship. For example, **Asahel the brother of Joab** was killed soon after David was declared king over Judah, several years before he became king over all Israel (2 Sam. 2:23). **Uriah the Hittite** died in battle after David had served as king over all Israel for several years (2 Sam. 11:17). A second reason why there were more than 30 in the group is because some of them died, thus necessitating the inclusion of others. Asahel and Uriah were two such men who died on the battlefield, and there may have been others.

𝐂 David Stops a Plague (24:1–25)

> **SUPPORTING IDEA:** *When God becomes angry with Israel, He causes David to take an improper census, resulting in a deadly plague that breaks out in Israel. David brings the plague to an end by offering a sacrifice on the outskirts of Jerusalem.*

24:1–4. At an unnamed point in David's reign as king over all Israel, God's anger **burned against Israel**. As a result of God's anger, he **incited David** to **take a census of Israel and Judah**. The parallel account of this event in 1 Chronicles 21:1–28 indicates that Satan incited David to take the census. The two passages are not in conflict. Second Samuel 24:1 recognizes that God is the ultimate authority of the universe and that all beings, even Satan, are subject to his dominion; 1 Chronicles focuses on the role Satan played in the event as an agent of God's judgment (see 1 Kgs. 22:19–23 for a similar instance).

Taking a census was never forbidden in the Old Testament. However, the law did have one requirement associated with census-taking that had to be followed in order to avoid a plague: Each person who was counted had to "pay the LORD a ransom for his life at the time he is counted" (Exod. 30:12). Apparently David failed to make his subjects pay the required ransom, thus bringing a catastrophic judgment on the land.

Since the census was military in nature, David ordered **Joab** to **go throughout the tribes of Israel** and count the fighting men. David's stated purpose for this was so he would know how many men were available for military service. The king's declared reason could indicate a second problem with the census. Perhaps he took the census because he was relying on military might more than God for success. Joab was concerned about the appropriateness of the census, because he asked his superior why David would **want to do such a thing**. But David **overruled Joab and the army commanders**, leaving them no choice but to take the census.

24:5–8. Joab and his officers traveled eastward from Jerusalem, **crossing the Jordan** River. They then made their way southward to the area east of the Red Sea, camping near **Aroer**. Questions about the original reading of the text leave us uncertain about exactly where they went after that. The NIV states that they went to the tribal region of **Gad**, whereas the Holman Christian Standard Bible indicates that the commanders went "south of the town in the middle of the valley" and then on to Gad.

The census takers also stopped in the tribal region of Dan, **Dan Jaan**, a village about 25 miles north of the Sea of Galilee. From there the group went westward to Sidon, situated along the Mediterranean Sea coast. Proceeding southward along the coast, the Israelite commanders then went toward **the fortress of Tyre**. Returning to the Galilee region, they next went to **all the towns of the Hivites and Canaanites**. The men continued on their way to Israel's southern region, visiting **Beersheba** in the **Negev of Judah**. To complete the counterclockwise journey around the land of Israel, the group finally came back to **Jerusalem**. Overall, the journey took **nine months and twenty days**, or 285 days (assuming that each month was a 29.5-day lunar cycle).

24:9–10. When the census was completed, Joab reported **the number of the fighting men** to David. Within Israel there were **eight hundred thousand able-bodied men who could handle a sword**. This number differs from the figure of 1.1 million stated in the parallel passage in 1 Chronicles 21:5. Likewise, the number given here for the total of fighting men in Judah—**five hundred thousand**—differs from the 470,000 of 1 Chronicles.

How are these discrepancies to be explained? Perhaps the two figures vary because different subgroups of Israel's population were included in each of the totals. Note that in 1 Chronicles 21:5 it is stated that the figure includes "all Israel," whereas no such claim is made in 2 Samuel. A second factor may be that the writer of 2 Samuel rounded the number of fighters in Judah, whereas the author of 1 Chronicles used a more precise figure. It is also possible that Joab reported inexact numbers to David in hopes of avoiding a divine curse.

After David was told the number of fighting men throughout the land, he was **conscience-stricken**. But he didn't let his wrongdoing destroy him. He confessed to the Lord that he had **sinned greatly** in what he had done, and then he begged the Lord to **take away the guilt** associated with his actions.

24:11–14. Even though David confessed his sin immediately after the census was completed, he could not escape the consequences of his wrongdoing. To announce his judgment the Lord sent **Gad the prophet**, David's trusted **seer** who had been with him since the early days of his career (1 Sam. 22:5). God gave David **three options** about the type of judgment that would result from the sin: **three years of famine** throughout the **land** or **three months** of overwhelming defeat on the battlefield or **three days of plague** in the land.

Each of the options was highly undesirable, and the prospect of any of them occurring left the king in **deep distress**. However, he knew that God is compassionate, gracious, loving, and forgiving (Exod. 34:6–7). So he chose to **fall into the hands of the LORD**. By selecting the three-day plague, he picked an alternative that omitted any direct human involvement and was shortest in duration.

24:15–17. As promised, the Lord sent **a plague** on Israel. A devastating outbreak of disease afflicted the population from **Dan** in the far north to **Beersheba** in the south. Within that three-day span **seventy thousand** Israelites died. While the plague might be explainable in medical terms, the Bible makes it clear that it was ultimately the handiwork of a supernatural being. An **angel stretched out his hand** in judgment against Israel.

As the angel prepared to destroy Jerusalem, however, divine grace intervened. The Lord was **grieved because of the calamity.** Exactly as David had predicted (v. 14), God's great mercy intervened, forcing the angel who was afflicting the people to **withdraw** his hand of judgment. Just outside the city wall at **the threshing floor of Araunah the Jebusite**, David pleaded with the Lord to let the hand of destruction fall on him and his family, and not on the rest of Israel. After all, it was he who had most directly **sinned and done wrong.** Perhaps it was David's willingness to die for his people that aroused the Lord's compassion. The parallel account in 1 Chronicles 21:16 indicates that David uttered his prayer after he saw a drawn sword in the angel's hand.

24:18–24. On the day that God directed the angel of judgment to spare Jerusalem, he also commanded David through the prophet Gad to **build an altar . . . on the threshing floor of Araunah.** This was an especially appropriate location for an altar, since it was the site of a significant act of divine mercy on Israel's behalf. So David and his men went outside the city to Araunah's threshing floor. David told him he had come to buy his threshing floor. On that site he would build an **altar to the LORD** so the plague, which had been temporarily suspended, might be stopped.

Araunah offered to let the king take **whatever** else he wanted, including oxen for the burnt offering and the heavy wooden threshing sledges and ox yokes. But this offer, though generous, was not one David could accept. He would not sacrifice to the Lord sacrifices that had cost him **nothing.** So he bought the threshing floor and the oxen for **fifty shekels of silver**, the assigned value for a sizeable piece of land that was dedicated to God (Lev. 27:16). According to 1 Chronicles 21:25, David paid Araunah 600 shekels of gold for the land. The large discrepancy in the amounts can be explained if the 50 silver shekels was payment for the altar site, animals, and implements, whereas the 600 gold shekels covered the purchase of the larger field in which the threshing floor was located.

24:25. Once the altar was constructed on this site, David made two kinds of sacrifices: **burnt offerings and fellowship offerings.** This pairing of offerings was utilized in solemn public situations apart from regular religious festival times (Num. 10:10; Judg. 20:26; 21:4; 1 Sam. 10:8; 13:9; 1 Kgs. 3:15; 9:25). Ezekiel 45:15 indicates that these sacrifices could be used to make atonement for people, and clearly they were part of the reconciliation in this situation.

As a result of these sacrifices offered at Araunah's threshing floor, the Lord answered prayer **in behalf of the land**, and **the plague . . . was stopped**. The king's decisive actions had halted the divine curse, just as his earlier actions had ended a three-year famine (2 Sam. 21:1–14).

The site of this sacred act of reconciliation between God and humanity involving wood and shed blood later became the location of the altar of burnt offering for Israel's temple to the Lord (1 Chron. 22:1). David's sacrifice that stopped a plague also foreshadowed the ultimate sacrifice made by Jesus, who shed his blood on a cross of wood outside Jerusalem. The actions of this ultimate son of David also brought an end to the plague of sin and resulted in a reconciliation between God and humanity (Rom. 5:10).

MAIN IDEA REVIEW: *A person who rules over others in righteousness is like the light of the morning at sunrise.*

III. CONCLUSION

A Tiger in a Pit in Winter

On December 25, 2007, seventeen-year-old Carlos Sousa Jr. and two of his friends were visiting the San Francisco Zoo. While the three young men were in front of the tiger exhibit, something happened that caused the 250-pound Siberian tiger known as Tatiana to become very disturbed. A twelve-foot-tall barrier separated the visitors from the tiger, but that wall was not enough to prevent Tatiana from leaping out of the exhibition pit and attacking the three teenagers. Within moments all three of the visitors had been mauled by the tiger. Each of them received deep bites and claw wounds on their heads, necks, arms, and hands. Carlos was fatally injured in the attack. As a result of the incident, officials at the San Francisco Zoo spent approximately one million dollars on the tiger exhibition pit to eliminate the possibility of such an incident happening again.

Tragic experiences such as this one involving large wild cats help us understand the great risk that Benaiah took when he attacked a lion in a pit. The animal he killed would have been panicked and extremely dangerous.

What's more, if Benaiah had not stopped the lion, it might have jumped out of the pit and injured or killed many men. Benaiah's actions were truly heroic.

PRINCIPLES

- The best leaders are those who view their position of leadership as a trust from God.
- God-fearing leaders who maintain justice throughout their land are a blessing to their subjects.
- The heroic efforts of a single person are sometimes the difference between success and defeat for a group.
- Good leaders reward those who perform exceptional deeds.
- God is not morally neutral; a nation's sins always lead to divine judgment.
- Good leaders take responsibility for the wrong they do and seek to fix the problem.

APPLICATIONS

- Pray that God will provide political leaders who view their position of leadership as a trust from God. Then work to get these people elected.
- Write a letter or send an e-mail to a politician who has taken a courageous stand for the right in a moral controversy; let him know that you are praying for him.
- When you become aware of a problem that needs to be dealt with at work or in the home, determine to face the issue and deal with it, even if no one else does.
- Do an inventory of self-sacrifice. Make a list of what you have given to God as part of your relationship with him; include money, time, and personal efforts that you have given to God.

IV. LIFE APPLICATION

Sacrifice for One's Nation

During America's Revolutionary War thousands of individuals paid dearly to help the fledgling nation achieve its independence. Out of an estimated population of three million citizens, approximately 25,000 soldiers died of battle wounds or disease. An additional 25,000 were seriously wounded or disabled as a direct result of the conflict. The comparable figure for the United States today, with its population of approximately three hundred million, would be about five million war casualties.

In addition to those who sacrificed life and health, many more people gave up property for the sake of freedom. Representative of the material sacrifices were those made by Lewis Morris, one of the 56 men who signed the Declaration of Independence in 1776. In order to support the war effort, Morris's home was taken over by the continental army and used as a barracks for soldiers. The horses and livestock on his farm were taken for use by the army as well. Philip Livingston, another of the signers of the Declaration of Independence, had several of his properties confiscated by the British. Because he died before the war ended, he never got them back. Thomas McKean, another of the Declaration's signers, was forced to move his family five times to avoid British forces.

Those engaged in the cause of freedom in behalf of the United States more than two centuries ago understood the importance of making costly personal sacrifices for a greater good. Similarly, King David knew that personal sacrifice was a vital part of a worthwhile relationship with God. Araunah the Jebusite offered to give David an altar site as well as the firewood and animals needed for an offering to the Lord. But David refused to take them. Instead, he insisted on paying the full price for these sacrificial necessities. David didn't believe in practicing discount religion.

V. PRAYER

Lord, thank you for leaders who confess you to be the giver of their political power and who use their God-given positions to pursue justice and righteousness in the land. Thank you for leaders who value their relationship with you more than they value great wealth. Thank you also for the gift of heroes who put their lives at risk to make ours safe. Lord, though we may never be a David, Eleazar, or Shammah, grant us the faith and resolve to stand strong for you in the daily battles of life. In the strong name of Jesus we pray. Amen.

VI. DEEPER DISCOVERIES

A. Israel's Military Organization in David's Time (23:8–39)

The Israelite military was mostly composed of temporary soldiers who were called to duty during times of national crisis; the modern counterpart in the United States today would be National Guardsmen, who are occasionally called up to help meet the nation's military needs. The army was divided into subunits called "thousands" and "hundreds" (Num. 31:14; 1 Chron. 13:1; 27:1; 2 Chron. 1:2; 25:5), which had commanders over them. At least some of these commanders were probably full-time soldiers employed by the king.

In addition to the nation's "National Guard," David's army contained smaller units of permanent soldiers. Prominent in the Bible were King David's personal bodyguards known as the Kerethites and Pelethites (2 Sam. 8:18; 15:18). These soldiers were probably non-Israelites whose loyalty lay only with the king. Another important group of full-time soldiers that David established was a kind of honor guard known as the Thirty (2 Sam. 23:1, 24; 1 Chron. 11:11; 12:4). These individuals, most of whom were Israelites, were fighters who had distinguished themselves through their skill and heroism in battle.

Above them was an elite group known as the Three (2 Sam. 23:18–23; 1 Chron. 11:20–21). Membership in this group was limited to those who had performed truly legendary feats in battle. A few select individuals, who had equally amazing battlefield performances, were given even greater honor than the Thirty. These individuals were honored with the positions of highest command over the troops (2 Sam. 23:19,23; 1 Chron. 11:6).

B. Censuses and Divine Anger (24:1–9)

On three occasions in the Old Testament, Israel took censuses to determine the number of adult males available for military service (Num. 1:1–49; 26:1–62; 2 Sam. 24:1–9). All men 20 years of age and older were counted, since these were the individuals considered essential to defend the nation in the event of war. The task of keeping up with the number of soldiers available for battle seems good and necessary for a nation. Yet the Lord warned that he would bring a plague against the people if each person who was counted did not pay a "ransom" (Exod. 30:11–16).

Why did the Lord threaten to bring a plague on his people simply because they counted their soldiers—a job that was vital for the good of the nation? No specific reason is provided in the Bible, so scholars can only speculate. The Hebrew term translated "ransom" (*kopher*) is related to a verb (*kaphar*) which means "to make a reparation to someone who has been deprived of what was due them" or "to appease anger." Scholars have suggested therefore that when a leader counted soldiers, he was in effect claiming the soldiers as his own. But the Israelite soldiers were really God's army; thus the leader had offended God and so had to appease God's anger.

VII. TEACHING OUTLINE

A. INTRODUCTION

1. Lead Story: Last Words of the Saints
2. Context: These final two chapters portray King David as a God-fearing, righteous ruler who identified and rewarded the most heroic defenders of the nation over which he ruled. He is also shown to be a leader who was capable of sin, but who repented and sacrificially interceded for the welfare of his people.
3. Transition: The righteous reign of King David and the heroism of his soldiers combined to produce a nation that experienced the blessing of God.

B. COMMENTARY

1. David's Final Oracle (23:1–7)
2. David's Most Heroic Soldiers (23:8–39)
3. David Stops a Plague (24:1–25)

C. CONCLUSION: SACRIFICE FOR ONE'S NATION

VIII. ISSUES FOR DISCUSSION

1. Is a God-fearing leader better than a leader who does not fear God? How can the fear of God make a person more fit to lead others?
2. How can Christians encourage people to take a stand against evil, even when doing so is unpopular?
3. When the nation of Israel sinned, God used a bad decision by King David to bring trouble on the nation. Does God use a leader's bad judgment today to punish nations for their sins?
4. King David insisted on making a financial sacrifice as part of his worship of God. What kinds of sacrifices should Christians make for God today?

Glossary

Abiathar—The son of Ahimelech and the only one to escape to David when Saul ordered the massacre of the priests at Nob

Abigail—Wife of Nabal who brought food to David after her husband rejected David's request. She later became David's wife

Abinadab—An Israelite who kept the ark of the covenant for a time before it was moved by David to Jerusalem

Abishai—A commander in David's army

Abner—Commander of the armies of Saul and Ish-Bosheth; murdered by Joab

Absalom—David's son who killed his half-brother Amnon and led a revolt against David

Achish—The Philistine king of Gath who befriended David

Agag—An Amalekite king who was spared by Saul, in disobedience of the Lord's command that all Amalekites should be killed

Ahimelech—A priest at Nob who provided food for David and his men

Ahithophel—One of David's aides who joined Absalom's rebellion against King David

Amalekites—Tribal enemies of the Israelites whom Saul was ordered by the Lord to destroy

Amasa—A commander in Absalom's army and then in David's army

Ammonites—A tribal people who fought against the Israelites during the days of Saul and David

Amnon—David's firstborn son who raped Tamar and then was murdered by Absalom, Tamar's brother

anointing—The pouring of oil on a person's head to set him apart for special service. Both Saul and David were anointed as kings of Israel

Araunah—A Jebusite from whom David bought a threshing floor. Here David built an altar to stop a plague that God had sent against his people

ark of the covenant—A sacred chest representing God's presence that was captured by the Philistines when Israel carried it into battle against them

Ashdod—A Philistine city where the Philistines placed the captured ark of the covenant for a time

Bread of the Presence—Twelve loaves of freshly baked bread, considered consecrated to the Lord, that were replaced in the tabernacle every Sabbath

covenant—An agreement between two parties that is regulated by established obligations, an example of which is the covenant between Jonathan and David

Dagon—A pagan god of the Philistines that fell before the ark of the covenant

Doeg—An Edomite who massacred the priests at Nob under orders from Saul

Eli—A priest who presided at sacrificial rituals at Shiloh and who trained the boy Samuel for the priesthood

ephod—A garment worn by priests and Levites in priestly service

fasting—A ritual of dedication that involved going without food for a period of time

forest of Ephraim—A wooded region in which David's forces defeated the army of David's rebellious son, Absalom

Gibeonites—A tribe or clan whom David allowed to kill seven of Saul's descendants in retaliation for Saul's campaign of annihilation against them

Gilboa—A mountain where Saul and his sons died in a battle with the Philistines

glory—Visible, radiant manifestation of God

Hannah—The wife of Elkanah and the mother of Samuel

Hebron—A city that served as David's capital city when he was king of the territory of Judah

Ish-Bosheth—Saul's only surviving son who attempted to succeed his father as king of Israel, in opposition to David

Jebus—Ancient name of Jerusalem when it was inhabited by a people known as the Jebusites

Joab—Supreme commander of David's army who killed Absalom

Kerethites—An elite unit of Israelite warriors who apparently served as David's personal bodyguards

Kiriath Jearim—An Israelite city where the ark of the covenant was kept after it was returned by the Philistines

lots—"Casting lots" was a decision-making process. Exactly how this was done is not known

Mephibosheth—The lame son of Jonathan who was befriended by David after he became king over all Israel

Michal—Youngest daughter of King Saul. She was apparently David's first wife

mighty men—A group of warriors loyal to David who were noted for their courage and fighting ability

Nabal—A wealthy Calebite who refused to provide food and other supplies for David and his men

Nazirite—A person who made a special vow of devotion to the Lord

Pelethites—An elite unit of Israelite warriors who apparently served as David's personal bodyguards

Philistines—A people who warred against the Israelites during the days of Saul and David

prophet—A spokesman for God who delivered God's message

Rabbah—Capital city of the Ammonites that was captured by Joab during David's time

Sheba—A Benjamite who led a revolt against David

Shiloh—A city where the tabernacle was located during Samuel's time

Shimei—A member of Saul's clan who hurled insults at David as he fled Jerusalem during Absalom's rebellion

Tent of Meeting—Another term for the tabernacle, the portable sanctuary where the Israelites worshiped before a permanent temple was built

Tyre—A non-Israelite seacoast city north of Israel that was ruled by King Hiram during David's time

Urim and Thummim—Gems or precious stones in the breastplate of the high priest that were used to determine God's will or make decisions in certain matters

Uzzah—An Israelite who was struck dead by the Lord when he touched the ark of the covenant while it was being moved

Ziklag—The city given to David and his men by Achish, the Philistine king of Gath

Zion—Another name for the city of Jerusalem

Ziphites—Residents of the desert of Ziph who told Saul that David was hiding in their territory

Bibliography

Andrews, Stephen J. "Holy War." In *Holman Illustrated Bible Dictionary*, ed. Chad Brand, Charles Draper, and Archie England, 774–75. Nashville: Holman Bible Publishers, 2003.

Arnold, Bill. *1 & 2 Samuel*. The NIV Application Commentary. Grand Rapids: Zondervan, 2003.

Bergen, Robert. *1, 2 Samuel*. The New American Commentary, vol. 7. Nashville: Broadman & Holman Publishers, 1996.

Blackaby, Henry T., and Claude V. King. *Experiencing God*. Nashville: Broadman & Holman Publishers, 1994.

Blackwood, Andrew W. *Preaching from Samuel*. New York: Abingdon-Cokesbury Press, 1946.

Bonhoeffer, Dietrich. *The Cost of Discipleship*. New York: Macmillan Publishing Co, 1963.

Davis, Dale Ralph. *Looking on the Heart*. Vol. 1, *Expositions of 1 Samuel 1–14*. Expositor's Guide to the Historical Books. Grand Rapids: Baker Book House, 1994.

Getz, Gene A. *David: Seeking God Faithfully*. Nashville: Broadman & Holman Publishers, 1995.

————. *Samuel: A Lifetime Serving God*. Nashville: Broadman & Holman Publishers, 1997.

Hays, J. Daniel. "Reconsidering the Height of Goliath." *Journal of the Evangelical Theological Society* 48 (2005): 701–14.

Kaiser, Walter. *Messiah in the Old Testament*. Studies in Old Testament Biblical Theology. Grand Rapids: Zondervan, 1995.

Phillips, J. B. *Your God Is Too Small*. New York: Macmillan Publishing Co, 1961.

Price, E. W., Jr. *ACTS in Prayer*. Nashville: Broadman Press, 1974.

Wakefield, Norman. *Listening: A Christian's Guide to Loving Relationships*. Waco: Word Books, 1981.

Walton, John, Victor H. Matthews, and Mark W. Chavalas. *The IVP Bible Background Commentary: Old Testament*. Downers Grove, IL: InterVarsity Press, 2000.

The Ultimate "Ever
for Study or Se

No other reference series gets to the heart of the Bible as efficiently as do Holman's Old Testament and New Testament Commentaries.

Designed to offer a detailed interpretation when time allows, or an essential understanding of the text when time is short, the Holman Old Testament Commentary series and the Holman New Testament Commentary series provide unsurpassed clarity and convenience.

OLD TESTAMENT

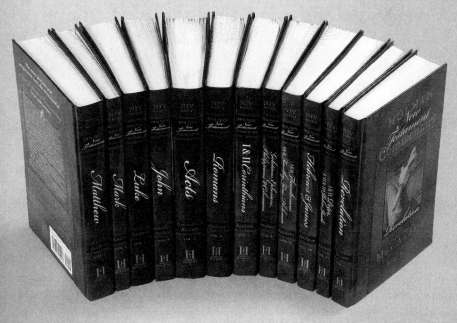